International Finance in the 1990s

International Finance in the 1990s

Challenges and Opportunities

Edited by
Joseph J. Norton SJD and Raymond M. Auerback

Centre for Commercial Law Studies
Queen Mary and Westfield College
University of London

Copyright © Basil Blackwell Limited 1993

First published 1993

Blackwell Publishers
238 Main Street, Suite 501
Cambridge, Massachusetts 02142
USA

108 Cowley Road
Oxford OX4 1JF
UK

All rights reserved. Except for the quotation of short passages for the purposes of criticism and review, no part of this publication may be reproduced, stored in a retrieval system, or transmitted, in any form or by any means, electronic, mechanical, photocopying, recording or otherwise, without the prior permission of the publisher.

Except in the United States of America, this book is sold subject to the condition that it shall not, by way of trade or otherwise, be lent, resold, hired out, or otherwise circulated without the publisher's prior consent in any form of binding or cover other than that in which it is published and without a similar condition including this condition being imposed on the subsequent purchaser.

Library of Congress Cataloging-in-Publication Data
International finance in the 1990s: global challenges and opportunities/
  edited by Joseph J. Norton and Raymond M. Auerback.
    p. cm.
  "Centre for Commercial Law Studies, Queen Mary and Westfield
College, University of London."
  Includes index.
  ISBN 0-631-18124-5. — ISBN 0-631-18876-2 (pbk.)
  1. International finance. 2. Asset-backed financing.
3. International finance—Law and legislation. 4. International
trade—Finance. I. Norton, Joseph Jude. II. Queen Mary and
Westfield College (University of London). Centre for Commercial Law
Studies. III. Auerback, Raymond M.
HG3881.I576333 1993
332.042—dc20   91-32847
                                                              CIP

British Library Cataloguing in Publication Data
A CIP catalogue record for this book is available from the British Library.

Typeset in Sabon on 10/12pt by Pure Tech Corporation, Pondicherry, India

This book is printed on acid-free paper

Contents

The Editors and Contributors	vii
Editors' Preface	ix
Part I Global Considerations	1
1 Prospects for International Finance Anthony D. Loehnis	3
2 Six Global Business and Financial Trends: A Lesson about Interconnectedness William B. Sechrest	13
3 Innovations in LDC Debt Conversions Carsten Thomas Ebenroth	32
4 Projecting Trends in International Bank Supervision: After BCCI Joseph J. Norton	64
Part II International Financial Arrangements	85
5 Project Financing Concerns Raymond M. Auerback	87
6 "Euromarket" Developments: Legal Aspects of Investing and Raising Finance in Russia, the Czech Republic and Slovakia, Hungary, and Poland Robert L. Drake, Philippe Max, Benedikt Weiffenbach, Wim A. Timmermans, Jan Grozdanovic, Timothy E. D. Gee, Kálmán Gyárfás, Anna Halustyik, Tomasz Ujejski, and Christopher Szpojnariwicz	109
7 US Legal Considerations Affecting Global Offerings of Shares in Foreign Companies Daniel A. Braverman	174

Part III Trade-Related Financings 237

8 Forfaiting 239
   Howard J. Waterman

9 Official Export Financing and Arrangements: US, UK, EC, and OECD 256
   Grant D. Aldonas

10 The Increasing Importance of Countertrade 275
   Adrian A. Montague

Part IV Niche Financings 291

11 Asset Securitization Developments: US and UK 293
   David Barbour and R. E. Parsons

12 Swap Financing 344
   Schuyler K. Henderson

13 Issues and Trends in Aircraft and Ship Financing from Current Methods 364
   Gordon C. C. Hall and Ian R. Siddell

Part V Special Legal Concerns 377

14 Confidentiality of Bank Records, Money Laundering, and Transaction Reporting Requirements under US Law 379
   Stephen K. Huber

15 International Coordination of Insolvency Proceedings: A Transatlantic Perspective 404
   Joel P. Trachtman

Index 434

The Editors and Contributors

The Editors

Professor Joseph J. Norton, Sir John Lubbock Professor of Banking Law, Centre for Commercial Law Studies, Queen Mary and Westfield College, University of London; Professor of Banking Law, Southern Methodist University School of Law, Dallas; Editor-in-Chief, *The International Lawyer*; Counsel, Jenkens & Gilchrist, Dallas

Raymond M. Auerback, Visiting Fellow (Banking Unit), Centre of Commercial Law Studies, Queen Mary and Westfield College, University of London; Partner, Radcliffes & Co., London; formerly legal counsel, Commonwealth Development Corporation

Other Contributors

Grant D. Aldonas, Partner, Miller & Chevalier Chartered, Washington, DC

David Barbour, Shareholder, Winstead Sechrest & Minick, PC, Dallas

Daniel A. Braverman, Associate, Cleary, Gottlieb, Steen & Hamilton, New York City

Robert L. Drake, Partner, Baker & McKenzie, London

Carsten Thomas Ebenroth, Professor of Law and Director of the Institute of International Economics, University of Konstanz

Timothy E. D. Gee, Baker & McKenzie, London

Jan Grozdanovic, Baker & McKenzie, London

Kálmán Gyárfás, Baker & McKenzie, Budapest

Gordon C. C. Hall, Partner, Norton Rose, London

Anna Halustyik, Baker & McKenzie, Budapest

Schuyler K. Henderson, Partner, Baker & McKenzie, London

Stephen K. Huber, Professor of Law and Director of LL.M. Program, University of Houston Law Center, Houston

Anthony D. Loehnis, Vice Chairman, J. Rothschild International Assurance Holdings, PLC, London

Philippe Max, Baker & McKenzie, Moscow

Adrian A. Montague, Partner, Linklaters & Paines, London

R. E. Parsons, Partner, Cameron Markby Hewitt, London

William B. Sechrest, formerly member and shareholder, Winstead Sechrest & Minick, PC, Dallas

Ian R. Siddell, Norton Rose, London

Christopher Szpojnariwicz, Baker & McKenzie, London

Wim A. Timmermans, Faculty of Law, University of Leiden, The Netherlands

Joel P. Trachtman, Associate Professor of International Law, Fletcher School of International Law and Diplomacy, Medford, Massachusetts

Tomasz Ujejski, Baker & McKenzie, Warsaw

Howard J. Waterman, Partner, Cameron Markby Hewitt, London

Benedikt Weiffenbach, Baker & McKenzie, Moscow

Editors' Preface

This volume is part of the efforts of the Centre for Commercial Law Studies at Queen Mary and Westfield College, University of London, to establish a collection of publications on international finance, commerce, and business. The cooperation of Blackwell Publishers in connection with this volume is greatly appreciated.

This volume is concerned with current themes and trends in international banking and finance as viewed from a perspective of practical challenges and opportunities for the private business sector. In Part I ("Global Considerations"), Anthony Loehnis (chapter 1) sets the tone and context with his prescient discussion (originally presented in 1990, but equally relevant today) of the financial implications arising from the dramatic global changes that have occurred over the past several years (including the reunification of Germany and the disintegration of the Soviet Union) and from the resulting demands on world capital resources and for financial innovation. William Sechrest (chapter 2) follows up this theme of search for capital by projecting a series of possible global trends, including one of global interdependence. Carsten Ebenroth (chapter 3) picks up the lingering and unresolved problem of Third World debt and explores certain innovations in LDC debt conversions that link the public and private sectors. Joseph Norton (chapter 4), drawing upon some preliminary lessons from the collapse of the Bank of Credit and Commerce International, speculates on trends in the development of international supervisory regimes for financial institutions.

In Part II, "International Financial Arrangements," some of the traditional international financing techniques are analyzed from a current vantage point. Insightful considerations are presented respecting project financing (by Raymond Auerback in chapter 5), lending facilities *vis-à-vis* Central Europe (by Robert Drake and his colleagues in chapter 6), and legal considerations on global securities offerings from a US viewpoint (by Daniel Braverman in chapter 7).

Trade continues to be the engine for world economic recovery: Part III discusses various "Trade-Related Financings" in light of current world circumstances. Howard Waterman (chapter 8) considers the continuing relevance of forfaiting, and Adrian Montague (chapter 10) brings to light the increasing importance of countertrade. Grant Aldonas (chapter 9) sets forth an analysis of official export financing arrangements from US, UK, EC, and OECD perspectives.

Innovation continues in international finance: certain areas of innovative "Niche Financings" are considered in Part IV. David Barbour and Robin Parsons (chapter 11) elaborate upon current and prospective developments in asset securitization in the US and UK. Schuyler Henderson (chapter 12) elaborates upon the complex structuring and mechanics of interest rate and currency swaps. Gordon Hall and Ian Siddell (chapter 13) discuss (from a UK point of view) issues and trends in aircraft and ship financing.

Part V considers two special, transnational legal concerns. The issue of money laundering and the rise of currency transaction reporting and regulation (in the context of US experience) are addressed by Stephen Huber in chapter 14, and the international coordination of insolvency proceedings by Professor Joel Trachtman in chapter 15.

The editors believe that this volume should be of special value to all major financial institutions and to corporations, accounting firms, law firms, and consulting firms having an international dimension or international interests.

In assembling this volume, the editors have been privileged to have worked in conjunction with the Centre for Commercial Law Studies at Queen Mary and Westfield College, University of London. Under the auspices of the Centre and its Director, Professor Brian Napier, the editors have been able to assemble in writing the analyses and views of many of the world's leading experts in the area of international banking and finance.

In addition to expressing sincere thanks to the Centre and to Professor Napier, the editors also thank the cooperating institution of the Southern Methodist University School of Law and its Dean, C. Paul Rogers III. Special thanks are also extended to the law firms of Jenkens & Gilchrist (Dallas, Texas) and Radcliffes & Co., London, which provided invaluable support for the production of this volume. The editors would also like to acknowledge the tireless efforts of Dee McKnight toward completing the manuscript.

Special thanks are expressed to Tim Goodfellow of Blackwell Publishers for his work in commissioning this project.

The Centre for Commercial Law Studies hopes that it will be able to continue to produce valuable and high-quality publications in the areas of international finance, commerce, and business.

Joseph J. Norton
Raymond M. Auerback

Publisher's Style Note

The publisher's preferred spelling style is the Oxford style. Accordingly, with respect to words that can be spelled with either an "s" or a "z," such as securitization, the preferred spelling for this volume is with the "z." The publisher and editors recognize that, in the investment and legal fields in the UK, the "s" version may be more commonly used.

Also, as some authors are American and some English, particular authors for particular chapters have been given the option to utilize standard English citation format or Harvard "Blue Book" style of citations.

The editors and publisher would like to point out that the use of the masculine pronoun "he" is not gender-specific.

Part I

Global Considerations

1

Prospects for International Finance

ANTHONY D. LOEHNIS

Chapter Outline

1.1 Introduction
1.2 Capital Shortages: The Demand Side
1.3 The Supply Side
1.4 The Risk of Financial Failure
1.5 Possible Structural Reforms
1.6 Conclusion

1.1 Introduction

As much of this volume is concerned with the micro-details of financing techniques and developments, the author suggests that it might be useful to say something about possible macro-developments over the next few years, which will provide the backdrop to the micro-developments to be discussed elsewhere. In particular, the author wishes to comment briefly on two themes: first, the risk (very much brought to people's minds by the incredible events of the recent past in Eastern Europe and the [now somewhat unravelled] Middle East) that the 1990s will see a huge shortage of capital; second, the fear that the fragility of the financial system – not just the US financial system, but the international financial system – will be a further hindrance to the satisfaction of those capital needs.

Mr Loehnis made the remarks in this chapter in July 1990. Already they can be seen to have been prophetic: witness, for example, the actual dismemberment of the Soviet Union. Major subsequent events consistent with Mr Loehnis' remarks have been inserted in square brackets by the editors.

1.2 Capital Shortages: The Demand Side

At any moment in time, one might have said that there was a shortage of capital. The only necessity of life in totally abundant supply is, one may suppose, air, and even that, as a result of environmental pollution, is seriously deficient in an increasing number of places. So one might say that *environmental demands* are largely a new claim on capital resources in the coming decade – both in cleaning up and improving the industrial processes and methods of transportation we already have, and in increasing the cost of those we will be putting in place. There is comfort to be had from the fact that the threat to the environment is now widely recognized. But differences of opinion as to the time-scale over which countries should pledge themselves to cut down their carbon dioxide emissions, or even claims by developing countries that they should be excused from the discipline because they have not caused the problem, indicate clearly how great the cost is anticipated to be.

Mention of *developing countries* points to a second major demand for capital over the decade. Economic development in the Third World and the need to alleviate the grinding poverty that afflicts so large a number of our fellow human beings is, of course, no new demand – but pressure in the 1990s to make up for the standstill, if not falling back, in the development process in many countries during the 1980s as a result of the debt crisis will be great.

The dangers and costs of neglecting investment and running down the capital stock of a country are nowhere more vividly illustrated than in Eastern Europe and the Soviet Union. We can all rejoice today at developments that would have been unthinkable to most of us only a short time ago – namely, that the former German Democratic Republic (GDR) should already be economically reunited with the Federal Republic, and well on the way to political reunification, and that the other countries of Eastern Europe should have overthrown their communist governments and embarked on the road to political pluralism and the establishment of market economies. Further east we have seen the continuation of Gorbachev's brave – one might almost say quixotic – experiment in the Soviet Union, where those twin goddesses "Perestroika" and "Glasnost" have ironically released the nationalist genie from the bottle, so that their most important result is at least as likely to be the dismemberment of the Soviet Union as its conversion to the market economy or a democratic political system.

The costs of economic restructuring in the former GDR, other East European countries, and the Soviet Union are literally incalculable. Those who claim to put even remotely meaningful figures on it are deceiving themselves as well as others. What is clear is that there will be substantial new demands, which will inevitably fall on the capital resources of the West, whether in the form of multilateral aid, bilateral aid, or private investment.

However, huge as the sums may be, it is important to remember that they are not all front-end loaded. What has still not really been fully realized is the time it will take for pluralist political systems to become established in the countries of Eastern Europe. After fifty years essentially of dictatorship or one-party rule, the process of restoring multi-party democracy, with parties reflecting genuine economic or class interests rather than intellectual fads or heresies, is bound to take time. Those now being elected to office substantially lack experience of politics or even administration. It will be possible to effect the necessary economic reforms only through strong governments with popular support and legitimacy. It will take time for such governments to become established. Until they are, and until the populations become accustomed to the legal structures and nexus of rights and obligations that go with market economies, the capacity of these countries effectively and productively to use aid and private investment will be limited. The political and the economic imperatives are unfortunately, as is so often the case, not synchronized. So while the additional demand for capital is huge and obvious, the speed at which it will seem sensible to either governments or private investors to meet that demand will be considerably slower than some people imagine.

As to the Soviet Union, the same is true, only more so. The country is, of course, enormously resource rich, but it is an empire in process of dismemberment. It will be some time before it is clear whether this process will unfold peaceably, resulting in a looser form of Commonwealth of more autonomous or even independent states, whether the process will involve a series of civil wars, or whether there could still be a second conservative comeback by a combination of the military and the remaining and newly created conservatives, reacting to the prospect of anarchy and civil war. If money alone could ensure the first outcome, then massive aid to the Soviet Union might be the answer. But it cannot and it is not.

The author's prediction would be that the process of real effective change in the Soviet Union will be much slower than in Eastern Europe; and that while there is an irreversibility about what has happened in Eastern Europe, one cannot so confidently say that of the Soviet Union. The best hope probably lies in some controlled and agreed process of independence for a number of peripheral states which can proceed with their own economic perestroika within a homogeneous ethnic group and with a fair degree of political consensus.

This should produce paradigms of successful development which can be followed and adapted in the much more unwieldy Russian heartland.

The author's first career as a diplomat in the Soviet Union and dealing with Eastern European countries has made him linger perhaps too long on the problems and prospects of these countries. His third career as a central banker induces him to comment briefly also on the capital demands likely to arise from the *process of economic integration in Western Europe*. We are approaching an important crossroads: forthcoming intergovernmental European Community (EC) conferences on such matters as economic and monetary union and political union should provide clearer answers to the vexed question of whether the EC should be concentrating on widening or on deepening, as well as to the question of the speed at which it is prudent and appropriate to move toward economic and monetary union.

Again, the political and economic imperatives are out of synchronization. Monetary union – that is, the locking of exchange rates, the introduction of a single currency, the establishment of a uniform monetary policy for all EC members, and the establishment of a European Central Bank or central bank system – will inevitably involve a substantial degree of union over a range of economic policies. It may not require full fiscal union; but it will require very close coordination in the fiscal and budgetary targets and results of member countries, and this will imply the sacrifice of sovereignty over a wider range of policies than is now the case – which will begin to look increasingly like federation or political union. If it is decided to implement Stage Three of the "Delors Report" – i.e. full monetary union – sooner rather than later [agreed to at Maastricht in December 1991, subject to a UK "opt-out"], while inflation rates, labor productivity, and a number of other economic indicators still diverge quite widely among member states, and when cultural, linguistic, and political differences are likely to inhibit the full mobility of factors of production which might otherwise compensate for the elimination of the exchange rate as a means of adjustment, then the political cost of such a move to the less-developed, peripheral countries of the Community will, in the author's judgment, be tolerable only if there is a far-reaching and generous regional policy emanating from the center. And this will bring additional budgetary implications and capital demands, which may well not be acceptable to all member states.

This is quite apart from the costs (and, of course, benefits) of the industrial rationalization and consolidation that are accompanying the whole "1992" process of establishing the internal market, including investment by non-EC members within the Community in order to share in the advantages of that internal market. So the process of EC integration will be another source of demand for capital likely to be greater than it would were the process not taking place.

[Also, with the Gulf War recently concluded, one can only speculate on the immediate and long-term capital demands not only to restore Kuwait and Iraq, but more generally to create the economic conditions for a broader Middle East peace settlement.]

There can be no doubt, therefore, that the capital demands of the 1990s will be enormous. What about potential supply?

1.3 The Supply Side

The starting point for concerns about a capital shortage or a credit crunch in the 1990s is observation of what is happening to savings. The most obvious statistical indicator is that of net household saving as a percentage of disposable household income, and whether one looks at countries with a high or low propensity to save, the thrift habit certainly seems to have slipped in the 1980s compared with the 1970s or earlier. In the 1970s that percentage for a low saving country like the US varied between a high of 9.6 percent and a low of 6.7 percent. In the 1980s the high was 7.7 percent and the low 3.3 percent. The figures for another low saver, like the UK, ranged between 12.2 percent and 9.6 percent in the 1970s, and in the 1980s between 13.5 percent (in 1980) and 4.1 percent (in 1988). A similar pattern can be seen in a high saver like Japan, whose range in the 1970s was 23.2 percent to 18.2 percent, and in the 1980s 18.3 percent to 14.8 percent.

Of greater significance, perhaps, is the measure of total national saving as a percentage of GNP. The differences are less stark, but the trend is similar. For all the OECD countries the figure comes down from over 25 percent at the beginning of the 1970s to just above 20 percent in the latter part of the 1980s. The decline includes high savers like Japan, where the figure dropped from 48 percent in 1973 to under 30 percent in 1983, as well as low savers like the US, where it fell from over 20 percent in the early 1970s to under 15 percent in the late 1980s. The UK's performance, thanks largely to the budget surplus of recent years, looks somewhat better, with figures around 15 percent in the mid-1970s giving way to averages nearer 17 percent in most of the 1980s. There is some encouragement to be found in the fact that recent trends in savings ratios have been upwards, but there is still a long way to go.

The theoretical observation that capital supply *should* be short because of this savings behavior is reinforced by empirical observation that long-term interest rates have been on a rising trend in most major industrial countries for the past few years (even in a year such as 1989 where there was a generally acceptable performance on inflation). The correlation of the rise in yields on the DM-bond with perceptions of increased capital demand by West German industry for investment in East Germany and of an increased budget deficit resulting from the adjustment costs of reunification is an obvious case in point. But the persistence of the US budget deficit and the extent to which that has to be financed by external savings, as well as demographic trends in Japan (and elsewhere), with aging populations seen as tending to perpetuate the secular decline in savings, point in the same direction.

Against this negative supply prognosis must be set two potentially positive factors. The first is the so-called *peace dividend*. Clearly the transformation of the geopolitical scene with the end of the Cold War means that defense budgets should be substantially reduced: indeed, this it is already happening. But by how much and how quickly depends on events in the Soviet Union, on the nature of the new international security framework that is hammered out within NATO, the CSCE, and the EC itself, and on the fallout from the Gulf War. Any reduction of the US contribution to defense in Europe may to some extent have to be matched by Europeans themselves taking a larger share of their own defense burden. This should, of course, be a substantially reduced defense burden, although the adjustment of defense strategy may well require new expenditure as different weapons systems and types of forces become more relevant. A worrying element in all this is the extent to which the potential proliferation of nuclear, chemical, or other catastrophic weapons among Third World countries (think, for example, of the recent Iraqi situation) could inhibit the simplification of the defense establishments that Western powers may think it appropriate to maintain to cope with the less cataclysmic threats to security deemed to face the world in the era after the end of superpower confrontation. Having said all that, national budgets generally should benefit from a reduced defense posture.

The second positive feature one would identify is the globalization of capital markets that has been such a feature of the 1980s and that seems set to continue in the 1990s. This can be positive in two ways. First, the wider the dissemination of information, and the wider the availability and variety of savings instruments, the more the savings habit will spread. Money removed from under the bed, or no longer available involuntarily to finance excessive budget deficits in regulated economies where a certain percentage of bank deposits is mandated to finance government expenditure, ought to become available for productive investment. Second, the globalization of the distribution channels, both of the information and of the products, should ensure that, on the whole, investment funds find their way toward the most productive investment opportunities.

Now, the globalization of financial markets is not necessarily an unmitigated good. There are two important potential negatives to it. The first is the fear that globalization may itself have substantially contributed to the decline in savings and the increased propensity to take on debt and consume. To be more precise, it is the process of deregulation in domestic financial markets, which is one of the key ingredients of the globalization process, that is alleged to have had this effect. The other key ingredient, which is the advance in information technology in all its facets, has also contributed in that it has opened up to so many people much greater opportunities to consume.

This phenomenon has been particularly marked in the US and the UK, suggesting that relaxation of previously existing credit restrictions combined with lower personal tax rates has led to a surge of consumption. This has been accompanied by an increase in these and other countries in levels of the net debt of households. It would be nice to think that this was a transitory phenomenon related to an adjustment process while households learn the virtues of self-discipline after years of the external discipline of restriction. The puncturing of a few property price bubbles, combined with the removal of fiscal incentives favoring property investment, might help in this respect. But there is a genuine paradox that deregulation stimulates competition, including competition in the granting of credit. To the extent that this leads to a lowering of credit standards, in the granting of credit to the personal or the corporate sector, it is hard not to share James Tobin's wish that there should be some grit in the machine.

1.4 The Risk of Financial Failure

The second potential negative of the globalization of capital markets is that the risk of financial failure, and more generally the danger of systemic failure as a result of the interdependence of markets and individual financial systems, is significantly increased.

To start on a cheerful note, the financial system in the 1980s survived both the shock of the international debt crisis, which broke the surface in 1982, and the stock market crash of October 1987 – not to mention the Tokyo stock market crash of the beginning of 1990. There is some comfort to be found in the ability of the national authorities to cooperate in the fields of monetary policy – particularly in relation to the aftermath of the 1987 crash – and of supervisory policy and practice. But the 1980s was by and large a period of unexpectedly sustained growth in most industrialized countries, and it is still uncertain how the globalized financial system would survive a prolonged recession. The fact that the business cycle seems to have reasserted itself to the extent that all industrialized countries are no longer at the same point of the cycle (related, perhaps, to the reduction in the dominance of the United States within the world economy) is encouraging in this respect; as is the fact that the demands for capital and investment discussed earlier ought to give some protection against prolonged recession, provided the lessons of generalized inflation in the 1970s are well remembered.

Perceptions of risk apply most obviously to two areas. First, the vulnerability of the international payments and settlements network to computer breakdown or financial failure. The author does not want to dwell on this complex subject other than to say that at least those involved are aware of the problem and practitioners themselves have contrived to produce an agreed set of principles aimed at the convergence of practice in different national markets and resulting in pressure on the relevant national authorities to bring about the necessary changes. As the recommendations are implemented, not only will the system become safer and more efficient, but also it will encourage cross-border trading in equities and other corporate instruments.

The second area where risk of failure is particularly salient concerns the *friction of transition to new financial structures*. The situation in the US financial system provides a good example. The need for new financial structures in the US (as elsewhere) has been dictated by deregulation, internationalization, innovation, and technological developments in data processing and telecommunications. In the US the process of deregulation has been partial, in that restrictions remain on the types of business that banks (and, for that matter, securities companies) can do, and on the geographical locations in which they can do them. To be sure, those restrictions have been obviated in a variety of ways, some with, some without, the connivance of the authorities; but the commercial banks are left in a position where much of their traditional commercial lending has been disintermediated away from them into new instruments and to new intermediaries. The general increase in competition among such intermediaries, nationally and internationally, has forced many banks to rely on business with weaker clients, to concentrate on those franchises still left to them – property lending and leveraged buyouts are examples – and thus to take greater risks. The new and more stringent internationally agreed capital adequacy rules, designed to reduce prudential risk, may perversely, in the conditions just described, increase risk by driving banks to look for earnings in non-traditional and sometimes off-balance-sheet activities.

1.5 Possible Structural Reforms

What the US banks want is the ability to compete with other providers of financial services without one hand tied behind their back by restrictions preventing them from emulating the universal banking model they see overseas, whether under one roof, as in a number of continental European countries, or within one holding company, as in post-Big Bang Britain. Efforts at regulatory change in Congress during the 1980s were mainly frustrated because there was no public opinion constituency, reflected through the legislators, that regarded it as necessary or desirable. The combination of the US Savings and Loans scandal, as well as the perceived, but possibly exaggerated, difficulties of a number of troubled US regional banks overexposed to the real estate sector, plus the possibility of a domestic credit crunch as a result of the knock-on effect of a weaker real estate sector, makes banks more reluctant to extend credit in anticipation of higher provisioning requirements and tighter inspection norms from the supervisors. These factors may combine eventually to create that constituency and enable Congress to pass legislation permitting financial groupings in the United States that closely resemble a "universal banking" model. That would probably result in a significant consolidation among deposit-taking institutions and in due course in a significant reduction in the banking sector's cost structure.

An analogous process is likely to be seen in Japan. Their post-war legislation – mindful in part of the power of the pre-war *zaibatsus*, the industrial and financial corporate conglomerates – followed the US model of separation of functions. But the consequences of the initiation of deregulation by the Japanese – although their culture enables them to control its pace more effectively than others – are moving inexorably in the same direction. Japanese securities companies do banking business overseas, just as Japanese banks deal in securities overseas. Once US legislation changes, Japanese will soon follow.

As regards Europe, the movement may, paradoxically, be in the opposite direction. The universal bank on the German or Swiss model, with all functions capable of being performed under the same roof, may react to the wider extension of securities markets in the Anglo-Saxon model by a tendency to spin off discrete activities, such as investment management or capital market activities, into separate subsidiaries. That has already happened as far as their international activities are concerned, but it could spread domestically as well. The pressures for this would be partly those of management logistics, partly supervisory. The supervisors in this process have a key role to play: at the end of the day they are the best, because the only, grit in the machine we have.

1.6 Conclusion

If the author were to draw together the strands of his argument, the conclusion might be this. There certainly are very considerable capital requirements foreseeable in the 1990s, although not necessarily greater than those that the world economy has faced at the beginning of other decades. The capacity of the system to supply those needs is certainly likely to be constrained by savings habits which may take some time to reverse. It should, however, be assisted by the improvement in the outlook for international security, and by the improved distribution and allocation of capital facilitated by the internationalization of the financial system. That process of internationalization has itself produced frictions and risks, which it is to be hoped are mainly a transitional phenomenon.

There is obviously a risk that governments may be induced by fear of financial fragility or breakdown to relax monetary policy. In the short run this may facilitate the satisfaction of capital requirements, but in the medium to long term it would unleash inflation, which could only end in a much more serious crisis and recession. The cautiously optimistic scenario thus painted, therefore, is dependent on the continuation of sensible macro-economic policies on the part of the main industrial countries, which means, *inter alia*, not giving way to every call for new capital. What is quite clear is that the 1990s will be an exciting time in the world of international finance.

2

Six Global Business and Financial Trends: A Lesson about Interconnectedness

WILLIAM B. SECHREST

Chapter Outline

2.1 Introduction

2.2 Trends in General

2.3 Trend No. 1: Major Inflationary/Deflationary Cycles for Hard Currency Countries

2.4 Trend No. 2: An Increasing Separation of Hard Currency Countries from Soft Currency Countries

2.5 Trend No. 3: The International Corporation

2.6 Trend No. 4: The Shrinking World

2.7 Trend No. 5: Supremacy of a New Power Source

2.8 Trend No. 6: An Existing Plague upon the Globe

2.9 Concluding Observations: Global Planning

2.1 Introduction

Let us be so presumptuous as to divide the countries of our world into two separate hemispheres. These will not be the traditional northern and southern hemispheres. Rather, we will define one hemisphere as consisting of those countries which have industrial-based economies and "hard currencies." The other hemisphere will therefore consist of all of those countries which are not in the first hemisphere. For purposes of this chapter, we will call the first hemisphere countries the "Hard Currency Countries"; we will call the other hemisphere countries the "Soft Currency Countries."

Let us even be more presumptuous and define the term "hard currency" as a currency backed by the full faith and credit of a country which not only has an industrial-based economy, but also has established a sufficient economic and political stability to warrant a confidence in its currencies by the holders thereof. The term "soft currency" will refer to all currencies other than hard currencies.

Let us also recognize that particularly over the last two decades, businesses previously grounded in regional economies have expanded either voluntarily or by necessity to become multinational or global in scope. The advances in transportation and communication technology have literally shrunk the world. These technologies are partially responsible for the continuously growing phenomenon of multinational and international corporate development. Certainly these technologies have been beneficial. Yet, within the domain of the multinational and international business worlds, their influences have forced a quickening of the necessity to assimilate cultural and linguistic differences.

Additionally, the information age, with its television, computer, fax, satellite communication, and electronic media, has accelerated the pace of this global shrinkage: again, not without severe consequences. Unfortunately, in this fast-paced information world, data flow at incredible speeds. Many times, actions are taken reflexively, based upon inaccurate information or rumor. Because of the fast pace, the necessary care and consideration before certain actions are taken are often neglected.

The above observations are well understood by most individuals doing business within the international community. However, occasionally it makes sense to step back from the fray and simply look at the existing global network to see if any trends can be spotted. Six trends appear to be evident.

2.2 Trends in General

Before we discuss these specific trends, a few words need to be said about the concept of "trends." First, trends are in the eyes of the beholder. The communication of trends imparts a perspective of the individual recognizing the trends. This perspective really constitutes a "frame of reference" which facilitates discussion.

Second, trends are general in scope. Trends evidence general tendencies as opposed to specific actions. There will always be exceptions to any trend.

Third, trends are set forth for purposes of establishing "frames of reference" from which people can act and to which people can react. Utilizing trends as a communication device simply allows the communicator to "frame" issues, much as a photographer frames a specific moment in time.

Finally, discussing events in terms of trends allows the participants in any such discussion to recognize the interconnectedness of specific actions, as opposed to the separateness of those actions. In the world of interconnected systems, if you "push down" in one sector of a system, something undoubtedly will "pop up" in another sector. Appropriate planning requires that you take into account not only the "push down" action, but also the resulting "pop up" action.

Enough about trends in general! Now let us talk about the six major trends which are evidencing themselves in the global business community.

2.3 Trend No. 1: Major Inflationary/Deflationary Cycles for Hard Currency Countries

There have been two major inflationary/deflationary cycles which have occurred in virtually every Hard Currency Country during the last two decades. One of these cycles is currency-based and has occurred in a subtle fashion throughout the 1970s and 1980s. This cycle has been brought about by (1) the removal of the dollar from the gold standard, hence (2) the removal of all currencies from the gold standard,[1] and (3) the extraordinary fluctuation of the dollar *vis-à-vis* other currencies.

The other major inflationary/deflationary cycle is real-estate based. This cycle has been caused by (1) a finance-pushed (in some cases complemented by a tax-pushed) pricing of real estate stimulated by the deregulation of at least four major economies (namely the US, the UK, Germany, and Japan) and then (2) a combination of the following reregulatory or other changes affecting those economies:

- in the US, a reregulation of financial institutions and a monumental change in tax policy resulting in an excessive tightening of credit;
- in the UK, a tightening of regulatory policy on real estate lending and a resulting tightening of credit by the Bank of England;
- in Germany, a consolidation of East and West Germany and the

allowance of conversion of the East German currency into the West German currency; and
- in Japan, a tightening of banking credit through the regulatory process.²

Each of these inflationary/deflationary cycles has fed upon the others in a reflexive manner. In essence, this "reflexive feeding pattern" is analogous to a balloon being inflated with air up to a certain point in time when the nozzle is then released. Think about what happens to the balloon! Apply that analogy to these economies.³

Recognize that all Hard Currency Countries communicate economically through their currencies. A relationship between these Hard Currency Countries develops; hence, the dollar can be "up" against the yen one day and the yen can be "up" against the dollar the next day. The pound can fluctuate with respect to the Deutsch mark and the Deutsch mark can fluctuate with respect to the dollar and the yen, and so forth. In other words, these Hard Currency Countries are interconnected through the ability of their currencies to trade with each other. This "ability to trade" will henceforth herein be called "communication."

Fluctuations in these currencies are supposed to be monitored by free-market concepts of supply and demand. And, when fluctuation becomes of concern, the members of the Group of Seven (the G7 countries) intervene to lessen the fluctuation and hence soften its effects. The G7 countries recognize this interconnectedness of hard currencies.⁴

The free-market balancing device of supply and demand and the intervention of the G7 countries assume some stability, both economic and political, within each of the Hard Currency Countries. As long as each country's policies remain stable, this combination of free market and intervention will work. Yet major changes in policy within a Hard Currency Country may have an inflationary or deflationary impact upon Hard Currency Countries through the hard currency market without any G7 country initially recognizing this impact. This arises by reason of the interconnectedness of all hard currencies.

Take, for example, the US. In 1973, the last vestiges of the gold-supported dollar were eliminated. From the perspective of the US, the dollar was left free to float with other currencies. From the perspective of all other countries, the dollar was no longer backed by gold and hence was more risky.

One such perspective was that of the OPEC nations, which five weeks after the closing of the gold window passed Resolution XXV.140 which declared:

The Conference,
having considered the report of the Secretary General concerning the recent international monetary developments and their adverse effect on the purchasing power of the oil revenue of Member Countries:
noting that these developments have resulted in a de facto devaluation of the United States dollar, the currency in which posted prices are established, vis-a-vis the currencies of the major industrial countries;
recalling Resolution XXI.122 which calls, inter alia, for adjustment in posted or tax-reference prices so as to offset any adverse effect resulting from de facto or de jure changes in the parity of monies of major industrialized countries;
resolves
1. that Member Countries shall take necessary action and/or shall establish negotiations, individually or in groups, with the oil companies with a view to adopting ways and means to offset any adverse effects on the per barrel real income of Member Countries resulting from the international monetary developments as of 15th August, 1971.
2. that the results of negotiations shall be submitted to the next Conference. In case such negotiations fail to achieve their purpose, the Conference shall determine such action as necessary for the implementation of this Resolution.[5]

Considering the fact that most oil contracts are priced in dollars, considering the fact that the dollar was taken off the gold standard, and considering the fact that many countries held the view that this action allowed the dollar to be "less valuable" than previously, the initial effect of "going off" the gold standard had to be inflationary.

As inflation grew, the need to regulate inflation grew, and hence higher interest rates were imposed through the monetary policies of Hard Currency Countries. In the short term, these higher interest rates were passed on to consumers and so were also inflationary. However, in the long term the high interest rates took the "steam" out of the economies of the Hard Currency Countries. A deflationary pull on prices ensued. (Remember our balloon analogy.)

Now consider the US in the 1980s. The United States deregulated financial institutions from 1980 through 1982 and passed the Economic Recovery Tax Act of 1981 (ERTA).[6] This resulted in finance-pushed and tax-pushed pricing which culminated in the reregulatory efforts of the Competitive Equality Banking Act of 1987, the 1989 FIRREA legislation, and numerous regulations, as well as a reversal through the Tax Reform Act of 1986 of ERTA's tax policies.[7] The result was first an inflationary spiral of real estate values and then a deflationary spiral of real estate values. (The balloon was blown up, then the nozzle was released.)

Each of these inflationary/deflationary cycles has had a great impact on the banking system of the US and thereby on the US dollar. And, because of the aforementioned interconnectedness, all currencies have been similarly impacted.

But do not jump to conclusions! It is not just the US inflationary/deflationary cycle and the dollar that have caused these inflationary/deflationary cycles in the Hard Currency Countries. In fact, the US influence is only one such influence. Any analyst would also have to look to the concomitant cycles occurring in each of the other Hard Currency Countries and the fiscal and monetary policies existing at that time. More importantly, because of this interconnectedness, it becomes easy for these Hard Currency Countries to mirror inadvertently each other's actions by first being enticed into a reflexive spiralling upward of values and then being caught in a spiralling downward of values. In this case, the exegesis of the free market of supply and demand and G7 intervention is overridden by this reflexive action.[8]

Where does this Trend No. 1 lead? There are at least two answers to this question. First, this trend has led and will continue to lead to major insolvencies and bankruptcies. Think about it! Have you noticed the ever-increasing numbers of these events? Second, it leads to the Soft Currency Countries and Trend No. 2.

2.4 Trend No. 2: An Increasing Separation of Hard Currency Countries from Soft Currency Countries

The second trend is an increasing separation of the Hard Currency Countries from the Soft Currency Countries, both politically and economically. This second trend results by reason of a curious preference of international creditors for unsecured lending.

Please note that each country's currency is supported by the "full faith and credit" of each country's government. In essence, when currencies were "taken off" gold, silver or other commodity support, the currencies became unsecured notes.[9] The fact that it is not backed by any commodity means that the note is unsecured and hence is backed only by the "full faith and credit" of the issuer of the currency.

A holder of a particular currency is a creditor of the issuer of that currency. And the issuer of that currency is a debtor to the holder of that currency. A debtor–creditor relationship is formed. Since each country's currency is backed only by the "full faith and credit" of its country, the credit is unsecured. Therefore, the question for any currency issuer becomes whether the international population of creditors will accept the "full faith and credit" of the issuer as a debtor state. The countries issuing currencies which the international population of creditors accepts are the "Hard Currency Countries"; all other countries are the "Soft Currency Countries."

Unfortunately, there is an increasing separation between the Hard Currency Countries (which, as seen above, are predominantly industrial, economic countries) and the Soft Currency Countries (which for the most part, provide the commodities and resources necessary to fuel the Hard Currency Countries).[10] As this separation continues to increase, a concomitant separation is also occurring: i.e., the Hard Currency Countries are achieving more, economically, while the Soft Currency Countries are falling into a further state of poverty.

We can see evidence of this trend by noting that virtually all the oil that powers Hard Currency Countries is imported from Soft Currency Countries. Even more ironically, these Soft Currency Countries, despite holding commodities that power the economies of the Hard Currency Countries, cannot communicate in the international monetary system with their currencies. You may ask: Why? The answer, quite simply, is that the international population of creditors, when evaluating "full faith and credit," values economic and political stability more than natural resources and available commodities.

What does this trend indicate? It indicates that there is a tendency for the international population of creditors to accept paper instead of commodities as evidence of value. This is neither good nor bad, right nor wrong. It only evidences this Trend No.2.

This certainly was not always the case. However, these creditors have been gradually weaned away from any commodity standard, including a gold or silver standard.

But do not become confused! This weaning applies only to the Hard Currency Countries. The Soft Currency Countries are still left with a commodity standard, albeit an indirect one. This indirect commodity standard is imposed by the international population of creditors through the pricing of goods and services by barter or in hard currencies.

Again, this is neither good nor bad, right nor wrong. Rather, what is important is that this phenomenon be recognized and dealt with in the context of international and global planning. Failure to do so will result in the Soft Currency Countries not having any chance at economic development. Once their resources and commodities are gone, they will not be able to barter or generate other hard currencies.

This leads to another factor to be gleaned from this trend. Quite simply, it is that at some point in time, unless the aforesaid imbalances are corrected through appropriate planning and action, they will continue to grow, leading ultimately to confrontation and perhaps global wars. In either event, there could be economic and social holocaust. The risk is simply too great to take: the only alternative is appropriate international and global planning that alleviates this trend.

2.5 Trend No. 3: The International Corporation

This leads to the third trend which is, simply, that the people populating planet Earth have moved from a system of separate independent tribes to separate independent countries, then to separate independent trading blocs, and now to an international, interconnected economy. At the same time, these people have moved from a system of separate cultures and languages to countries composed of an amalgamation of these separate cultures and languages, then to an amassing of these countries into trading blocs with multiple cultures and languages, then to the evolution of these countries and their trading blocs into what is now an international economy.

Also at the same time, major corporations have become "multinational" and have come to wield more political, social, and economic power (in real terms) than the governments of those countries in which they operate. These "multinational" corporations are really multicultural corporations since they must deal with multiple cultural and language differences within the context of their own corporate culture.

This trend leads to the following observations:

- Because of technological changes such as the airplane, the computer, the television satellite network, the fax, etc., a global network of instantaneous information has been established, bridging these separate traditions of culture, religion, and socioeconomic history – indeed, in some cases threatening their very existence. Destruction of these traditions must not be allowed to occur.
- All people are, for the most part, proud of their cultural, religious, and socioeconomic traditions. And they should be! These traditions have provided a framework of support for these people. These traditions have provided these people with a "frame of reference" by which they could express themselves effectively, thereby allowing for their survival. These traditions must not be forgotten. Indeed, within a global plan there must be enough time and space for each culture and religion to be celebrated.

- Nevertheless, protectionism and separation based upon traditional cultural, religious, and socioeconomic demographics must be de-emphasized. Clearly, people cannot be interconnected in every other way and remain isolated by reason of cultural and religious preferences. A global plan must allow for differences without fear for loss of soul. Multinational corporations appear to be the vehicle available to bridge that fear.

However, notwithstanding this need to de-emphasize cultural, religious, and socioeconomic differences, there nevertheless has been over the past two decades a continued effort to resist this trend toward an integrated, international business community. Hence, a certain type of schizophrenia exists, as evidenced by the following observations:

- The European Economic Community is a bold step and makes sense for each of its participants. As a trade bloc, the Community as currently structured would have a GNP substantially greater than that of the United States (which is also a trade bloc, consisting of fifty states and some territories, although it is not usually thought of as such). Nevertheless, there continues to be resistance to the Community because of social and political protectionism. Resistance is particularly harsh when it comes to the currency issues. This prompts a British chap when communicating with a US fellow about the Community's "currency," the ECU, to respond: "How would you feel if you had to trade in your dollars for another currency which had not yet proved itself?"
- Another bold effort is underway with the creation of a free trade pact between Mexico, Canada, and the US. Positive steps are being taken in this regard. These steps, quite frankly, are steps which should have been taken some time ago. More likely than not, they are only now being pushed along by the US because of the consolidation of the EC and the potential competition it represents. Will this continue if the Community loses impetus?
- Japan continues to be protectionist in many respects, but at the same time is very accommodating of other cultures in economic ways. Because of commodity resource issues (namely, the lack thereof), Japan will ultimately have no alternative but to form an alliance with some country or group of countries. The protectionist tendencies of this Asian economic power will ultimately succumb to the shrinkage of the world. Ultimately, its tendency will be to require its people to "cross over" from one culture and one language to multiple cultures and languages to allow for continued economic development. The issue is not whether, but when!

■ This leads to the Soviet Union (which is a real question mark). Since it still remains in the aftermath of having its economic trade bloc (the Eastern bloc countries) virtually disintegrate over night, chaos is approaching. The distress being felt by the Soviet Union, particularly Mikhail Gorbachev, reflects the ultimate downside of an economic protectionist policy that collapses. Quite simply, when such protectionist policies disintegrate, "full faith and credit" for any of the currencies of these countries, among themselves and others, is eliminated. The result is that currencies of these countries (in the Soviet Union's case, the rouble) are relegated to soft currency status and face an inability to communicate within the international monetary system. The result is exactly what has happened in the Soviet Union: namely, the Hard Currency Countries and their business organizations are entering into the Soviet Union to produce products and render services which can be paid for only in other hard currencies or in commodities through barter. The result is that the Soviet people, who hold the soft currency rouble, have no ability to acquire the services or products priced in hard currencies. The outcome is first criticism of perestroika and then economic and social despair.

■ In the Middle East, the protectionist characteristics of religious and cultural traditions place these countries and their people in a state of constant conflict. This area has become a "powder keg" because the most critical natural resource upon which the Hard Currency Countries depend, namely oil, resides as an ocean under the Middle East's sand. The politics of this region have been debated for years and will continue to be debated as long as the Hard Currency Countries' economic viability is dependent upon oil. If that dependency is ever alleviated (see Trend No. 5), then the "powder keg" will be defused. At that time, the Middle East may find itself an area of continual conflict over cultural and religious issues but with no economic viability.

Any global economic plan must embrace all cultures using their strengths, not their weaknesses, to pull together one political, social, and economic fabric upon which a world economy can be based. The international and multinational corporations recognize this.

In other words, the international and multinational corporations recognize that the cultural, religious and socioeconomic traditions of all of the people operating within their corporate culture must be nurtured, not ignored. And each person within that corporate culture must be encouraged to develop his or her talents and skills (so-called personal mastery) not only within the context of the corporation's culture, but also within his or her cultural, religious, and socioeconomic traditions. Governments must learn the same lessons. This is a monumental responsibility of global politics and global business to work together in this regard. Many multinational and international corporations recognize this responsibility and are attempting to fulfill it. Others are lagging behind. Governments are lagging still further behind and may lose out. However, this trend is clear. Because they can and will continue to address these issues proactively, the era of the multinational and international corporation has arrived.

2.6 Trend No. 4: The Shrinking World

Of course, the concept of a "shrinking world" has already been incorporated into several other trends previously discussed. Nevertheless, the "shrinking world" is a trend in itself which must be reckoned with. Of course, this "shrinking world" trend results from a facilitation in transportation and communication emanating from air travel, television satellite networks, the computer, and other inventions. However, these elements are the technologies that have given rise to the global shrinkage. These technologies are not themselves the "global shrinkage."

Rather, the global shrinkage is a phenomenon that has arisen by reason of the voluminous data which flow through these technologies into the minds of people who control and run not only our governments, but also multinational and international businesses. There is a flood of information which is spewed forth every day from numerous sources utilizing these technologies. Whether we like it or not, we are affected by this flood of information in either of two ways: we can respond to it reactively and take action accordingly; or we can respond to it proactively and take action accordingly. In other words, this flood of information must be dealt with by its recipients through some "clearing house" procedure, be it reactive or proactive.

This is nothing new for executives and government bureaucracies. They must respond to voluminous information all the time.[11] But what this trend of global shrinkage produces is a flood of information which requires immediate action, but which in many cases does not allow time for verification. This is a difficult point to grasp. Let us elaborate!

In essence, what Trend No. 4 reflects is a world which, while trying to bridge cultural, religious, and socioeconomic traditions, must also at the same time distinguish out of a flood of information (1) fact from fiction, (2) accuracy from rumor, (3) objectivity from subjectivity, and (4) grounded communication from inflammatory hyperbole. Therefore, within this shrinking world, while cultural, religious, and socioeconomic traditions are being bridged, there is also the need to exercise caution when taking actions based upon this flood of information.

In certain languages, different tonal inflections change the nature of the communication. In different cultures, a gesture, meant in one to compliment may embarrass in another. And in this information age, action based upon misinformation is nevertheless an action with its attendant consequences. Hence, beware of the information age: always recognize the value of accurate information as its bright side and the dangers of inaccurate information as its dark side.

2.7 Trend No. 5: Supremacy of a New Power Source

We can talk about the dark side of anything. In essence, the dark side is considered the "bad side"; the light side is considered the "good side." Every invention has the potential of being interpreted as constituting a part of either the dark side or the light side. It depends on your perspective.[12]

Probably no invention can be portrayed as darker than the invention of nuclear power. The human tragedies brought about by the dropping of the atomic bomb or the Chernobyl incident must not be forgotten. Yet nuclear power also has a light side. This is evidenced over and over again in medicine, in the providing of electrical power, and in many aspects of science. But the question always remains as to whether nuclear power can be safely harnessed.

Accepting for the moment as true the second law of thermodynamics, which contemplates that all systems have a tendency to entropy, one can only conclude that all methods of harnessing nuclear power would have this same tendency and hence, from moment to moment, create the potential of another nuclear disaster. Nevertheless, in the short term the harnessing of nuclear power becomes very important to a number of Hard Currency Countries which are detached from the oil and natural gas reserves needed to power their economy.[13] Hence, France and Belgium have a number of nuclear power facilities and other countries such as Germany, Japan and the United States are following in their footsteps.[14]

However, lurking in the background is another power source. Although not yet totally identified, this power source will replace the dependency upon nuclear power and fossil fuels. Perhaps the efficient economic production of this power source is only one year away; perhaps it is a decade or more away. But it is coming. Do you know what it is?

In a sense, the reader's mind is being played with in the preceding paragraph. The reader is being requested to consider a "paradigm shift." "When the rules change, your world changes"; a paradigm shift occurs, like it or not![15]

What if the "hydrogen car" is perfected? What if water can be converted to energy in a much more efficient manner than oil? What if so-called "cold fusion" is possible? Where does that leave the Hard Currency Countries? How do they adjust? What happens to the oil industry? Where does this leave the Middle East?

A new efficient power source is coming. The question is only when. Perhaps we should consider that eventuality in our global planning.

2.8 Trend No. 6: An Existing Plague upon the Globe

This sixth trend reflects the consequences of the continuing failure of economic and political planning for the people of the globe. This trend is evidenced by the numerous social issues which are plaguing the globe, including, but not limited to:

- issues involving economics;
- issues involving energy;
- issues involving the environment;
- issues involving hunger and starvation;
- issues involving health;
- issues involving the homeless;
- issues involving education; and
- issues involving drugs and crime.

We all recognize these issues. What we do not recognize is that each of the previous five trends has led to this sixth trend. All of these six trends are interconnected. Each trend has caused adjustments in cultural, religious, and socioeconomic traditions around the globe. Some cultures have prevailed at the expense of others. Some religions have prevailed at the expense of others. Some societies and economies have prevailed at the expense of other societies and economies.

Let us look at one example of this "interconnectedness." Take the Third World countries which typically now exist as Soft Currency Countries. Many of these countries were provided with international financing through loans by international lenders, including the US banking industry. Consider that this lending occurred mostly in the mid-1970s, at which time this type of international lending was emphasized by monetary policies of Hard Currency Countries as well as their governments.[16] Then consider the upheaval caused by the inflationary/deflationary cycles described in the first trend discussed.

The failure of these loans resulted in economic chaos for certain money-centered banks in the United States and in other Hard Currency Countries. The underdeveloped countries, having received these loans, defaulted since they could not pay them back. In exploring why these defaults occurred, the questions arose not only (1) what economic and political events within these countries created the necessity for default, but also (2) what was happening to the hard currencies in which repayment of these loans was denominated?[17] The point is that each of these factors was undoubtedly connected with the other. Taken together the recipient countries could not repay the loans and hence defaulted.

The results of these defaults are well documented. Many underdeveloped countries are no longer able to borrow in the international monetary market. What initially appeared to be thriving economic reform disappeared into economic chaos. This economic chaos has exhibited itself in the form of hunger, starvation, homelessness, lack of education, illness, drugs and crime. It is all "interconnected."

2.9 Concluding Observations: Global Planning

What these six trends indicate is an immediate need for global planning taking into consideration the interconnectedness of these six trends. Abstractly and practically, planning globally for both social and economic issues is simple. We all know the issues and there are a range of solutions to each of these issues.[18] The difficulty is that politically each government, its members and its bureaucracy, is entrenched in its own survival and in some cases, in the survival of its people and its culture.

Under the rule of law, a government is subject to the rule of the people, not vice versa. Hence, entrenchment in survival issues by the members of a government and its bureaucracy is violative of the rule of law.[19] Clearly, it is the government's obligation to support its people and their culture to the extent the people want this support. This function is easily achievable in the context of global planning.

Now, what would global planning look like? It would not have to be complex, but it would incorporate the following:

■ A method of allowing all currencies to communicate. This could be done in conjunction with a world bank or an international monetary fund operating on a debit/credit type of formula pursuant to appropriate treaties. Each currency would be backed by a basket of commodities on a margin basis allowing for some leverage. This structure would be superimposed upon all economies and would give some discipline to what are now unfettered hard currencies circling the globe.[20] Controlling the money supply through government intervention is simply not enough. These controls will not stop the reckless or desperate printing of money. Economies must have the right to communicate with other economies and do so through commodity-backed disciplines.[21]

■ An international legal framework functioning politically, much as contemplated by the United Nations or the League of Nations. This framework must be based upon the rule of law (which in principle would be adopted by treaty). In his excellent book on *The Rule of Law*, Geoffrey De Q. Walker postulates twelve principles that would be included in this treaty: these are reproduced here (with a prelude).

> ... most of the content of the rule of law can be summed up in two points: (1) that the people (including, one should add, the government) should be ruled by the law and obey it and (2) that the law should be such that people will be able (and, one should add, willing) to be guided by it. From these two basic propositions one can deduce the twelve requirements listed and explained below....
> 1. Laws against private coercion: There must be substantive laws prohibiting private violence and coercion and of such a character as to give the citizen protection against general lawlessness and anarchy ...
> 2. Government under law: The government must be bound by substantive law, not only by the constitution, but also as far as possible by the same laws as those which bind the individual ...
> 3. Certainty, generality, equality: The substantive law must be guided by the principle of "normativism." This notion means that the substantive law should possess characteristics of certainty, generality and equality ...
> 4. General congruence of law with social values: There must be some mechanism for ensuring that the law is, and remains, reasonably in accordance with public opinion. Otherwise, there may be widespread disrespect for the law and pressures for violent change may build up and find expression in arbitrary and lawless actions ...
> 5. Enforcement of laws against private coercion: ... The fundamental requirement here is for institutions and procedures that are capable of speedily enforcing the substantive laws mentioned

in (1) above, those which prohibit private violence, coercion, general lawlessness and anarchy . . .

6. Enforcement of government under law principle: There must be effective procedures and institutions, such as the judicial review of executive action, to ensure that government action is also in accordance with law . . .

7. Independence of the judiciary: An independent judiciary is an indispensable requirement of the rule of law, indeed of all known methods of controlling power . . .

8. Independent legal profession: Some system of legal representation is required. Experience suggests that, except in most underdeveloped societies, this should take the form of an organized and independent legal profession . . .

9. Natural justice; impartial tribunals: The principles of natural justice, as that term is understood in law, must be observed in all trials . . . The rules of natural justice are defined today as including the requirement of an unbiased tribunal, the hearing of both sides of the case, and open courts with the possibility of press reporting. In criminal cases there should preferably be a presumption of innocence; at the very least, denial of a charge or allegation must not be held against a party in a criminal matter or in any other case . . .

10. Accessibility of courts: The courts should be accessible, so that a person's ability to vindicate legal rights is not made illusory by long delays or excessive costs . . .

11. Impartial and honest enforcement: The discretion of law enforcement agencies or of other government officials or of political officeholders should not be allowed to pervert the law . . .

12. The twelfth ingredient: an attitude of legality: The above eleven items embody the main requirements of the rule of law in terms of substantive law, procedures, practices and institutions. But there is still one element missing, one that is difficult to articulate with precision . . .[22]

This last point is to remind us that the health and strength of the rule of law does not ultimately depend on the efforts of lawyers, judges, or police, but on the attitudes of the people. There must be a legal *Geist*, an attitude of legality: "The true source of the values of the Rule of Law, even in those countries having written constitutions is to be found in the patterns of behavior and belief of the people, and their crystallization through the institutions of the legal system is a continuous process."

This legal framework would also set forth in a general structure a property code which covers not only issues of ownership, condemnation, and appropriation, but also enforcement of ownership and compensation rights through appropriate tribunals. Property rights would include intellectual and other intangible property rights perfected through an appropriate legal process of international patent, copyright, trademark, and trade secret protection. An international tribunal would be formed solely to deal on a consistent basis with infringement issues involving these rights.

- A method by which the Hard Currency Countries help the Soft Currency Countries in this time of transition. There must be a coalescing of economic, political, and military energy among the Hard Currency Countries and the Soviet and Eastern bloc countries for purposes of helping all nations. There must be a unified support (economically and politically) of the rule of law and the democratic principles arising therefrom. Each culture and religion must allow its own expression and the expression of others.

Of course, this plan is idealistic, but it is also practical. Virtually everything is in place, including the existing regional and tribal cultures, the framework for an international global system (the United Nations and the League of Nations), models for civil and criminal codes (both substantive and procedural), etc. It does take some effort to "cross over" from a regional, protectionist mentality to one with an international, egalitarian emphasis. But if an international plan for our planet can be developed based upon a common vision and collective action by all peoples, supporting that vision with their underlying cultures and support systems still remaining in place, then we will have taken the first step toward a transition from a regional economic existence based on the fight for survival to a global, unifying, proactive push for an expression of individual rights and a recognition of the interconnectedness of all things.

Notes

1 As long as the US dollar was on the gold standard, all other currencies were indirectly tied to the gold standard. Once the dollar was removed from the gold standard, this had the effect of removing all currencies from the gold standard.
2 Recognize that this real-estate based cycle, though existing in each of these countries, is not identical in all of them. By far the most dramatic is the fluctuation that has occurred in the United States. Yet the cycle does not appear to be complete in any of these countries. The ultimate patterns for

each country may prove to be closer in similarity than the existing patterns reflect.
3 You may react in disbelief to this analogy. But, support for it may be obtained from WINCO Asset Services, Inc., an affiliate of Winstead Sechrest & Minick located in Washington, DC. See also the December 1990 Report of McKinsey & Company, Inc. entitled "Restoring Health and Profitability to the U.S. Banking System."
4 The G7 countries are the US, the UK, Germany, France, Italy, Japan and Canada.
5 See *Wall Street Journal*, July 10, 1990, editorial by Robert L. Bartley: "The Great International Growth Slowdown."
6 Economic Recovery Tax Act of 1981, Pub. L. No. 97–34, 95 Stat. 172.
7 Competitive Equality Banking Act of 1987, Pub. L. No. 100–86, 101 Stat. 552; Financial Institutions Reform, Recovery and Enforcement Act of 1989, Pub. L. No. 101–73, 103 Stat. 183; Tax Reform Act of 1986, Pub. L. No. 99–514, 100 Stat. 2085.
8 This type of reflexive action is described in George Soros, *The Alchemy of Finance* (Simon & Schuster, 1987). Mr Soros described his theory of reflexivity in the first chapter of his book, juxtaposing this theory to the free-market theory of supply and demand.
9 In fact, if you read the fine print on any currency, you will discover that every currency is a note. The US dollar bill is described on its face as a Federal Reserve Note and states the following: "This note is legal tender for all debts, public and private." The result is that if you seek redemption of a dollar bill by the US Treasury, you will, if successful, not receive gold, silver, or any other commodity. Rather, you will receive another dollar bill. A similar result arises with Britain's various sterling notes. For example, the five pound note declares "I promise to pay the bearer on demand the sum of five pounds." Turn a five-pound note in, get a five-pound note back.
10 For an excellent portrayal of oil consumption, which countries are net importers and which countries are net exporters, see "The Beginning of the End for Oil," *Fortune*, September 10, 1990.
11 Numerous books are being written dealing with this very issue. One good example is Michael J. McCarthy, *Mastering the Information Age* (Tarcher, 1991).
12 For an interesting portrayal of the light side vs. the dark side, see Patrick Tilley, *Mission* (Little, Brown, 1981).
13 For an excellent article on this aspect of nuclear power, see *Time*, April 29, 1991, p. 54.
14 Ironically, two Soft Currency Countries show up also. One is the Soviet Union; the other is Bulgaria, which must have received support from the Soviet Union. See ibid., p. 61.
15 The quotation is from Joel Barker's excellent series "Discovering the Future," specifically the video tape *The Business of Paradigms* produced by Charthouse Learning Corporation.
16 These loans are usually referred to as the "less developed country loans" or the "LDC" loans.

17 In other words, a change in the value of a hard currency relative to other hard currencies could have a great impact on repayment of an LDC loan, depending upon the hard currency in which the loan is denominated. The following quote from the editorial by Robert L. Bartley in the *Wall Street Journal*, July 10, 1990, entitled "The Great International Growth Slowdown," reflects this interconnectedness: "For perspective on this issue, though, I once asked the helpful folks at Cyrus J. Lawrence to program up the price of oil in terms of gold. At the historic price of $35 gold and $2.75 oil, an ounce of gold bought 12.73 barrels of oil. This ratio prevailed so long as the London Gold pool lasted. In 1969, the price of gold started to creep up, and an ounce of gold would command 13 barrels of oil. In 1972, it would buy 16 barrels of oil. By the eve of the Arab oil embargo in 1973, an ounce of gold commanded 26 barrels of oil. After the embargo, in the first half of 1974, an ounce of gold was worth 12.76 barrels of oil."
18 These issues and their solutions have been pursued by innumerable task forces, "white paper" committees, investigative committees, etc. The solutions have been proposed; we simply cannot get the solutions put into practice.
19 For an excellent discussion of the "rule of law," see Geoffrey de Q. Walker, *The Rule of Law: Foundation of Constitutional Democracy* (Melbourne University Press, 1988).
20 For an excellent portrayal of currencies circling the globe, see Hazel Henderson, *Politics of the Solar Age: Creating Alternatives to Economics* (Knowledge Systems, Inc., 1988).
21 Three possible approaches to realizing this commodity-backed discipline were set out by Edouard Balladur in the *Wall Street Journal*, February 23, 1988, under the title "Rebuilding an International Monetary System." For another approach, see Soros, *The Alchemy of Finance*, ch. 18, p. 5.
22 See Walker, *The Rule of Law*, pp. 23–42 and n. 21.

3

Innovations in LDC Debt Conversions

CARSTEN THOMAS EBENROTH

Chapter Outline

3.1 New Developments in the Management of Debt Restructuring
    3.1.1 New Practical Strategies in the Management of Debt Restructuring
    3.1.2 Departure from the Principle of Equal Treatment of Creditors
    3.1.3 The Brady Plan and its Implementation in the Management of Debt Restructuring

3.2 LDC Merchant Banking
    3.2.1 The Object of LDC Merchant Banking
    3.2.2 Preconditions for LDC Merchant Banking

3.3 Opportunities for the Employment of Financial Innovations
    3.3.1 Innovative Forms of Securities
    3.3.2 Euronote Facilities
    3.3.3 Interest and Currency Swaps
    3.3.4 Innovative Forward Market Instruments

3.4 Corporate Finance Activities

3.5 Debt Conversions

3.6 High-Interest Government Bonds

3.7 The Segmentation of Debts and the Settlement of Conflicts
    3.7.1 The Problem
    3.7.2 The Mechanism of Conflict Settlement

3.8 Summary

Appendix   Section 11.08 of 1989–92 Credit Agreements from 1990 with Mexico

---

This article is written from the viewpoint of summer 1990.

3.1 New Developments in the Management of Debt Restructuring

3.1.1 New Practical Strategies in the Management of Debt Restructuring

Around 1987 international management of the rescheduling of debts entered a second phase with the implementation of new strategies.[1] The introduction of these strategies stemmed from the realization that the management of debt as practiced up to that time had had too little success and, consequently, could not provide a satisfactory basis for a permanent solution of the debt crisis.[2] The outbreak of an international financial crisis had indeed been avoided. But a permanent solution of the problem required the re-establishment of a reasonable balance between contractual obligations, on the one hand, and on the other the ability to service debts and a subsequent return of the debtor countries concerned to the international financial markets, goals which had not been achieved.

There are, in principle, three possible approaches to the problem of indebtedness:

- re-establishment of the ability to service debts by means of adjustments in the debtor countries;
- financing the debt service by means of rescheduling and the provision of new credits;
- complete or partial debt relief.[3]

Within this framework, a variety of theoretical approaches was developed before 1987, but none of them was fully applied in practice to the rescheduling of debts.[4] The various methods did, however, influence the development of new strategies for the management of debts,[5] based on the so-called case-by-case approach, which provided for the treatment of each individual debtor country in accordance with its particular situation.[6] This approach was followed with the debtor countries of the sub-Saharan African group, whose external debts were substantially reduced by means of partial remission of the debts to official creditors.

The situation is different, however, for the debtor countries of the Latin American group, whose debts are owed primarily to private creditors and, in particular, to international commercial banks. Here, a combination of adjustments and financial measures was pursued, which involved to an increasing degree elements of debt relief under market conditions. In the implementation of this strategy the so-called "menu approach" was used, according to which a wide variety of different measures of adjustment and financing was introduced: the aim was to improve the economic situation of the debtor countries concerned and to provide incentives for the provision of new credits and debt relief by the private creditors.[7] These incentives were generated by elements of the menu system, which in the course of time were coordinated more and more with the varying business interests and strategies of the private creditors, particularly the commercial banks.

The development of a market-oriented strategy was made possible by the continuous expansion of the secondary market in developing country debt, which opened up around 1980.[8] Even today, this market is still relatively limited in scope, its activities being restricted primarily to London and New York. It consists mainly of trade in the principal and interest from syndicated Eurocredits involving substantial discounts with a weighted average of 40–50 percent off face value.[9] The main forms of transaction on the secondary market are different kinds of loan sales and loan swaps.[10]

Among the elements of the menu approach there are financial instruments which were already implemented, at least in part, during the first phase of debt management. In the meantime, however, their application has been extended and refined. The most important of the menu elements introduced before 1987 are probably the so-called debt–equity swaps.[11] These are transactions which allow an investor to transform foreign currency debts acquired on the secondary market, usually with a considerable discount off face value, into equity holdings in the debtor country.

Further elements of the menu are options on onlending and relending, which permit creditors to distribute their commitments in debtor countries among several debtors without increasing their overall commitment.[12] Onlending includes the possibility of transferring both the agreed credit and the terms of repayment from an original to a new debtor. Relending, on the other hand, permits the transfer to a new creditor of a debt which has been repaid by the original debtor but cannot be converted into foreign currency because of foreign exchange problems of the state. The right of creditors to exercise these options is established by means of so-called onlending and relending rights, which are traded on the secondary market, as they are, in principle, transferable.

Deposit facilities are mechanisms which are often used to reschedule the debts to creditors in the private sector.[13] In this case, the debtor is required, when payment is due, to pay into the central bank of the debtor country an equivalent in local currency of his foreign currency debt. Instead of converting these payments into foreign currency, the bank deposits an equivalent in foreign currency in accounts opened for the benefit of the creditor.

Other elements of the menu developed during the first phase in the management of debt restructuring are:

- currency diversification by means of redenomination of the debts to be rescheduled in other currencies or international currency units;[14]
- changes related to interest, involving, in particular, rates (above all conversion from floating to fixed rates), levels, and interest payment periods;[15]
- the establishment of trade facilities.[16]

It was only in the second phase of debt management, however, that securitization was introduced on a wide scale as an element of the menu approach.[17] This involves the replacement of credits by securities in exchange for existing credits (debt-for-bonds swaps as a subcategory of debt-to-debt swaps) or as an alternative to new credits. The bonds are usually obtained by means of auction.

A further element of the menu is the buy-back of debts, which permits a debtor country to repurchase debts owed by the state or by debtors domiciled in the state at current market rates of discount off face value.[18] By their very nature, such transactions involve anticipatory redemption of a debt coupled with a partial remission of the debt.

Other elements of the menu include new forms of debt swaps which function as mechanisms for the reduction of debts.[19] This is achieved in particular by means of debt-for-export and debt-for-nature swaps, in which existing debts are redeemed by means of export consignments or by ecological measures carried out in the debtor country in return for the relief of debts previously acquired on the secondary market by non-profit-making organizations.[20]

Capitalization of interest is yet another element of the menu which has been put into practice. In this case, the usual practice of financing interest due by new credits is replaced by adding the accrued interest to the outstanding capital. Further elements include short-term trading credits, new forms of financing external trade (in particular the advance financing of exports and medium-term revolving financing of foreign trade), sale/lease-back mechanisms, and the extension of interbank lines.[21]

3.1.2 Departure from the Principle of Equal Treatment of Creditors

Although the menu approach is based on earlier methods of restructuring debts, it also involves a departure from them. By aiming to create incentives for the financing and remission of debts, its various elements imply the abandonment of the principle of equal treatment of all creditors and the rise of different classes of creditors enjoying different degrees of preference.[22] Consequently, the menu approach conflicts with the mechanisms ensuring equal treatment of creditors traditionally contained in rescheduling agreements.

The implementation of debt–equity swaps or of actions to buy back debts can, for example, lead to claims arising from mandatory prepayment clauses and sharing clauses.[23] In the case of buy-back actions, this results from the anticipatory redemption of debts. With debt–equity swaps this situation can arise if the debtor country pays out the equivalent value fixed for the acquisition of equities in local currency, or if the equities acquired through a debt–equity swap are disposed of before the due date originally fixed for the converted debt. Similarly, the exchange of credit claims for partially collateralized securities in debt-for-bond swaps can lead to claims arising from negative pledge clauses.[24]

Consequently, it became necessary to overcome the incompatibility between individual elements of the menu and the corresponding regulations of the rescheduling agreements.[25] This is generally done by including these menu elements in new rescheduling agreements, by making the necessary changes in existing agreements – usually through the introduction of clauses permitting the menu elements – and by procuring waivers from the creditors in particular cases.

As a rule, rescheduling agreements provide for a graduated scale in the percentage of creditor votes necessary for the adoption of changes in rescheduling agreements or in the procurement of waivers.[26] Changes in stipulations of payment – usually including the sharing clauses – or waivers in regard to them affecting all the creditors involved in the restructuring of a debt can, in principle, only be taken unanimously (the so-called unanimity requirement) or virtually unanimously (the so-called virtual unanimity requirement), virtual unanimity sufficing in only very few rescheduling agreements.[27] But a majority decision is, in principle, sufficient for all other changes or waivers affecting all the creditors, where they refer to other conditions of the agreement, including those regulating the equal treatment of the creditors.[28] The majority required usually varies between 50 percent and 66.67 percent, depending on the rescheduling agreement. In determining the majority, voting is weighted in accordance with the share of individual commitment to the sum total of the debt under the rescheduling agreement. In the case of waivers, it should also be noted that they apply only to individual cases and require written notice.

3.1.3 The Brady Plan and its Implementation in the Management of Debt Restructuring

Recently, fresh impulses toward a further reorientation in the management of debt restructuring have come from the US administration. At the conference of the Bretton Woods Committee held in Washington, DC on March 13, 1989, the US Treasury Secretary, Nicholas Brady, presented new proposals for easing the debt problem. This initiative, now termed the "Brady Plan,"[29] was based on the prior Baker Plan,[30] which is generally regarded as having failed. In the opinion of the US administration the Brady Plan should permit a reduction of the repayment and interest liabilities of the debtor countries toward private creditors of up to 20 percent and thus make a substantial contribution to the mitigation of the debt problem. As with the Baker Plan, the Brady Plan also pursues a differentiated, case-by-case approach. The menu is designed to establish a reasonable balance between the ability of the debtor countries to service their debt and the obligations entered into, by encouraging cooperation between the debtor countries, creditor banks, multilateral financial institutions, and creditor countries.[31] What is new about the Brady Plan, however, is that it accepts debt reduction under market conditions as a fundamental approach alongside adjustment and financing, by envisaging a combination of debt relief and the provision of new credits.[32]

In order to create incentives for commercial banks to participate in the reduction of debts and the provision of new credits, both a quantitative and a qualitative extension of the elements of the menu approach are carried out.[33] In the case of debt reduction there is, in particular, provision for the increased use of the menu elements of buying back and converting debts. To this end, incentives are to be created by granting preferential treatment to the creditors concerned in the form of securities or other similar measures. The same concept can be seen at work in the measures taken to promote the issue of new credits, which also provide for the preferential treatment of new credits over old claims.

The implementation of the Brady Plan involves a change in the basic conditions governing the management of debt rescheduling. Here the contractual conditions arising from rescheduling agreements and credit contracts are of fundamental importance.[34] The Brady Plan envisages measures for a quantitatively and qualitatively substantial preferential treatment of existing creditors. This, in turn, strengthens the existing tendency favoring the creation of different classes of creditors, which contradicts the principle of equal treatment of creditors laid down in the rescheduling agreements. The removal of such obstacles to the implementation of the Brady Plan, however, requires the approval of the majority of the creditors concerned, or even their unanimous consent. Consequently, the greater the degree of approval on the part of the creditors which a rescheduling agreement requires, the more difficult the implementation of single elements of the Brady Plan in the process of restructuring becomes.[35]

Apart from changes in the basic contractual conditions, the Brady Plan also requires changes in other general conditions.[36] The differing national regulations on bank supervision, accounting, and taxation in the various countries of domicile present an obstacle which needs to be overcome by measures of adjustment and harmonization, if the creditor banks are to be motivated to participate in the measures envisaged by the Brady Plan to relieve debts, reduce interest, and issue new credits.

During the recent rescheduling of Mexico's external debt to private creditors, the Mexican government and the advisory committee appointed to lead the negotiations reached an agreement, at the end of July 1989, on a financing package which provides for the implementation of fundamental elements of the Brady Plan. The core of the package is the provision that rescheduling should be implemented by means of three options which can be freely combined by the creditor banks concerned.[37]

The first option (capital variant) enables debt relief on capital repayment liabilities by means of debt-for-bonds swaps. It provides for a discount of 35 percent on the face value of the original debts and their conversion into bonds with a term of thirty years and variable and partially collateralized rates of interest at the current market level. The second option (interest variant) enables debt relief on interest repayment liabilities, also by means of debt-for-bonds swaps. It provides for the conversion of the original debt at face value into bonds with a term of thirty years and also with partially collateralized rates of interest, although in this case the rates are fixed and, at 6.25 percent, lie below the current market level. As a third option, the creditor banks can take the traditional step of providing new credits, which have to be granted within four years and amount in volume to 25 percent of the total commitment in each case.

The rescheduling package with Mexico was signed on February 4, 1990, at a meeting chaired by the Mexican President Carlos Salinas de Gartari, in the presence of the Minister of Finance, Pedro Aspe, and the US Treasury Secretary, Nicholas Brady, the author of the Brady Plan, on which the rescheduling negotiations were based. This package brought about a reduction in the Mexican external debt of

$14.67 billion, leaving a total debt of $80 billion. Of the reduction, $6.82 billion was made available by direct debt relief and a further $7.76 billion by means of capitalized reductions of interest. The $80 billion external debt makes up 40 percent of Mexico's GDP. This represents a substantial reduction in the level of debt in relation to GDP, when compared with the external debt of $108 billion in 1987, which was 60 percent of GDP, and $100 billion in 1988, which was 57 percent of GDP.

In 1989 more than $4 billion was liquidated by means of sales of state companies, debt-for-equity conversions carried out before November 1987, net amortization of the public sector, and currency gains over the US dollar.

The annual interest burden will be reduced between 1990 and 1994 by an average of $1.63 billion, as Mexico has to pay a fixed rate of interest of 6.25 percent on $22.5 billion from the second option, instead of the 9–10 percent it had to pay previously. The annual repayment of $2.164 billion has been extended over thirty years, the full amortization of capital coinciding with the maturity of the US zero coupon bonds. Annual external net transfer payments have been reduced on average by $4.07 billion up to 1994. Mexico will receive approximately $1.25 billion fresh money from the banks between 1990 and 1994.

The principal of the discount and par bonds is completely covered by zero bonds of the US Treasury with the same maturity. Mexico acquired these bonds at the closing of the deal and can use them when they mature to repay the discount and par bonds.

Although the debt crisis began in Mexico in October 1982, Mexico has always been a model debtor. It has never been in arrears with the payment of interest and it has even liquidated small amounts of the principal debt. By 1985 Mexico had paid $150 million of the $1.2 billion promised in the rescheduling package. The remaining sum could no longer be repaid, as a consequence of an earthquake which paralysed the economy.

The Mexico package is regarded as a very important milestone in debt management, not only for Mexico itself but also for other countries for which it can serve as a model.[38] In spite of strong American influence, the package was negotiated without any confrontations. This may encourage other countries faced with debt rescheduling. With the help of this rescheduling package Mexico will try to gain free access to the capital markets. A major precondition for the achievement of this aim is the further privatization of the state sector. In addition, Mexico intends to carry out annual debt–equity auctions to the value of $1 billion until 1992.

A day after this huge financial package of $48.5 billion was formally ratified, Mexico successfully negotiated a bridging loan of $1.2 billion. Thirty-four banks participated in this thirty-month facility, which is designed to secure the large American enhancement package of $7 billion.[39] It is to be paid back in tranches, when Mexico has completed the arrangement of the enhancement package with the help of the IMF and the Japanese Exim Bank.

The new contracts also involved a series of changes in the clauses regulating the equal treatment of creditors. In particular, Mexico can buy back the discount, par, and new money bonds introduced in this package without triggering off sharing responsibilities of the banks concerned or an obligation on the part of Mexico to make corresponding payments to other creditors. Conditions have also been eased to some extent in regard to the unbonded debts to the banks providing new money. Although the agreements with them still contain sharing and mandatory prepayment clauses, they have been extended to include exceptions in two new cases. On the one hand, a debt buy-back is now possible, provided that Mexico makes the buy-back offer pro rata to all the banks involved in a particular agreement. The buying back is, however, limited to a maximum amount annually, which is calculated on the basis of the Mexican currency reserves, import costs, the level of current interest payments, and the new credits to be awarded in the future.

On the other hand, conditions for debt-for-debt exchanges have also been eased. The old contracts permitted only those conversions which involved the exchange of existing liabilities for new ones with a longer life or which were offered pro rata to all creditor banks.[40] A new, third variant has also been introduced, permitting conversions into new debts with a shorter life than the old liabilities, provided that they are linked with a sufficiently large reduction of debt in Mexico's favor. Calculations are made on the basis of a detailed formula contained in the contracts, according to which the term of a new debt can be shortened in proportion to the size of the reduction accepted by the creditor.

A modification in the negative pledge clause had led to a further possibility of differentiating among the various creditors. Whereas hitherto securities were permissible only within the framework of the customary financing of projects and external trade, Mexico now has numerous possibilities open to it to furnish securities for both new credits and liabilities arising from debt-for-debt exchanges.

The Philippine debt agreement concluded at the beginning of the year also severely restricted the principle of equal treatment of creditors. In an initial phase, the Philippines can use $1.5 billion for any debt reduction or debt service reduction transactions it chooses, with total exemption from the sharing, mandatory prepayment, and negative pledge clauses. The funds must, however, stem from public sector multilateral or bilateral sources. Once these are exhausted, the amount which can be employed is reduced to $300 million annually, although the Philippines could then have recourse to its own currency reserves.

In addition, the raising of new credits is made easier by a further exception to the negative pledge clause. This exception permits the Philippines to furnish securities for new credits annually to the value of $200 million.

3.2 LDC Merchant Banking

3.2.1 The Object of LDC Merchant Banking

In view of the development of these new practical strategies in debt restructuring, with their increasingly market-oriented approach to questions of financing and debt reduction, a growing number of commercial and investment banks have seized the opportunity of doing profitable business in "LDC merchant banking" on the basis of already existing business links with the debtor countries.[41] This is a new field of business activity, which is generally pursued alongside the traditional activities of commercial export and foreign investment transactions.

This business field is primarily concerned with advisory and service functions for clients outside the banking sector in connection with financing in debtor countries. It deals in particular with the implementation of debt–equity swap operations from the acquisition of debts on the secondary market to the conversion of the debts in the debtor country.[42] An aspect of growing importance in this field is the advising of debtor countries on the planning and implementation of actions to reduce debts, especially by means of debt-for-bonds swaps.[43] Another field of activity to be opened up is the management of the portfolios of other banks, which, in view of their information deficits, would incur heavy costs if they entered into transactions on their own account. These banks are also advised on the optimum exploitation of the options arising from rescheduling. The banks in this field also operate as brokers for the debts of the debtor countries[44] and arrange arbitrage dealings on the secondary market. A further aspect of LDC banking activities is the issuance by some investment banks of LDC junk bonds.[45] These investment banks acquire the debts of debtor countries as the separate assets of companies especially created for the purpose. These companies subsequently issue underlaid high-interest and high-risk bonds, which are termed junk bonds because they have low credit standing.

LDC merchant banking operates predominantly on a commission basis and is off-balance-sheet.[46] Transactions affecting the balance sheet occur regularly only in so far as the bank's own assets are employed in the form of short-term debts held in a trading portfolio especially created for this area of business. On the other hand, the employment of debts from the bank's own credit portfolio normally occurs only when conditions on the secondary market are unfavorable.[47] The banks active in LDC merchant banking also need to protect themselves against price risks on the secondary market and to have the debts of debtor countries at their disposal in a form and size suited to the needs of their customers, independently of the conditions prevailing on the secondary market. These two problems have led some of the banks, particularly US investment banks which, because of the separate banking systems in the US, do not have their own credit portfolios, to conclude master agreements with commercial banks. On the basis of these agreements they can avail themselves of the debts of the debtor countries by means of carrying over business in the form of loan sale and repurchase agreements (repos) and asset loans.[48]

3.3.2 Preconditions for LDC Merchant Banking

In order to achieve the best possible range of services in the sphere of LDC merchant banking, a bank must establish a separate division for this business field.[49] This division must do business in LDC merchant banking at a global level in the leading international financial centers, particularly New York, London, Frankfurt, or Zürich, and must have the entire technical know-how at its finger tips. It must also possess precise knowledge of the opportunities arising from the various menu elements employed in the debtor countries and be well acquainted with the general legal framework. It must take into account, on the one hand, the restructuring agreements arrived at in each country and, on the other hand, the restrictions arising from the general legal regulations on bank supervision, accounting, and taxation. The division must, furthermore, be continually present on the secondary market, if it is to survey this highly volatile area adequately.

Those involved in LDC merchant banking must also have contacts with local insiders in the debtor countries, who can ensure that the desired transactions, particularly debt–equity swaps, can be carried out locally.[50] It is particularly important that these agents in the debtor countries should have good contacts with the authorities, who need to be convinced of the advantages of a transaction for the stabilization of export earnings. The implementation of transactions with the help of a local insider is preferable to the establishment of a foreign branch, as the local insider personally guarantees an identity of interest between the external goals of the debtor country and their optimum realization. In the complex process of completing a transaction, a foreigner or the representative of a foreign subsidiary company would have far less influence over the processes of implementation.

3.3 Opportunities for the Employment of Financial Innovations

There is a powerful drive to innovate in LDC merchant banking, which requires the employment of the entire range of financial techniques. Financial innovations introduced from outside the field of developing country debt financing are growing in importance, the most significant of them being innovative forms of bonds, Euronote facilities, interest and currency swaps, and forward market instruments.[51]

3.3.1 Innovative Forms of Securities

In the case of innovative forms of securities the mutual claims of creditors (interest and capital payment claims) and debtors (liberation and capital prepayment claims), and thus the terms of the security, are fixed in a manner which deviates from the traditional forms.[52] Whereas the conditions of the security (particularly the kind of interest rate, due date for interest payment, maturity, and bond issue currency) were originally regarded as fixed in accordance with the arrangements for traditional securities, in the development of new forms of security modifications have been made and new rights introduced. The employment of these variations singly or in combination, as required, had led to the creation of a variety of innovative forms of securities. Deviations from the traditional forms of bondholder claims have resulted in the appearance of a torrent of innovative equities, which secure these claims in a special form of bond. They have in common the basic form of the fixed interest bond (straight bond) of the traditional kind. Of the forms which are innovative in regard to interest rates, the most important are floating rate notes, step downs, and zero bonds, whereas innovations in regard to currency are to be found mainly in bonds denominated in international currency units, dual currency bonds, and bonds with currency options.[53] Of the innovations in regard to maturity, mention should be made, on the one hand, of perpetual bonds and, on the other, of bonds of variable duration.[54] As innovations in the area of capital payments, partly paid bonds and serial bonds have been developed.[55] Reference should also be made to innovative convertible bonds and warrant issues in which the object of the right to opt or convert deviates from that of the traditional form.[56]

Innovative loan forms can be employed in LDC merchant banking, particularly in the framework of debt-for-bonds swaps. They must be taken into account, above all, in advising debtor countries as to the form of actions to be taken in debt conversion. In order to create the strongest possible incentives for the participation of as large a number of creditors as possible in such actions, the needs of the various creditor groups must be carefully analyzed and taken into account in fixing the terms for the bond to be issued by the debtor country in exchange for existing claims. These requirements can be fulfilled with optimal effect by the use of innovative loan forms, as they permit a wide variety of combinations of features in their terms. The adjustment of the issue to the varying needs of the creditors can also be carried out in such a way that several differently arranged bonds are placed at the disposal of the creditors as options.

3.3.2 *Euronote Facilities*

Euronote facilities[57] are financing instruments which permit a debtor to raise capital in a way tailor-made to suit his needs by means of a medium- or long-term agreement. This involves the issue on a revolving basis of money-market papers through other distributors in accordance with a clearly laid down distribution procedure, usually linked to a financial guarantee in the form of an underwriting or credit commitment.[58]

Because of this basic structure, Euronote facilities are a mixed form, which combine money-market and bond-market instruments on the one hand (medium- to long-term capital raising through the issue of short-term papers) and, to the extent that they provide a financing guarantee in the form of a credit commitment, credit-market instruments on the other (provision of standby credits), thus blurring the hitherto clearly defined borders between these markets.[59]

The money-market papers issued to raise funds are usually notes, which are called Euronotes on the Euromarket. These papers are debenture bonds with maturities ranging from a few days to several years, and they have a relatively high face value. Normally they are bearer instruments with maturities current on the money market of three to six months and face values of $500,000 upwards. They are often issued in the form of promissory notes of the debtor corresponding to the commercial papers. In discount form they are commercial papers of a kind which has been available for a long time on the US money market.[60] If the arrangements are with a bank, certificates of deposit are often issued instead of notes, involving repayment claims from bonded promissory notes for short-term deposits on deposit accounts.

The funds are made available by the issue of a financing guarantee on the part of a guarantee consortium especially established for this purpose. In the event of a non-complete placement, its members commit themselves to cover the consequent financial deficit for the duration of the Euronote facility. This financial guarantee can take the form of either an underwriting commitment or a standby commitment.[61]

In LDC merchant banking, advising debtor countries to set up Euronote facilities as a substitute for the traditional financing by means of syndicate credits is worth consideration. This is particularly true in regard to the provision of "fresh money" in connection with debt restructuring. In this case Euronote facilities can be implemented as menu elements in the rescheduling package as an alternative to the traditional credit financing. This innovative financial instrument offers the debtor country more favorable conditions than traditional credit financing, whereas the creditor enjoys the benefit of a balance-sheet improvement if the credit standby is not utilized.

3.3.3 Interest and Currency Swaps

Interest and currency swaps are among the most significant financial innovations of the eighties.[62] Although they come in a variety of forms, they follow three basic types: interest rate swaps,[63] currency swaps, and cross-currency interest rate swaps.[64] Interest rate and currency swaps are contracts between two parties concerning the mutual exchange of money payments over a fixed period of time. Interest rate swaps involve the mutual exchange of interest payments calculated at different rates based on a nominal principal amount. In the case of pure currency swaps, on the other hand, the parties agree to exchange equivalent amounts of principal in different currencies at a particular time, and to change them back at a later point in time at a predetermined rate of exchange. Finally, in cross-currency interest rate swaps, the parties concerned agree not only to exchange capital, but also to pay the interest on the amounts exchanged.

Beyond these basic forms swap agreements of the second generation were developed, for example, extendable swaps, puttable swaps, step up swaps, and amortizing swaps, in which the exchanged principal increases or decreases during the life of the agreement.[65] These forms can also be combined in a variety of ways. In addition, chain or cocktail swap agreements were developed, in which several independent swaps were combined back to back.

A further variant is provided by the options on swaps called swaptions, in which one party is granted the right to conclude an agreement with fixed conditions. Relatively new is the development of so-called commodity swaps, in which one party pays a fixed amount or an amount dependent on a money-market index, while the other party contributes variable amounts related to a commodity index.[66]

Interest rate and currency swaps can be employed in LDC merchant banking as instruments of arbitrage for the achievement of relative cost advantages. In addition, they are a suitable means of hedging interest and currency risks. These financial instruments can also be used in portfolio management to control and adjust the portfolio structure. The employment of interest-rate and currency swaps should also be taken into account in advising debtor countries. In this area, more intensive use could be made of commodity swaps, which can provide protection against fluctuations in the price of important export commodities.

3.3.4 Innovative Forward Market Instruments

First place among the innovative forward market instruments is taken by financial futures and options. Financial futures are forward operations involving the purchase or sale at a fixed price of a specified amount on the money, capital, or currency markets, in which the quantity and the future settlement date are standardized.[67] They are contracted on futures markets by authorized members on their own account or for others, with the interposition of a clearing house as the actual counterparty. Particularly important types of financial futures are interest rate futures,[68] stock index futures, currency index futures, and precious metal futures, which differ from each other only in regard to the standardized specified amount.

In the case of options the purchaser of the option pays an option premium in return for the right to buy or sell at an agreed strike price a specified amount of a given security at any time during a fixed period or at a designated future date.[69] A call option confers the right to buy, a put option the right to sell the financial instrument, which can be traded on the money, capital, or currency market. In recent years interest rate options,[70] currency options, and stock index options have been developed as innovative forms of financial options. The financial instruments they are based on differ from those of traditional share options.

Forward deposits[71] and forward rate agreements are futures deals on the over-the-counter market. Forward deposits are agreements between two parties in which one party commits itself to investing, at an agreed future date, a specified principal amount at a fixed rate of interest for a fixed period of time, whereas the other party agrees to accept this investment on the specified conditions. In forward rate agreements, on the other hand, two parties agree that the losing party should pay to the winning party an amount arrived at by calculating the difference between the interest achievable on the fictitious investment of a notional deposit of specified maturity at a specific future time and the interest on this investment as determined by a reference rate specified in the contract.[72] In contrast to forward deposits, forward rate agreements do not involve any actual investment. The difference between the interest according to the rate specified in the contract and the interest on a fictitious investment at the current market rate at an agreed future date is equalized.

Caps, floors, and collars are further forms of futures on the over-the-counter market.[73] Caps are contractually agreed top limits on interest rates for a specified principal amount over a designated period of time. If during this period a specified reference rate increases beyond a fixed maximum rate, the "seller" of the cap is required, in return for the payment of a premium, to repay the "buyer" the additional interest on the specified amount of principal. Floors, on the other hand, involve contractually agreed bottom limits for the interest on a specified amount of principal over a designated period of time.

Collars are a form which combines caps and floors, establishing by contract agreed margins for the interest on a specified amount of principal over a designated period of time. Caps and floors are fixed for the highest and lowest rates of interest on principal for the agreed period of time. Depending on whether the agreed reference rate sinks below the minimum or exceeds the maximum, either the seller of the caps or the seller of the floors must pay the difference in interest to the counterparty. For the guarantees on maximum and minimum interest they give, both parties receive a premium, which is usually set off against the loss. The net cost of a collar results from the difference between a cap premium and a floor premium, which means that the cost of financing a collar is lower than that of an isolated cap or floor.

Innovative futures can be suitably employed both in portfolio management and in advisory services to debtor countries as a security against interest, exchange, and other price risks. An important field of application lies in the hedging of debtor countries against fluctuations in the price of raw materials, a primary source of export earnings. In view of the variety of instruments available and the numerous possibilities for their employment, an optimum protection against individual risks can be achieved in this way.

3.4 Corporate Finance Activities

Apart from LDC merchant banking, the field of corporate finance has also seen a growth of new activities which might enable the debtor countries and their companies to return gradually to the international capital and credit markets. Because of the lack of creditworthiness of the debtors, however, the capability of the banks to give unsecured credits under a voluntary lending agreement has dwindled. On the other hand, the debtors are by and large forbidden to provide securities by the negative pledge clauses contained without exception in the syndicate loan and rescheduling agreements.[74] Consequently, forms of financing have been developed which indicate a solution to the problem. A very recent example provides a good illustration of this: To secure the financing needs of an institution in the public arena of a debtor country a trust was established which placed any substantial funds in hard currency at the disposal of the debtor. The trust was then refinanced by the sale of fixed interest trust shares to interested banks. The debtor, for his payment, assigned payment claims from long-term export commitments to foreign clients to the trustees. These were then used by the trustees to meet the payments agreed with the banks. The debtor himself remained collaterally liable for possible losses on claims.

These transactions, which are a kind of fictitious factoring, do not establish a security interest forbidden by the negative pledge clause.[75] As a rule, however, negative pledge clauses in restructuring agreements cover not only the security interests expressly acknowledged in common law, but also other measures which amount to a security from an economic point of view. This was also the case in the example under discussion.[76] Consequently, the old creditors were called upon to renounce the negative pledge clause, a demand for which the necessary majority was found. However, risks still remain, because the debtor country itself is also forbidden to grant securities by the terms of the restructuring agreements in which it is directly involved. Furthermore, it is forbidden not only to grant securities on its own account, but also to tolerate securities granted by specific institutions of the public sector.[77] Violation of the stipulation would entitle the creditor to the immediate repayment of the loan and, because of the cross-default clauses, could also lead to a disastrous reaction.[78] Previous experience has shown, however, that the termination of an existing contract is highly unlikely. A more serious risk for the second creditor is probably the possibility that the old creditors will accuse him of inducing breach of contract and claim compensation for damages.

3.5 Debt Conversions

Debt conversions offer wide scope for innovative banking. A well-known example is the Mexican exchange action of 1988, in which Mexico offered the creditor banks an exchange of existing indebtedness for newly issued, partly secured bonds with longer maturities than the old liabilities.[79] Similar conversions with other debtor countries have followed this model. This was rendered possible by a change in existing restructuring agreements, permitting preferential treatment of conversions in return for new indebtedness with longer maturity. The modalities of such transactions have in certain respects been very much refined. The following variant deserves particular attention: The debt exchange is not carried out directly between the creditor banks and the debtor; instead, an intermediary is positioned between them, who exchanges bonds he has issued in return for the existing credit claims. The credit claims are used for a conversion with the debtor in return for new indebtedness with a longer maturity. Furthermore, the intermediary is provided with additional funds by the creditor banks, which he uses to acquire securities for the bonds he has issued. There is no violation of the negative pledge clause in this case, as the securities do not stem from the assets of the debtor country. Although, in effect, the creditor banks involved pay for these securities on their claims out of their own pockets, the existence of the securities can, nevertheless, lead to substantial advantages in regard to taxation, accounting, and banking supervision, depending on the degree of value adjustment of the bank concerned and the overall legal conditions in its country of domicile.

Parallel to this development, other completely different forms of debt exchange have been adopted which aim at a premature payment of existing credit claims in return for a discount off face value. A straightforward buy-back of debts by the debtor is often not lucrative for the creditor banks, as they are required by the sharing clause to share profits arising before the agreed due date with the other banks involved in the banking syndicate or the restructuring agreements. Consequently a number of banks have chosen to take an alternative path. Reduced to its economic core, it involves the creation of a new security of the debtor, with a one-sided and not a reciprocal commitment, which would link payments to the sharing clause. These liabilities have shorter maturities than the existing credit agreements and payments on them – through the interposition of one or more banks – lead to the retransfer of credit claims of the creditor which mature at a later date and at a higher face value. From a formal point of view, the debtor does not perform payments on the credit claims, and only such payments require sharing under the sharing clause. It is, however, very questionable whether this objection would be of the utmost importance in a lawsuit instituted by one of the adversely affected banks. It is more likely to be seen as an unlawful circumvention of the contractual obligation to share.

3.6 High-Interest Government Bonds

The process of securitization, which has developed out of the increasingly refined structuring of the menu approach to debt conversion, has a further aspect in addition to the questions closely related to the contractual regulations in rescheduling agreements.

The volume of secured government debts in bond form has risen in the last few years to over $50 billion and will probably multiply in the near future. According to Salomon, bonds, in contrast to syndicated Eurocredits, have been restructured in only 3.5 percent of all cases in the last ten years.[80] And even though there have been well-publicized problems with the servicing of indebtedness, the most important debtor countries (Mexico, Brazil, Argentina, and Venezuela) have serviced their external bonds properly. For this reason investment in such bonds is very attractive for non-bank creditors. The commercial banks, acting as intermediaries, can pass on all the risks at a high commission to capital investors.

In fact, in the recent past, the return to the capital market of state enterprises, which were hitherto permanently excluded, has been successfully achieved. For example, at the beginning of April 1990, the Westdeutsche Landesbank managed the placement of a DM 100 million loan of the Potroloos Mexicanos with a coupon of 1.25 percent and a five-year maturity at par. At the end of May 1990 the Nacional Financiera Mexico issued a loan with a volume of DM 125 million (which has since been increased to DM 150 million) on the German capital market. The five-year issue with a government guarantee, which is managed by the Dresdner Bank, has a coupon of 11 percent and was offered for sale at par.

In spite of the by and large very positive estimates of the development of LDC government loans and loans issued by state enterprises, there are some critical remarks to be made:

■ The high servicing quota in payment on exit bonds is dependent upon the relatively slight share of government loans in the sum total of external debt. The higher the share of the bonds in external debt, the more improbable a proper servicing becomes. This is definitely the case if the bonds have come from a debt conversion.

■ In servicing, bonds enjoy preferential treatment over syndicated credits. Without knowledge of this fact, conversion into bonds could not be implemented. It seems reasonable to assume, therefore, that if only limited amounts are available for the repayment of debts and servicing of interest, the old stock can only be partly serviced. Consequently, there is a danger that the value of the credit claims will sink. This risk is clearly expressed in the higher risk premium which the debtor is willing to pay the creditors and in the fact that the interest rates are higher than for exit bonds. The risk of loss to a creditor who does not participate in a debt exchange conversion to bonds also tends to be reduced the more the burden of principal and interest payments is reduced for the debtor country by conversion.

■ Direct issue of bonds by state enterprises brings them fresh money which is desperately needed precisely for new investments and replacement investments (as in the case of Pemex). In view of the resultant increase in rentability, it can generally be expected that the ability to service the debt properly will also increase. In fact, however, there is a danger that the additional foreign exchange earnings deriving directly from the growth in productivity will be diverted and used for other purposes as a result of government intervention.

3.7 The Segmentation of Debts and the Settlement of Conflicts

3.7.1 *The Problem*

The developments discussed above involving the abandonment of the principle of equal treatment of creditors by the introduction of new contractual relationships between debtors and creditors already contain in themselves an increased potential for conflict. This is true not only of the creditors themselves, who have different interests in the pursuit of their business policies. Both the wide-ranging restructuring contracts and the individual syndicating contracts contain regulations which suggest that the conversion of, for example, old stock into bonds could, under certain conditions, be regarded as a violation of existing contractual terms. Partial agreements between sub-groups of the creditors, on the one hand, and the debtor country or the state enterprise concerned, on the other hand, are also potential sources of conflict. Apart from the claims of creditors against the debtor, claims of creditors against each other are also conceivable, as has been discussed above.

3.7.2 The Mechanisms of Conflict Settlement

Almost all restructuring agreements contain agreements regulating the place of jurisdiction, which permit disputes arising from the restructuring agreement to be settled before the federal or state courts in New York or the High Court of Justice in London. This is also true of the recent Mexico Agreement.[81] The agreement on the competence of the courts mentioned is not exclusive.[82] Actions can also be brought before the courts of the debtor country. In order to deprive the debtor country of the claim to immunity, the contracts usually contain the stipulation that the debtor (and in most cases also the state or national bank acting as guarantor) make an explicit and unrestricted waiver of immunity for all claims relating to the contract.[83] As in earlier agreements,[84] the new Mexico Agreement also takes the interests of British banks into account. Apart from accepting the jurisdiction of the High Court of Justice, the waiver of immunity specifically includes the UK State Immunity Act of 1978 alongside the US Foreign Sovereign Immunities Act of 1976.

In spite of the fact that most contracts contain these or similar agreements on the place of jurisdiction, there has, in the past, hardly ever been a conflict between debtors and creditors fought out and decided in state courts. This is in no small measure due to the experience of individual banks. The decisions of two US federal courts in 1983, which as a matter of fact dealt with the influence of currency control regulations on commercial loan contracts, are well known.[85] The state-owned Costa Rican banks which were sued had recourse in these proceedings to the Act of State Doctrine, and in one case this led first to a dismissal of the action.[86]

Why so few actions have been taken in this area has never been thoroughly investigated. The following reasons can, however, be assumed:

- The institution of advisory bodies led in the rescheduling negotiations to a far-reaching sharing of the burden associated with restructuring and refinancing carried out parallel to economic reform.

- The interest payment by the debtor countries was, in most cases, continued.
- The external assets of the debtor countries which the creditor banks might hope to have seized are limited.
- Because of the sharing clause, the proceeds of a successful claim would have to be shared with another bank.
- The filing of an action might lead to write-off, at least under American accounting law. This might not be necessary, if an action were not filed.[87]

The poor participation of the creditor banks in the fresh money option of the Mexico package clearly indicates their unwillingness to supply new credits, although these were needed. A burden-sharing in accordance with the previously negotiated solutions is, therefore, improbable. This suggests that there will be an increase in legal proceedings between creditor banks and debtor countries in addition to the conflicts arising from the disruption of the creditor committees.

In this connection, Brazil enjoys special status. Although the Multi-Year Deposit Facility Agreement of September 22, 1988 contains in section 12.07 an agreement on the place of jurisdiction which corresponds by and large to traditional contracts, section 12.08 provides for arbitration procedures in the event of conflict between the creditor banks and the Brazilian State as the guarantor of the claims of the banks.[88] The clause also contains special regulations in regard to the waiver of immunity.[89] The enforcement of claims by means of arbitration in Brazil is, however, a very uncertain matter, because of the aversion to arbitration clauses in Brazilian legislation.[90]

In comparison to proceedings in state courts, however, arbitration proceedings have considerable advantages, which have led to a clearly recognizable international spread of such proceedings.[91] Apart from the expertise, the quicker completion of the proceedings, the right of the parties concerned to determine the form of the proceedings, and the generally lower costs, the irrelevance of precedent and the confidential nature of arbitration proceedings seem to render them particularly suitable for the settlement of conflicts arising from commercial loan contracts. The confidentiality which is so essential in debtor–creditor relations is guaranteed even when disputes occur. Coercion reactions involving other creditors may thus be avoided, even if a creditor does not succeed in enforcing a repayment claim. Data on debtor–creditor relations, which are so important for all participants, remain concealed from other competitors to a degree exceeding the customary protection of business secrets.

In view of the frequent participation of US banks in conflicts between creditor banks, it is indispensable that the Arbitration Law of the State of New York and the Federal Arbitration Act should be taken into account in this context. The laws regulating debtor–creditor relations and syndicate relations are in any case mostly subject to New York law. Although a variety of individual questions arises in connection with the regulation of arbitration law at a state and federal level,[92] it can safely be said that there are no convincing objections to the introduction of arbitration proceedings, from the point of view of either state or federal law. In all cases where the claims of creditor banks against debtor countries are a source of conflict, arbitration agreements are both conceivable and meaningful. This is in no small measure due to the fact that the US Foreign Sovereign Immunities Act has restricted the claims to immunity of states in proceedings concerned with the recognition and implementation of arbitration awards.[93]

3.8 Summary

LDC merchant banking is a new field of business for banks operating internationally, in which long-term fixed sources of profit can be opened at a time when the financial markets are becoming more and more restricted. It presents a challenge for all banks wishing to operate in global banking and thus to improve their future prospects.

The increasing segmentation of creditors who, when illiquidity or insolvency threatens, are willing to enter into fresh money commitments in return for debt-for-bonds conversions, will lead to a preferential satisfaction from the foreign exchange earnings secured by these transactions. This might give rise to possible future conflicts between creditors. The scope of pari passu, negative pledge, and sharing clauses and the conditions determining waivers present new challenges for innovative financial arrangements. The secondary market for LDC claims will, consequently, be further segmented. Banks which keep their old stock without further new money commitments will have to accept the fact that these old commitments lose value more rapidly and that the future foreign exchange earnings of a debtor country will, in the first instance, be reserved for those creditors who, in spite of growing insolvency of the debtor, are willing to supply new money, because they expect higher returns from this capital transfer.

Banks which wish to become active in this increasingly complicated field need a world-wide infrastructure in the industrial countries, so that they can entrench themselves solidly in the global financial centers. This must be paralleled by a similarly strong entrenchment in the debtor countries, where the banks as insiders must ensure that the financial arrangements they make and their implementation are in accordance with the supervisory regulations of the host country. It does not matter whether the necessary penetration of the market is achieved extensively by a universal bank or selectively by global exploitation of gaps in the market in investment or merchant banking for corporate finance activities. The growing privatization of state enterprises in the highly indebted countries also makes mergers and acquisition activities of merchant banks attractive and necessary.

In order to guarantee an optimum range of services, participation in LDC merchant banking requires an extensive global presence on the market in this field of business. All the technical know-how must also be available. In particular, a good overall knowledge of the general legal conditions relating to contracts, bank supervision, accounting, and taxation is necessary. Furthermore, all the relevant financing techniques, including the financial innovations developed outside developing country financing, must be employed.

The great challenge for banks active in LDC merchant banking lies in linking the experience and banking "culture" of the various global centers of finance and inside knowledge of the highly indebted countries. In this area English and French investment and merchant banks have acquired experience and knowledge from which other banks might benefit by means of cooperation.

Notes

1 See C. T. Ebenroth, "The Changing Legal Framework for Resolving the Debt Crisis: A European's Perspective," *International Lawyer*, 23 (1989), p. 629; U. Messer, *Rechtliche Rahmenbedingungen für die Betätigung von Geschaftsbanken im internationalen Forderungshandel* (Konstanz, Hartung-Gorre, 1989), p. 60; M. A. Corti, "Tritt das internationale Verschuldungsproblem in eine neue Phase?," *Finanzmarkt und Portfolio Management*, 2 (1988), pp. 23, 27; S. Griffith-Jones and L. Nichols, "New Directions in Debt Management," *Case Western Reserve Journal of International Law*, 19 (1987), pp. 53, 66.
2 See Messer, *Rechtliche Rahmenbedingungen*, p. 58; Corti, "Verschuldungsproblem," p. 23.
3 See C. T. Ebenroth, "Internationale Verschuldungskrise – Lösungsansätze und unternehmerische Chancen aus Sicht der Landesbanken" (Westdeutsche Landesbank, 1988), p. 12.
4 See Ebenroth, "The Changing Legal Framework," p. 639; C. T. Ebenroth, "Neue Instrumente in der Umschuldung," Diskussionsbeiträge Sonderforschungsbereich 178, *Internationalisierung der Wirtschaft*, series 2, no. 37

(Konstanz, 1987), p. 13; H. J. Huss and P. Nunnenkamp, "Finanzinnovationen und Schuldenerlass – Wege zu einem effizienten Management der Auslandsschulden von Entwicklungslandern?," *Die Weltwirtschaft*, 38 (1987), p. 110; W. Cline, *Mobilizing Bank Lending to Debtor Countries* (Institute for International Economics, 1987), p. 80; K. Clark and A. Yianni, "Are There Solutions to the Debt Problem?," *International Financial Law Review* (Sept. 1988), pp. 9, 10.

5 See Messer, *Rechtliche Rahmenbedingungen*, p. 63.
6 See Clark and Yianni, "Are There Solutions?," p. 9.
7 Ebenroth, "The Changing Legal Framework," p. 640; Messer, *Rechtliche Rahmenbedingungen*, p. 63.
8 See also Messer, *Rechtliche Rahmenbedingungen*, p. 81; J. Wulfken, *Juristische Strukturen und ökonomische Wirkungen von debt equity swaps* (Konstanz, Hartung-Gorre, 1989), p. 43; J. Wulfken and W. Berger, "Juristische und ökonomische Grundlagen des internationalen Handels mit Kreditforderungen," *Zeitschrift für vergleichende Rechtswissenschaft*, 87 (1988), p. 335.
9 See Messer, *Rechtliche Rahmenbedingungen*, p. 84.
10 On the different forms of transactions see ibid., p. 88.
11 On this point see Wulfken, *Juristische Strukturen*, p. 23; G. Franke, "Debt–Equity Swaps aus finanzierungstheoretischer Perspektive," *Zeitschrift für Betriebswirtschaft*, 58 (1988), p. 187; L. C. Buchheit, "The Capitalization of Sovereign Debt: An Introduction," *University of Illinois Law Review*, 40 (1988), p. 401; S. Rubin, *Guide to Debt–Equity Swaps* (London, Economist Publications, 1987), p. 11; T. Roth, *Bankenfonds für Debt Equity Swaps* (Konstanz, Hartung-Gorre, 1989), p. 50 with further notes; A. Marton, "The debate over debt-for-equity swaps," *The Banker*, February 1987, p. 115; T. A. Layman and T. F. Kearney, "Debt for Equity; A Solution to the LDC Debt Crisis," *Journal of Commercial Bank Lending* (January 1988), p. 33.
12 On this point see Messer, *Rechtliche Rahmenbedingungen*, p. 32.
13 Ibid., p. 30.
14 K. P. Regling, "Neue Finanzierungsansätze beim Management der Schuldenkrise," *Finanzierung und Entwicklung* (March 1986), p. 6.
15 Ibid.
16 Ibid., pp. 6, 7; W. Berger, "Neue Ansätze im Schuldenmanagement für Entwicklungsländer," *Die Sparkasse*, 105 (1988), pp. 123, 126.
17 See Messer, *Rechtliche Rahmenbedingungen*, p. 65; R. Plehn, "Securitization of Third World Debt," *International Lawyer*, 22 (1988), p. 161; Regling, "Neue Finanzierungsansätze," pp. 6, 8; L. C. Buchheit, "Alternative Techniques in Sovereign Debt Restructuring," *University of Illinois Law Review*, 40 (1988), pp. 371, 394; D. Bender, "Financial Innovations and International Debt Problems," *Intereconomics* (May/June 1989), pp. 103, 107; A. R. Dombret and L. Vossenberg, "Schuldenkrise und Securitization," *Österreichisches Bank-Archiv*, 35 (1987), p. 861.
18 See G. Franke, "Institutionelle Gestaltungsmöglichkeiten zur Erleichterung des LDC-Portefeuille-Managements der Gläubigerbanken," Diskussions-

beiträge Sonderforschungsbereich 178, *Internationalisierung der Wirtschaft*, series 2, no. 74 (Konstanz, 1988) at 14; Regling, "Neue Finanzierungsansätze," pp. 6, 9; Clark and Yianni, "Are There Solutions?," pp. 9, 13.
19 Messer, *Rechtliche Rahmenbedingungen*, p. 66 with further notes.
20 C. T. Ebenroth and S. Bühler, "Verschuldungskrise und Umweltschutz – Debt-for-Nature Swaps, eine Lösung für zwei Probleme?," *Natur und Recht*, 12 (1990), p. 260.
21 See Berger, "Neue Ansätze," pp. 123, 125.
22 See Ebenroth, "The Changing Legal Framework," p. 640; Messer, *Rechtliche Rahmenbedingungen*, p. 67.
23 Clark and Yianni, "Are There Solutions?," pp. 9, 13; Buchheit, "The Capitalization of Sovereign Debt," pp. 401, 407; Wulfken, *Juristische Strukturen*, p. 147.
24 See C. T. Ebenroth and M. Cremer, "Mexikos Umschuldungsangebot – ein Ansatz zur Lösung der Schuldenkrise?," *Die Bank*, 28 (1988), pp. 488, 490.
25 See Messer, *Rechtliche Rahmenbedingungen*, p. 69.
26 Ibid., and see L. C. Buchheit and R. Reisner, "The Effect of the Sovereign Debt Restructuring Process On Inter-Creditor Relationships," *University of Illinois Law Review*, 40 (1988), pp. 493, 506.
27 See Messer, *Rechtliche Rahmenbedingungen*, p. 70; Buchheit and Reisner, "Sovereign Debt Restructuring," p. 508.
28 See Messer, *Rechtliche Rahmenbedingungen*, p. 70; Buchheit and Reisner, "Sovereign Debt Restructuring," p. 508.
29 See Messer, *Rechtliche Rahmenbedingungen*, p. 71; M. Frenkel, "The International Debt Problem: An Analysis of the Brady-Plan," *Intereconomics* (May/June 1989), p. 110; G. Maier, "The Brady Plan – A Vicious Circle or a Way out of the Debt Crisis?," *Intereconomics* (May/June 1989), p. 116.
30 On this point see C. T. Ebenroth, Code of Conduct, *Ansätze sur vertraglichen Gestaltung internationaler Investitionen* (Universitäts verlag Konstanz, 1987), annot. 108–21; Ebenroth, *Globale Herausforderungen durch die Verschuldungskrise* (Universitäts verlag Konstanz, 1987), p. 17; P. Conway, "Baker Plan and International Indebtedness," *World Economy* (July 1987), p. 193.
31 See Frenkel, "The International Debt Problem," p. 110; Maier, "The Brady Plan," p. 116.
32 Ibid.
33 Messer, *Rechtliche Rahmenbedingungen*, p. 73.
34 Ibid.; and Frenkel, "The International Debt Problem," p. 112.
35 See P. Norman and S. Fidler, "The West takes a Leap in the Dark of Debt," *Financial Times* (London), April 5, 1989, p. 4.
36 Frenkel, "The International Debt Problem," p. 112; "US-Kongressresolutionen für Brady-Plan," *Neue Zürcher Zeitung*, Fernausgabe, July 2–3, 1989, p. 15; "US-Strafgesetze zur Forderung des Brady-Planes," *Neue Zürcher Zeitung*, Fernausgabe, June 30, 1989, p. 13; "Official Tells Banks to Assist Brady Plan," *Washington Post*, May 25, 1989, p. C13.
37 Messer, *Rechtliche Rahmenbedingungen*, p. 78 with further notes.

38 On this point see C. T. Ebenroth and S. Bühler, "Die Implementierung der Brady-Initiative in Mexico und den Philippinen," *Recht der Internationalen Wirtschaft*, 36 (1990), pp. 23, 24, 26.
39 These funds were necessary in order to secure the bonds of those creditors who had decided in favor of options I and II and had thus renounced a part of their claims. Apart from the commercial bridging loan mentioned in the text, credits were also provided by the World Bank, the IMF, and the Japanese Export-Import Bank.
40 See M. Chamberlin, M. Gruson, and P. Weltchek, "Sovereign Debt Exchange," *University of Illinois Law Review*, 40 (1988), pp. 415, 463.
41 See also Ebenroth, "Internationale Verschuldungskrise," p. 26; Messer, *Rechtliche Rahmenbedingungen*, p. 109; L. Glynn, "The New Latin Beat in Investment Banking," *Institutional Investor* (October 1987), p. 91; K. Handschuch, "Blühendes Geschäft," *Wirtschaftswoche*, October 2, 1988, p. 54.
42 See also Ebenroth, "Internationale Verschuldungskrise," p. 26.
43 See Ebenroth and Cremer, "Mexikos Umschuldungsangebot," p. 488; and Messer, *Rechtliche Rahmenbedingungen*, p. 110.
44 See Wulfken and Berger, "Juristische und ökonomische Grundlagen," p. 349.
45 This process is a kind of securitization. See Plehn, "Securitization," p. 173. On securitization generally, see chapter 11 in this volume.
46 See Messer, *Rechtliche Rahmenbedingungen*, p. 110.
47 See Ebenroth, "Internationale Verschuldungskrise," p. 26.
48 In the case of loan sale and repurchase agreements, claims are sold and the parties at the same time agree to a subsequent reacquisition of the same or a similar claim by the seller at a specified price and time. See Messer, *Rechtliche Rahmenbedingungen*, p. 102. In the case of asset loans, a claim is transferred to another party for a specified time in return for the payment of interest or fees, depending on the kind of loan. See ibid., p. 103.
On this cost-intensive practice see R. Evans, "Anomalous but Profitable," *Euromoney*, 25, Special Supplement, January 1988, pp. 25, 31.
49 See Ebenroth, "Internationale Verschuldungskrise," p. 26.
50 Ibid.
51 C. T. Ebenroth, "Die international privatrechtliche Anknüpfung von Finanzinnovationen aus deutscher und schweizerischer Sicht," in P. Forstmoser et al., eds, *Festschrift für Max Keller zum 65. Geburtstag* (Schulthess Polygraphischer Verlag, 1989), p. 391.
52 See Ebenroth, "Anknüpfung von Finanzinnovationen," p. 394 with further notes.
53 Ibid., pp. 394, 399 with further notes.
54 Ibid., p. 400 with further notes.
55 Ibid., p. 401 with further notes.
56 Ibid., p. 402 with further notes.
57 Ibid., p. 409 with further notes.
58 See N. Dungan, "The Structure of Euronote Facilities," in L. Bankson and M. Lee, eds, *Euronotes* (Euromoney Publications, 1985), p. 9.

59 See Ebenroth, "Anknüpfung von Finanzinnovationen," p. 409; H. E. Büschgen, "Finanzinnovationen," *Zeitschrift für Betriebswirtschaft*, 56 (1986), pp. 301, 329.
60 On this point see R. Felix, "The US Commercial Paper Market," in R. Felix, ed., *Commercial Paper* (Euromoney, 1987), p. 1.
61 On this point see Ebenroth, "Anknüpfung von Finanzinnovationen," p. 441 with further notes.
62 Ibid., p. 417; C. T. Ebenroth and U. Messer, "Die vorzeitige Beendigung von Zins- und Währungsswaps bei Eintritt von Vertragsverletzungen aufgrund vertraglicher Lösungsklauseln," *Zeitschrift für vergleichende Rechtswissenschaft*, 87 (1988), p. 1 with further notes; and U. Jahn, "Klauseln internationaler Swap-Verträge," *Die Bank*, 29 (1989), p. 395.
63 Specifically for interest swaps see chapter 12 in this volume; also C. N. Strupp, "The Mechanisms of Interest Rate Swaps," in B. Antl, ed., *The Management of Interest Rate Risk* (Euromoney Publications, 1988), p. 117.
64 See Ebenroth, "Anknüpfung von Finanzinnovationen," p. 417; Ebenroth and Messer, "Zins- und Währungsswaps," p. 2.
65 On this point see Ebenroth, "Anknüpfung von Finanzinnovationen," p. 419; Strupp, "Interest Rate Swaps," p. 122.
66 For 'swaptions' and commodity swaps see Jahn, "Swap-Verträge," p. 400.
67 See Ebenroth, "Anknüpfung von Finanzinnovationen," p. 422; C. T. Ebenroth and D. Einsele, "Rechtliche Hindernisse auf dem Weg zur 'Goffex'," *Zeitschrift für Wirtschaftsrecht und Insolvenzpraxis*, 9 (1988), p. 205 with further notes.
68 See especially R. A. Hutchison, "The Mechanisms of Interest Rate Futures", in B. Antl, ed., *The Management of Interest Rate Risk* (Euromoney Publications, 1988), p. 89.
69 See Ebenroth, "Anknüpfung von Finanzinnovationen," p. 423; and Ebenroth and Einsele, "Rechtliche Hindernisse," p. 205 with further notes.
70 See especially I. Cooper, "The Management of Interest Rate Options," in B. Antl, ed., *The Management of Interest Rate Risk* (Euromoney Publications, 1988), p. 179.
71 See Ebenroth, "Anknüpfung von Finanzinnovationen," p. 426.
72 Ibid., p. 409 with further notes; R. D. Brown, "The Mechanisms of Forward Rate Agreements," in B. Antl, ed., *The Management of Interest Rate Risk* (Euromoney Publications, 1988), p. 219.
73 On caps, see Ebenroth, "Anknüpfung von Finanzinnovationen," p. 426 with further notes; S. Oakes, "The Mechanisms of Caps and Collars," in B. Antl, ed., *The Management of Interest Rate Risk* (Euromoney Publications, 1988), p. 243. On floors, see Ebenroth, "Anknüpfung von Finanzinnovationen," p. 427 with further notes; Oakes, "Caps and Collars," p. 245. On collars, see Ebenroth, "Anknüpfung von Finanzinnovationen," p. 427 with further notes; Oakes, "Caps and Collars," p. 245.
74 On negative pledge clauses see L. C. Hinsch and N. Horn, *Das Vertragsrecht der internationalen Konsortialkredite und Projektfinanzierungen*, (Berlin, de Gruyter, 1985), p. 104.

75 These securities are regularly listed in the contracts and include liens, pledges, mortgages, deeds of trust, charges, and other encumbrances, i.e. all burdens on the debtor's assets.
76 See A. S. Pergam, "The Borrower's Perspective on Euroloan Documentation," *International Financial Law Review* (August 1983), pp. 14, 15.
77 On this common feature of debt conversion terms, see Buchheit and Reisner, "Sovereign Debt Restructuring," p. 513; Pergam, "The Borrower's Perspective," p. 15.
78 Cross-default clauses entitle a creditor to withdraw a credit if the debtor gets into arrears with other creditors. Otherwise, if the debtor is in economic difficulties, the creditor with whom he first falls into arrears could levy execution on the assets of the debtor earlier than other creditors. See Hinsch and Horn, *Vertragsrecht*, p. 95.
79 See Ebenroth and Cremer, "Mexikos Umschuldungsangebot," p. 488; A. Mudge, "Mexico Leads the Way," *International Financial Law Review* (June 1988), p. 25.
80 Salomon Brothers, *Developing Country Sovereign Bonds: Opportunity in a New Asset Class* (April 1990).
81 See s. 11.08 of the 1989–92 Credit Agreements from 1990 with Mexico; in the same words s. 12.08 of the Onlending and Trade Credit Agreement from 1990 with Mexico.
82 S. 11.08 (c) of the 1989–92 Credit Agreements from 1990 with Mexico.
83 S. 11.08 (d) of the 1989–92 Credit Agreements from 1990 with Mexico.
84 S. 13.08 of the New Restructure Agreements of 1985; and S. 14.08 of the Multi-Year Facility Agreements from 1987.
85 570 F. Supp. 870 (S.D.N.Y 1983); *Libra Bank Ltd.* v. *Banco Nacional de Costa Rica*, 566 F. Supp. 1440 (S.D.N.Y 1983), aff'd, 733 F.2d 23 (2nd Cir. 1984), rehearing granted July 3, 1984, reversed 757 F.2d 516 (2nd Cir. 1985), certiorari denied 473 US 934, 87 L Ed 2nd 706, 106 S.Ct. 30 – *Allied Bank International* v. *Banco Credito Agricola de Cartago*.

Only brief reference can be made here to questions which arise in connection with the suability of claims and article VII, s. 2b of the Agreement on the IMF. On this point see, for instance, Oberlandesgericht Düsseldorf, Verdict of September 28, 1989, *Wertpapiermitteilungen*, 43 (1989), p. 1842.
86 On these problems, see C. T. Ebenroth, *Banking on the Act of State* (Universitäts verlag Konstanz, 1985).
87 R. E. Dineen, "The Brady Plan: The Siren Song of Debt Forgiveness?," *International Financial Law Review* (November 1989), pp. 22, 23; Ebenroth and Bühler, "Implementierung," p. 23; *Handelsblatt* (Düsseldorf), January 12, 13, 1990, p. 2; *Financial Times* (London), January 12, 1990, p. 1.
88 S. 12.08 (a) of the Multi-Year Facility Agreements of September 22, 1988.
89 S. 12.08 (b) of the Multi-Year Facility Agreements of September 22, 1988.
90 For more details on this, see J. Samtleben, "Aktuelle Fragen der internationalen Handelsschiedsgerichtsbarkeit in Brasilien," *Recht der Internationalen Wirtschaft*, 35 (1989), p. 769; J. A. Clare, "Enforcement of the Arbitration Clause in Brazilian Loan Agreements," *International Financial Law Review* (November 1982), p. 18.

91 See R. A. Schütze, D. Tscherning, and W. Wais, *Handbuch des Schiedsverfahrens*, 2nd edn (Berlin, de Gruyter, 1985), annot. 3–20.
  This is valid for all questions of international economic relationships; see the references in U. Rieder, "Kaum eine Alternative zum internationalen Schiedsrecht," *Handelsblatt* (Düsseldorf), February 15, 1990, p. 10.
92 On this point, see C. Borris, *Die internationale Handelsschiedsgerichtsbarkeit in den USA* (Köln, Carl Heymanns, 1987); D. Rahmann, *Ausschluss Staatlicher Gerichtszuständigheit* (Köln, Carl Heymanns, 1984).
93 Public Law 100–640 of November 9, 1988, and Public Law 100–669 November 16, 1988.
  See K. P. Berger, "Internationale Schiedsgerichtsbarkeit und Staatsimmunität," *Recht der Internationalen Wirtschaft* (1989), p. 956 with further notes; see also C. N. Brower, "Jurisdiction over Foreign Sovereigns: Litigation v. Arbitration," *International Lawyer*, 23 (1989), p. 681.

Appendix

Section 11.08 of 1989–92 Credit Agreements from 1990 with Mexico

SECTION 11.08. Consent to Jurisdiction; Waiver of Immunities. (a) Each of the parties hereby irrevocably submits to the jurisdiction of any New York State or Federal court sitting in New York City and the High Court of Justice in London, and any appellate court from any thereof, in any action or proceeding arising out of or relating to this Agreement, and each of the parties hereby irrevocably agrees that all claims in respect of such action or proceeding may be heard and determined in such New York State or Federal court, or in the High Court of Justice in London. Each of the parties hereby irrevocably waives, to the fullest extent it may effectively do so, the defense of an inconvenient forum to the maintenance of such action or proceeding and any right of jurisdiction in such action or proceeding on account of the place of residence or domicile of such party. The Borrower and Banco de Mexico each hereby irrevocably appoints (i) the person for the time being and from time to time acting as or discharging the function of the Consul General of Mexico in New York, New York (the "New York Process Agent"), with an office on the date hereof at 8 East 41st Street, New York, New York 10017, United States, as its agent to receive on behalf of the Borrower, Banco de Mexico and their respective property service of copies of the summons and complaint and any other process which may be served in any such action or proceeding brought in New York State or Federal Court sitting in New York City and (ii) the person for the time being and from time to time acting as or discharging the function of the Consul General of Mexico in London, England (the "London Process Agent"), with an office on the date hereof at 8 Halkin Street, London SW1, England, as its agent to receive on behalf of itself and its respective property service of copies of the summons and complaint and any other process which may be served in any such action or proceeding brought in the High Court of

Justice in London. Such service may be made by mailing or delivering a copy of such process to the Borrower or Banco de Mexico, as the case may be, in care of the appropriate Process Agent at the address specified above for such Process Agent, and the Borrower and Banco de Mexico each hereby irrevocably authorizes and directs such Process Agent to accept such service on its behalf. As an alternative method of service, each party also irrevocably consents to the service of any and all process in any such action or proceeding in such New York State or Federal Court sitting in New York City or the High Court of Justice in London by the mailing of copies of such process to such party, at its address specified in Section 11.02. A final judgment in any such action or proceeding shall be conclusive and may be enforced in other jurisdictions by suit on the judgment or in any other manner provided by law.

(b) In connection with any action or proceeding commenced by a Bank, or by the Borrower or Banco de Mexico against any Bank, arising out of or relating to this Agreement, each of the Borrower, Banco de Mexico and such Bank further hereby irrevocably submits to the jurisdiction of any competent court in the jurisdiction in which the principal office of such Bank is located and each of the Borrower, Banco de Mexico and such Bank irrevocably agrees that all claims in respect of such action or proceeding may be heard and determined in such court. The Borrower, Banco de Mexico and such Bank each hereby irrevocably waives, to the fullest extent it may effectively do so, any defense to the maintenance of such action or proceeding in such jurisdiction; and each of the Borrower and Banco de Mexico further agrees upon the request of any Bank to appoint the Consul General or comparable official of the United Mexican States as process agent for the Borrower and Banco de Mexico in any such jurisdiction in which the principal office or Lending Office of such Bank is located on a basis comparable to the appointment of the New York Process Agent and the London Process Agent pursuant to Section 11.08(a).

(c) Nothing in this Section shall affect the right of any party to serve legal process in any other manner permitted by law or affect the right of any party to bring any action or proceeding against any other party or its property in the courts of other jurisdictions.

(d) To the extent that the Borrower or Banco de Mexico has or hereafter may acquire any immunity from jurisdiction of any court or from any legal process (whether through service or notice, attachment prior to judgment, attachment in aid of execution, execution or otherwise) with respect to itself or its property, the Borrower and Banco de Mexico each hereby irrevocably waives such immunity in respect to its obligations under this Agreement and, without limiting the generality of the foregoing, (i) agrees that the waivers set forth in this subsection shall have the fullest extent permitted under the Foreign Sovereign Immunities Act of 1976 of the United States and are intended to be irrevocable for purposes of such act; and (ii) consents generally for the purposes of the State Immunity Act of 1978 of the United Kingdom to the giving of any relief or the issue of any process.

(e) Each of the Borrower and Banco de Mexico will maintain in New York, New York and in London, England, a person acting as or discharging the function of Consul General or, if such person shall not be maintained, the Borrower and Banco de Mexico will each appoint CT Corporation System to act as their respective New York process agent and The Law Debenture Trust Corporation p.l.c. to act as their respective London process agent as provided in subsection (a) above.

4

Projecting Trends in International Bank Supervision: After BCCI

JOSEPH J. NORTON

Chapter Outline

4.1 Introduction

4.2 The Background for International Supervision
    4.2.1 The Policy Underpinnings
    4.2.2 The Linkage to Legal Regulation
    4.2.3 The Strains of the Convergence Process
    4.2.4 International Cooperative Activities

4.3 Probable Trends
    4.3.1 An Enhanced Framework for International Bank Supervision
    4.3.2 Linking Banking and Securities Supervisory Standards
    4.3.3 Effective Consolidated Supervision
    4.3.4 Qualified Home Country Supervision
    4.3.5 An International Institutional Structure
    4.3.6 Greater Transparency and Disclosure
    4.3.7 Increased Role of Auditors and Converging Account Standards
    4.3.8 Inevitability of Greater Legalism
    4.3.9 International Insolvency Laws
    4.3.10 Coordinated and Effective Enforcement

4.4 Concluding Observations

Appendix BCCI: Timetable of Events, 1972–1991

4.1 Introduction

The debacle of the collapse of the Bank of Credit and Commerce International has unfolded as an ongoing financial "soap opera" of unprecedented dimensions. Jet-setting financiers, Arabian sheiks, Caribbean resorts, a former Panamanian general, Colombian drug dealers, crafty money launderers, catnapping and disarrayed government officials, a suspecting but unsure Bank of England and Federal Reserve Board, unsuspecting Scottish Highland councilors, scrambling auditors, CIA provocateurs, and dysfunctional regulators of a tiny continental duchy supposedly overseeing the BCCI flagship: all make for spicy and eye-opening copy in the otherwise turgid financial pages of the daily papers.[1]

It is the objective of this chapter to use this scenario as a reference point and then (after considering underlying policy, legal, and convergence issues and the current cooperative activities of the international bank supervisors) to attempt to project probable trends that might occur during the remainder of the 1990s in the area of international supervisory concerns respecting banking institutions and standards.

4.2 The Background for International Supervision

Before trying to project trends in international supervision, one first needs to consider: (1) What are the driving policy considerations? (2) What is the linkage to legal regulation? (3) What is the relationship to the convergence process? and (4) What international cooperative activities have occurred to date?

4.2.1 The Policy Underpinnings

International concerns of bank regulators have rested largely on policy means of facilitating the "safe and sound" development of an "international banking system" through the promotion of stability within such system, and of ensuring competitive equality among international banking institutions. An example illustrating these policy objectives is the issue of capital adequacy.[2]

Safety and soundness The expansion of international banking operations has required large amounts of support capital. These capital needs and the impact of converging international money and capital markets have led to substantial product innovation which, in turn, has entailed new and different risks being assumed (on- and off-balance-sheet) by such institutions. For instance, in certain transactions, banks are now assuming market and other non-credit risks, as well as traditional credit risks.[3]

Such risk-taking raises concerns over the possible adverse impact upon the "safety and soundness" of the international banking system and upon the financial soundness *inter se* of the banking institutions operating within this system by distorting prudent capital bases for these institutions (many of which have suffered already a qualitative deterioration in their asset portfolio). Further, the rise of global competition in the international financial markets has extended the financial and managerial wherewithal of these international banking institutions and has led to more "cut-throat" bank pricing practices and more aggressive business policies.[4] Moreover, as noted below, there have been various bank scandals or crises of international dimensions, which have led to reform of regulatory practices in the prudential supervision area.

The difficulty with hinging capital adequacy regulations for international banking institutions on the "safety and soundness" of the international banking system is that there exists no such system as a formal coordinator, nor does there exist any comprehensive framework for the orderly conduct of banking activities on an international level. What do exist are national banking systems: the so-called "international banking system" is currently a non-system (notwithstanding the existence of "international financial markets"). Thus, when one speaks of concern for the "safety and soundness" of the international banking system, one is really talking about an apprehension that a major disruption in the marketplace network of international banking activities or in the financial condition of a major domestic banking institution engaged in significant international operations will jeopardize somehow the "safety and soundness" and systemic stability of particular domestic banking systems (as in the "contagion" and "domino" theories).

Yet none of the recent international banking crises was rooted in a capital adequacy problem. For example, Herstatt failed because of fraudulent book-keeping concealing exposed foreign exchange positions; Franklin National, because of a volatile wholesale deposit base and excessive speculation in foreign exchange markets; the "secondary banking crisis" occurred because of the decline in the UK property market and the large wholesale deposit base of the unsupervised "fringe banks"; Ambrosiano failed as a result of excessive concealed losses on foreign loans (which did lead to a capital deficiency and insolvency) and serious gaps in prompt and effective international cooperation among the relevant national supervisory authorities; Continental Illinois, because of imprudent international and energy lending practices and a volatile wholesale deposit base;[5] Johnson Mathey, because of excessive concentrations in shipping loans and lending limit violations;[6] and BCCI and BNL because of fraud and abuse of a weak supervisory framework.[7]

Certain of the domestic policy justifications for capital adequacy standards may be applicable, roughly speaking, to the international arena; however, these justifications are also vulnerable to similar types of criticism. For example, these standards can be seen as enhancing the solvency of banks operating internationally. However, such standards increase an institution's costs of doing business, which might lead to a non-competitive position in the international financial marketplace, to greater risk-taking, or to underpricing for such institutions. Also, it is inconceivable that higher, uniformly accepted standards would have made any real difference in protecting international banks against the unexpected and monumental strains of the Third World debt crisis.[8]

Arguably, higher uniform capital requirements might increase public confidence in international markets. But many banks (the Japanese, for example) have operated very successfully internationally without having high visible levels of capital. The confidence that is increased by these standards is that of the regulators, who subjectively believe these standards will provide a needed buffer to avoid or to minimize shocks or "contagion" effects of a financially distressed or failed international banking institution, especially in the absence of any international regulatory structure, international lender of last resort, or governmental or intergovernmental deposit protection scheme.

Certainly, the bank regulators had a genuine concern in the late 1970s and in the 1980s for the trend indicating erosion of bank capital internationally and for the severe detrimental effect the Third World debt crisis was having on the capital bases of the international banks.[9] Undoubtedly, international prudential supervision concerns of the bank regulators are on the increase, with events such as those surrounding BCCI and BNL, and "safety and soundness" questions will remain prominent for these regulators. However, notions of "safety and soundness" and "system stability" based solely on the apprehensions of the regulators lend themselves to broad, catch-all, and possibly uncritical policy supports – as is perhaps the case with the currently hyper-complex capital adequacy standards.[10]

Competitive Equality and Transparency Perhaps more convincing as policy rationales for international supervisory standards are the twin needs of transparency and competitive equality within the international banking system. This is not to say that the "safety and soundness" goal is not important, at least in terms of regulatory concern. Certainly, these three policy needs are interrelated, as a non-transparent and competitively unequal system may tend to erode safety and soundness, solvency, and stability within the system. However, transparency and competitive equality by themselves possess greater specificity for formulating sustainable governmental policies to support international capital adequacy that can be implemented in a meaningful manner.

As to *transparency*, internationally, product innovation has accelerated at a rapid pace and has largely been off-balance-sheet; thus, the transactions have been largely non-transparent. In addition, with the absence of any internationally uniform regulatory framework, limited transparency has existed concerning the nature and impact of related bank regulations or examination and supervision practices – whether for banking institutions, bank customers, the financial markets, or the regulators themselves. A transparent international banking system is desirable as it helps the private participants better evaluate transactions and financial instruments and their inherent risks, the pricing of such transactions and instruments, and the implications of any regulatory requirements or burdens.[11]

Again using capital adequacy as an example, a uniform framework for internationally acceptable capital adequacy standards (particularly a risk-based system) in one sense encourages transparency for and among the regulators as it gives a visible concentration to the entire gamut of banking activities in a risk context (at least for regulatory accounting purposes), brings the growing off-balance-sheet activities back within a uniform financial framework, and adds clarity and consistency to the regulatory rules respecting the capital issue. In effect, the regulators are not operating in the dark. Increased transparency, where the rules are known by all parties, also should encourage impartial and consistent implementation of the rules. Conversely, it is easier to detect whether a foreign banking institution is being "hometowned" by the domestic regulators (i.e. being treated less fairly than domestic counterparts under the same rules). But where the rules, though uniform, are so highly complex and dense, transparency may be defeated or rendered meaningless for the public.

As to *competitive equality*, internationally, the precept is that an efficient international banking system requires a "level playing field" for all banking institutions, with the national rules to be applied as uniformly as possible. Divergent national rules or gaps in rulemaking or supervision are to be eliminated, or at least minimized so that neither discriminatory regulatory burdens nor unfair competitive advantages can be exploited. A uniformly consistent regulatory system also promotes system fairness and equity: all who are similarly situated are treated the same. Moreover, international competitive equality tends to create domestic symmetry in the domestic regulators' work on capital adequacy and other prudential standards by adjusting national interests for broader international objectives, which will aid ultimately the economic strength and competitiveness of the national systems and banking institutions.[12]

4.2.2 The Linkage to Legal Regulation

Given that there may be one or more substantial governmental policy justifications for international supervisory standards, it still requires a long mental leap to conclude that such standards should be formalized into legal regulations. Although the making and explanation of this leap into formal regulations are outside the scope of this chapter,[13] the author would like to express certain preliminary observations concerning why there appears to be a growing tendency, domestically and internationally, toward embodying supervisory standards in formal legal regulation:

- *Public and political significance* It appears that, more often than not, when matters of bank supervision acquire a considerable public visibility and ensuing political significance, the national legislature will seek formal statutory criteria. This clearly has been the case in the US with the enactment of the International Lending Supervision Act of 1983 (ILSA), the Competitive Equality Banking Act of 1987 (CEBA), the Financial Institutions Reform, Recovery and Enforcement Act of 1989 (FIRREA), and the Federal Deposit Insurance Corporation Improvement Act of 1991, and their statutory supervisory and enforcement requirements. With these measures, the US Congress has placed statutory duties upon the bank and thrift regulators to promulgate formal legal regulations regarding capital adequacy and other prudential supervisory standards.[14]

In the United Kingdom the intervention of parliament has been more indirect. However, with respect to both the secondary banking crisis and the Johnson Mathey affair, parliament reacted by enacting major banking legislation, which conferred considerable prudential supervision and enforcement powers upon the Bank of England; and most likely the BCCI affair will bring further parliamentary enactments. Although the Bank of England has continued to resist the obvious pressures for enactment of formal regulations and directives under the new UK legislation (which power the Bank has been granted by the legislation), it has taken a much more public and formal position with respect to capital adequacy and other supervisory standards through the publication of various formal notices and statements (although these do fall short of true legal statements).[15]

■ *Improvement of quality of regulation* The quality of regulation is considered to be improved when the process leading to the regulation has broad informational input from various sections of the economy and society, and where the management of and compliance with the regulation can be enhanced through a greater transparency. Clearly, under the law-making processes in the US and the UK, while there may be shortcomings, the enactment of legislation goes through a rather extensive formal and informal public process of scrutiny and analysis. Accordingly, the very process of creating laws adds a considerably greater breadth of information than might otherwise be the case if the regulators were to formulate their policies only internally. In addition, once enacted into formal legal regulations, prudential supervision policies become transparent both to the regulators and to those affected by the regulators. Thus, there is an objective medium by which the regulators can begin effectively to manage their day-to-day regulation and by which the affected parties can effectively begin to comply with the objectives and requirements of the regulatory policy.[16]

■ *Consistent fulfillment for regulatory policy* Although formal regulations have a tendency to inject rigidity into supervisory practices, they do have the countervailing effect of providing for the consistent fulfillment of regulatory policies. In effect, everyone, from the regulators to the affected parties, knows what the regulatory requirements are.

■ *Greater transparency* In addition to the advantages referred to above of the transparency provided by formal legal regulations, from an economic analysis standpoint, the more transparent regulations and regulatory policies are, the more likely they are to be effective and efficient.

■ *Conditions for competitive equality* Particularly with the present domestic and international complexities impinging on the role of banks and other competing financial intermediaries, the use of formal legal regulations can help to ensure "competitive equality" among differing institutions from differing jurisdictions, by placing everyone, in a legal sense, on the same "level playing field" (at least to the extent the legal regulation purports to do so).

■ *Effective regulatory enforcement* By having clear legal standards on supervision, the regulators then should be in a better position, when such standards are not complied with, to enforce legally these supervisory requirements.

■ *Fairness and protection of private rights* The importance of legal regulation relates not only to the regulators but also to those affected by the regulations. Rather than being subjected to *ad hoc*, non-transparent regulatory discretion, the affected party is in a position to evaluate its rights and obligations under the regulations. Thus the desired element of fairness in regulation becomes enhanced by the legal regulation. Also, with legal regulation, a decision of a regulator touching a particular party or class of parties may well be justiciable under some form of administrative review procedure.[17]

■ *Stable convergence vehicle* Perhaps even more significantly, legal regulation becomes a more stable vehicle for implementing goals for the international convergence of bank supervision standards. In addition to aiding achievement of these goals, in a regional situation such as that of the European Community the formal harmonization directives in the banking area can be seen as a way to assure the EC treaty requirements for the accomplishment of the single market and the right of establishment and supply of services throughout the Community.[18]

Accordingly, although it is possible (as evidenced by the historical practices of the Bank of England) to pursue regulatory policies and objectives on bank prudential supervision without resorting to formal legal regulations, the above summary considerations (along with the historical realities occurring in the US and in other countries as Germany and elsewhere through EC legislation) seem to suggest a discernible trend and logical progression toward greater legalism in bank prudential supervision generally and specifically with respect to issues such as capital adequacy standards.

4.2.3 The Strains of the Convergence Process

It is becoming clear that an international process of "convergence" of bank prudential supervision standards is unfolding. But the notion of "convergence" is more directional than substantive: that is, the term indicates a movement toward regulatory uniformity, but it tells one very little about the end result or about the means and process toward the end.[19] For example, is the end result actually identity of, or an approximation to, or a functional similarity or equivalence of, supervisory regulation? Moreover, there is no guidance as to how convergence is to be achieved – from the bottom up, from the top down, bilaterally, or multilaterally.

In addition, the legal content of the convergence process is largely undeveloped. In fact, it is questioned at certain levels whether there is or should be any legal content. The international efforts of the Basle Committee on Bank Supervision are portrayed to be non-legal; the efforts of the EC are being effected through legal "directives" that set prescribed ends to be met by the member states, but leave them with discretion and latitude in meeting the goals;[20] in the US there appears to be a concept of "equivalency" for similar regulations by the different domestic regulators;[21] but in the UK, the Bank of England clings to its non-legal traditions of "moral suasion."[22]

Not only is the concept of "convergence" ambiguous and obscure, it is non-unitary and multidimensional. For instance, convergence is being carried out internationally through the *ad hoc* Basle Committee,[23] is happening regionally through the bureaucracy of the European Commission,[24] and is occurring domestically through national regulatory practices (in the US, with its multiple regulators of banking institutions, through multiple national regulatory processes).[25]

Yet (as discussed in section 4.2.4 below) there is a thread that appears to be running through these multiple, complex, and obscure processes; and that is, the recognition among bank regulators that there is a real need (for the policy reasons discussed above) to attempt to approximate prudential supervision standards for banking institutions.[26]

4.2.4 *International Cooperative Activities*

The primary international cooperative activities in the bank prudential supervision area have come about through the Basle Committee and the EC authorities. The Bank of England and the US Federal Reserve Board of Governors have been singularly important in promoting these cooperative activities.[27]

The Basle Committee The international bank supervisors of the OECD jurisdictions have for several decades been highly sensitive to the existence of significant gaps in international supervision and to the resulting possibility of a domino effect on erosion of public confidence within a banking system and on banking systems internationally.[28] The 1974 failure of Bankhaus Herstatt led the governors of the central banks of the Group of Ten to establish the informal and low-key Basle Committee of Bank Supervisors. The first task of this committee was to prepare a "Concordat" addressing the division of bank supervision between home and host countries and the question of consolidated supervision.[29]

The inadequacies of this Concordat surfaced with the Ambrosiano scandal in the early 1980s and a revised Concordat was prepared which attempted to address the problems of consolidated supervision of holding companies and non-banking companies as part of banking groups. The goal was that no international banking operation should escape effective supervision. The Basle Committee addressed the matter of supervisory responsibilities, but not that of a lender of last resort nor that of deposit insurance.[30]

The Basle Committee in the 1980s sought also to improve communication and sharing of information among supervisors, to understand better the risks of the international banking system, and to develop objective supervisory standards (e.g. respecting capital adequacy ratios and treatment of off-balance-sheet transactions). The Committee's 1988 Report on "International Convergence of Capital Measurement and Capital Standards" is its most significant accomplishment to date.[31]

The Committee has recently been working with the International Federation of Accountants (IFAC) to develop acceptable standards in the auditing of international commercial banking (but not respecting the nature and quality of audit reports for regulatory purposes);[32] and has been studying money laundering matters, coordinating international supervisory standards with the international securities supervisors, and further revising its consolidated supervision positions in the wake of the BCCI collapse. The Committee has also been influential in helping to inform and coordinate other regional groups of bank supervisors.[33]

The EC authorities The EC bank supervisors, in implementing the "1992" goal of a common internal financial market, embarked upon deployment of a "mutual recognition" concept whereby duly licensed banking institutions in one EC country will have Community-wide privilege of operations (assuming they meet certain minimum "safety and soundness" criteria). In a move which complements this approach, the EC will institute a supervisory network largely based on "home country" control and a comprehensive system of consolidated supervision for holding company and affiliated operations (revised post-BCCI). The EC programme also envisions EC directives on deposit insurance and large exposures of banking institutions.[34] The EC efforts may well entail creation of a European central bank ("Eurofed") and an EC bank supervisory authority.[35]

4.3 Probable Trends

As the domestic dust of the UK parliamentary and independent (Bingham) enquiries and Bank of England "bashing" subsides in the wake of the BCCI debacle, we will undoubtedly see new UK banking legislation and enhanced UK supervisory practices (as in the cases of the secondary banking crisis and the Johnson Mathey affair), just as we have witnessed substantial revisions of the US banking law and practices under the 1991 Foreign Bank Supervision Act.[36] However, the pervasive and gnawing dilemma left by BCCI is not so much a domestic question of bank fraud, money laundering, and domestic bank regulation and supervision, as it is a question of the necessity, nature, and viability of the incipient network of international bank supervision emanating from the Basle Committee and the coordination of this evolving international supervisory framework with the newly unfolding EC framework, the yet-to-be-enhanced UK framework, and the regulatory frameworks of the other major domestic banking systems (such as those of the US and Japan).

In looking through and projecting beyond this complex, multidimensional matrix of international bank supervision after the BCCI affair, one can discern certain probable trends.

4.3.1 An Enhanced Framework for International Bank Supervision

Although BCCI involved the failure of a $20 billion financial institution, it does not appear that such a failure (even if left unattended by the international regulators) would have created any serious systemic problems for the international banking community. Nevertheless, it is clear that for London, New York, and other world financial markets to continue to prosper there must be a level playing field that instills integrity and confidence on a global basis. This decade will offer further evidence that we are in a global financial market transcending national and regional boundaries. Increasingly supervisors will be required to act jointly if they are to create and to preserve integrity in what has become a world-wide banking system.[37]

4.3.2 Linking Banking and Securities Supervisory Standards

The linkage of banking and securities supervision will become more apparent and coordinated. First, many of the European banking models (e.g. Germany), as well as the EC Second Banking Directive, embrace the "universal banking concept that permits securities activities as legitimate banking activities."[38] Even in the US, where there long has been a federal statutory dichotomy between commercial and investment banking (enshrined in the Glass–Steagall Act), considerable regulatory and judicial erosion of this division has occurred in recent years, and considerable pressure is being placed on the Congress by the US Treasury and others to repeal the Glass–Steagall Act.[39] Second, as prudential concerns continue to focus on a "risk evaluation" of bank activities, it becomes clear that "market risks" (particularly respecting securities), and not simply credit risks, will need to be addressed by the regulators.[40]

However, substantial disparities exist as to how securities firms treat market risks and capital adequacy.[41] To avoid conflict between the securities and bank regulators will require each to minimize competitive advantages between securities firms linked to investment banks and those linked to other banking institutions by a coordinated development of a workable and prudent approach to such market risks and related capital issues.[42]

In recent years, the Basle Committee and the *ad hoc* International Organization of Securities Commissions (IOSCO) have begun to address these issues regarding traded debt and equity securities and related "capital" definitions. It is envisaged that a joint consultative paper on these subjects may be issued by the end of 1992 or early in 1993.[43]

4.3.3 *Effective Consolidated Supervision*

The international bank supervisors have developed principles of "consolidated supervision" under the original and revised (1983) Basle Concordats (as supplemented in 1990).[44] The utilization by BCCI of affiliated bank holding company structures in jurisdictions self-avowedly incapable of any effective consolidated supervision (Luxembourg and the Cayman Islands) and the operation of a hidden "bank within a bank" made evident the existence of persisting and glaring gaps in this supervision. The new EC Consolidated Supervision Directive[45] and pending pronouncements by the Basle Committee should go a long way toward closing these remaining gaps (though, most likely, all gaps cannot be sealed). But the realities of consolidated supervision operate on the national level; it requires effective coordination and convergence of regulatory and supervisory standards and flows of quality information between home and host country regulators. The recent US statute and regulations on foreign bank supervision incorporate the principles of "effective" consolidated supervision into the application, termination, and examination processes for foreign banks.[46]

4.3.4 *Qualified Home Country Supervision*

As the baby should not be thrown out with the bath water, so the principle of home country supervision as espoused by the Basle Committee and the EC Second Directive should not be abandoned.[47] What BCCI makes clear is that home country supervision only makes sense where that jurisdiction has comparable supervisory standards, has a capacity to implement and enforce such standards, and has a deposit insurance and/or lender of last resort dimension. Before 1993 comes upon us, the EC authorities will undoubtedly rethink and refine the "mutual recognition" vehicle for convergence of national supervisory standards. The US authorities have already given their Federal Reserve the powers to step into the breach where home country supervision is unfeasible or inadequate.[48]

4.3.5 An International Institutional Structure

The recent Key and Scott Report of the Group of Thirty has pondered possible international supervisory structures; some commentators even suggest a multilateral treaty approach.[49] What appears realistic and feasible is a continuing maturation and enhancement of the currently informal Basle Committee structure so that this vehicle can assume a broader role in the overall convergence process of supervisory standards; in the assembly, coordination, analysis, and dissemination of relevant supervisory information; in the uniform interpretation of the standards and practices; and in the ultimate surveillance of compliance with and effective implementation of national jurisdiction. The Basle Committee also most probably will accelerate its attempts to influence and to assist the practices of non-OECD bank supervisors and its dialogue with international securities supervisors.[50] On an EC level, it is probable that when Economic and Monetary Union approaches, so also will proposals for an umbrella EC bank supervisory authority appended to the new EC central bank.[51] On a national level, effective linkages will need to be created between national authorities, regional authorities, and the Basle Committee.

4.3.6 Greater Transparency and Disclosure

Secrecy and confidentiality traditionally have been ingrained into the temperament of bankers and central bankers. However, this can lead to an opaque and non-transparent system, as witnessed by the BCCI affair. A radical review of the possible benefits of greater transparency (not only on a supervisory level, but on public and marketplace levels) is what is needed, in a somewhat similar way as it was needed with securities firms and markets. Clearly, there needs to be a better informed and more transparent international banking system respecting both quantitative and qualitative data and respecting an appropriate international vehicle for digesting, evaluating, and disseminating such information. Market disclosure may be the best form of market and institutional discipline.[52] However, broad disclosure can in some jurisdictions (such as the US) greatly complicate and impede international supervisory cooperation in exchange of information.[53]

4.3.7 Increased Role of Auditors and Converging Account Standards

Related to the issue of transparency is the proper role of auditors in the supervisory processes. In BCCI, we found different auditors auditing different affiliated entities under differing national auditing standards. In a consolidated and transparent supervisory network this situation cannot be permitted. But though it may be possible to require one reputable independent auditor (or at least a coordination of audits) for an affiliated group, it will be a long-term project to try to harmonize or converge the disparate accounting and auditing principles and standards existing world-wide (though the Basle Committee and IFAC's International Auditing Practices Committee have begun this dialogue). Also, the relationship of auditors to the official supervisory and regulatory examination processes will need to be sorted out.[54]

4.3.8 Inevitability of Greater Legalism

Because of the complexities of the issues, the multiplicity of the parties involved, the needs for transparency and fairness of application, and the inherent "culture" of various jurisdictions (e.g. the US and certain European countries), greater legalism will creep into international and EC bank regulation. Such legalism has been anathema to the Bank of England, which prefers the more informal method of "moral suasion" and participative discussions with relevant parties. However, it was (in part) this inability to come to terms with the legalism of the 1987 Banking Act and an apprehension of judicial review that stymied the Bank from acting sooner and more decisively in respect of BCCI. Certainly, the density of regulation that exists in the US is not a desired international norm, but some reasonable level of legalism in bank regulation and supervision is needed to ensure transparency, uniformity of application, and fairness within the international banking system.[55]

4.3.9 International Insolvency Laws

Multilateral work will need to be encouraged respecting acceptable international solutions to transnational insolvencies such as BCCI. Such attempts have proven to be protracted and most difficult, as can be seen in the efforts to harmonize EC bankruptcy laws. These attempts become even more problematic when dealing with financial institutions. But for an international supervisory network to work at an optimum level, such problems will need to be addressed on a regional and broader multilateral basis.[56]

4.3.10 Coordinated and Effective Enforcement

An international supervision network cannot ensure effective national supervision, on a ground level, or prompt and effective national enforcement action (both civil and criminal). These aspects will remain in the hands of national authorities; and, as such, the chain of international supervision will always ultimately be subject to the problem of weak or uncoordinated national links in the chain. However, more coordinated efforts and better cooperation of the Basle Committee, the EC authorities, and the dominant national authorities (e.g. of the US, the UK, Germany, and Japan) can promote better national enforcement and examination practices.[57] International cooperative activities in the money laundering area are only a starting point.[58]

4.4 Concluding Observations

Perhaps the efforts of the Bank of England, the *ad hoc* "college" of international supervisors, and the Federal Reserve Board in the BCCI affair were too little, too late. But the broader observation is that the only feasible approach was through a working international network of cooperating supervisors. Over this decade, something better than this *ad hoc* crisis-oriented approach will emerge with respect to international financial services generally, with EC efforts in these areas serving as a centrifugal force for international reform.

Notes

1 For a serious discussion and analysis of the BCCI affair, see the "Perspectives" section of *The International Lawyer*, Winter 1992, which contains an article by Professor Richard Dale, remarks by Messrs Mattingly and Taylor of the Federal Reserve and Mr Corrigan of the New York Federal Reserve, and a summary of the recommendations of the New York Superintendent, Advisory Committee on Transnational Banking Institutions, chaired by Mr Heinman. See also the appendix to this chapter for a summary of the main dates in BCCI's history.
2 See generally R. M. Pecchioli, *The Internationalization of Banking: The Policy Issues* (OECD, 1983). For discussion of the policy, practical, and legal significance of the capital adequacy issue, see, *inter alia*, J. J. Norton, "Capital Adequacy Standards: A Legitimate Regulatory Concern for Prudential Supervision of Banking Activities," 49 *Ohio St. L.J.* 1299 (special symposium, Winter 1989).
3 See generally Study Group established by Central Banks of the Group of Ten Countries (Sam V. Cross, Chair), *Recent Innovations in International Banking* ("Cross Report"; BIS, 1986).

4 See M. Watson, et al., *International Capital Markets: Developments And Perspective* (IMF World Economic and Financial Survey), pp, 40–4.
5 For further discussion, see, *inter alia*, R. Dale, *The Regulation of International Banking*, (Woodhead-Faulkner, 1983), pp. 156–7.
6 Ibid.
7 See note 1 above.
8 On the Third World debt crisis see, *inter alia*, J. J. Norton, ed., *Prospects for International Lending and Rescheduling* (1988).
9 See e.g. Basle Supervisors Committee, *Report on International Developments in Banking Supervision 1981* (1982), p. 7.
10 See Norton, "Capital Adequacy Standards."
11 For discussion of international aspects of the transparency issue, see Pecchioli, *Internationalization of Banking*, pp. 96–100.
12 See Cooke, "Capital and Competition," remarks made at the 1988 London International Capital Markets Conference; and Lamfalussy, "Issues for Banking Supervisors Arising from Worldwide Competition in Financial Markets," remarks printed in BIS. REV. No. 201 (October 23, 1986).
13 For certain legal implications, see generally J. J. Norton, ed., *Bank Regulation and Supervision in the 1990s* (1991).
14 On recent US bank regulation, see *inter alia* J. J. Norton and S. C. Whitley, *Banking Law Manual*, esp. chs 2, 2A (1992).
15 See Norton, "The Bank of England's Lament: The Struggle to Maintain the Traditional Supervisory Practices of 'Moral Suasion,'" in *Bank Regulation*.
16 See, e.g., on US administrative practices, *inter alia*, B. Schwartz, *Administrative Law*, 3rd edn 1991.
17 Ibid.
18 See generally, R. Cranston, ed., *The Single Market and the Law of Banking* (1991).
19 On the notion of "convergence" see E. P. M. Gardener, *Regulation and Convergence of Capital Adequacy*, IEF Research Paper 89/1 (1989).
20 On the nature of EC directives, see P. J. G. Kapetyn and P. V. Van Themaat, *Introduction to the Law of the European Communities – After the Coming into Force of the Single European Act*, 2nd edn L. W. Gormly) (1989), chs. VI–VII.
21 See Norton and Whitley, *Banking Law Manual*, chs 2 and 3, particularly regarding the work of the Federal Financial Institution Examination Council, and Norton, "Capital Adequacy Standards."
22 See Norton, "The Bank of England's Lament."
23 On the Basle Committee's efforts, see, *inter alia*, P. Hayward, "Prospects for International Co-operation by Bank Supervisors (with Background note on the Basle Committee on Banking Supervision)," in Norton, ed., *Bank Regulation*, ch. 5.
24 See Cranston, *The Single Market*.
25 See note 21 above.
26 See, *inter alia*, Kapstein, *Supervisory International Banks: Origins and Implications of the Basle Accord*, Princeton Essays in International Finance, no. 185 (December 1991).

27 See J. J. Norton, "The Convergence of Banking Laws and Standards Within and Without the European Community: An Example of the Efficacy of Emerging International Banking Law," in J. J. Norton and W. Ebke, eds, *Festschrift für Sir Joseph Gold* (1990).
28 See Dale, *Regulation of International Banking*.
29 The first public printing of the 1975 Concordat was as an Annex ("Supervision of Banks' Foreign Establishments") to R. C. Williams and G. G. Johnson, *International Capital Markets: Recent Developments and Short Term Prospects*, IMF Occasional Paper no. 7 (IMF, 1981), pp. 29–32.
30 A copy of "1983 Revised Concordat" was published in (1983) 22 *Int'l Leg. Mat.* 900. The Basle Committee has since supplemented the Revised Concordat in April 1990: see *Supplement to the Concordat: The Ensuring of Adequate Information Flows Between Banking Supervisory Authorities*, published and attached to *Information Flows Between Banking Supervisory Authorities* (BIS, April 1990).
31 See, *inter alia*, J. J. Norton, "The Work of the Basle Committee on Bank Capital Adequacy and the July 1988 Report on International Convergence of Capital Measurements and Capital Standards," (1989) 12 *Int'l Law* 245.
32 See "The Audit of International Commercial Banks," *International Statement on Auditing*, February 1990, issued by the International Auditing Practices Committee of the International Federation of Accountants after consultation with the Basle Committee on Banking Supervision.
33 See Hayward, "Prospects for International Co-operation."
34 See Gruson and Feuring, "A European Community Banking Law: The Second Banking and Related Directive," in Cranston, ed., *The Single Market*, ch. 2.
35 J. J. Norton, "The EC Banking Directives and International Banking Regulation," in Cranston, ed., *The Single Market*, ch. 8.
36 See Pub. L. No. 102–242, 105 Stat. 2236 (1991), tit. II.
37 See, e.g., BCCI testimony of Messrs Mattingly, Taylor and Corrigan of US and NY Federal Reserve before the Committee on Banking, Finance and Urban Affairs, US House of Representatives (September 13, 1991).
38 See E. P. M. Gardener and P. Molyneux, *Changes in Western European Banking: An International Banker's Guide* (1991).
39 See Norton and Whitley, *Banking Law Manual*, ch. 16.
40 See Hayward, "Prospects for International Co-operation."
41 See US General Accounting Office, "Securities Markets: Challenges to Harmonizing International Capital Standards Remain" (Report GAO/GGD-92-41-1992); and Haberman, "Capital Requirements of Commercial and Investment Banks: Contracts on Regulation," *Fed. Res. Bd. of N.Y. Q. Rev.* at 1 (Autumn 1987).
42 Cf. R. Dale, "Banking and Securities Business: The Separation Issues," and Trachtman, "Perestroika in Bank Regulation: Advantages of Securities Regulation for a Market Economy," in Norton, ed., *Bank Regulation*, chs 7, 9.

43 See joint statement by Richard C. Breeden, Chairman, Technical Committee of IOSCO, and E. Gerald Corrigan, Chairman of Basle Committee (released January 29, 1992).
44 See note 30 above.
45 See, Gruson and Feuring, "A European Community Banking Law."
46 See Foreign Bank Supervision Act of 1991, note 36 above. For discussion of this Act see *The International Lawyer*, Winter 1992, "Recent Developments."
47 See EC Council Directive (Second Banking Directive). 89/646/EEC (1989) O. J. L. 38611.
48 See note 46, above.
49 See S. J. Key and H. S. Scott, *International Trade in Banking Services: A Conceptual Framework* (Group of Thirty, 1991).
50 See Hayward, "Prospects for International Co-operation."
51 See Norton, "The EC Banking Directives."
52 See, e.g., remarks by Iain Murray on "International Bank Supervision" for Euromoney Conference on International Banking Regulation After BCCI: What's Wrong and How it Can be Put Right (London, November 20–1, 1991). See also Trachtman, "Perestroika."
53 See Mattingly, Taylor, and Corrigan, testimony to House of Representatives Committee.
54 See remarks by Michael Fowle on "Role of Auditors," Euromoney Conference on International Banking Regulation.
55 Remarks by J. J. Norton on "International Bank Supervision," Ibid.
56 See Goode, "The Insolvency Implications for Banks," in Cranston, ed., *The Single Market*, ch. 7.
57 See remarks by Sturmer on "Practical Problems of Enforcement and Compliance," Euromoney Conference on International Banking Regulation.
58 See, *inter alia*, W. C. Gilmore, *International Efforts to Combat Money Laundering* (1992).

Appendix

BCCI: Timetable of Events, 1972–1991[1]

1972	BCCI SA (owned directly by its shareholders) incorporated in Luxembourg.
1974	Current structure of BCCI (a number of subsidiaries below a Luxembourg holding company) created.
1976	New York regulators turn down BCCI's attempts to buy a US bank using an intermediary because of BCCI's lack of a lead regulator.

[1] *Source*: UK Parliamentary Report (1992).

1978	US court affidavit shows Bank of America (30 percent shareholder in BCCI) critical of BCCI's lending. Bank of America decides to dispose of its shareholding in BCCI. (Divestment completed in 1980.)
1978	UK branch expansion blocked by Bank of England.
1980	Bank of England turns down BCCI's request for recognized status under Banking Act 1979. Instead accorded licenced deposit taker status.
1985	Huge losses revealed in BCCI's Treasury Division (legally part of BCCI (Overseas) Ltd, the Cayman Island Company). This division transferred to Abu Dhabi.
1985	Bank of England discourages Luxembourg's suggestion that BCCI set up separately incorporated company in UK so that Bank of England takes on role of lead regulator.
1986	Ernst & Whinney writes to BCCI complaining about excessive management power and weakness of BCCI's accounting controls.
1986	BCCI's Treasury Division losses (see 1985 above) revealed to Bank of England.
1987	Price Waterhouse appointed sole auditor.
1987	Establishment of College of Regulators for BCCI agreed.
1987	BCCI, as licenced deposit taker recognized under 1979 Banking Act, is automatically authorized under 1987 Banking Act.
June 1988	First meeting of College of Regulators.
October 1988	Drug indictment against BCCI (relating to Tampa branch) issued in US. BCCI's UK management sets up investigation. Bank of England kept informed. Bank of England insists on daily balances and liquidity statistics, and on weekly meetings.
February 1989	Bank of England's meeting with BCCI becomes monthly, with weekly figures.
January 1990	Bank of England institutes formal review of UK operations of BCCI in respect of drug money laundering.
Early 1990	Bank of England becomes aware of terrorist finance accounts at BCCI.
March 1990	Evidence of poor banking emerges from Price Waterhouse's work on BCCI's 1989 report and accounts.

March 1990	Section 39 report commissioned by Bank of England from Price Waterhouse on adequacy of BCCI's accounting systems to detect drug money laundering.
March 1990	Under pressure from Price Waterhouse, BCCI sets up task force to review bad loans and related transactions, using Price Waterhouse's report of March 14 as briefing note.
April 1990	Price Waterhouse's report to the Board of BCCI (received by Bank of England on April 18) sets out task force findings, including confirmation of previously identified problem loans, but also finds evidence of accounting transactions and statements, mainly offshore, being "either false or deceitful." Recommends contingency provisions. Bank of England later argued this report contained no evidence of systematic fraud.
4 April 1990	Governor of Bank of England briefs the Chancellor of the Exchequer on aftermath of Tampa.
20 April 1990	College of Regulators meets. Considers Price Waterhouse's report. Leads to injection of capital (in mid-1990) by Abu Dhabi, which gives it shareholding of over 75 percent.
30 April 1990	College of Regulators meets. Still not satisfied by current provisions, wants $600 million. Reported to College that in-house reorganization committee has been set up to reorganize BCCI. Headquarters to be moved to Abu Dhabi.
16 May 1990	Governor briefs the Chancellor on BCCI's reconstruction plans.
June 1990	Luxembourg gives BCCI a year to move its operations.
June 1990	Price Waterhouse's Section 39 report shows BCCI's systems and controls are satisfactory.
October 1990	Follow up to Price Waterhouse's April report shows need for additional financial support of $1.5 million[2] needed to cover potential losses. Said previous management may have colluded with customers to misstate transactions. Abu Dhabi agrees to meet liabilities and make management changes. Naqvi and Abedi step down. Bank of England later says it still had no evidence of fraud to justify revocation of license at this stage.
December 1990	In last week of December, BCCI executive tells Price Waterhouse of substantial unrecorded deposits.

[2] Figure revised from that given by the Governor in *HC Debates* (1991–92), col. 26, q. 1.

January 1991	In first week of January, Bank of England is told of these unrecorded deposits. Abu Dhabi agrees to make good any shortfall in respect of these deposits. Price Waterhouse informs Bank of England that some irregular transactions may have gone through UK branches and investigates, keeping Bank informed.
25 January 1991	Bank of France bans BCCI from taking new deposits because of inadequate capital requirements.
4 March 1991	Price Waterhouse commissioned to investigate BCCI under Section 41 of Banking Act.
April 1991	Bank of England briefs the Chancellor that BCCI's UK branches in "pretty sound shape."[3]
May 1991	Financial package signed by BCCI's shareholders.
24 June 1991	Bank of England receives Price Waterhouse's draft Section 41 report. Report reveals "massive and widespread fraud" going back a number of years and involving not only past but existing management, even after the reconstruction. Uses evidence provided by Naqvi's 6,000 personal files, previously concealed from Price Waterhouse.
28 June 1991	Governor of the Bank of England receives the Section 41 report.[4]
1 July 1991	Bank of England alerts Serious Fraud Office.
2 July 1991	College of regulators meets. Abu Dhabi not informed.
4 July 1991	Governor informs Prime Minister and Chancellor of decision to close BCCI.
5 July 1991	Coordinated closure of BCCI.

---

[3] Date revised from that given by the Governor in *HC Debates* (1991–92), col. 26, qq. 22–3.

[4] Date revised from that given by the Governor in *HC Debates* (1991–92), col. 26, q. 70.

Part II

International Financial Arrangements

5

Project Financing Concerns

RAYMOND M. AUERBACK

Chapter Outline

5.1 The General Outlook
    5.1.1 Introduction
    5.1.2 The Economic Background
    5.1.3 Prospects for the 1990s

5.2 Debt Servicing: Hedging the Political and Economic Risks
    5.2.1 The Particular Hazards of Project Financing
    5.2.2 Currency Undertakings
    5.2.3 Retention Accounts and Trust Accounts
    5.2.4 "Take or Pay" and other Future Payment Agreements
    5.2.5 Indirect Risk Hedging
    5.2.6 The Multilateral Investment Guarantee Agency (MIGA)

5.3 Security Concerns for Project Lenders
    5.3.1 Segregation of Risk
    5.3.2 Sellers' Liens and Reservation of Title
    5.3.3 "Equal and Rateable" Security

5.4 Enforceability and Legal Opinions
    5.4.1 The Backdrop
    5.4.2 The Limitations of Legal Opinions
    5.4.3 Enforceability Checklist
    5.4.4 Future Trends

5.5 Environmental Issues
    5.5.1 How Environmental Issues Affect Project Lenders
    5.5.2 Risks for the Project
    5.5.3 Lender Liability

5.1 The General Outlook

5.1.1 Introduction

Project finance is distinguished from general corporate financing mainly by its ultimate dependence on the revenues earned by the project for the repayment and servicing of the loan. All true project financing involves at least some degree of risk in one or more of the following categories:

- *physical risk* – e.g., the risk of non-completion or late completion, of machinery breakdown, of crop failure, or of shortages of labor or materials;
- *economic risk* – the viability of the project may be based on incorrect assumptions as to the project implementation costs, market, exportation costs, or currency movements;
- *technical risk* – assumptions as to the suitability of soils, the quality of extractable metals or minerals, or the cost of production or extraction may prove incorrect;
- *political risk* – the possibility of civil disorder, changes in exchange control regulations or in government policy, the cancellation of tax advantages, or the removal of preferential quotas or tariffs; or
- *legal risk* – sophisticated contracts governed by "user-friendly" common law systems may need to be understood and enforced in Third World countries, the development of whose commercial laws may be at a relatively primitive stage.

Moreover, the project lender is frequently unable to take full advantage of the status or general creditworthiness of the project sponsors, since the borrower is likely to be a separate company incorporated under the laws of the place where the project is to be carried out especially for the purpose of implementing the project. Consequently, the assets available for securing the loan are likely to be confined to:

- the physical assets of the project, such as land, buildings, plant, and equipment, some or all of which may have little intrinsic value other than as part of a going concern, and the alienation of which may be severely restricted, particularly to non-nationals;
- the sponsor's shares in the company, which may have little value in those circumstances in which a lender is likely to want to enforce its security and the marketability of which may be practically impossible or even prohibited by local laws;
- inventories and raw materials, which may be subject to sellers' liens or the ownership of which may not vest in the project

company until the full purchase price of the equipment or materials in question has been paid (and possibly not even then, if the transfer of ownership is subject to the "all moneys" type of title retention clause); and
- sales, proceeds and receivables, which may arise in several countries and which the lender may need to "capture" before the proceeds are repatriated to the home country of the project.

The lawyer's task is to create the safest and most predictable legal environment reasonably available to his client in the circumstances. His attention in this respect during the next decade is likely to be concentrated in three traditional areas, namely:

- debt servicing;
- security;
- enforceability;

and one relatively new one:

- environmental problems.

5.1.2 The Economic Background

From about 1983, revenues generated from the utilization of loan funds supplied by the international financial community to a number of sovereign borrowers and their agencies became insufficient to repay and service those loans. This problem particularly affected borrowers in middle- and low-income countries, notably in Latin America and sub-Saharan Africa. In these circumstances, the threat of default could force the lender to the negotiating table, but the resultant inevitable rescheduling of debt and capitalization of interest simply increased the debt burden and made the prospect of ultimate discharge, without some important concessions on the lender's part, even more remote.

Problems affecting sovereign borrowers adversely affect private sector projects in many ways, since they can result in such problems as:

- exchange rate volatility;
- cancellation of public expenditure programmes;
- labor unrest; and
- depletion of foreign currency reserves.

The situation was exacerbated in the 1980s by the increasing dominance of floating interest rate debt, or more specifically by the increase in real interest rates. According to a recent authoritative report, real interest rates were on average nearly six times higher in the 1980s than in 1974–9 when developing countries borrowed much of their debt.[1] The effect was most marked in Latin America: for example, in Argentina floating rate debt as a percentage of all long-term debt increased from 6.6 percent in 1973–5 to 80.2 percent in 1988.[2]

At the same time, low-income countries have become increasingly reliant on official credit, i.e. that supplied by foreign governments or multilateral institutions such as the World Bank. As a result, sovereign borrowers in these countries became, and will remain for a long time to come, "off limits" to many commercial lenders.

5.1.3 Prospects for the 1990s

The 1990s began with a recession which, if not global, will at the very least seriously affect every developed country and will therefore exacerbate the problems of less developed countries which rely on the proceeds of trade with developed countries to service their foreign currency payment obligations. Private sector finance to the developing countries will be concentrated in those middle-income countries targeted by the US "Brady initiative" for Third World debt restructuring, many of which have serious, though (it is to be hoped) reversible, debt problems. Lawyers everywhere acting for commercial investors and lenders will need to be particularly creative and flexible in their approach to project financing in these countries, since they will need to achieve two basic objectives, which may at first sight appear to conflict: first to protect the lender's money, and second to develop a more flexible and less confrontational response to default and potential default.

Ideas have already been floated – and in some cases put into practice – to achieve these objectives. One such idea is the issue of commodity-linked bonds which provide for the risks of reduced commodity prices to be spread between the lender and borrower, and another is the use of "recapture" clauses whereby debt service requirements are variable, and move according to project-related economic circumstances, such as fluctuations in export prices achieved by the goods or commodities produced by the project.

More solutions of this nature will need to be found. Some will involve changes to the substance of transactions, but others will be changes of form, many of a highly technical nature.

The early years of this decade, therefore, will present a much tougher environment in which to operate than the early 1980s. Recent experience of defaults, in the repayment of both sovereign debt and corporate debt, coupled in some countries with the introduction of increasingly restrictive capital adequacy requirements for lenders, will make lending everywhere more difficult. In some countries it has or will become practically impossible for all but the multilateral agencies such as the International Bank for Reconstruction and Development (World Bank or IBRD). However, lending money is the business of banks and financial institutions, and despite past experiences, sooner or later project implementation, and with it project financing, will recommence in earnest. At that stage, financial institutions will look to their lawyers to help them avoid repeating past mistakes.

5.2 Debt Servicing: Hedging the Political and Economic Risks

5.2.1 *The Particular Hazards of Project Financing*

Most project finance is in essence limited recourse financing. Not only is the borrower frequently incorporated solely for the purposes of the project, with no revenues, property, or assets other than those derived from the project, but sponsor support tends to be concentrated in the period up to completion – either by way of guarantees of project completion or undertakings to provide or procure the provision of funds as required to complete the project. Consequently, although the period up to project completion is objectively speaking the most hazardous for the lender, it is, paradoxically, the easiest period for which to obtain effective risk coverage.

Moreover, in the event of the physical failure of the project, it is easier for the lender to find common cause with the borrower, the project sponsors, and even the host government. Thus in many cases the damage can be limited and both the project and its financing restructured. On the other hand, if a project which has been running successfully for a period runs into problems the lender risks finding itself isolated and caught between project sponsors who would rather see the project fail than devote thousands of hours of management time to saving it mainly for the lender's benefit, and an unsympathetic host government indifferent to the project's inability to meet its debt servicing costs.

Assuming the lender has taken security over the moveable and/or immoveable property and assets of the borrower, its position will theoretically become much stronger once the project is completed and those assets have acquired a commercial value as part of a going concern. However, that value may be difficult to translate into cash proceeds of sale, particularly where enforcement involves pursuing a borrower or a guarantor through various domestic tribunals in its own jurisdiction. In practical terms, therefore, receivables and revenues are far more important than buildings, plant, equipment, and even inventory.

The key objective must be to ensure that the debt service costs of the project are met out of the sales proceeds of the project or are otherwise assured and not dependent on the general foreign currency reserves of the host country. In many African countries, for example, foreign currency "pipelines" became so long that debt service payments were increasingly subject to delay, while dividends payable to overseas shareholders in foreign currency became practically irrecoverable.

The following subdivisions of this section illustrate some of the ways in which lenders may protect themselves against these economic and political risks.

5.2.2 Currency Undertakings

Currency undertakings are sometimes available from the government and/or central bank of the country in which the project is to be carried out. These undertakings are addressed to the lender and constitute promises to make available to a borrower or guarantor amounts as required from time to time to enable the borrower or guarantor to perform its debt servicing obligations to the lender in the currency of payment provided for under the loan agreement or, as the case may be, guarantee.

Legal opinions should specifically confirm that such undertakings are valid and enforceable against the party giving the undertaking in the courts of that party's country.

Currency undertakings are not usually drafted so as to constitute guarantees of payment or indemnities against non-payment. They are simply undertakings to sell to the borrower sums in the currency of payment as required to meet the borrower's debt servicing obligations.

It is advisable to stipulate the rate at which the currency of payment will be purchased – usually the "official" rate, i.e. the rate at which the central bank sells the currency of payment in the money market. Particular attention should be paid to this aspect where parallel rates of exchange are in force. Currency undertakings will be easier to obtain if projects are co-financed by institutions such as the International Finance Corporation.

5.2.3 Retention Accounts and Trust Accounts

"Retention accounts" and "trust accounts" are two methods used to procure the servicing of debt out of the foreign currency proceeds of export sales of the goods or commodities produced by the project company.

Retention accounts are bank accounts opened in the name of the borrower in the country in which export revenues are earned, or through which payments are channeled, being accounts into which the sales proceeds are paid and out of which the following are paid:

- project expenditure payable in foreign currency;
- repayments of principal and payments of interest and other charges in relation to foreign currency loans;
- amounts transferred to debt service reserve accounts as a cushion to meet future debt service requirements;
- surplus funds (if any) to the borrower.

The purpose of the retention account is to apply foreign currency sales proceeds directly toward payment of debt servicing, particularly where sales proceeds are paid in the same currency as that required to service the loans.

The essence of a retention account is that the movement of funds between the various sub-accounts is predetermined in as much detail as possible and leaves the banker operating the account with very limited discretion. Indeed, bankers are concerned to see that they cannot be called upon to exercise more than a very limited discretion, since their role involves a potential conflict between their normal duties as bankers to act on their customers' instructions and in those customers' best interests, and their contractual obligations under the agreement providing for the operation of the retention account to apply the provisions of that agreement.

Lenders will normally reinforce their rights and remedies under the agreement by taking a charge over the proceeds of the various accounts constituting the retention account. In England and other jurisdictions where "floating charges" are permitted, there is some scope for argument as to whether a charge over such bank accounts should be a fixed or a floating charge. The distinction may be of some importance (e.g. in the event of insolvency of the borrower), but the dilemma is usually resolved in practice by creating both a fixed and a floating charge over the retention account moneys.

Alternatively, the documentation can provide for the assignment of the borrower's right, title, and interest in and to the retention account and all moneys from time to time in the retention account to the lender, with a proviso that when the loan, together with interest thereon, is repaid, the lender reassigns the same to the borrower. The effect of this is to transfer ownership of the funds rather than to create a security interest over funds remaining in the ownership of the borrower.

In choosing between the two methods, some essential aspects to clarify are:

- *registration*: assuming the borrower is a company, a charge will require registration in any register maintained in the name of the company; an assignment may not require registration;
- *stamp duties*: a charge will obviously be dutiable as such; an assignment may be dutiable as a sale;
- *tax treatment*: an assignment may be treated as a disposal for tax purposes (but probably not if there is a proviso for reassignment);
- *balance sheet treatment*: an assignment effectively reduces the borrower's assets; a charge merely creates a corresponding liability;
- *exchange control*: exchange control regulations applicable to the borrower may permit the creation of a security interest over assets maintained overseas but prohibit the disposal of those assets.

In practice, the major disadvantage of the assignment method for the borrower, namely the relinquishing of ownership, can be neutralized as long as the provision for reassignment is included.

Trust accounts work in exactly the same way as retention accounts, but introduce an independent trustee into the arrangements as the chargee or, as the case may be, assignee, on behalf of the lenders.

The advantages of a trustee are:

- the borrower may feel happier if the account holder is an independent trustee rather than a lender;
- the exchange control and central bank authorities in the borrower's jurisdiction may consent more easily to the arrangements if the account holder is a trustee, particularly a well-known and reputable trust corporation;
- the bankers controlling the account may prefer to deal with a locally based trustee rather than an overseas borrower or lender;
- the legal formalities can be simplified where a number of lenders are involved if they are prepared to rely on the trustee's lawyers to prepare documentation;
- the trustee will be familiar with the laws of the place where the account is maintained, which will usually be chosen to govern the relevant legal documents;
- in the case of a default, a local trustee is better able to take or authorize immediate remedial or enforcement action.

Disadvantages are:

- the introduction of a trustee adds another layer of bureaucracy, e.g. one more party to receive notices and execute documents;

- lawyers in many civil law countries are unfamiliar with the trust concept, and may dislike the idea of a trustee who has no connection with any of the lenders;
- the officer responsible for administering the trust on behalf of the trust corporation will be less aware of the background to the investment than an officer of the lender, and may be less able to anticipate a potential problem;
- additional time and expense are incurred, particularly in the initial stages, both *directly*, e.g. the trustee's fees and those of the trustee's lawyers; and *indirectly*, e.g. the additional time spent by lawyers acting for lenders in dealing with the documents required to set up the trust arrangements.

It has been said that retention account and trust account arrangements are disliked by some governments and central banks on the grounds that they override both the duty of the borrower to repatriate foreign currency sales proceeds and the right of the government to apply those funds in accordance with the political and economic criteria laid down by government policy. For the same reason, such arrangements can run contrary to the policies of the International Monetary Fund (IMF). Lenders should therefore take particular care to ensure that their arrangements are legally binding and enforceable within the borrower's jurisdiction. A legal opinion to this effect will be of some comfort, but the ideal solution is to join the government or central bank as parties to the documents establishing and securing the arrangements.

5.2.4 *"Take or Pay" and other Future Payment Agreements*

These arrangements include:

- *Take or pay contracts*, which are agreements for the purchase of goods or services where the purchaser agrees to pay a specified minimum price for goods or services whether or not he takes delivery of them. The purchaser's obligation is effectively that of an unconditional guarantor, although in some ways it is even stronger since a guarantor can avail himself of certain technical defenses arising out of the relationship between the lender and borrower. The take or pay purchaser's obligations are absolute, however, and cannot be excused even by events of *force majeure*.
- *Through-put contracts*, which are take or pay contracts for services such as pipeline or other transportation services (also called tolling agreements, or deficiency agreements).

- *Take and pay contracts*, which oblige the purchaser to pay for goods or services only if delivered, but regardless of whether the purchaser uses them or not.[3]

The assignment of the seller's rights under these agreements to a lender, or a trustee on behalf of a number of lenders, provides potentially excellent security. They are most often encountered in production, refining, and distribution projects in the mining and energy sectors.

These arrangements are not, however, totally secure in practice. The credit risk has not been removed, but has simply moved from the project company to the contractual purchaser. Some purchasers are public utilities, and they introduce an element of risk, since breaches by them of their obligations – e.g. to take advantage of lower prices on spot markets – may not be actionable under local law. Accordingly the comfort of a reliable legal opinion will certainly be required as to the binding and enforceable nature of such obligations, but lenders should also consider the need for additional comfort or security from an appropriate governmental source.

Recent problems have also arisen as a result of extreme fluctuations in product prices, encouraging purchasers to repudiate their obligations under take or pay and take and pay contracts, and risk litigation. The lender must therefore always be aware of the political and economic dimensions. Does the seller have an alternative market if the buyer repudiates the contract? Will he be allowed to seek an alternative market, if the buyer is a public utility? Is the product saleable without a government license or consent? Is the license general or limited to sales under the contemplated arrangements?

The value of the security should be realistically discounted by lenders in light of the above factors.

5.2.5 Indirect Risk Hedging

There are a number of ways in which the project lender may be able to manage, or even reduce, the risk of default, delay, or rescheduling. The opportunities will vary, depending on the individual circumstances of the project, but any checklist of options should include the following:

- Cost-effective funding of local costs. The use of hard currency loans converted at unrealistic "official" exchange rates to fund local costs of the project, such as labor and transport, is highly undesirable. If no or insufficient sources of local funds are available, and circumstances permit, there may be scope to reduce the effective cost of funding by arranging for the project sponsor to:

(a) purchase hard-currency-denominated sovereign debt having a poor credit rating at a deep discount;

(b) allow the sovereign borrower to settle the debt at face value, or a lesser discount, but in local currency, pursuant to arrangements previously agreed between the sponsor and the sovereign borrower; and

(c) use the proceeds of settlement to fund the local costs possibly with a "hard currency" tag, i.e. agreeing with the government to treat the proceeds as funds brought into the host country in hard currency for exchange control and repatriation purposes.

- Utilize debt countertrading. If a project sponsor has more than one existing project in the same country earning foreign currency through export sales, it may be possible to agree with government that sales proceeds of one project be set aside for debt servicing of the other project.
- Co-finance with a multilateral or bilateral development institution. Institutions like the World Bank, European Investment Bank, and Asian Development Bank can have considerable political "muscle" and projects co-financed by these institutions are less likely to run into problems resulting from macro-economic factors such as government policy. More direct advantages include the increased likelihood of government guarantees being made available and, in the case of many development institutions, loans at fixed rates of interest, possibly "soft loans" or a mix of loan and equity funds.

Disadvantages include the length of time taken by many development institutions to appraise projects and approve investment proposals and, in the event that the project runs into trouble, the possible reluctance of development institutions to accelerate the maturity of their loans or take other decisive action promptly, due both to overall political considerations and to the inherently bureaucratic nature of the internal management of such institutions.

Despite these disadvantages, it is likely that in the short term at least, lenders considering participating in the financing of projects in a number of low-income countries would be well advised to seriously question the wisdom of lending without the benefit of an institutional co-financier.

5.2.6 *The Multilateral Investment Guarantee Agency (MIGA)*

MIGA was established in 1988 by the World Bank to provide, *inter alia*, guarantees to foreign investors in developing countries against all or any of the following risks:

- currency risks, i.e. losses resulting from "a deterioration in the conditions for converting local currency" and delays in remitting foreign currency abroad;
- expropriation, i.e. measures taken by the host government to "deprive the investor of his ownership or control of, or substantial benefits from, his investment";
- war, revolution, and civil disturbance, i.e. physical damage and interruption to the investor's business;
- breach of contract, i.e. the repudiation or breach by a host government of a contract "where the investor is denied justice."

The breach of contract guarantee could prove the most far-reaching of these guarantees. Guarantees are given under contracts of guarantee up to a maximum of fifteen (or in some cases twenty) years, but can be terminated by the investor at any time after the third anniversary. MIGA cannot terminate other than as a result of default by the insured ("Guarantee Holder").

The General Conditions of Guarantee were issued on January 25, 1989. These provide that disputes between MIGA and the Guarantee Holder (with one exception) shall be settled by a special arbitration tribunal set up under the Arbitration Rules of MIGA, whose decision shall be final and binding and "enforceable in any court of competent jurisdiction" (section 3.3). The Arbitration Tribunal shall apply – apart from the specific terms of the Contract of Guarantee, and the provisions of the convention establishing MIGA – "general principles of law" (section 3.4).

It is far too early to judge the practical usefulness of MIGA, but potentially it could provide services similar to those currently offered by existing political risk insurers such as ECGD (UK), COFACE (France), and HERMES (Germany), but for investors as well as suppliers. Cooperative schemes between MIGA and such insurers are already on the agenda.

5.3 Security Concerns for Project Lenders

5.3.1 Segregation of Risk

Although some projects are carried out through joint venture or partnership arrangements, as we have already seen most are implemented by specially created and locally incorporated companies. In some cases this will be a requirement of the host country, particularly where the project company is required to acquire an interest in real property, or to hold a license to exploit minerals or other natural resources. It may also be necessary to enable the company to benefit from tax holidays. In many cases, however, the establishment of a local corporate vehicle will be the most attractive option for the project sponsor. In particular, it will enable the sponsor to segregate the risks attached to the project from the sponsor's other business operations, and remove or limit the lender's right of recourse to the sponsor in the event of default by the project company in its capacity as a borrower.

Assuming that segregation of risk is an important objective, the sponsor is unlikely to agree to guarantee the project company's obligations to lenders. The lender may therefore have to be content with more remote or indirect support, e.g. a comfort letter, a share retention undertaking, or an obligation to provide or procure facilities to meet cost overruns.

This leaves the lender looking to the assets of the project itself as the main, or even sole, source of security. If that security is to have tangible worth, it must (a) be realizable and (b) have an ascertainable value.

Evaluating the true worth of asset security is difficult, partly because the apparent value of security may differ from its real value. Two contemporary examples of this problem are discussed below, one taken from English law, and the other of more general application.

5.3.2 Sellers' Liens and Reservation of Title

The development of English law and practice in relation to sellers' liens shows how assets which may appear to belong to a project company may nevertheless not be owned by it.

The right of a seller to impose a lien over goods as security for the payment of the purchase price of those goods has long been generally acknowledged. Indeed, it is usual for negative pledge clauses to specifically exclude such liens from the general prohibition against the creation of encumbrances over the borrower's assets.

However, rather than create a security interest over goods, the ownership of which has passed to the buyer, sellers operating under English law generally prefer to "reserve title" to the goods: that is to say, to retain ownership of the goods until the purchase price has been paid in full.

"Reservation of title" clauses have been a feature of contracts for the sale of goods under English law particularly since 1976.[4] In recent years, however, their scope has often been extended so that ownership of the goods remained "reserved" to the seller until not only the purchase price of those goods but all other indebtedness of the buyer to the seller arising out of all other transactions between the parties had been discharged.

It has been argued that these so-called "all moneys" clauses effectively create a charge over the goods, which, being registerable under the UK Companies Acts, would be void unless duly registered. It appears, however, that the House of Lords has rejected these arguments in favor of the argument that reservation of title clauses create, in effect, conditional sales contracts, so that if the condition is not fulfilled the buyer never acquires title to the goods and has therefore no legal interest over which security can be created.[5]

The logic of this decision certainly appears sound, but the effect is that where the seller and the buyer have a number of parallel ongoing contractual relationships, the point, if any, at which the buyer actually acquires ownership of the goods supplied under a specific contract (and can therefore grant an effective security interest over them in favor of the lender) may be extremely difficult to identify.

It also means that permitting a seller to use a reservation of title clause, even on an "all moneys" basis, may not constitute a breach of a borrower's negative pledge since such a clause creates no security interest in the goods.

Accordingly, if lenders wish to avoid financing the purchase of goods to which the borrower may not ultimately acquire a title and over which they in turn may not acquire a valid security interest, they must specifically prohibit the use of loan funds to purchase goods under contracts containing "all moneys" type retention of title clauses.

5.3.3 *"Equal and Rateable" Security*

The basic negative pledge covenant is a feature of most international loan agreements. It comprises a covenant by the borrower not to "create or permit to subsist" any mortgage, charge, pledge, lien, or other encumbrance over its assets or revenues (with standard exceptions, e.g. liens arising by operation of law and pre-existing encumbrances).

There are two variations of the basic covenant which are frequently seen in international loan agreements, and which might be more properly termed "positive pledges."

The first variation allows the borrower to create security in favor of third parties but provides that if the borrower does so, it must grant "equal and rateable" security to the lender – either the same security over the same assets or equivalent security (i.e. other security accepted by the lender as no less beneficial than the security granted to the third party).

The second variation is similar to the first, but rather than providing for the creation of equal and rateable security, provides that the creation of the third party security will automatically, equally, and rateably secure the borrower's indebtedness to the lender.

The basic difference appears to be that the first variation constitutes an agreement to create security[6] but implicitly accepts that further action will be required before that security can be effectively created, while the second variation assumes that effective security can be automatically created by the act of creating third party security (which may or may not be a dubious legal proposition).

The project lender will need to assess the value of negative and positive covenants not only if it seeks to impose them but equally if it wishes to take an immediate security interest over the project assets itself, since it may be affected

- by negative and positive pledges in other loan agreements entered into by the borrower, the existence of which may not be known to him; and
- by the uncertainty surrounding the effectiveness and enforceability of positive pledges, particularly of the automatic type (which appear, for example, as a standard provision in loan and guarantee agreements to which the IBRD is a party[7]). For example, if such a provision can effectively and automatically create a charge, how will the third party lender know when this has occurred and how can he ascertain that it was registered within the prescribed period? Does the borrower have an implied duty to register the charge? How can the date of creation be determined in any event?

The project lender in this situation is arguably worse off than one whose co-lenders insist on equal security being granted to them *ab initio*. At least in the latter case the lenders can all enter into a trust deed or a security sharing agreement, regulating priorities *inter se* and coordinating enforcement procedures.

It is tempting to play down the potential hazards. Enforcing the lender's right to equal and rateable security promptly and effectively will require the borrower's cooperation, which might not be forthcoming. Provisions for automatic security may well prove impossible to enforce or take effect only as a lesser security interest or one ranking below that of the secured lender. Nevertheless, the obligation to create security should be taken seriously, like any contractual obligation, if only because of its potential as a weapon to defeat the enforcement by the secured lender of its security or to delay the enforcement to such extent that the security becomes practically worthless.

Consequently, lenders and their lawyers should resist the temptation to play down the importance of these covenants, or accept facile arguments that they are "standard" or "never used in practice," and should always evaluate them, unless reliably advised otherwise, on the basis that they are (a) enforceable and (b) likely to be enforced.

5.4 Enforceability and Legal Opinions

5.4.1 The Backdrop

Nowhere is the distinction between capital market transactions and project financing more apparent than in relation to the governing law and enforcement of agreements.

In capital markets the accent is on negotiability; and loan agreements or notes, participation agreements, and transfer documents tend to follow a predictable and uniform format and to be governed by the law of the market in which they are intended to circulate. Thus a Scandinavian bank (acting through its London branch) will happily lend to a Korean borrower on the London market under an agreement or note governed by English law.

Project finance agreements, however, are rarely designed for ease of transferability.

Additionally, agreements for the provision of loans to finance projects are frequently governed by the law of the lender's domicile. However, some peripheral but crucial documents may necessarily be governed by laws with which the lender is unfamiliar, e.g. charges over immovable property (which are normally governed by the *lex situs*) or by no specifically chosen law, e.g. undertakings given by governments.

Even where the lender is happy with the chosen law, it needs to be satisfied that the borrower's obligations are enforceable against the borrower in the courts of the borrower's domicile. This means that the lender will need to obtain a legal opinion as to the validity, binding nature, and enforceability of the agreement and the borrower's obligations.

5.4.2 The Limitations of Legal Opinions

It is ironic, but nevertheless a fact of project financing life, that assumptions as to the enforceability of a borrower's or guarantor's obligations under a complex and highly sophisticated set of documents drafted under, say, English law may ultimately be based on the opinion of a lawyer in a civil law jurisdiction who is unfamiliar with the project, unused to dealing with sophisticated international finance transactions, and under pressure to produce an opinion in a predetermined form within a certain time limit in order to meet conditions of disbursement in the loan agreement.

Consequently, there are a number of key areas that should be investigated before a legal opinion can be safely relied upon. These include:

- The calibre and experience of the giver of the opinion. The lender's lawyer should avoid using local counsel whose knowledge, experience, and diligence he or she has not had the opportunity to assess face to face or at least in the course of lengthy discussions by telephone.
- The assumptions made as to the authenticity of signatures and the conformity of copy documents with originals. This standard formula of words may disguise the failure to make reasonable enquiry.
- Statements by the lawyer that he has "examined such other documents as we have deemed necessary or relevant." It may be unwise to place too much reliance on such a statement, and it may be more prudent to ask for specific details.
- Statements that the borrower or guarantor has taken the necessary corporate action and has the corporate power and authority to enter into and perform its obligations under specified agreements. This statement may be based solely on the receipt of a certificate to that effect from an officer of the borrower or guarantor. Does the opinion state the consequences of *ultra vires* action?
- Statements that agreements are legally binding and enforceable in accordance with their terms. This opinion will often be qualified, e.g. by reference to overriding bankruptcy legislation or equitable principles. This is the heart of the opinion, and the elements of this statement should be tested to see if they are based on knowledge and experience or merely inserted because they are standard.
- Statements that the chosen law of the agreement represents a valid choice of law which would be recognized and applied by the local courts. Can this statement be supported by concrete evidence such as an Article of a Statute or a decided case?

5.4.3 *Enforceability Checklist*

It is impossible in one brief passage to enumerate all the considerations which lawyers should bear in mind in testing the likely consequences of seeking to enforce an agreement in a foreign (to the lender) jurisdiction. However, some basic considerations are:

- *The language of the agreements.* This is arguably the most important practical consideration. How can an agreement under New York law in the English language be enforced in the courts of, say, a province of Indonesia? The lender should consider the merits of obtaining a first-class translation of vital documents and asking the other parties to initial the translation as evidence of its authenticity.
- *The familiarity of concepts around which legal relationships are created.* See, for example, the discussions earlier in this chapter regarding the use of a trustee or trust corporation. Would it be more practicable to use an alternative with which local lawyers may be more familiar?
- *Public policy considerations.* To what extent could these override the provisions of the agreement? Is this covered in the legal opinion?
- *The enforceability of obligations and undertakings of governments or their agencies.* Can a government or government agency be sued, or have a judgment enforced against it in its own courts?
- *Sovereign immunity.* Can a sovereign borrower or guarantor claim immunity against a suit brought in another country? It may be more relevant here to investigate the law of the country in which the sovereign entity habitually maintains assets, rather than that of the jurisdiction to which the sovereign entity has specifically submitted.
- *Formalities.* A document may be unenforceable because it has not been duly stamped or registered.
- *Incompatibility with basic legal principles*, such as equitable principles (in common law jurisdictions) or good faith principles (in civil law jurisdictions). A specific "no conflict" legal opinion should highlight problems.
- *Usury laws.* Do the interest provisions risk violating usury laws or, in countries applying Islamic law principles, prohibitions against the charging of interest?
- *Exchange control.* All necessary consents must be obtained to ensure that funds can be repatriated and that Article VIII, 2(b) of the Articles of Agreement of the International Monetary Fund[8] cannot be invoked. In some territories, sovereign borrowers or guarantors require exchange control consent in the same way as private sector entities.

5.4.4 Future Trends

The twin dominance of the English language as the first international business language and of Anglophone bankers and lawyers as leaders of the international financial community during the post-war decades has brought about two separate but related consequences in relation to the drafting of international financial agreements. The first is the increasing acceptance of English law and the laws of certain US states (mainly New York State) as the governing law of the agreement, even where the connection of one or both of the parties with the chosen legal system is not immediately apparent.

This approach, though it has the advantage of predictability and universality, may produce a situation which is far from that which was intended. The document may appear impeccable, but how far does it reflect the lender's wishes? English law, for example, is no longer truly English. It incorporates, by adoption, a mass of European Community legislation. It encompasses, potentially, law from the whole of the Commonwealth, decided cases from which can be persuasive in English courts, particularly in deciding new issues.

The second consequence can best be demonstrated by the following (fictitious) example:

> The Commercial Bank of Ruritania, involved in project financing throughout the (largely Anglophone) Third World, produces its loan, guarantee, and security documentation in English. The documentation is obviously based largely on standard English agreements, incorporating many familiar provisions, but with the occasional addition of what appear to be echoes of Ruritanian law. Loan and guarantee agreements are governed by Ruritanian law (which is based on a civil law system) and the borrower submits to the jurisdiction of the courts of the Western Province of Ruritania. There is no translation of the documents into the Ruritanian language accepted as authentic by the parties.

Sounds far-fetched? On the contrary, it is the normal practice of certain continental European institutions, and not out of choice. They know that if the documentation is not (a) in English and (b) in a form with which the borrower is familiar, they will not be able to successfully conclude the transaction.

On the other hand, these lenders may be commercial banks determined to lend only under agreements governed by the laws of their domicile, or maybe para-statal institutions required by their statutes to apply their national laws to all basic financial agreements. As a result the legal *pot-pourri* described above is only too easily achieved in practice.

These practices may well change during the course of the next decade. For one thing, the emerging countries of Eastern Europe have legal systems which are far closer to those of many continental European countries than to the common law systems of many English-speaking countries, so it may be illogical to use a "neutral" common-law-based governing law, or an Anglo-American format, for investment documentation in those cases.

Alternatively, documentation of universal application, subject to no stated governing law but to general principles of international law, may eventually come to replace the existing Anglo-American models.[9]

The idea of an agreement governed by general principles of international law may seem revolutionary, but there are already in existence a number of supranational institutions which effectively apply such principles, as well as numerous conventions providing for the universal adoption and application of standard terms and conditions of contract. Moreover, the laws of many countries, e.g. Israel and Mauritius, contain elements of both common law and civil law.

Finally, there are models which already exist (such as the IBRD General Conditions) and which constitute a well-tried platform from which to develop a comprehensive and generally understood set of basic rules governing international project finance agreements.

5.5 Environmental Issues

5.5.1 How Environmental Issues Affect Project Lenders

There has been an increasing awareness during recent years of the impact of environmental legislation, but the law in this area is bound to develop exponentially throughout the 1990s. There are two separate ways in which the environmental aspects of a project can impact upon lenders:

- by affecting the project company or the project sponsors, e.g. if project costs have to be increased to ensure compliance with environmental legislation, or a license is not granted, or is revoked, due to non-compliance, or a large fine is imposed for contravention, or the value or marketability of an asset over which a lender has security is impaired;
- by making the lender directly liable for non-compliance, as a result of the lender's direct participation in the project, e.g. in the course of enforcing security or of an attempt to rescue a project which is in a critical condition.

5.5.2 *Risks for the Project*

At present, US lenders' and investors' consciousness of and sensitivity to environmentally related risks are greater than those of their British and other European counterparts, since US laws have been more stringent, and more stringently applied; but that will change when existing and proposed municipal and European Community legislation begins to bite. In most developing countries, environmental legislation either does not exist or has no teeth as yet.

However, project financing is largely medium- to long-term, and lawyers acting for lenders should be already inserting suitable provisions into loan and guarantee agreements to ensure:

- compliance with present and future legislation;
- that revocation of vital licenses, or the imposition of substantial fines, are events of default;
- that actual and potential action by environmental agencies against the project company is disclosable, and subject to appropriate warranties, in the same way as major litigation;
- that where applicable and if negotiable, indemnities are obtained from project sponsors (or that the additional cost of compliance is covered under the agreement providing for the funding of cost overruns by the project sponsor).

The insertion of suitable contractual safeguards does not remove the need to make due enquiry directly, or through expert consultants, or to consider other protective measures, e.g. insuring against liability.

5.5.3 *Lender Liability*

Generally speaking, the lender will only risk direct liability by:

- taking possession of assets, particularly land, in the course of enforcing security; or
- being deemed to be in the position of managing or controlling the operations of the project company.

It may be difficult to avoid these situations arising, particularly where liability is "strict," i.e. where it arises because the lender is, or is deemed to be, a "possessor" of land or a "producer" of substances on that land.

However, since potential liability will invariably arise in the course of enforcing, rather than simply holding, security, particular care should be taken to ensure that persons appointed to carry out enforcement functions should be, in so far as is possible and practicable, deemed for all purposes to be acting as agents of the borrower rather than of the lender.

Notes

1 *World Development Report 1990* (Oxford University Press), p. 15.
2 Ibid., p. 168.
3 For a detailed analysis of the subject see P. K. Nevitt, *Project Financing*, 5th edn (Euromoney, 1989).
4 Following the decision of the Court of Appeal in *Aluminum Industrie Vaassen BV* v. *Romalpa Aluminium Ltd* [1976] IWLR 676.
5 *Armour* v. *Thyssen Edelstahlwerke AG* 1990 3 AER 481 (October 1990).
6 See R. M. Goode, *Legal Problems of Credit and Security*, 2nd edn (Sweet & Maxwell, 1988), pp. 19–21.
7 See s. 9.03(a)(i) of the IBRD General Conditions Applicable to Loan and Guarantee Agreements, dated January 1, 1985.
8 Article VIII, 2(b) states: "Exchange contracts which involve the currency of any member and which are contrary to the exchange control regulations of that member maintained or imposed consistently with this Agreement shall be unenforceable in the territories of any member."
9 See, e.g., s. 10.01 of the IBRD General Conditions Applicable to Loan and Guarantee Agreements, dated January 1, 1985.

6

"Euromarket" Developments: Legal Aspects of Investing and Raising Finance in Russia, the Czech Republic and Slovakia, Hungary, and Poland

ROBERT L. DRAKE, PHILIPPE MAX, BENEDIKT WEIFFENBACH, WIM A. TIMMERMANS, JAN GROZDANOVIC, TIMOTHY E. D. GEE, KÁLMÁN GYÁRFÁS, ANNA HALUSTYIK, TOMASZ UJEJSKI, AND CHRISTOPHER SZPOJNARIWICZ

Chapter Outline

6.1 Russia
    6.1.1 Applicable Laws
    6.1.2 Company Law
    6.1.3 Privatization
    6.1.4 Foreign Investment
    6.1.5 Foreign Exchange
    6.1.6 Public Fund-raising
    6.1.7 Property Law
    6.1.8 Security
    6.1.9 Creditors' Rights
    6.1.10 Leasing
    6.1.11 Execution of Documents
    6.1.12 Law and Jurisdiction
    6.1.13 Sovereign Immunity

6.2 The Czech Republic and Slovakia
    6.2.1 The Czech Republic and Slovakia
    6.2.2 Company Law
    6.2.3 Privatization
    6.2.4 Foreign Investment
    6.2.5 Foreign Exchange
    6.2.6 Tax
    6.2.7 Property Law
    6.2.8 Security
    6.2.9 Creditors' Remedies
    6.2.10 Leasing
    6.2.11 Execution of Documents
    6.2.12 Law and Jurisdiction

6.3 Hungary
    6.3.1 Company Law
    6.3.2 Privatization
    6.3.3 Public Fund-raising
    6.3.4 Foreign Investment
    6.3.5 Foreign Exchange
    6.3.6 Property Law
    6.3.7 Security
    6.3.8 Creditors' Rights
    6.3.9 Tax
    6.3.10 Leasing
    6.3.11 Execution of Documents
    6.3.12 Law and Jurisdiction
    6.3.13 Sovereign Immunity

6.4 Poland
    6.4.1 Company Law
    6.4.2 Privatization
    6.4.3 Foreign Investment
    6.4.4 Taxation
    6.4.5 Foreign Exchange
    6.4.6 Property Law
    6.4.7 Leasing
    6.4.8 Security
    6.4.9 Insolvency and Liquidation
    6.4.10 Law, Jurisdiction, and Arbitration
    6.4.11 Sovereign Immunity

6.1 Russia

6.1.1 Applicable Laws

The Russian parliament has been enacting legislation since 1990. That legislation is quite independent of the legislation passed by the Supreme Soviet of the USSR. The Minsk Agreement of December 1991 (by which the Commonwealth of Independent States was founded) provided, *inter alia*, that legislation of other states (including the USSR) would not apply in the territory of the new independent states. In its decree ratifying the Minsk Agreement, the Russian parliament modified the effect of the agreement by stating that legislation of the former USSR would continue to apply in circumstances where there was no applicable Russian law so long as the application of the relevant law of the former USSR would not contradict the Russian constitution and other relevant Russian legislation.

Unless otherwise stated, references to legislation in section 6.1 of this chapter are to legislation of the Russian Federation.

6.1.2 Company Law

State and municipal enterprises Most enterprises in the Russian Federation are state enterprises which are owned by either the Russian governmental authorities or the municipal authorities. The proportion of state enterprises to the total number of enterprises is, however, decreasing as the privatization process continues.

Private enterprises The Law on Enterprises and Entrepreneurship of December 25, 1990 regulates all forms of enterprises and lists, among other things, the various types of private enterprises. Because they provide limited liability, to date mostly joint stock companies (and, to a lesser extent, limited liability companies) have been used by foreign investors. The forms of private enterprises are as follows:

- *Private (family) business [individualnoe (semeinoe) chastnoe predpriatie]* This type of enterprise owns and deals either with the property of only one citizen, or with that held in common by members of a family. The owner of the private business is liable for the obligations of the business to the extent defined in the by-laws of the enterprise.
- *Partnerships [polnoe tovarishchestvo]* This type of enterprise is briefly referred to in one article of the Law on Enterprises and Entrepreneurship. As in most Western jurisdictions, all partners in a partnership bear unlimited joint liability for the obligations of the partnership.

■ *Limited partnerships [smeshannoe tovarishchestvo]* As is the case with partnerships, the Law on Enterprises and Entrepreneurship gives little information about this type of enterprise. Limited partnerships consist of one or more full members with full joint liability and one or more investing members who are liable only to the extent of their investment in the enterprise.

■ *Limited liability companies [tovarishchestvo sogranitchenoi otvetstvennostiu]* A limited liability company is a form of entity that is largely unregulated. In the view of the Russian authorities, it is the successor to the joint venture that existed under the legislation of the former USSR. Therefore it is the structure most favored by companies that had established joint ventures in the former USSR and that now want to restructure into a Russian entity. A limited liability company does not issue shares or stock, and there is no requirement to maintain a minimum amount of capital. Each limited liability company is managed by a board of directors who are appointed by the company's owners or participants and a general director who is appointed by the board.

The lack of legal requirements relating to limited liability companies does create some uncertainties for both the limited liability companies and persons dealing with them. However, the lack of such requirements also enables a limited liability company to be established and managed in a way which best suits its owners and other participants.

■ *Joint stock companies [actsionnernoe obshestvo]* Joint stock companies are regulated by Decree No. 601 of December 25, 1991, and are similar to corporations in many Western countries. It is the form of entity most favored by Western investors. A joint stock company which issues shares may be (a) closed, where its shares may not be transferred without the approval of the other shareholders; or (b) open, where its shares may be freely traded.

Joint stock companies are administered and managed by a shareholders' meeting, a board of directors and a management consisting of company officers and an auditing commission. The auditing commission, which is a relic of the former USSR's legal structures, is a body that can be convened at any particular time to investigate financial and other issues concerning the company. Decree No. 601 contains some cumbersome technical rules as to how joint stock companies must be governed in the absence of alternative provisions in the company's foundation documents. The foundation documents will include a charter or set of by-laws, a protocol (which is signed by the founders and which states that the company is being founded and provides for the appointment of its first directors), and other information about the shareholders (which may include references or evidence of solvency).

The minimum capital for a closed joint stock company is 10,000 roubles, and for an open joint stock company 100,000 roubles. The number of members of the board of a joint stock company must be equal to the number of its founders. The shares in an open joint stock company can be freely transferred without the necessity to obtain consent or approval from the other shareholders or the shareholders' meeting. In cases where the shareholders include both Russians and Westerners, the Russians often object to the free transferability of shares.

A joint stock company is, pursuant to Decree No. 601, allowed to establish a wholly-owned subsidiary. That subsidiary must also be in the form of a joint stock company. As a Russian legal entity, it has the same rights as any Russian organization and may engage in a wide range of commercial activities.

Representative offices A Western company can establish a representative office in the Russian Federation without any requirement to become accredited or obtain any governmental approval. There would, however, be advantages for a company in its business activities if the company were to become accredited.

Branch offices A Western company can also register as a branch in the Russian Federation. There is little law on the subject and the Russian authorities have not yet conclusively determined how to treat a branch office – whether simply as an office of a foreign legal entity or as a legal entity in its own right. There are a number of advantages, including tax advantages, in establishing a branch, but, because of the current uncertainties, it might not be prudent for a Western company to establish a branch office.

Corporate information There is no central companies registry in the Russian Federation where the by-laws, other corporate documents, or accounts of a Russian company may be reviewed. It is therefore practically impossible to conduct an objective "due diligence" review of a Russian company as the only source for such information is the company itself.

Acts of authorized officers The Civil Code (1964) provides that a company is not usually bound by the acts of its officers in the event of its officers not acting within the rights accorded to them by the law or by the charter of the company. Therefore, before entering into any type of agreement with a Russian legal entity, it is advisable to verify the powers of such company officers.

From a legal point of view, there is no general duty for officers to act with due care, but in practice such requirement may be included in the charter or foundation documents of the company.

Maintenance of capital and financial assistance

- Increase or decrease in the capital of a joint stock company is dealt with in Decree No. 601. There is no prohibition or regulation concerning maintenance of capital following the initial registration of the joint stock company.
- The Law on Foreign Investment of July 4, 1991, states that enterprises which have raised capital from foreign sources may use their assets to provide security for all types of obligations which they may incur, including borrowing.

6.1.3 Privatization

General The privatization process in the Russian Federation is principally governed by the Law on Privatization of State and Municipal Enterprises in the Russian Federation of July 3, 1991, as amended on June 5, 1992. This law sets the general principles and framework for privatization. The Fundamental Provisions of the Programme for Privatization of State and Municipal Enterprises in the Russian Federation for 1992, which were adopted on December 29, 1991, and modified on June 11, 1992, establish priorities for privatization in the Russian Federation for 1992. They aim to facilitate the transition to a market economy through the accelerated privatization of enterprises and attraction of foreign investment, and by removing from the state the burden of maintaining ineffective and unprofitable enterprises.

Regulations which were adopted in June 1992 include those which (a) require transformation of large state enterprises into joint stock companies by November 1, 1992, with shares subsequently to be made available to the enterprise labor staff, and then to the general public, and (b) permit sales of land which is used or needed in running an enterprise during the course of its privatization.

Legislation has recently been introduced to provide for the issue of vouchers to Russian citizens which would entitle such persons to acquire interests in privatized businesses and properties.

In the months to come, further regulations are expected to clarify the privatization process relating to foreign investors' participation, privatization vouchers, share sale, and investment funds.

The Russian Federation State Property Management Committee (the GKI) supervises and controls the privatization process, in which the local council of people's deputies and the labor staff of enterprises also have significant influence.

Methods of privatization There are various methods for carrying out the privatization of a state-owned enterprise, and although some criteria for the choice of privatization method have been determined by the Fundamental Provisions (referred to above), such choice remains at the discretion of the GKI. These methods are:

- the sale of shares of enterprises which are being transformed into joint stock companies;
- the sale of enterprises at auction;
- the sale of enterprises through competitive bidding;
- the sale of enterprises through non-commercial investment tenders (called investment bidding);
- the sale of property and other assets of enterprises in the process of being, or having been liquidated; and
- the redemption of property of an enterprise that was leased to the labor collective of the enterprise, prior to the Privatization Law of July 1991 being adopted.

The Privatization Law gives the employees of an enterprise the right to purchase shares in their enterprise on preferential terms. It also allows, and encourages, foreign parties to participate in the privatization of certain facilities and enterprises, although some restrictions remain.

Compensation There is no legislation entitling individuals who suffered loss as a result of the 1917 Revolution and the nationalization of privately owned property to any compensation.

6.1.4 Foreign Investment

Permits and authorizations Generally, no special permission, other than in connection with the registration of the relevant enterprise, is required for a foreign person to make an investment in the Russian Federation.

The Law on Foreign Investment allows foreign investors to make almost any type of investment in the Russian Federation. However, prior to a foreign person conducting certain activities (including mining, banking, insurance, and brokering connected with the circulation of securities), that foreign person must first have obtained a license from the appropriate Russian ministry.

Foreign debt–equity ratio There is no restriction under Russian law on the level of foreign debt to foreign equity to be maintained by an enterprise in the Russian Federation.

Tax New and comprehensive Russian tax legislation has been enacted to replace the earlier tax system, which was based largely on

USSR law. All taxes are payable in roubles. The four main elements relating to taxation are:

- *Profit tax* Profit tax is payable by an enterprise at a rate of 32 percent on the enterprise's net profits from most of its business activities. Certain other activities are taxed at different rates. For example, profits on commission-based intermediary and brokerage activities are taxed at the rate of 45 percent. Banking and insurance activities are each taxed under separate laws.

Tax concessions, such as tax holidays for enterprises with foreign investment, have now largely been eliminated. The elimination of the differences between the taxation of enterprises with foreign investment and enterprises which are owned by Russian interests has also removed the prior distinction between joint ventures with more than 30 percent foreign ownership and other types of enterprise.

An income (or revenue) tax law has also been passed. It has been assumed that the income tax law would supersede the profit tax law sometime during 1992. However, as time goes by, it appears less likely that the income tax law will ever come into force.

- *Value-added tax* Value-added tax, at the rate of 28 percent, is imposed on the sale of most goods and services. The rate of value-added tax applicable to basic food and consumer items was recently reduced to 15 percent. The tax does not apply to export or import sales, but it does apply to services rendered in the Russian Federation for foreign companies and to the resale of imported goods. The tax also applies to barter transactions and to the rental of land and buildings. Value-added tax which has been paid on operating expenses and inputs in connection with goods and services may be refunded, so that the relevant enterprise is obliged to pay to the state only the difference between the value-added tax paid and the value-added tax that has been collected.

- *Dividend withholding tax* Pursuant to the Law on Dividends, dividends to be paid by Russian companies to foreign shareholders are subject to a dividend withholding tax of 15 percent. This tax may be reduced or eliminated by a tax treaty. Most of the former USSR's tax treaties are treated as being in force in the Russian Federation.

- *Export tax* An export tax is levied on exports on certain listed products. It is assessed in ECUs by volume or weight and paid in roubles, according to the prevailing ECU–rouble exchange rate. The rate is higher for the exporter if mandatory currency conversion requirements (discussed in section 6.1.5 below) do not apply to the relevant transaction (which includes barter transactions).

6.1.5 Foreign Exchange

Introduction As yet, there is no Russian law relating to foreign exchange. There was a USSR Law on Currency Regulation of 1991 which introduced internal convertibility of the rouble and liberalized foreign exchange regulations. It is unclear whether the USSR law still applies, but given the many new Russian regulations dealing with the issue it is generally considered that it does not. However, the internal convertibility of the rouble, which permits the conversion into foreign exchange of roubles which have been lawfully earned in Russia, has been maintained.

A new Russian law, which is intended to consolidate all existing currency regulations, was adopted in May 1992 by the Russian parliament. The law states, *inter alia*, that payments in foreign currency within the Russian Federation are prohibited. This prohibition is also effective in relation to salaries and other remuneration. For this reason, Western companies usually elect to do business in the Russian Federation through two entities: (1) an accredited representative office (which can transact business in foreign currencies); (2) a joint stock company or a limited liability company (which transacts business, as required, in roubles).

The law provides that Russian citizens and legal entities will be entitled to open foreign currency accounts with Russian banks which are authorized to transact foreign exchange transactions. Such authorized banks and no other entities or persons will be entitled to offer foreign exchange within the Russian Federation. Currently, Russian authorities are considering the introduction of the full convertibility of the rouble. This was due to occur on July 1, 1992 but has been postponed.

Permissions required Under the laws of the USSR, it was expressly provided that joint ventures were permitted to borrow and raise credits in foreign currency with foreign banks and corporations if they had obtained the prior consent of Vnesheconombank (the Foreign Trade Bank of the USSR). Although the Foreign Investment Law of the Russian Federation does not contain a similar provision, it is probable that the same requirement exists and the prior consent of the Russian Foreign Trade Bank should be obtained.

According to a presidential edict of November 1991, all persons or entities dealing in foreign currency exchange must be licensed by the Central Bank of the Russian Federation.

Convertibility of Russian roubles Under the 1991 Foreign Investment Law, a foreign investor may, following payment of applicable taxes and fees, freely transfer foreign currency revenues (including profits, dividends, proceeds from the liquidation or sale of an investment, and compensation moneys resulting from nationalization) obtained in connection with its foreign investment. Profits in roubles payable to foreign investors in connection with the production of import-substituting goods (the category of which is determined on a case-by-case basis but would include certain consumer goods and pharmaceuticals) may be transferred in foreign currency following the granting of permission from the Russian Ministry of Foreign Economic Relations, the Russian Cabinet of Ministers, and the Council of Ministers of the relevant republic within the Russian Federation.

A foreign employee of a company having a foreign shareholder may, after all applicable income taxes have been paid, transfer, to a place outside the Russian Federation, that part of his salary which is denominated in a foreign currency.

Pursuant to a presidential decree of June 14, 1992 (No. 62), each Russian company (including each joint venture and wholly-owned foreign company) is required to convert into roubles an amount equal to 50 percent of the amount in foreign currencies held by it which has been derived from its export sales at the market rate of exchange, such conversion to be made through certain authorized banks. Such conversion is required to be effected within fourteen days of the receipt of the amount in foreign currency by the Russian company. Unless an exemption is obtained from the Central Bank of the Russian Federation, export revenues must be settled in foreign currency accounts held with authorized Russian banks. There are also reports that another mandatory rate of exchange will be introduced in connection with privatization transactions, and rates as low as 5 roubles to US $1 have been mentioned. The Foreign Investment Law is likely, however, to continue to provide that foreign investors may use lawfully obtained roubles for the purchase of state assets.

Enterprises with more than 30 percent of their shares held by foreign persons are permitted to exchange currency at market rates.

Consent for offshore payments and location of bank accounts As was the case under the law of the former USSR, both residents (including foreign legal entities registered within the Russian Federation) and non-residents are entitled to open foreign currency accounts with authorized Russian banks. Residents may also open bank accounts with foreign banks outside Russia in accordance with the procedures and requirements from time to time determined by the Central Bank of the Russian Federation.

6.1.6 Public Fund-raising

Russian companies There is no Russian legislation relating to the issue of shares to the public or to the trade in shares in Russian companies outside the territory of the Russian Federation. It may therefore be assumed that such activities are permitted under the same conditions that would be applicable to issues of shares and trading of shares within the Russian Federation. The issue of shares within the Russian Federation requires the prior registration of such issue by the Russian Ministry of Finance. The trade in securities of Russian companies outside the Russian Federation is subject to quotas established from time to time by the Russian Ministry of Finance.

Foreign companies In principle, under applicable Russian securities regulations, a foreign company registered in Russia is allowed to issue shares in Russia under the same conditions that are applicable to a Russian company. Securities of foreign companies which are issued outside Russia can be traded in Russia only if they have been registered with the Russian Ministry of Finance.

Offers to the public Securities may only be offered to the public in accordance with a prospectus which must contain the information required by, and be issued in accordance with, the procedures of the Russian Ministry of Finance. If the issuer of the securities is a bank, the requirements of the Russian Central Bank must also be complied with.

A prospectus for an issue of securities by a company must contain, *inter alia*, the following particulars: the details of the issuer; details of the securities offered for sale; and particulars of the financial position of the issuer (including a balance sheet for the three preceding financial years and for its last quarter, certified by the company's auditors).

The company and the sponsoring broker are responsible for the reliability of the information contained in the prospectus. The Russian Ministry of Finance and its local agents are responsible only for the completeness of the information contained in the prospectus and not for its reliability.

The Stock Exchange The Moscow Central Stock Exchange was founded in 1991. The Stock Exchange is governed by the Statute on the Issue and Circulation of Securities and Stock Exchanges in the RSFSR, Decree No. 78 of December 28, 1991. A new law on the subject is expected to also be enacted before the end of 1992. The Moscow Central Stock Exchange has issued its own rules of admission of securities to trading. These rules introduce two criteria for admission: (1) the minimum capital of an issuer must not, in the case of commercial banks, be less than 50 million roubles, and in the case of other issuers of securities, must not be less than 100 million roubles; (2) the number of listed securities must not, in the case of commercial banks, be less than 2,500 and, in the case of other issuers of securities, be less than 5,000.

6.1.7 Property Law

Property ownership and title issues Foreign persons are generally not permitted to own real estate in the Russian Federation. However, pursuant to a presidential decree of June 14, 1992 (No. 631) which deals with the sale of land owned by privatized state and municipal enterprises, foreign persons and enterprises are permitted to purchase real estate from privatized enterprises. They are not, however, allowed to own agricultural land, land used for communal purposes, or land used for national parks and national monuments. Foreign persons are also permitted to lease land on a long-term basis. Pursuant to the Law on Ownership and the Land Law, Russian citizens may own plots of land only for agricultural and housing purposes. To date there is no law permitting Russian citizens to own land for industrial or commercial purposes. It has recently been announced that a referendum on real estate ownership will take place in the future.

Environmental issues The 1992 Law on the Protection of the Natural Environment provides for the preservation of "the natural wealth and living environment of man, the prevention of ecologically harmful effects of economic and other activity, [and] the cleaning and improvement of the quality of the natural environment." This law provides performance standards for enterprises, the breach of which could in some circumstances entail civil and criminal liability.

6.1.8 Security

The 1992 Law on Security supplements the Civil Code, which also contains several provisions on security. The Law on Security provides that:

- assets and rights (including intangible property and future rights) may be the subject of a security interest;
- upon mutual agreement, an asset that is the subject of a security interest may be held by, or transferred to, the pledgee;
- securities that are the subject of a security interest may be deposited with a notary public or a bank;
- assets that are joint property may be secured only with the consent of all the joint owners;

- floating security may be taken over the assets of an enterprise;
- unless it is otherwise provided in the document creating the security interest, the pledgee of an asset must give its consent prior to the disposal of such asset;
- the pledgor shall be entitled to the return of the pledged asset if the pledgee fails to comply with its obligations;
- a *droit de suite* in respect of land is provided for in the event of the security being granted over property on which a building is situated; and
- if the rights of a pledgor are interrupted as a result of nationalization or other action of the state, all losses suffered by the pledgor will be compensated by the Russian Federation or the relevant republic within the Russian Federation.

6.1.9 Creditors' Rights

Enforceability of documents generally Pursuant to the 1964 Civil Code, agreements can be set aside when:

- all the parties to the agreement so agree;
- all the mutual obligations are able to be set-off; and
- the party obliged to perform an obligation finds it impossible to perform that obligation for reasons beyond its control.

Russian law does not contain any provision to the effect that an agreement may be cancelled in the event of there being force, mistake, or fraud. The Civil Code also provides that an amount of liquidated damages (which is a sum determined by statute or contract) may be payable by a debtor in the event that the debtor fails to perform or improperly performs the obligations which it is required to perform. A creditor may also claim its actual losses in the case of improper performance or non-performance of the debtor's rights. Such losses may also include lost profits. Losses in excess of an amount of the liquidated damages are fully recoverable. The amount of liquidated damages may be reduced by the court if the sum is extraordinarily large in comparison to the actual losses of the creditor. Therefore, it is not considered to be very likely that losses in excess of liquidated damages may be successfully claimed.

Bankruptcy The Russian Federation does not yet have a law on bankruptcy. In May 1992, the Russian parliament rejected a draft bankruptcy law.

Both the 1990 Law on Enterprises and Entrepreneurship and the 1990 Statute on Joint Stock Companies provide for liquidation in the event of bankruptcy and for voluntary liquidation. Both laws refer to bankruptcy regulations, which to date do not exist. A presidential decree which deals with state-owned enterprises is in effect. It is intended to be temporary and provides that a state-owned enterprise that fails to pay its debts for a period of three months can be made bankrupt on the application of any creditor.

Voluntary liquidation The 1990 Law on Enterprises and Entrepreneurship provides that an enterprise may be liquidated voluntarily if the owner of the enterprise or the authorized state body so decides, and the personnel of the enterprise consent. An enterprise is considered to be liquidated at the moment it is deleted from the State Register.

The liquidation procedures are performed by a liquidation commission that is composed of persons nominated by the owner or the authorized state body and who have been approved by the personnel of the enterprise. The liquidation procedures may also be executed by the board of the enterprise. The liquidation commission or any other body that effects the liquidation procedures announces the liquidation in the local press and specifies the procedures and terms within which the enterprise's creditors should submit their claims. The commission is required to establish a list of all outstanding claims of the enterprise and is obliged to collect such claims. Creditors who have contractual relations with the enterprise are required to receive written notice of the liquidation. The liquidation commission values the assets, settles accounts with the creditors, draws up a liquidation balance sheet, and makes a final report.

The 1990 Statute on Joint Stock Companies also contains other provisions on liquidation. The voluntary liquidation of a joint stock company is initiated following the decision of its shareholders. The shareholders are also entitled to appoint a liquidation commission. The liquidation commission has the same duties as are set out above. It reports its findings to the shareholders' meeting and the Ministry of Finance. After settling all accounts, the balance of the assets is required to be distributed among the shareholders.

6.1.10 *Leasing*

Lease terms There is no Russian law relating to leasing. In the absence of a Russian law, the applicable law is a USSR law, the 1989 Fundamentals of Legislation on Leasing. That law provides that both movable and immovable property, including land, may be leased to both Russian and foreign persons. The law provides that a lease contract must provide (*inter alia*) for: a description and the value of the property; the lease payments; the term of lease; and the various mutual obligations (including the obligations to repair and the right to quiet enjoyment). The parties are also free to include other terms and conditions. The term of lease for immovable property cannot, in principle, be less than five years, unless the character and purpose of the lease necessitates a shorter period. With the consent of the lessor, the lessee may grant subleases in respect of the leased asset or property.

The lessee's rights under a lease contract include the protection of his rights on a basis equal to the right of ownership. The lessee may demand:

- the return of the leased asset from anyone unlawfully holding such assets;
- the removal of any impediments to the use of the leased asset; and
- compensation of damage inflicted to the leased asset by all persons (including the lessor).

Enforcement If one party defaults in its obligations under a lease, the other party may file a claim with an appropriate court for the leasing contract to be cancelled. A lessor would be able to retake possession of a leased asset only with a court order. A court order can be executed voluntarily or by the court's bailiff.

Upon its expiration, the lease period may be renewed if the parties so agree. If upon expiration of a lease the lessor or lessee fails to terminate the lease the leasing contract is deemed to continue on the same terms as the initial leasing contract.

6.1.11 Execution of Documents

Under the Civil Code, contracts may be concluded either orally or in writing. Contracts which are required to be made in writing include:

- contracts made between the state, cooperative, and public organizations and Russian citizens; and
- transactions between citizens involving sums in excess of 100 roubles or having a duration of longer than one year.

It should be borne in mind that at the time that the Civil Code was passed, the economy was totally controlled by the state. It is probable that privately owned companies and enterprises will now be considered to be within the category of Russian citizens. Failure to comply with the requirements of the Civil Code may result in the invalidity of the contract.

Contracts between a Russian party and a foreign party, in the Civil Code called "foreign trade contracts," must, in the case of the Russian person, be executed by two persons authorized to represent the relevant contracting party. The law requires notarial authentication of certain documents (including documents relating to land transactions, and foundation documents relating to companies), which are required to be registered. Failure to do so renders such documents invalid.

6.1.12 *Law and Jurisdiction*

Proper law As a rule, contracts providing for acts and things to be done outside the Russian Federation may provide for a proper law which may be either Russian law or an applicable foreign law. The contract can also provide for the submission of the parties to the jurisdiction of foreign courts. Russia does not have a separate law on private international law. Typical private international law provisions are contained in various other laws.

Jurisdiction There is generally no provision in Russian law requiring the exclusive jurisdiction of Russian courts in disputes between parties to contracts. Article 119 of the Code of Civil Procedure provides that the following disputes must be dealt with by the courts of the Russian Federation:

- cases regarding immovable property situated in the Russian Federation;
- proceedings involving the estate in the Russian Federation of a deceased person; and
- claims against a carrier which has its registered office in the Russian Federation.

Arbitration The Russian Federation, as the legal successor of the former USSR, is a member of the New York Convention on the Recognition and Enforcement of Foreign Arbitral Awards (1958), which provides for the recognition and enforcement of foreign arbitral awards.

Currency of judgments The Civil Code provides that debts must be expressed and paid in roubles and that judgments should be expressed in roubles. The Civil Code, however, provides that subject to other legislation, debts may be paid in foreign currency. Accordingly, if the debt is in a foreign currency it is possible that judgment can also be rendered in that currency.

Execution of foreign judgments   The Code of Civil Procedure and the 1988 USSR Decree on the Recognition and Enforcement in the USSR of Decisions of Foreign Courts and Arbitration Tribunals (which is most likely still in force) provide for the recognition and enforcement of foreign judgments. The general rule is that foreign court decisions may be recognized and enforced if it is so provided in accordance with international agreements concluded between the USSR and the jurisdiction where the judgment was rendered. There are conditional agreements for the reciprocal enforcement in the Russian Federation of judgments rendered in all countries of the former socialist bloc, as well as in Finland, Italy, Greece, and Cyprus.

The 1988 Decree on the Recognition and Enforcement in the USSR of Decisions of Foreign Courts and Arbitration Tribunals is still in force. Article 5 of that decree provides that the enforcement of foreign judgments rendered in other treaty states will be refused in the USSR (Russia) where:

- under the legislation of the jurisdiction where the judgment was rendered, the judgment did not come into effect;
- the party against whom the judgment was entered did not receive due procedure;
- the hearing of the case is subject to the exclusive jurisdiction of a Soviet (Russian) court or body;
- there is already a Soviet (Russian) court decision that was legally binding on the same parties and on the same subject, or a procedure was commenced before a Soviet (Russian) court between the same parties and on the same subject;
- a period of three years has elapsed after the filing date of the claim; and
- the enforcement of the judgment would contradict the sovereignty of the USSR (Russia), or threaten the security of the USSR (Russian Federation), or contradict the basic principles of the laws of the USSR (Russian Federation).

6.1.13 Sovereign Immunity

Under Russian law, there is no concept of state immunity from civil law. The new Russian constitution has introduced a concept under which claims can be filed against the state for compensation of damage inflicted by state bodies or their officials. The state and its agencies and state-owned enterprises are not responsible for the obligations of a state-owned enterprise.

6.2 The Czech Republic and Slovakia

6.2.1 *The Czech Republic and Slovakia*

The Czech and Slovak Federal Republic will split into two separate independent republics (the Czech Republic and Slovakia) on January 1, 1993. How this will be effected is not clear, as at the time of writing, the law to effect the separation has not been passed. It is uncertain whether the two new republics will continue to apply the current federal laws or whether new laws, which would supersede existing laws, will be passed. The separation will also have a dramatic impact on the current programme by which the economy is being transformed from a command economy into a market economy. The ambitious privatization programme (in which more than 2,000 enterprises are due to be privatized) and Czechoslovakia's request for membership of the EC will also be affected. Another consequence of the separation will be the transfer of the authority of ministries and governmental agencies from the Federal Republic to the new republics.

6.2.2 *Company Law*

Commercial Code The Commercial Code came into effect on January 1, 1992. On that date, the Economic Code, the Joint Stock Companies Act, the Foreign Trade Code, and the Act on Enterprises with Foreign Property Participation were all repealed.

The Commercial Code is divided into four parts:

- Part 1 contains provisions on the concept of enterprises, commercial names, entrepreneurial activities, and commercial secrets. Importantly, there are provisions regulating the business activities of foreign persons. This part also deals with the commercial register, accounts, and economic competition.
- Part 2 contains detailed provisions relating to commercial companies (including limited liability companies and joint stock companies as well as less commonly used types of corporations). A section also deals with cooperatives.
- Part 3 contains detailed provisions relating to the law of contract, including obligations in international trade.
- Part 4 deals with transitional provisions.

Types of corporate entities The most commonly used corporate entity in Czechoslovakia is the limited liability company [společnost s ručením omezeným] and the joint stock company [akciová společnost].

Other corporate forms less often used include the public commercial company [veřejná obchodní společnost] and the limited partnership [komanditní společnost].

Limited liability companies Quotaholders are not personally liable to the company's creditors for the company's debts. The minimum capitalization of a limited liability company is 100,000 Kcs. In addition the company must form a reserve fund initially amounting to 5 percent of capital stock. The value of quotas must be divisible by 1,000. A board of directors must be appointed, although there does not have to be more than one director. There is an option to elect a supervisory board.

Joint stock companies The minimum capitalization of joint stock companies is 1 million Kcs (increased from 100,000 Kcs under the Joint Stock Companies Act). A joint stock company must elect a supervisory board. A reserve fund has to be created equal to 10 percent of capital stock.

Other entities A public commercial company must have at least two participants. A limited partnership can have one or more partners with each limited partner being liable to the extent of his participation and one or more partners who are liable to the extent of all their property.

Registration A limited liability company is established pursuant to a foundation document. A joint stock company is established pursuant to both a foundation document and a statute.

Registration is effected by filing the relevant application form and the company's foundation document, in the form of a notarial deed, which will contain information on the company's capital stock, the names of shareholders/quotaholders, and their rights and obligations. In addition a joint stock company must file its statutes.

Public fund-raising The Czechoslovak stock exchange is due to open shortly. Foreign companies may offer shares to Czechoslovak persons with the consent of the State Bank of Czechoslovakia. A new Securities Act, which will deal with disclosure and trading rules, is due to come into force on January 1, 1993.

Ultra vires A company is able to perform only acts that are permitted in the objects, which are contained in its statutes or foundation documents. The statutes or foundation documents cannot contain objects that the company is not capable of performing. Therefore, if a company wishes to change its scope of business activity from those activities specified in the objects, it is required to amend its statutes or foundation documents. This change must be authorized by a resolution passed by two-thirds of its shareholders or quotaholders.

Directors' activities Unless the company's statutes specify otherwise, directors may not conduct certain activities which are set out in the Commercial Code. Such activities include concluding transactions relating to the business of the company in the directors' own names or on their own account, and mediating business. A company may request the director to give up the benefit of the relevant transaction. In addition, the company may sue a director for compensation.

Financial assistance Although it is in theory possible, in practice the giving of financial assistance to a company is not common in Czechoslovakia.

6.2.3 *Privatization*

Small businesses The Act on the Transfer of the State Ownership of Some Property to Other Juridical or Natural Persons (generally known as the "Small Privatization Law") provides for the privatization of small businesses such as shops, restaurants, and roadside stalls which are controlled by the state. This privatization was effected by way of auctions, the first round of which was reserved for Czechoslovak citizens only. Most of the small privatization has been completed.

Large businesses The Act on Conditions of Transfer of Property of the State to Other Persons (generally known as the "Large Privatization Law"), which came into effect on April 1, 1991, established a framework for privatization of large state enterprises. Other regulations were passed which put the process into effect.

Privatization is triggered by the approval of a document called the "privatization project" by the Ministry of Privatization of the republic in which the enterprise is situated. The privatization project must be recommended by the founding ministry first. The privatization project contains important information regarding the enterprise, including a description of the enterprise and the property which is the subject of the proposed privatization, details of the way in which the state acquired the property, any restitution claims from previous owners, valuation of the property, proposed manner of privatization, details of the successor who will take over the business and assets of the enterprise, intellectual property, main contract to which the enterprise is a party, and a timetable for the implementation of the privatization transaction. A new amendment was passed in February 1992, under which each enterprise has to prepare a summary of environmental issues, any penalties to be paid for environmental damage, and quantification of environmental damage caused by the enterprise.

After preparation and approval of the privatization project, the responsibility for the enterprise and the implementation of privatization will be transferred to either: (1) the Federal Fund of National Assets (if the relevant enterprise was operated or founded by federal organs) or (2) either (a) the Czech Republic Fund of National Assets or (b) the Slovak Republic Fund of National Assets (depending on where the relevant property is situated). The assets of the enterprise (or the shares of its successor company) will be transferred by the founder to the relevant fund and the former enterprise will be dissolved without liquidation. The funds are not part of the federal or republican budget and their assets may be transferred to newly incorporated companies, sold to investors, or transferred to municipalities or to coupon-holders. The funds coordinate the sales of businesses and shares in their successor companies.

Privatization is being effected in two waves; the first wave was completed by the end of June 1992 and the second wave is not planned to be completed until the end of 1992 (depending on the implications of the split of the Federation).

The Large Privatization Law provides that each Czechoslovak citizen above the age of 18 is entitled to purchase a coupon book for 35 Kcs and, on registration of these coupons for a fee of 1,000 Kcs, will be entitled to exchange these coupons for shares in certain Czechoslovak companies. Alternatively, the coupon-holder may exchange his or her coupons for shares in a Privatization Investment Fund (working broadly on the principles of unit trusts or mutual funds). Each holder has 1,000 points to invest.

The coupon privatization programme is well under way, and the shares in some well-regarded companies have been fully subscribed. Those less favored companies must offer their shares in several rounds, with the offered price for the shares being reduced (e.g. three shares for 100 points in the first round; ten shares for 100 points in the second round).

6.2.4 Foreign Investment

Under the Commercial Code, a foreign person (which includes a person with his residence, and a legal entity with its domicile, outside Czechoslovakia) may conduct its business activities under the same conditions that would apply to a Czechoslovak person. In certain spheres of business (including banking), approval of relevant regulatory bodies is required. A foreign person or other legal entity may acquire interests in a Czechoslovak company, establish a wholly-owned subsidiary, invest in a new company with Czechoslovak persons, and establish a branch in Czechoslovakia.

Article 25 of the Commercial Code provides that the property of foreign persons is protected under the law and can be expropriated only on the basis of statutory provisions for reasons of public interest which cannot be satisfied in any other way. There is an appeals procedure, and if the property of a foreign person is expropriated, the foreign person can claim compensation equivalent to the full value of the affected property. The amount of compensation is freely transferable into foreign currencies.

Although a foreign investor is no longer required to obtain an approval from the Ministry of Finance, it must obtain a trading license from the relevant local authority (in respect of its place of business) and from the Small Business Office (in respect of its business activities).

6.2.5 Foreign Exchange

Convertibility of local currency The applicable law relating to foreign exchange rules is contained in the Foreign Exchange Act. The Act introduced the concept of internal convertibility, under which a Czechoslovak person or other legal entity which becomes registered in the Commercial Register has, subject to sufficient liquidity, the right to have any amount of Czechoslovak crowns exchanged into foreign currencies in order for its import activities to be financed. The Act also provides that any amount in a foreign currency that is earned by a Czechoslovak person from its export activities must be converted by the relevant Czechoslovak bank into Czechoslovak crowns.

Lending Czechoslovak state-owned enterprises and privately owned companies may borrow money from foreign banks. Amounts borrowed in foreign currencies must however be converted into Czechoslovak crowns.

Consents for offshore payments and location of bank accounts The prior consent of the State Bank of Czechoslovakia is required before a Czechoslovak person is permitted to open a foreign exchange account with a foreign bank. Such consent is also required for the opening of a foreign currency bank account in Czechoslovakia. These requirements do not however apply to investments that may be made by foreign investors (which may be made in foreign currencies) or Czechoslovak natural persons. It should be noted that a joint venture with foreign participation, including a 100 percent foreign-owned Czechoslovak company, is considered to be a Czechoslovak legal person and thus subject to the Foreign Exchange Act.

Generally, all Czechoslovak companies are obliged to transfer any funds in foreign bank accounts to Czechoslovak banks promptly after their receipt in such accounts. If a Czechoslovak company wished to maintain funds in a foreign bank account then it would be required to obtain the prior permission of the State Bank of Czechoslovakia.

6.2.6 Tax

Withholding tax Withholding tax is, subject to applicable double taxation agreements, levied at the rate of 25 percent on dividends, interest, royalties, and rent paid to a foreign person. Double taxation agreements have been entered into with some eighteen countries. In addition, agreements with more than twenty other countries have either been signed but not yet ratified, or are currently being ratified. In the latter category are agreements with the United Kingdom, the United States, Switzerland, and Australia.

Tax holidays Tax holidays, whereby companies which otherwise would be liable to pay Czechoslovak tax are excused from such taxes, are available for periods of up to two years, or longer in the case of companies involved in certain industries which are of strategic importance to the national economy. Generally, a company seeking a tax holiday must be incorporated prior to any application for a tax holiday and no dividends may be paid during the tax holiday. The right to apply for tax holidays (and the discretion to grant them) will be repealed by the new Tax Code.

New Tax Code A new Tax Code is due to come into force on January 1, 1993. It will introduce a whole range of new taxes including value-added tax, real estate tax, inheritance and gift tax, environment tax, and new rates of personal and corporation taxes. Corporation tax is due to be set at 45 percent and the maximum personal income tax at 47 percent. Value-added tax will be charged at 23 percent with a reduced rate of 5 percent on essential goods. The Tax Code will also introduce a new concept of loss carry-forward for up to five years.

6.2.7 Property Law

Property ownership and title issues The law relating to property is fragmented and there is currently no comprehensive property code. Land may be owned by the state, cooperatives, or other legal persons or individuals. Foreign individuals may not own land, although it is possible to acquire land by way of registration of a wholly-owned Czechoslovak subsidiary. Land has to be valued by an expert specially appointed by the Ministry of Finance in accordance with special regulations.

Restitution There are three laws relating to restitution of ownership of property:

- The Small Restitution Law (Act No. 403/1990) (so-called because it relates to a short period of time) relates to the restitution of property (which includes non-agricultural land) expropriated between 1955 and 1959 and under certain later government decrees. Under this Act, both Czechoslovak and foreign nationals may apply for restitution (they may recover the property or receive financial compensation under purchase price or the difference between the financial compensation and the purchase price). The deadline for claims under this Act expired on April 30, 1991.
- The Large Restitution Law (Act No. 37/1991 on Extra-Judicial Rehabilitations) (so-called because it relates to a longer period of time) relates to the restitution of property (which includes non-agricultural land) expropriated between February 25, 1948 and January 1, 1991. Only Czechoslovak nationals with permanent resident status in Czechoslovakia may apply for restitution under this Act. Compensation includes the return of the relevant property or financial compensation (which could, for example, be provided by the issue of shares in the privatized company). The deadline for claims under this Act expired on September 30, 1991.
- The Act No. 229/1991 on land regulates the restitution of agricultural land and buildings on such land. The deadline for claims under this Act will expire on December 31, 1992.

Environmental issues New environmental laws came into force on October 1, 1991. These laws are similar to environmental laws that have been adopted in the European Community jurisdictions.

6.2.8 *Security*

General Under the Civil Code (as revised with effect from January 1, 1992), pledges, mortgages, and liens can be created and enforced in Czechoslovakia. Article 151(a) of the Civil Code provides that a security interest may secure any claim and right resulting from that claim (which would include interest and the right to reimbursement of any costs that were incurred). The property that may be secured may include real and personal property, including intangible property and other choses in action.

Security interests must be created pursuant to a written agreement signed by the party creating the security interest. The document creating the security interest must, pursuant to article 151(b) of the Civil

Code, in addition to the property being secured, identify the debt or the claim that is being secured.

Real property Article 151(b)(2) of the Civil Code provides that a mortgage over real property must, in order to be an effective security interest, be filed with, and stamped by, a notary in the local district where the real property is situated. After a notary has validated and stamped a mortgage, the mortgage documents are returned to the mortgagee who is required, pursuant to article 151(b)(6), to file such documents with the local real property registry.

The major problem with this procedure is that, in practice, a notary can take several months to stamp and return the mortgage documents to the mortgagee. Because a mortgage is unenforceable until stamped, a lender should wait until the mortgage documents have been returned to it before disbursing any loan.

Where a mortgage has been granted by one business organization to another (which could include a bank), the mortgagee can sell the mortgaged property at auction, retaining an amount equal to the amount that it is owed and paying any balance to the mortgagor. There are different procedures to be applied when an individual has granted a mortgage.

Personal property A security interest can be taken over personal property. Such a security interest is required to be evidenced by a written agreement, signed by the party granting the security interest. In order to perfect the security interest, the property must be marked, or otherwise sufficient steps must be taken in order that the property will be able to be sufficiently identified. In addition, with two exceptions, actual possession of the property must be taken, either by the beneficiary of the security interest or, alternatively, its agent. The two exceptions are:

- an asset which itself has a separate title document (which would include a motor vehicle or an aircraft), where the title document is itself marked to evidence that the asset is secured; and
- accounts receivable, choses in action, intangible property, and other contract rights.

It is therefore impractical and very difficult to take effective security over inventory, machinery, or other equipment that is required to be used by the party granting the security.

Security interests over accounts receivable may be created if a written agreement is entered into between the parties. Although there is no legal requirement to notify a debtor that its debt has been encumbered, it would be advisable, in order to prevent the debtor paying the party which granted the security interest instead of the beneficiary of the security interest.

Security can be created over shares in a joint stock company (which may be in the form of bearer shares or registered shares), by entering into a security agreement, taking possession of the share certificates, and marking the share certificates to the effect that they are held as security.

Security over ownership interests in a limited liability company (which are not evidenced by share certificates) can be effected by entering into a security agreement and recording the terms of that agreement in the register of members of the company. The validity of this form of security is, however, doubtful as it is not expressly provided for in the Civil Code.

Void security Under article 14(1)(f) of the Bankruptcy and Settlement Act (discussed in section 6.2.9 below), a security interest (including a right of pledge, lien, mortgage, or other restriction imposed on the transfer of immovable property) over the assets of a bankrupt person or liquidated company which is acquired by a creditor within two months of the date of a proposal for the bankruptcy declaration of such person or company is rendered null and void.

6.2.9 Creditors' Remedies

Voluntary winding-up of a company The Commercial Code provides for the voluntary liquidation or dissolution of a company. The company in general meeting may resolve, by resolution of a majority of two-thirds of the members present, to be liquidated.

The liquidation resolution is entered into the Commercial Register, and a liquidator is appointed to settle all claims and fulfil commitments of the company. As well as informing all known creditors of the liquidation, the liquidator is obliged to make a public announcement appealing for all creditors and affected persons to present their claims within a specified period (which is to be of not less than three months). The liquidator will prepare closing accounts and proposals and present them to the members for approval. The claims of all known creditors must be satisfied before the remaining assets after liquidation may be divided among the members. If the liquidator discovers excessive indebtedness of the liquidated company, he must without undue delay apply for receivership.

Within thirty days of the completion of the liquidation, the liquidator must apply to have the company removed from the Commercial Register.

Voluntary winding-up without liquidation If a company is to be transformed into a different form of company or is to be acquired by another company, then it may be wound up without being liquidated. Application for registration of a new company must be made, together with application to remove the wound-up company from the Commercial Register. If the conditions are fulfilled, the assets of the wound-up company are transferred to the new company.

Bankruptcy and liquidation The Bankruptcy and Settlement Act (No. 358) of July 11, 1991 came into force on October 1, 1991. It is the first major Act of its kind as the concept of bankruptcy was virtually unknown under the previous regime.

The Act applies the concept of insolvency to both individuals and companies. It provides that a debtor will be deemed insolvent if he is unable to meet his financial obligations to his creditors for a given period of time.

■ *Compulsory winding-up* Before the Act came into force, winding-up proceedings could only be instigated by the debtor applying to a court of bankruptcy, with the debtor paying the costs of the court proceedings. After October 1, 1992, proceedings can also be instigated by creditors and liquidators of companies. The court will then appoint an administrator to administer the property. A creditors' meeting will be convened by the court (or requested by the administrator), where the creditors' views are sought. At the meeting, a committee of creditors can be appointed with the court's approval. That committee will supervise the administrator's activities. If the court is satisfied that the conditions for an insolvency declaration have been met, it will issue a ruling to that effect.

■ *Process of compulsory winding-up for reasons of insolvency* Creditors are given thirty days from the declaration of insolvency to register their claims. Once their claims are presented, the court will order an examination of the affairs and assets of the debtor. The insolvent debtor is obliged to prepare a list of his assets and liabilities. The list is handed over to the administrator, along with accounting books and all necessary documents, and the administrator then compiles a statement for the court. Once the debtor's property has been liquidated, the court will issue a distribution ruling.

■ *Compulsory settlement* After the examination procedure, but before the distribution ruling, the insolvent debtor may propose to the court that the proceedings be terminated by a compulsory settlement.

The debtor's proposal will set out the terms of the settlement. Judicial proceedings, attended by the debtor, administrator, creditors, and guarantors to the settlement, are held in order for the court to consider the proposal. The agreement of a majority of the creditors is required before the court can accept the compulsory settlement. As a result of a compulsory settlement:

- the right to dispose of property is returned to the insolvent debtor; and
- all other rights curtailed by the insolvency declaration are returned to the debtor.

■ *Settlement* Before bankruptcy of a debtor may be declared on the application of the debtor, the court may allow the settlement of the creditors' claims. Such a settlement involves a plan specifying the proposed settlement terms together with a list of the assets and liabilities of the debtor being presented to the court. If the court decides to permit the settlement proceedings, then a settlement administrator is appointed and creditors are invited to register their claims. During the course of the proceedings the debtor and creditors may not propose a declaration for the compulsory winding-up of the debtor.

If the creditors accept the debtor's settlement terms, and the conditions for settlement under the Act are met, then the court will allow the settlement. The effects of a settlement include the following:

- unlike bankruptcy, the debtor retains some power to dispose of property, and the administrator transfers the agreed settlement direct from the debtor to the creditor;
- the approval of the court, which is confined to the terms of the settlement, enables the debtor to discharge his debts even to those creditors who did not approve the settlement; and
- neither the debtor nor the creditors can then propose the bankruptcy of the debtor.

■ *International aspects* Unless stipulated otherwise by an international agreement, a bankruptcy declared by a Czechoslovak court shall also apply to those of the debtor's movable assets which are located abroad.

If bankruptcy has not been declared in Czechoslovakia in respect of a debtor abroad, the transfer of movable assets in Czechoslovakian territory to a foreign court may be ordered, subject to the rules regarding the reciprocity between the relevant countries, and subject also to any prior rights that have already been established in Czechoslovakia when the foreign court's request is received.

Void contracts and legal acts Pursuant to article 14(1)(a) of the Bankruptcy and Settlement Act, any person who has concluded a contract with the bankrupt person or company may withdraw from it unless he knew about the bankruptcy declaration at the time when the contract was made.

Under article 14(2) of the Act, either party (including the bankrupt person or company) to a contract of "reciprocal fulfillment" may withdraw if the contract has not yet been performed either partially or fully. In addition, the administrator in bankruptcy may withdraw from a lease or hire contract concluded by the bankrupt person or company as a lessee or hirer even if the lease or hire contract was concluded for a fixed period of time.

Under article 15 of the Act, a creditor may initiate legal action to determine that the legal acts of the debtor alleged to have been performed within the last three years with a view to curtail enforceable claims of the creditor are null and void. This applies to acts of the debtor curtailing creditors' claims the intention of which was known to the relevant third party. This also applies to transactions between the debtor and persons connected with him. If a creditor is successful, his remedy is equal to the value of property by which his claim was curtailed; if this cannot be met, compensation is payable by the third party.

Priority of payments Payments to be made following the bankruptcy or liquidation of a debtor are payable in the following order:

- costs of bankruptcy or liquidation, including the fees of the administrator, taxes and fees incurred during the bankruptcy proceedings, and claims of creditors from contracts concluded with the administrator;
- claims of the bankrupt's employees from within three years prior to the declaration of bankruptcy proceedings;
- taxes, fees, duties, and social insurance contributions paid within three years prior to the declaration of bankruptcy proceedings and during the time of the bankruptcy proceedings, unless satisfied by liens; and
- other claims.

6.2.10 Leasing

Lease terms The Czechoslovak Civil Code covers lease agreements. Leases are not required to contain any special terms. These will be implied by the Code unless expressly stated in the agreement. The subject matter of a lease may be movable or immovable property. One of the implied terms of leases is the requirement to pay rent, not necessarily in cash. The lessor of immovable property automatically acquires a right of lien to movables which are situated on the leased assets and which belong to the lessee.

Termination The Civil Code provides that the lease term terminates by effluxion of time unless the parties agree otherwise. If the lessee continues to use the leased property after the lease has terminated and the lessor does not object in court within thirty days of the termination date of the lease, the lease will be renewed under its original terms. It is possible to terminate a lease that has an indefinite lease term if one party gives the other party notice of termination.

The lessor may terminate a lease if the lessee continues to use the leased property following its receipt of a notice specifying default under the lease or if the lessor suffers, or is likely to suffer, damage resulting from the lessee's activities. In addition, unless the leased property comprises flats or non-residential premises, the lessor may terminate the lease if the lessee has not paid all or part of the rent that is payable. The lessee may also terminate when the leased property is not fit for the use to which it is required to be put under the lease or for the usual use of the leased asset.

If the lease is for a definite term and the leased property is movable property, the lease may be terminated by the lessee if the lessor transfers the ownership of such property.

When the lease is terminated, the leased property must be returned to the lessor in the condition required pursuant to the lease or, if such condition has not been agreed in the lease, in its original condition, taking into account normal wear and tear.

6.2.11 *Execution of Documents*

Valid execution Article 40 of the Civil Code sets out the requirements for the validity of execution of documents. Generally, documents are validly executed on behalf of a company if such execution is in accordance with the company's foundation documents or statutes.

The Commercial Code requires that the execution of certain documents must be officially certified by either the State Notary Office or the District Court. To be valid, agreements are not required to be written in Czech or Slovak. However, as Czech and Slovak are the official languages of Czechoslovakia it is necessary, when dealing with governmental authorities, to submit documents in either Czech or Slovak; or, if in another language, the relevant documents must be submitted with an official Czech or Slovak translation.

6.2.12 *Law and Jurisdiction*

Recognition of choice of a foreign law as the proper law The Code on International Civil Procedure and Law (Act No. 97 of 1963) provides that the parties to a contract may choose the proper law for that contract. The law that is to apply in respect of transactions, arrangements, and contracts entered into when no proper law is chosen is determined in accordance with the rules relating to each type of transaction:

- the law in respect of a sale and purchase agreement will be the law of the place of domicile of the seller;
- the law in respect of a sales representative or trade agency agreement will be the law of the place of domicile of the relevant customer;
- the law in respect of a claim for compensation or damages arising from a breach of contract will be the law of the place where the damage was incurred;
- the law in respect of transactions, arrangements, or contracts entered into where none of the above rules apply will be the law of the place where the relevant transaction, arrangement, or contract was concluded.

Enforceability of a foreign judgment Czechoslovakia has entered into bilateral and multilateral treaties which provide for the mutual recognition of judgments of courts of a large number of countries, including the United Kingdom. It has not, however, entered into such a treaty with the United States.

Currency of judgments Monetary judgments may be rendered only in Czechoslovak currency.

Sovereign immunity The Act on State Enterprises (Act No. 111 of 1990) provides that, subject to limited exceptions, the state is not liable for the liabilities and obligations of state enterprises and state enterprises are not liable for obligations and liabilities of the state.

The Foreign Trade Code provided that the state is also immune from the liabilities of foreign trade corporations. Foreign trade corporations are liable to the extent of the value of their assets.

6.3 Hungary

6.3.1 Company Law

State-owned enterprises State-owned enterprises currently constitute between 80 percent and 85 percent of enterprises and business organizations that have been established in Hungary. The foundation and organization of such enterprises are regulated primarily under the Civil Code (Act IV of 1959, as amended) and the Act on State-owned Enterprises (Act VI of 1977, as amended).

Business organizations There are six forms of business organization in Hungary. They are all regulated by the Act on Business Organizations (Act VI of 1988, as amended). The following points are relevant to each form of business organization:

■ *Limited liability companies [korlátolt felelósségú társaság or kft]* A kft is similar to a German GmbH. Capital is divided into quotas of predetermined value which must be at least 100,000 forints each. The minimum capital is 1 million forints (the current exchange rate between forints and the US dollar being approximately HUF 80 to US$1). Each quota-holder is obliged to pay up his quota in cash or in kind, as set out in the kft's contract of association. Offering quotas to the public is prohibited. The managers of a kft (and the members of its supervisory board and its auditor, if any) are all elected by the quota-holders' meeting.

■ *Companies limited by shares [részvénytársaság or rt]* An rt is similar to a German AG. Capital is divided into a number of shares having a predetermined nominal value. Shares may be issued at a premium and may be in bearer or registered form. However, foreigners and financial institutions (where up to 90 percent of the registered share capital is in the hands of foreigners) may own only registered shares. Companies may issue (*inter alia*) ordinary shares, preference shares, and convertible bonds. The shareholders, at their general meetings, elect the board of directors, the members of the supervisory board, and the auditor.

■ *Joint companies [közös vállalat or kv]* Only legal (as opposed to natural) persons may be partners in a kv. Each partner is liable for the obligations of the kv in the proportion which its own contribution bears to the total contributions. A kv has separate legal personality. The council of directors is the governing body of the kv. Each member nominates one representative to the council of directors. The council of directors elects and dismisses members of the committee of directors (if any) and the members of the supervisory board (if any). Foreigners usually do not participate in kvs.

This form of business organization is about to disappear. Its original purpose was to be a vehicle whose participants were predominantly state-owned enterprises and, as a result of the privatization programme, it is no longer being utilized.

■ *Partnerships [közkereseti társaság or kkt]* Each partner of a kkt has full joint and several liability for the obligations of the kkt. Each partner in a kkt is entitled to manage and represent the partnership unless the partners agree otherwise in the contract of association.

■ *Limited partnerships [betéti társaság or bt]* In a bt, at least one partner must have unlimited liability (a full partner) and at least one partner must have limited liability (a limited partner). The liability of the limited partner is limited to the amount of his capital contribution. There is no separate board of management as full partners deal with all relevant management issues. Full partners are obliged actively to participate in the activities of the bt. A limited partner is not entitled to manage or represent the bt.

■ *Business unions [egyesülés]* An *egyesülés* is established by legal persons to enhance their profitability, to harmonize their business activities, and to represent their business interests. An *egyesülés* should not carry on business with a view to making a profit but may in fact make a profit. The members are jointly and severally liable for the obligations of the *egyesülés*. An *egyesülés* is governed by a council of directors to which each member nominates a representative. The council of directors elects and dismisses the members of the board of directors (if any).

Acts of authorized officers In each type of business organization, the managers or directors represent the business organization towards third parties. The actions of a manager or director in his dealings with third parties are binding on the business organization, even if there is an inherent restriction in the power of that manager or director to bind the business organization.

Each manager, director, member of the supervisory board, and auditor has a duty to act with all the due care generally expected of a person holding such an office. In the event of his failing to do so and causing damage to the business organization, the general rules of civil law liability apply.

Maintenance of capital and financial assistance

- Generally, the maintenance of capital by an rt or a kft is a less significant principle under Hungarian law than under English law. For example, although an issue of shares or quotas at a discount is not permitted, there are fewer restrictions on the purchase by an rt or kft of its own capital and the reduction of its own capital.
- Unlike English law or the law of any other jurisdiction in the European Community, there is no prohibition on an rt or a kft giving financial assistance for the purchase of its own capital.
- Therefore, an rt or a kft may provide security over its assets to a person which has provided finance to a purchaser of the shares in the rt or quotas in the kft. This applies whether or not the provider of the financial assistance is a bank or any other type of entity and whether or not it is a Hungarian or a foreign entity. A loan

cannot, however, be provided for the acquisition of a banking institution's own shares or for the acquisition of interests in a business organization where the banking institution holds a controlling interest.
- In practice, the provision of financial assistance is not common in Hungary, but this will no doubt change as the sophistication of transactions increases.

6.3.2 Privatization

General The Act on Transformation of State-owned Enterprises and Business Organizations (Act XIII of 1989, as amended) governs the process by which state-owned enterprises are transformed into forms of business organizations. The State Property Agency supervises the transformation process.

Methods of privatization The programmes for the privatization of state-owned property include the following:

- An active privatization programme which was launched in 1990 and is managed by the State Property Agency. It focuses on obtaining investments from foreign investors in the pharmaceutical, hotel, department store, tourist, and manufacturing sectors. A secondary programme, which is not actively managed by the State Property Agency, has also been introduced.
- A privatization programme which was primarily directed towards Hungarian individuals was provided for in Act No. LXXIV of 1990. That Act provided the means for the privatization of small state-owned operations in the fields of retail sales, hospitality, and consumer services.
- An investor-initiated programme also exists where state-owned enterprises and assets can be privatized on an *ad hoc* basis by foreign investors purchasing state-owned enterprises or assets from the State Property Agency.

Compensation The Compensation Act provides that individuals who can prove that they suffered loss as a result of the nationalization of land and other assets will be compensated by means of vouchers which can be used to purchase shares in privatized state-owned enterprises and land set aside by the government for this purpose. The value of the vouchers to be distributed will be of unequal amounts and disproportionately less than the actual loss suffered. The maximum amount payable may not exceed HUF 5 million.

6.3.3 Public Fund-raising

Hungarian business organizations Before a Hungarian business organization can issue shares to the public outside Hungary or its shares can be dealt in outside Hungary, the prior permission of the Securities Supervisory Board and the National Bank of Hungary is required. Dealing in securities outside Hungary is normally only permitted if such securities are listed in Hungary.

Foreign companies Foreign companies may, under the Foreign Exchange Code, issue securities in Hungary. Securities which are issued outside Hungary may be dealt in within Hungary only with the permission of the Securities Supervisory Board and the National Bank of Hungary.

Offers to the public Offers of securities to the public may only be made pursuant to a prospectus which has been approved by the Securities Supervisory Board.

Each prospectus for an issue of securities by a company must contain information, *inter alia*: relating to its management and business; on its financial position (not more than six months old) certified by auditors; on the current and any previous issue; and an assessment of the major risk factors in the company's business.

The company, its directors, and its broker are liable for losses incurred by the holder of a security acquired pursuant to a prospectus that is found to contain false information.

Budapest Stock Exchange The Budapest Stock Exchange was reopened in 1990. The shares of some nineteen companies are currently listed. The Stock Exchange is regulated by Act VI of 1990, which also deals with the issue of securities and dealing in them by brokers.

In order for securities to be listed on the Stock Exchange, the relevant company must satisfy the following rules of the Stock Exchange (which were introduced in January 1992): (1) the listed securities must, in aggregate, have a market value of at least 200 million forints; (2) at least 20 percent of the securities must be owned by the public; (3) there must be at least fifty persons holding the securities; (4) the accounts of the company (or its legal predecessor) must be audited by an accounting firm approved by the Stock Exchange for three consecutive years (although until 1993 this requirement is for two consecutive years); and (5) the listed securities shall be traded only on the Stock Exchange. Each listed company must maintain, as its minimum share capital, at least 5,000 shares in a minimum amount of 200 million forints.

6.3.4 *Foreign Investment*

Permits and authorizations No permission is required for the establishment of a joint venture or for a foreign person to buy shares in an existing business organization, even if the level of foreign ownership is 100 percent. However, the permission of the Hungarian government and the approval of the National Bank of Hungary are needed to acquire shares in, or establish, a commercial bank or other financial institution.

Debt–equity ratio requirements There is no restriction under Hungarian tax or foreign exchange legislation on the level of foreign debt to foreign equity that must be maintained in a Hungarian business organization.

However, the National Bank of Hungary can effectively regulate the ratio of foreign debt to foreign or local equity (see section 6.3.5 below).

As regards domestic debt, a kft must have a minimum capital of 1 million forints and an rt must have a minimum share capital of 10 million forints at the time of its establishment. Theoretically, so long as it has capital in those minimum amounts, a kft and an rt may each have any ratio of domestically raised debt to equity.

6.3.5 *Foreign Exchange*

Permissions required Domestic Hungarian business organizations may borrow freely from domestic banks or foreign joint venture parties. Business organizations that are totally owned by foreigners may borrow from such banks and parties but only with the permission of the National Bank of Hungary if the loan is to be made in Hungarian forints.

Pursuant to the Foreign Exchange Management Code (Law Decree No. 1 of 1974) and the Decree of the Minister of Finance No. 1/1974 (I/17), each Hungarian business organization needs permission from the National Bank of Hungary:

- to borrow from foreign financial institutions or other lenders outside Hungary (such a loan is called a finánc hitel);
- to enter into leases with foreign financial institutions or other lessors outside Hungary; and
- to grant a mortgage over any of its real property in Hungary to a foreign person.

When the National Bank approves the raising of a loan in a foreign currency, it undertakes to the relevant Hungarian business organization that the relevant foreign currency will be made available for the repayment of the loan. As a result, the situations in which the National Bank of Hungary is willing to agree to the raising of such loans are relatively limited.

Convertibility of Hungarian forints No permission is required for a foreign investor to transfer dividends or the proceeds from the sale or liquidation of an investment in the same currency in which the investment was made to an account outside Hungary.

A foreign employee of a joint venture can convert and remit outside Hungary 50 percent of his after-tax income in the currency of the country of his permanent domicile without the need to obtain any permission.

A Hungarian business organization must offer to the National Bank of Hungary, through a commercial bank, all amounts of foreign currency received in the ordinary course of its trading activities.

In the event that a foreign investor makes a capital investment in a joint venture business organization in a foreign currency, the joint venture may hold amounts in such currency in a foreign exchange account and may use such amounts for the acquisition of assets that are to be used for the production of goods in its business as well as durable goods and spare parts to be acquired and other incidental costs.

Consent for offshore payments and location of bank account The permission of the National Bank is needed before a Hungarian business organization may open a bank account outside Hungary. Commercial banks which are authorized by the National Bank to deal with foreign exchange transactions may open bank accounts outside Hungary.

6.3.6 *Property Law*

Property ownership and title issues Real property ownership is regulated by the Civil Code (Act IV of 1959, as amended) and the Act on Land (Act I of 1987, as amended) which provide (*inter alia*) that:

- a foreign entity may acquire real property only if it has first obtained the permission of the Ministry of Finance;
- a joint venture (including a joint venture which includes one or more foreign persons) may acquire or lease real property in connection with the operations specified in its constitutional documents without any requirement to obtain any permission from any governmental authority.

Environmental issues The Act on the Environment (Act II of 1976, as amended) provides for the protection of land, water, air, living nature, and inhabited areas against harmful interference, pollution, and damage. Persons who cause pollution, harm, or damage to such protected property are under an obligation to either limit or terminate the offensive conduct or take appropriate protective measures. Offenders are also liable to pay fines and may be liable for the damage caused to other persons. Some offenses carry criminal liability. Lenders are generally not liable for the actions of their borrowers.

6.3.7 *Security*

General Hungarian law generally permits security to be taken over any negotiable or transferable assets, whether tangible or intangible. In all cases, creation of the security requires an instrument in writing.

The usual method by which security is provided is for the pledgor to grant a pledge and deliver the physical possession of the pledged assets to the pledgee or a mutually acceptable third party. A pledge cannot be granted over only part of an asset (except in the case of a mortgage over a severable part of real estate). Once a pledge has been granted, no further pledges over the pledged asset may be granted. A pledgee is obliged to keep the pledged asset in good condition and cannot use it for his own benefit but is entitled to proceeds from the pledged asset.

Priorities are determined in accordance with the respective times at which competing securities were created. There is no public procedure or place where pledges or assignments by way of security can be registered. The only registry that is available for the registration of security documents is the land registry, where mortgages have to be registered.

Section 57 of the Act on Bankruptcy, Liquidation Procedure, and Voluntary Liquidation 1991 (discussed in detail in section 6.3.8 below) provides that securities granted by a business organization within six months of liquidation do not confer any priority over unsecured creditors.

Mortgages Although Hungarian law provides that mortgages can be created over land, pledges can be created over personal property, and floating charges can be created over other property in favor of banks, it does not allow a mortgage to be created over personal assets.

A mortgage over personal property could however be created by a Hungarian person in favor of a foreign entity if its proper law was the law of a jurisdiction which recognizes the validity and enforceability of mortgages. Such mortgage may be enforceable in the courts of

Hungary if the mortgage was enforceable in the jurisdiction of its proper law. However, as there is no Hungarian law or practice on the subject, it is unclear whether it would be enforceable. The usual practice is that the judgment or order of a foreign court (or the decision or award of arbitration proceedings) is admissible in evidence in Hungarian court proceedings.

However, if a mortgage over personal property with a foreign proper law provided for disputes to be resolved in accordance with arbitration proceedings in Hungary, the arbitrators would (subject to principles of Hungarian public policy) recognize the choice of the proper law and the mortgage would be enforceable in accordance with that law.

Choses in action and intangible assets Security can be provided over choses in action, or "rights" (being any right or interest which is transferable and which has a material value), as that term is used in the Civil Code. Such rights (including receivables or interests in a joint venture) are usually secured by way of an assignment. In order for the assignment to be valid and enforceable the debtor or party who is obliged to perform the obligation that is inherent in the chose in action must be notified of the creation of the assignment. There are no specified formalities for the giving of notice.

Where the secured asset is not a chose in action, but is nevertheless an intangible asset (e.g. intellectual property rights), no additional formalities beyond written evidence of the assignment are required.

Floating security Where the assets are tangible but the owner wishes to continue to deal with them (as would be the case with items of inventory), security is available only in the event that the security is being given to a bank to support a loan. No other type of creditor can take advantage of this type of floating security. The Civil Code does not, however, provide for floating charges. For this reason, and because of the problem caused by there being no registration procedure, floating charges should be used with caution.

Real property A mortgage can be created over real property. A mortgage must secure a stated maximum amount of money and is rendered null and void if it entitles the mortgagee to possess, use, or collect the proceeds from the mortgaged property. Mortgages can be registered at the relevant land registry. In order to be valid and enforceable, a mortgage must be registered.

Shares and quotas Shares in an rt can be pledged. A quota in a kft is an intangible asset but it is capable of being pledged. There are statutory pre-emption rights in favor of quota-holders of a kft so that a pledgee is required to offer the pledged quotas to the other members of the kft before exercising a power of sale to third parties.

Rights of enforcement by secured creditors

■ *Initiation of action* The Act on Bankruptcy, Liquidation Procedure, and Voluntary Liquidation 1991 (discussed in detail in section 6.3.8 below) does not provide for a secured creditor to appoint a receiver, administrator, or similar person in respect of a business organization.

For enforcement purposes, it is irrelevant whether the document containing the financial or other obligations is notarized or in a particular form, but, as specified in section 6.3.11 below, it should in some cases be annotated.

The legal procedures regulating enforcement of securities are constantly changing. The legal position is therefore uncertain, and before taking action, a secured creditor should obtain specific legal advice on the steps that should be taken. The general position is that a mortgagee which is a bank can enforce any security over real property or a movable asset either by initiating the enforcement action itself or by doing so with the assistance of the executor of the court (which is a government officer affiliated to the court). A mortgagee which is a bank does not have to obtain a judgment or court order in order to enforce its rights under a mortgage unless enforcement of the mortgage is contested by the mortgagor. In that case the mortgagee can apply for a court order for specific performance or liquidated damages. If an order is made for liquidated damages to be paid and such liquidated damages are not paid after the expiration of fifteen days after such order, further orders may be sought and obtained for the sale of the assets of the mortgagor.

At the request of a defendant, a foreign plaintiff must lodge a guarantee to cover its costs at the time that it initiates court proceedings to enforce the relevant obligation, unless: (a) it is otherwise agreed pursuant to a relevant international convention; (b) the plaintiff's claim *prima facie* provides or constitutes a sufficient guarantee; or (c) the plaintiff receives an exemption from the requirement to provide the guarantee.

If both the defendant and the plaintiff are present in court when the complaint is raised, then, at the request of both parties, the court shall hear the case at that time unless another court has exclusive jurisdiction to hear the complaint. If the court has jurisdiction for the action but the defendant is not present at the time that the complaint is recorded in the court, then a future date shall be specified at which time the case will be heard.

■ *Contesting mortgagee's actions* A mortgagor may contest a mortgagee's actions and seek the termination or limitation of such mortgagee's actions by producing documentary and other evidence to the court. Such mortgagee can, if it accepts the mortgagor's position, elect to terminate the court action. The court may stop such mortgagee's proceedings if a third party (who has no knowledge of such mortgagee's claim before the commencement of such mortgagee's proceedings) brings an action against the mortgagee claiming that he has a right to the mortgaged property.

■ *Execution of judgments* On a default by a mortgagor, a mortgagee may file relevant documents requesting the sale of the relevant mortgaged asset or property with the executor of the court. The executor of the court can then authorize a sale of the mortgaged asset or property by public auction. The mortgagee could however agree with the mortgagor that the sale is to be completed by a private sale. A Hungarian purchaser of such asset or property cannot pay for such asset or property in a foreign currency unless it first obtains the consent of the National Bank of Hungary. A foreign purchaser is required to pay for the movable asset or property in a foreign currency. The mortgagee could purchase the asset or property but is under an obligation to account to the mortgagor.

Voidable security The Civil Code provides that a contract can be rendered null and void if there is evidence of fraud or bad faith by one of the parties.

6.3.8 Creditors' Rights

Enforceability of documents generally An agreement can be set aside on the basis of mistake, deception, or fraud. A payment due under an agreement could also be unenforceable if it is deemed by a Hungarian court to constitute a penalty. A penalty would include an obligation to pay interest calculated at an annual percentage rate that is more than double the prime rate for the time being of the National Bank of Hungary (which is currently 22 percent; i.e. interest at more than 44 percent would constitute a penalty). Additionally, a penalty would constitute a payment which would be in excess of the amount of loss or damage that was proven to result as a consequence of the breach.

The Bankruptcy Act The Act on Bankruptcy, Liquidation Procedure, and Voluntary Liquidation (Act IL of 1991) generally applies to all types of business organizations that are recognized under Hungarian law. The Bankruptcy Act does not apply to individuals and certain provisions do not apply to financial institutions. The Act on Banks and Banking Activities (Act LXIX of 1991) sets out relevant laws on the liquidation of banks and financial institutions. The Bankruptcy Act generally sets out how bankruptcy, voluntary liquidation, and compulsory liquidation procedures are able to be implemented in Hungary:

■ *Bankruptcy* Bankruptcy procedures against a debtor may be instituted as soon as the debtor encounters any financial difficulty. When a debtor is unable to satisfy a debt within ninety days the debtor is obliged, by notice to the court, to declare its own bankruptcy within eight days. The court is obliged, within fifteen days of such notice, to issue a writ as to the commencement of the bankruptcy proceedings and to publicize the writ in the *Firm Registry Gazette*. The bankruptcy procedure commences on the date that the writ is publicized in the *Firm Registry Gazette*. Once such a notice is issued in respect of a debtor then another notice cannot be issued in respect of the same debtor for a period of three years. If an act of bankruptcy occurs during such three-year period, then, instead of procedures being implemented for the bankruptcy of the debtor, liquidation procedures must be commenced in respect of such debtor.

The purpose of the bankruptcy proceedings is to normalize the debtor's arrangements with its creditors. This is done in either of two ways:

- a moratorium in respect of the debtor's debts may be implemented: the moratorium lasts for a period of ninety days following the date of the publication of the bankruptcy notice;
- an agreement may be entered into between the debtor and all its creditors whereby the debtor is obliged to agree to a programme for the payment of its debts and for the debtor to become solvent again.

If a moratorium cannot be entered into or no agreement can be reached with creditors, then the debtor is obliged to report this fact to the court, together with the reasons, within three days. Within fifteen days of the receipt of the report (or, if no report was submitted, after the expiry of the moratorium period) the court shall commence the liquidation procedure on an ex officio basis, with a writ issued to that effect. During the course of such liquidation procedure the court can, at the request and expense of the creditors, appoint an administrator who would supervise the liquidation procedure. The creditors may appoint a committee to represent their interests to the administrator.

■ *Voluntary liquidation* A business organization may resolve, by resolution of a 75 percent majority of its members, to be liquidated.

Notice of such members' resolution is required to be given to the court within eight days. The court then publicizes the resolution and the business organization's creditors then have thirty days from the date of such publication to notify the accountant appointed by the members to effect the liquidation of the amounts that they are owed by the business organization.

The accountant who has been appointed to effect the liquidation is entitled to terminate all contracts or other arrangements (other than certain contracts that are specified in the Bankruptcy Law, including agricultural leasing contracts, collective contracts, and loan contracts relating to certain non-economic activities) that have been entered into by the business organization; or, if none of the parties to a contract had performed the contract, the liquidator is entitled to rescind the contract on behalf of such business organization.

The liquidator must examine all the business organization's assets and liabilities in order to determine whether its assets exceed its liabilities. The results of the liquidator's examination and its proposal for the division of the business organization's property and assets are presented to the members of the business organization. If following such examination the liquidator determines that the business organization is insolvent or in all probability will become insolvent, then the liquidator must immediately petition the court to liquidate such business organization. In that event, the rules relating to compulsory liquidations would apply.

■ *Compulsory liquidation* Prior to the passing of the Bankruptcy Law it was difficult to liquidate state-owned enterprises and business organizations in Hungary, it being more usual to effect a reconstruction. Under the Bankruptcy Law, a business organization can be liquidated if it remains insolvent after:

- creditors do not receive payment of their debts following bankruptcy proceedings in respect of such business organization; or
- a creditor, the business organization, or the liquidator of such business organization (where voluntary liquidation procedures have been instituted) petitions for the liquidation of such business organization; or
- the Court of Registration notifies the court authorizing the liquidation.

The court then examines the solvency of the business organization and, if it finds that the business organization is insolvent, then an order will be made for it to be liquidated. A liquidator will then be appointed and notice of the liquidation will be made in the *Company*

Gazette. The creditors of the business organization may appoint a committee to represent their interests.

The liquidator or a creditor may, within ninety days of the liquidation of the business organization, apply to have any burdensome, gratuitous, or onerous contract or other arrangement entered into by the business organization within the previous twelve months set aside. During the period during which the business organization is being liquidated, the organization's creditors may enter into an agreement with the liquidator in connection with the payment of debts. An agreement is binding on all creditors of the business organization if creditors who number one-half of all creditors and who are all owed at least two-thirds of the amount of total debts so agree.

During the course of the liquidation, the liquidator is obliged to examine all the business organization's assets and liabilities. Following such examination the liquidator is obliged to prepare a balance sheet and a proposal for the distribution of the business organization's assets. The liquidator then must forward the balance sheet and proposal to the court and, within thirty days of receipt of such documents, the court must set a date for a meeting at which a decision will be made as to the payment of creditors and the business organization's liquidator. The court's decision can be the subject of an appeal if application for the appeal is lodged within eight days of the court's order.

Voidable contracts Section 40 of the Bankruptcy Law provides that within ninety days following the commencement of the liquidation procedures, a creditor or the liquidator of the liquidated business organization may initiate legal action to contest contracts or other documents made within the previous twelve months if the object of the contract or other document was (1) alienation without compensation from the property of the debtor or the incurrence of uncompensated liabilities encumbering the property; or (2) an onerous legal transaction concluded to benefit a third party, with a striking disparity of values.

Priority of payments A creditor can, when a business organization is put into liquidation, receive the amount that is secured to it after the payment of: (1) the costs of the liquidation; (2) other secured creditors who have priority pursuant to security granted at least six months prior to the date of the liquidation; (3) alimony, life annuity, payments relating to compensation for damages, and termination payments to employees of the business organization; (4) amounts outstanding by the business organization to certain unpaid consumers; (5) social security contributions and unpaid taxes; (6) amounts of principal payable to creditors; and (7) amounts of interest payable on overdue payments to creditors and fines payable to the tax authorities.

6.3.9 Tax

Tax on dividends and interest Pursuant to the Personal Income Tax Act 1988, as amended, when a dividend is paid on shares, or interest is paid on loans, bonds, or other debt instruments, the payer must deduct and pay, by way of personal income tax, an amount equal to 10 percent (which rate has been reduced from 20 percent as from January 1, 1991) of such dividends or interest.

Tax on profits Hungarian business organizations and other entities carrying on business in Hungary must pay corporate tax on profits earned in Hungary. The rate of the tax is 40 percent.

Tax allowances There is a series of tax incentives for foreign investors. Although the normal rate of Hungarian corporation tax is 40 percent, there are substantial tax concessions for business organizations and other entities in which foreign shareholders hold at least 30 percent of the capital.

Until December 31, 1993, if such a company has been established with share capital of at least HUF 50 million and has more than half of its income derived from the manufacture of products, its taxes will be reduced by 60 percent for the first five years of its existence and 40 percent for the following five years.

If such a company operates in certain defined areas of major economic importance (including certain areas of the tourism, telecommunications, electronics, engineering, vehicle manufacture, and pharmaceutical industries), it will enjoy a full tax holiday for the first five years of its existence and a 60 percent reduction in its tax bill for the following five years.

6.3.10 Leasing

Terms and conditions of leases Hungarian law recognizes the concept of leases over Hungarian real and movable property. Leases are not required to contain any special terms, the terms of the lease being freely determined by the parties. If however the lease is silent, Hungarian law will infer certain provisions from the Civil Code into the lease. Such provisions could include: that the leased asset is generally able to be used for the purposes of the lease for the lease period; that the lessee is able to use the leased asset without restriction from the lessor; and that the lessee may sub-lease the leased asset without the consent of the lessor.

Enforcement Hungarian law recognizes the right of a lessor in a lease to retake possession of the leased asset on certain occurrences. If a lessee objected to the actions of the lessor, then the lessee or the lessor could apply to a Hungarian court for relief. Generally no governmental or other consent is required in order for a lessor to enforce its rights under a lease. As mentioned in section 6.3.7 above, executor of the court can assist in the enforcement of the lessor's interests in the lease.

If the lease was for a specific term and provided that the lessor could terminate the lease in certain circumstances, then Hungarian law would not interfere with the lessor's rights. If the lease period was not fixed then the lease would be determinable on fifteen days' notice. A lessee could apply to a Hungarian court to prevent the lessor from terminating the lease if it objected to the grounds on which the lease was being terminated. Under the Civil Code, either the lessor or the lessee could also seek to have the lease set aside on the grounds of mistake, deception, or intimidation.

In the case of most types of movable assets being leased by a foreign lessor to a Hungarian lessee, an export license is not required when the movable asset leaves Hungary upon the expiration of the lease, unless the lessor had requested an "end-user certificate" from the Hungarian Office of Export Supervision. Such a certificate may be required by the country to which the movable asset is being sent, and it serves as an assurance to the lessor that the movable asset would not leave Hungary unless a certificate was obtained from the Office of Export Supervision. If the end-user certificate had in fact been issued, then an appropriate export certificate must be obtained before the movable asset may be taken out of Hungary (as this is considered a re-export by the Hungarian authorities). An export certificate is usually provided as a matter of course by the Hungarian Office of Export Supervision.

6.3.11 *Execution of Documents*

A loan agreement, lease, or other document entered into in connection with a financing transaction by a Hungarian person or business organization must be in writing but it is not required to be in the Hungarian language. Pursuant to paragraph 196 of the Civil Procedure Code, a document will be deemed made, accepted, or assumed to be binding on a party if the following conditions have been satisfied: (1) the party (or an attorney on behalf of that party) signed the document itself; (2) two persons certify, by their signatures in the document (with their addresses stated), that the party signed the document in their presence or otherwise acknowledged their signature in their presence; (3) the party's signature or mark is authenticated by a court or a notary public; and (4) in the case of a document to be executed by a state-owned business organization, the document has also been signed in accordance with its own regulations.

The Civil Procedure Code does not expressly provide that a document that fails to comply with paragraph 196 is invalid and other provisions may provide for certain documents to be validly submitted as evidence in transactions. Pursuant to paragraph 198(a), if a document is executed in a place outside Hungary it will be deemed to be duly executed if it is binding in accordance with the laws of such place. Pursuant to paragraph 198(b), the Minister of Justice can require certain documents to be legalized by the Hungarian representative authority in the relevant foreign jurisdiction.

6.3.12 Law and Jurisdiction

Proper law In contracts which are to be wholly or partially performed outside Hungary or which involve one or more foreign persons, it is usual to provide for the choice of a proper law, which may or may not be Hungarian law, and the submission to a jurisdiction.

Recognition of judgments The Law Decree of the Presidential Council on Private International Law (Act XIII of 1979) generally deals with the recognition and enforcement of foreign judgments.

The Law Decree provides that Hungarian courts or other relevant authorities have exclusive jurisdiction in the following: (1) cases relating to the personal status of Hungarian nationals, except Hungarian nationals domiciled outside Hungary; (2) cases involving immovable property situated in Hungary; (3) proceedings involving the estates of deceased Hungarian persons resident in Hungary; (4) proceedings against the Hungarian state, state authorities, or administrative organs; (5) proceedings against Hungarian nationals acting as diplomatic representatives abroad; (6) proceedings for the invalidation of a negotiable instrument or deeds executed in Hungary; and (7) proceedings concerning intellectual property rights in Hungary.

There are conditional agreements for the reciprocal enforcement in Hungary of judgments obtained in Syria, France, Yugoslavia, Greece, Albania, Algeria, Bulgaria, Cyprus, Iraq, Cuba, Poland, Romania, the former Soviet Union, Tunisia, Vietnam, Korea, Mongolia, and the former East Germany.

In other cases, judgments of foreign courts or other authorities are recognized unless: (1) such recognition would violate Hungarian public policy; (2) the person against whom the judgment was entered did not receive a fair trial (based on Hungarian criteria); (3) a Hungarian court or other relevant authority made an earlier decision on similar facts; or (4) proceedings involving similar facts are at that time before an Hungarian court or another relevant Hungarian authority.

Hungary is a member of the New York Convention on the Recognition and Enforcement of Foreign Arbitral Awards (1958), which provides for the recognition and enforcement of foreign arbitral awards.

Currency of judgments A judgment of a Hungarian court can be obtained in a foreign currency if the claim arose in that foreign currency and permission has been obtained from the National Bank of Hungary.

Execution of judgments Final judgments or decisions given by a foreign court or other authority in matters relating to property or contract may be executed so long as there is an international convention or agreement providing for the reciprocity of the enforcement of judgments between Hungary and the relevant country. The Minister of Justice has the right to issue a binding decision on the question of reciprocity.

Stamp taxes on enforcing securities and loan documentation Stamp taxes are, pursuant to the Act on Stamp Taxes (Act XCIII of 1990, as amended), payable on the enforcement of a judgment or a decision. The rate of such stamp tax is 3 percent of the value of the judgment or decision, as calculated at the time that the enforcement action is taken.

6.3.13 Sovereign Immunity

State-owned enterprises are liable for their own obligations and cannot, under Hungarian law, claim sovereign immunity in connection with commercial transactions entered into by them.

6.4 Poland

6.4.1 Company Law

Types of corporate entity Although much of the law governing Polish business and commerce has been adopted since 1989, many fundamental aspects of company and commercial life continue to be governed by the Polish Commercial Code, 1934. The Commercial Code is currently being reviewed but the timing of any proposed amendments is at present uncertain.

The limited liability company [spółka z ograniczoną odpowiedzalnością] and the joint stock company [spółka akcyjna] were adopted as the two main Polish company entities by the Commercial Code and that Code still governs their status and form. The Polish versions of both types of company are based on the continental European model which was developed prior to the Second World War. Both have legal personality, and in each case the liability of investors is limited to the amount of their contribution to the company's equity. A limited liability company may have one or more shareholders.

The structure of Polish companies, as set out in the Commercial Code, will be familiar to Western lawyers and businesspeople. A company can be established by one or more persons. It is managed by a board of directors (which may consist of only a single director) and by the shareholders, who exercise that management in shareholders' meetings. In addition, the management of a joint stock company will, in most cases, be overseen by a supervisory board which is elected by the shareholders of the company in general meeting and which performs a non-executive role.

Each of the two types of company is incorporated by registration of its statutes in the Commercial Company Register. These documents are first reviewed by a Commercial Registration Court which will consent to, or refuse, their registration. The company statutes are a contractual document which are signed by the subscribing shareholders and notarized by a Polish notary public before they are submitted to the Commercial Registration Court for approval. If the statutes have not been properly notarized, they will be considered null and void and thereby negate the company's legal status. The company will not be a recognized entity in law until the statutes have been approved by the Registration Court and entered in the Commercial Register. Once registered, a third party is deemed to have knowledge of the contents of the statutes. As in most Western jurisdictions, the statutes contain the business objects and powers of the company. Such objects and powers can be amended, but, to be legally valid, the amendments must also be registered.

Stock Exchange The Stock Exchange opened (or re-opened, as there was a Stock Exchange in Poland before the Second World War) in April 1991. At present the shares of approximately fourteen companies are trading on the Stock Exchange, although applications for new issues are becoming more and more frequent and the number of companies trading on the Stock Exchange has been steadily increasing.

Raising capital Joint stock companies may raise equity capital either by issuing shares to the public or by private placement. Under the Act on Public Distribution of Securities and Managed Funds the term "public distribution" is defined as "an offer made via the use of the mass media or in the form of a written document where the offer or invitation is addressed to more than 300 people." That Act does not deal with "non-public" distribution. Thus Polish law has no regulation of private placements of shares other than the essential general provisions related to issue and registration of shares that are found in the Commercial Code.

If capital is to be raised by public subscription, the following procedures must be followed under the Commercial Code and the Act on Public Distribution of Securities and Managed Funds.

The Commercial Code provides that:

- the statutes of the company should be published in a local or national newspaper indicating when and before which notary public they were executed;
- an announcement of the public subscription should be made in a local or national newspaper indicating:

    (a) the number and type of shares offered for subscription;
    (b) the nominal value and issue price of the shares;
    (c) the opening and closing dates of the offer for subscription;
    (d) any special rights or benefits connected with the various classes of shares on offer;
    (e) any obligations on the shareholder other than payment of amounts due for the shares;
    (f) the name and date of the newspaper in which the statutes were published;
    (g) the principles to be applied in allocating shares to subscribers; and
    (h) the persons announcing the subscription.

The Act on Public Distribution of Securities and Managed Funds provides that:

- the consent of the Securities Commission to a public distribution of shares must be obtained;
- applications to the Securities Commission should contain:

    (a) the name and address of the issuing company;
    (b) the size and value of the issue, including its proposed date;
    (c) the name of the broker who will undertake the public distribution;
    (d) a written prospectus;
    (e) a copy of the issuing company's statutes; and
    (f) a copy of the issuing company's resolution authorizing the issue;

- the Commission must approve or reject the application within two months of its filing; and
- once an application for public distribution has been approved, the issuing company is then obliged to publish in a minimum of two daily national newspapers sufficient information to allow prospective subscribers to assess the shares.

Consents required A foreign company offering shares in Poland must first obtain the consent of the Ministry of Industry and the Securities Commission. A resident Polish citizen requires a permit from the National Bank of Poland to purchase shares in such a foreign company, as does a Polish company.

Financial assistance The Commercial Code prohibits a Polish company from purchasing its own shares or being a "pledgee" of its shares. The Commercial Code does not, however, provide any specific prohibition against financial assistance by Polish companies in relation to the purchase of their own shares.

6.4.2 Privatization

The Privatization Act 1990 provides the basis for the Polish government's stated aim of privatizing all its state-owned enterprises. Under the Privatization Act, a state-owned enterprise can be privatized in a number of ways, including the following:

Sales of shares When a state-owned enterprise is privatized via a sale of shares the intent generally is that it will be transformed into a limited liability company or a joint stock company. Initially, the shares in each newly formed company will be held by the State Treasury. The shares are then, in accordance with Article 23 of the Privatization Act, sold either: (1) on an auction basis, (2) on a public offer basis, or (3) on a negotiated basis following a public invitation to tender.

Once a former state-owned company has been privatized and transformed into a commercial company, it is governed by and subject to all of the provisions of the Commercial Code.

The Polish government is proposing to stimulate public participation in the privatization process within Poland by issuing vouchers to the public. Members of the public will redeem the vouchers in return for interests in investment funds which will in turn invest in shares of newly privatized companies. It is envisaged that the investment funds themselves will invest in a broad range of privatized companies in order to spread and reduce risk.

Liquidation An alternative method of privatization, which is gaining favor among investors and the Polish government, is liquidation.

Under Article 37 of the Privatization Act, with the prior approval of the Minister of Ownership Changes, a state-owned enterprise may be liquidated and its assets disposed of by means of a sale, lease, or contribution to the capital of another existing or newly formed company. This method has some advantages, including the fact that it is generally a quicker and simpler procedure. Although the liquidation method was originally intended for the privatization of small state-owned enterprises, it is increasingly being applied to larger ones.

The privatization process has occurred partly on an *ad hoc* basis, with individual state enterprises being privatized as a result of proposals from, and on the initiative of, private business interests. However, the Polish government has also attempted to structure and accelerate the privatization process by means of a number of programmes.

In the autumn of 1991 the government announced a "sectoral" privatization programme under which some 143 state enterprises, covering thirty-four industrial sectors, are to be privatized. Under the "sectoral" programme, the Polish government has appointed professional advisers (including foreign consultants, merchant banks, and law firms) to advise it on the most appropriate course for the privatization of each industrial sector and to negotiate the sale of state enterprises on its behalf.

At the same time the Polish government has been developing its "mass" privatization programme which involves the formation of numbers of investment funds designed to provide for and encourage wide public share ownership of shares in "transformed" former state enterprises.

6.4.3 *Foreign Investment*

The Act on Companies with Foreign Participation The Polish government has recently overhauled the foreign investment regime, creating new advantages for foreign parties wishing to invest in Poland. The Act on Companies with Foreign Participation came into force in July 1991 and replaces the Act on Commercial Activity with the Participation of Foreign Parties of 1988, as amended. The Act on Companies with Foreign Participation further liberalizes the investment regime, although in respect of tax it favors larger enterprises and removes, in the case of smaller companies, the tax incentives which were previously available to all joint ventures with foreign participation.

The main thrust of the Act on Companies with Foreign Participation is to remove some of the procedural obstacles which previously faced a foreign party wishing to form or invest in a Polish company, and to increase the amount of profit that the foreign investor can repatriate.

Permit requirements Procedurally, one of the major changes made under the Act on Companies with Foreign Participation is that a foreign party is not, in the usual case, required to obtain a permit to incorporate a Polish company or to acquire shares of an existing company. Article 4 of the Act limits the permit requirement to those companies which will operate in the fields of:

- operation of seaports and airports;
- real estate agency;
- the defense industry;
- import of consumer goods; and
- the provision of legal services.

The requirement to obtain a permit also applies where shares in the company are to be acquired by a Polish state entity in return for a non-cash contribution to the company's capital in the form of all or part of a business, or non-movable assets. Companies falling outside these parameters will no longer require a permit.

When a permit is necessary, it is now provided by the Minister of Ownership Changes. The Foreign Investment Agency is abolished by the Act on Companies with Foreign Participation, although in fact much of the old agency is being transferred to the Ministry of Ownership Changes and will continue with its previous functions within the more limited scope of jurisdiction set out in the Act.

Repatriation of profits Under the Act on Companies with Foreign Participation, 100 percent of after-tax profit may be repatriated. Article 25 of the Act provides that the foreign party, after all relevant taxes have been paid, is entitled to convert its portion of the company's profit into foreign currency in a Polish foreign exchange bank and then to transfer it out of Poland.

A foreign party may also, pursuant to article 26 of the Act, export in hard currency the proceeds from the sale of its shares in a Polish company (less any taxes that may be owing).

Protection against expropriation Although, in the current political climate, expropriation and nationalization of private assets are not contemplated by the Polish government or any Polish political group or governmental authority, the Polish government is none the less mindful of the country's past nationalization policies. In this vein, it has sought in the Act on Companies with Foreign Participation to provide assurances to foreign investors that their investment will be guaranteed against expropriation and nationalization.

The Act contains provisions which provide the basis for guarantees to the foreign investor of payment of damages in the event of expropriation of its Polish business or assets. Article 22 provides for a general guarantee of this nature which is made by the Minister of Finance in the name of the State Treasury. The State Treasury will be responsible for making good any loss.

6.4.4 Taxation

Income tax Currently, the maximum corporate income tax rate is 40 percent. The amount of tax is calculated on the basis of gross operating income, less allowable expenses (which include interest paid on a cash basis). The Corporate Income Tax Law distinguishes operating income from income obtained from investments and dividends. A company which pays a dividend is required to deduct an amount equal to 20 percent of the amount payable under the dividend and remit such amount to the tax authorities. If tax is deducted from investment or dividend income then it may be set off against the company's other tax liabilities.

Tax holidays Whereas, under the Act on Commercial Activity with the Participation of Foreign Parties, 1988, most companies or joint ventures with foreign participation automatically enjoyed a three-year tax holiday, this is no longer the case. Under the Act on Companies with Foreign Participation, eligibility to apply for a tax holiday is limited to companies in which foreign shareholders hold share capital in an aggregate amount of not less than an equivalent of 2 million ECU. Additionally, the company must satisfy at least one of the following criteria: (1) it must maintain its operations in an area of actual or potential high unemployment; (2) it must introduce new technology to Poland; or (3) it must export not less than 20 percent of its products. A company may apply to the Minister of Finance for a preliminary opinion on the likelihood that it will obtain a tax exemption.

There is no time limit to the income tax holiday under the Act on Companies with Foreign Participation. Rather, it is based on the amount of equity capital invested in the Polish company. One dollar of equity capital will provide the company with an exemption from tax of one dollar of its taxable income. The company can extend the tax holiday if further amounts of equity capital are injected into the company.

Withholding tax Withholding tax on interest paid to a foreign lender is currently payable at a maximum rate of 30 percent on payments made from Poland to sources outside Poland. Amounts payable under leases where the leased asset is used in Poland (which may not include aircraft, ships, and other assets used by a Polish lessee outside Poland) are subject to withholding tax at the rate of 20 percent. Withholding tax is also payable on dividends paid to a foreign shareholder at the rate of 5 percent. Double taxation treaties do, however, provide that withholding tax on interest paid to lenders and lessors who are resident outside Poland and dividends paid to investors outside Poland may be reduced or, in some cases, eliminated. A provision in a contract providing for a gross-up in the event of the imposition of a Polish withholding tax will be effective under Polish law.

Documentation taxes Stamp duty of 1 percent is payable on rentals payable under an ordinary lease and stamp duty of 2 percent on the purchase price payable pursuant to an option granted under a lease. Otherwise there is no registration fee, documentation tax, or stamp duty payable on the execution, or prior to enforcement, of financing documents or security documents. The only fees which arise are notarial and registration fees on the transfer of land or other assets, which are calculated on a percentage basis.

6.4.5 Foreign Exchange

Convertibility Poland was the first country in Eastern Europe to introduce the free internal convertibility of its currency. As a result, the rate of exchange is subject to some extent to market forces, though it fluctuates in a relatively narrow range determined by a trading band attached to a basket of leading foreign currencies. Although over the past two years the overall trend has been a depreciation of the zloty against hard currencies, the fact that it is tied to a basket of hard currencies has resulted in the occasional appreciation against various of the currencies that make up the basket. During the recent significant depreciation of the US dollar against European currencies, the zloty appreciated against the US dollar by nearly 10 percent.

The Foreign Exchange Law 1989 has authorized the operation of foreign exchange bureaux [kantors] by persons who have obtained foreign exchange permits under rules established by the President of the National Bank of Poland. There are numerous kantors and they each trade freely in all major currencies at variable rates which are established by market forces.

Foreign banks are permitted to make loans to Polish government-owned entities and privately owned entities. Individuals may take out loans of up to the equivalent of US$1 million without the prior consent of the National Bank of Poland. Polish borrowers must convert loans that are made in foreign currencies into local currency.

Debt–equity ratios There is no law or rule regulating the ratio of foreign debt to foreign equity that must be maintained in a Polish company or joint venture.

The minimum share capital of a limited liability company is 10 million zlotys (approximately US$740, at current exchange rates) and that of a joint stock company is 250 million zlotys (approximately US$18,519). Subject to that requirement, decisions regarding debt–equity ratios are at the discretion of the company.

6.4.6 Property Law

Property ownership and title issues Poland has a comprehensive legal regime dealing with land transfer, together with a well developed system of land registration and transfer.

■ *Title and interests in land* The following types of title and interests in respect of land are recognized under Polish law:

- *Ownership* Ownership, as it is referred to in Poland, is an absolute title over real property equivalent to freehold title in the English system. Ownership conveys freedom of use and transfer for an unlimited period of time.
- *Perpetual usufruct* Perpetual usufruct is a transferable right of use which may be granted by the state in relation to state-owned land. It conveys a free right of use of the land for a set period of time. The word "perpetual" is misleading as the perpetual usufruct may be granted for a maximum of ninety-nine years, although it is renewable.
- *Limited rights in property* There are the following limited rights in property which are effective and mandatorily applied (not being able to be avoided or altered by agreement between the parties) not only with respect to the owner of property but also with respect to other persons:

    (a) *Usufruct* Usufruct is a limited right in property entitling the holder to use and take profits from property. This right is not transferable and expires with the death of the person entitled (and presumably in the case where the holder is a company, with the liquidation of the company) or earlier if granted for a time period which expires prior to the death or liquidation of the holder.

    (b) *Real easement* A real easement is a limited right to the use of real property granted by the owner of one parcel of real property to another person. Conversely it may limit the owner of the other in the use of his property. A real easement may be acquired by various means with the most common being by adverse possession.

(c) *Personal easement* A personal easement is a limited right to the use of real property which is created in favor of a specific person and is not transferable. It expires if and when the individual waives his right to the easement, or upon the death or liquidation of the holder.

(d) *Cooperative right to premises* A cooperative right to premises is a limited right in property regulated by the Law on Cooperatives. This right derives from membership in a cooperative and conveys freedom of use and transfer of premises subject to restrictions defined in the Law on Cooperatives and the individual statutes of the cooperatives themselves.

(e) *Mortgage* A mortgage is a limited right in property involving a charge against real property securing a given claim. A mortgage allows a creditor to satisfy a claim over real estate regardless of who has title to that real estate. A valid mortgage will have priority over personal creditors of the owner of the real property. The mortgage can be created by contract, by a judicial or administrative decision, or by documents issued by a bank which are then registered in the mortgage register. This however does not apply to mortgages which are established by virtue of statute, such as for example a mortgage that arises out of arrears of taxes. Such mortgages are not required to be registered and, despite non-registration, may have priority over a previously registered mortgage.

- *Possession* A person may possess a property either with or without having legal title to that property. Rights of possession are to some extent protected by law. For example:

(a) possession must not be wilfully infringed, even though the party holding possession of the property acted in bad faith;
(b) a party holding possession of the property may employ any necessary defense in order to repel a wilful infringement of possession; and
(c) a party holding possession of a property is entitled to claim against the person who wilfully infringed his rights to possession, such claim being for an order for the restoration of his rights to possession and for the forbearance from any further infringement.

- *Rights arising from obligations* Except in respect of certain mandatory rules pursuant to the Civil Code, parties to a contract are free to regulate their relationship in relation to real property. The following contracts are commonly used in relation to real property:

    (a) *Leasehold* As in English law, a leasehold is a contract under which the lessor is obliged to convey the use of property to the lessee and the lessee is obliged to pay the lessor an agreed rent. A lease of real estate or premises for a period exceeding one year must be made in writing. In the event of the parties failing to do so the contract is considered to be concluded for an unspecified period of time.

    (b) *Tenancy* Tenancy is a contract according to which the person granting the tenancy (the landlord) is obliged to grant the tenant the relevant property for the tenant's use and the taking of profits. In consideration of such grant of tenancy the tenant shall be obliged to pay an agreed rent to the landlord. The most important difference distinguishing a tenancy from a leasehold is the entitlement of the tenant to take profits arising from the property. As a result land is usually the property that is the subject of a tenancy and premises the property that is the subject of leasehold.

■ *Registration* Freehold title and perpetual usufruct are both registered in a public register referred to as the "eternity register." The limited rights in property, claims or any interests may also be registered. The eternity register is conclusive and is governed by the registration courts. In addition to this there is the "annotated land register" which is maintained by local municipalities. The annotated land register is used for reference only and is not conclusive in all circumstances.

■ *Interests related to land* Other legal interests which may affect title to land are as follows:

- *Co-ownership (common ownership)* When two or more persons have title to the same property they are deemed to hold the property as co-owners. Polish law recognizes two types of co-ownership: co-ownership in fractional shares and joint ownership.

    (a) *Co-ownership in fractional shares* In the case of co-ownership in fractional shares, each owner is entitled to the property in proportion to the amount of his share. Each owner may be required to divide the relevant property and each owner can freely dispose of its share in the property.

(b) *Joint ownership* Joint ownership is regulated by the relevant rule from which such ownership arises (for example, family law regulates co-ownership arising from marriage).

- *Pre-emptive rights* Pre-emptive rights are the rights of priority of purchase of certain property reserved for a specified person in the event that the owner of the property sells the property to a third party. The property may be sold to a third party on the condition that the person entitled to pre-emption does not enforce its own rights.

  Pre-emptive rights are created either by contract or by virtue of law. The State Treasury is, in principle, reserved pre-emptive rights in respect of all Polish property.

- *Options*

  (a) Under an option, a property may be sold on the condition that ownership to such property will be transferred only after the full price is paid [*pactum reservati dominii*]; or
  (b) a property may be sold on the condition that the purchaser agrees at a later time that the property is acceptable to it.

- *Buy-backs* A property may be sold on the condition that the seller shall have the right to buy back such property.

■ *Effects of registration* Once an interest in land has been registered, such interest will *prima facie* be treated as being valid. When an interest is deleted from the register it will *prima facie* be deemed no longer to exist.

Where there is a divergence between the register and facts related to title (as evidenced in other documents or circumstances), the register will prevail. This applies particularly in respect of third parties who receive a transfer of title from such person who is the registered title-holder. Thus any rights registered on a title will be effective against and have priority over:

- any unregistered rights in interests; and
- any rights in interests which are registered subsequently.

Registered interests will be effective only where a third party is relying on the register and has no actual notice of any fact which would cause it to believe or suspect that the register was incorrect. Additionally, when a purchaser of property obtains title to a property without paying any consideration, such purchaser is not able to rely upon the register if another person who has a *bona fide* interest in the property objects to his title.

■ *Adverse possession* A person who does not hold title to property but is in possession of that property for a period of no less than twenty years may acquire title to the property unless he originally gained possession of the property as a result of an act of bad faith. If he did gain possession as a result of an act of bad faith the person holding possession may acquire title to the property if he is in possession for a period in excess of thirty years. Where a person possesses the real property under some form of legal instrument or contract, that person is not treated at law as an "adverse" possessor and cannot claim title on that basis.

Foreign purchasers A foreign person may purchase real estate in Poland only with the prior consent of the Ministry of Internal Affairs. The Law on Real Estate Acquisition deems a person to be a "foreign person" if such person is:

- a natural person who is not a Polish citizen;
- a legal person incorporated outside Poland; or
- a legal person incorporated in Poland which is, directly or indirectly, controlled by a person in either of the two previous categories.

A direct or indirect holding of at least 50 percent in the proposed purchaser would constitute control.

Proving title The title to land which was never expropriated by the Polish government can usually be ascertained by an examination of the land register in the relevant locality.

As regards land which has been expropriated by the Polish government, many difficult title issues can arise, including potential claims to title by persons who had an interest or claims to an interest in the property at the time of expropriation. The Polish government has indicated that it will be adopting legislation to deal with these issues in a comprehensive fashion. Until that legislation is passed, however, the situation related to ownership and title is relatively uncertain.

This uncertainty has, quite understandably, caused difficulties in relation to both privatizations of state-owned enterprises and foreign investment projects where land is to be acquired or used as security for financial transactions.

Environmental issues Poland's environmental laws require standards similar to those found in the European Community. To date, enforcement of these laws has been lax. Pursuant to a new law which was passed in 1991 the Polish government has provided a legal basis for the formation of a new Environmental Enforcement Agency which is to have broad powers of investigation and sanction.

6.4.7 Leasing

General The Civil Code provides that parties to a contract can generally agree among themselves as to the content of that contract. This principle is generally applicable to leases. The Civil Code does however provide that a lessee in an "ordinary lease" is entitled to certain rights:

- article 664(1) of the Civil Code provides that a lessee is entitled to demand a reduction in the rent which is payable under the ordinary lease if the leased asset has defects which limit the lessee's ability to use such leased asset; and
- article 664(2) of the Civil Code provides that a lessee is entitled to terminate an ordinary lease if the leased asset was not able to be used for its intended purpose either at the time of its delivery or at a later time, following notice to the lessor.

Ordinary lease or finance lease In some circumstances it will be in the interest of the lessor that the lease is not categorized as an "ordinary lease." It is unclear whether or not a Polish court would categorize a Western-style finance lease as an ordinary lease.

Transfer of title It is often the case that the lessor will not want to assume the risks attached to owning a depreciated asset at the end of the lease term. In such circumstances the lease may provide that the title to the leased asset is automatically transferred to the lessee at the end of the lease term or that the lessee is obliged to purchase the leased asset at the end of the lease term. In such cases, the lease may be interpreted as being not a lease but a conditional sale agreement. This has the consequence that the provisions in the Civil Code that apply to sale and purchase contracts (including implied warranties on fitness for purpose and no defects) will apply to the lease.

Title to leased assets As is the case in Western countries, there is always the danger that the lessee could fraudulently sell the leased asset to another person. Article 405 of the Civil Code provides that a lessor, in the event that a leased asset is sold for no consideration, is entitled to recover the leased asset. In other cases, where consideration has been paid and the purchaser believed that the seller had title, the purchaser will obtain title to the leased asset.

Import licenses and duties An import license from the Ministry of Foreign Economic Cooperation must be obtained for the importation of equipment which is to be leased in Poland. No import duty is payable if the equipment is to be leased but duty is payable if the lease is classified as being a conditional sale agreement.

Repossession of leased assets   Articles 342, 343, and 344 of the Civil Code provide protection to a lessee or another possessor of a leased asset, even in the event of it acting in bad faith. These articles could serve to impede a lessor taking possession of a leased asset following a default by a lessee. A lessor would therefore require a court order to retake possession of the leased asset.

6.4.8 Security

General   As most real property and assets used in connection with commerce have in the past been owned by state-owned enterprises, the law in relation to security is not well developed and opinion as to the benefit accruing to secured creditors varies. Accordingly, the Polish government is currently considering comprehensive legislation to provide for the granting and enforceability of security.

Types of security   Currently, security can be created over the following types of assets in the following ways:

- *Tangible and intangible property*   Security can be granted to banks over movables, or tangible property (including items of inventory) and rights, or intangible property and rights (including accounts receivable, shares and intellectual property rights). In practice, a bank which takes security over an asset such as an item of equipment attaches to such item of equipment a plaque stating that the equipment is pledged to that bank.
  The Civil Code provides that banks (but not other creditors) can take floating security over assets. For example, security over intangible property rights such as accounts receivable would be effected by way of security being granted. In such case, in order to be enforceable, notice of the assignment would be given to the debtors and payments would be made to a bank account nominated by the creditor. Creditors can take security over shares by way of lien, with the share certificates being held by the creditor.
- *Real property*   Real property can be mortgaged. A mortgage over land can, pursuant to the Civil Code and the Law on Mortgages, be registered against the title to such land in the land registry in the district in which the land is located. The respective priorities of competing mortgages are determined by the respective dates on which they were created.
- *Documentation and registration*   Other than a bank's floating security over a company's assets and a mortgage over a company's shares (which are both registered in the relevant company's own register), a

security interest over a ship or an aircraft, and a mortgage over real property, Polish law has no registration procedure for any security.

Accordingly, a borrower could grant security over the same asset more than once, albeit fraudulently. For this reason, security by way of lien, where possession of the relevant asset is taken by the lender, is the best form of security. To be enforceable, all forms of security must be in writing, dated, and preferably notarized.

■ *Enforcement rights* The Civil Procedure Code provides that a mortgagee can enforce its rights by first obtaining judgment against the mortgagor and then selling the real property by public auction. Similarly, a creditor seeking to enforce its security over intangible assets such as shares would, pursuant to the Commercial Code, be required to obtain judgment and then sell the assets either under the supervision of the court or by public auction.

■ *Voidable security* There is no specific law to the effect that security can be set aside if the borrower was insolvent at the time that the security was created or a creditor otherwise gained a preference over other creditors. The only relevant law provides that if there is fraud then the security can be rendered unenforceable.

Promissory notes A lender or financier holding promissory notes evidencing the required payments from a borrower would, pursuant to articles 485–97 of the Civil Procedure Code, be entitled to obtain a summary judgment against such borrower, in the event of borrower's default. Accordingly a lender or financier would be obliged to take promissory notes.

6.4.9 Insolvency and Liquidation

Polish bankruptcy law dates back to 1934. The 1934 legislation (the Bankruptcy Law 1934 and the Arrangement Proceedings Acts 1934) was passed with individuals, rather than incorporated bodies, in mind. Therefore, many conceptual difficulties are encountered when this law is applied to incorporated bodies. This law has been updated in a somewhat piecemeal fashion, most recently in the Bankruptcy Act 1991. This Act sets out an amended bankruptcy law and procedure.

The law governing winding-up is governed principally by the Commercial Code, with particular provisions applicable to state enterprises in the Rehabilitation and Liquidation of State Enterprises Act 1983. Both a limited liability company and a joint stock company may be dissolved in the following circumstances:

- for reasons specified in the company's statutes;
- by a resolution of the shareholders to dissolve the company; and
- the company being declared insolvent.

It is unclear under Polish law what is meant by "insolvent," but it is understood to include the fact that the company is unable, or ceases, to pay its debts and that it has negative net assets.

A limited liability company (and not a joint stock company) may, in addition, be wound up by a court order at the request of a shareholder or member of the company's governing bodies where the fulfilment of the company's objectives becomes impossible.

An application to wind up a company may be brought by a creditor, by a director of the company, by the company's governing body, or by the company's financing bank. A creditor may apply for winding-up proceedings only if he has a judgment which is capable of execution or acknowledgment of a debt which is unsatisfied for six months.

The winding-up is supervised by the district court, which appoints a liquidator. The liquidator's first duty, having established the assets and liabilities of the company, is to attempt to reach an arrangement with a view to paying off the creditors. During the winding-up the company retains its legal personality. The winding-up is conducted under the company's business name with the addendum "in liquidation." Dividends cannot be paid to the shareholders until all obligations to third parties have been satisfied. Directors or managers of the company may find themselves personally responsible for liabilities caused by their mismanagement.

6.4.10 Law, Jurisdiction, and Arbitration

Proper law Documentation providing for the granting of security over land must be governed by Polish law. Other documentation or transactions can be governed by a foreign law, as agreed by the parties to such documentation or transactions.

Foreign judgments A foreign judgment can only be enforced in Poland if there is an international treaty in force between Poland and the relevant country. Although there are treaties with Italy, Greece and Austria and some other countries, treaties do not currently exist with the United States or the United Kingdom.

Arbitration Poland is a party to the New York Convention on the Recognition and Enforcement of Foreign Arbitration Awards (1958). Accordingly, in determining how disputes are to be resolved in a contract, the best solution is for disputes to be dealt with by arbitration. The Civil Procedure Code provides for the enforcement of arbitration awards subject to several conditions which include the following:

- the award is final and binding;

- the award is not against Polish public policy;
- the award is recognized in the country where it was given; and
- neither a Polish court nor any foreign court has exclusive jurisdiction.

6.4.11 Sovereign Immunity

Poland recognizes the accepted principles of international law in relation to governments acting in their sovereign capacity on the one hand and in a commercial capacity on the other.

Where a contract was entered into with a Polish company whose shareholders included Polish government entities, the Polish company would not be able to claim sovereign immunity.

7

US Legal Considerations Affecting Global Offerings of Shares in Foreign Companies

DANIEL A. BRAVERMAN

> **Chapter outline**
>
> 7.1 Introduction
>
> 7.2 US Laws and Regulations
>   7.2.1 Public Offerings in the US
>   7.2.2 Private Placements in the US
>   7.2.3 Offerings Outside the US
>
> 7.3 The Impact on a Global Equity Offering
>   7.3.1 Standard Global Equity Offering
>   7.3.2 Global Equity Offering Involving a US Private Placement
>   7.3.3 Global Equity Offering Involving Public Offerings in the US and in other Countries
>
> 7.4 Conclusion

The author is indebted to Messrs George M. Cohen and Leslie N. Silverman (partners in the New York office of Cleary, Gottlieb, Steen & Hamilton), to Messrs Edward F. Greene and Manley O. Hudson, Jr (partners in that firm's London office), and to Mr Alan L. Beller (partner in its Tokyo office). This chapter has drawn significantly on their work, and has also benefited from the thoughtful comments of Messrs Greene and Hudson and Mr Sebastian R. Sperber, an associate in the London office of Cleary, Gottlieb, Steen & Hamilton. Any weaknesses or errors are of course attributable to the author alone.

This article considers the situation as at January 1, 1992.

7.1 Introduction

The 1980s witnessed the emergence of so-called "global" equity offerings as part of the increasing internationalization of the world's capital markets. An equity offering can be said to be "global" when it involves simultaneous offerings of shares in a number of countries, one or more of which may be made to the public in accordance with the regulations of national markets. The capital markets of the US can be included in a global equity offering in one of two ways: shares may be offered to the public in accordance with the registration and disclosure requirements of the US Securities Act of 1933 (the Securities Act) and the regulations of the Securities and Exchange Commission (SEC) thereunder; or shares may be offered on a private basis in accordance with Rule 144A under the Securities Act or pursuant to traditional private placement procedures.

When a public offering or private placement is made in the US as part of a global offering, the structure of the offering as a whole will be significantly affected both as a result of the requirements that will apply in the US with which the requirements of other countries will have to be coordinated, and as a result of the extraterritorial effect of US laws and regulations on the activities of the participants in the portion of the offering being made outside the US. This chapter first outlines the most important laws and regulations that apply to public offerings and private placements in the US and then analyzes how they can affect the structure and conduct of the offering outside the US. The extent to which the existence of a US tranche will affect the rest of a global equity offering will be seen to vary significantly depending on whether a public offering or private placement is being made.

It must be stressed at the outset that the SEC's response to the internationalization of the world's capital markets has been dynamic, its regulations changing significantly to accommodate global offerings. In the early 1980s, the SEC attempted to facilitate US public offerings of shares in foreign companies by tailoring disclosure requirements more closely to home country requirements, and in 1990 the SEC adopted Rule 144A under the Securities Act, which simplifies the procedures for making private placements to large US institutions, and Regulation S under the Securities Act, which ensures that offerings can be made outside the US without registration with the SEC under the Securities Act. Throughout the 1980s and into the 1990s the SEC also took steps to limit the extraterritorial application of its restrictions on market activities by participants in an offering while a US distribution is under way, thereby reducing the impact of a US tranche on the activities of foreign underwriters in foreign markets in a global offering.

Other measures, such as allowing a foreign securities broker or dealer to solicit business in the US in certain circumstances without having to register with the SEC as a broker or dealer, and permitting a foreign bank or insurance company to offer its securities to the US public without having to register with the SEC as an investment company, were also part of the SEC's multifaceted response to internationalization. Finally, in a move that bears little on this chapter but foreshadows things to come, the SEC adopted a bilateral multijurisdictional disclosure system with Canada, permitting certain large issuers to use the offering documents of their home country when making a public offering of securities in the other country. In light of these developments, all of which are discussed in what follows, it is important to emphasize the protean character of the US regulatory system and its effect on global offerings. This chapter thus represents a snapshot of a dynamic system, the engine of change being commercial innovation and regulatory response, the forward thrust being toward the accommodation of international capital flows and the integration of the US capital markets with those of the rest of the world.

7.2 US Laws and Regulations

The Securities Act is the principal piece of legislation governing the distribution of securities in the US. Any offer or sale of securities in the US must be registered with the SEC under the Securities Act unless an exemption is available. In the context of a global equity offering, the only relevant exemption is the one for a private placement that is made either under Rule 144A or on the basis of traditional private placement procedures. We consider first the US laws and regulations for registered public offerings and then turn to private placements.

A prefatory word may be in order here. The discussion that follows outlines the relevant US laws and regulations in considerable detail, more in fact than might be expected. There are two important reasons for doing this. First, many of the interesting and difficult questions that arise in a global offering relate to conflicts between the US and foreign regulatory regimes, and between US regulatory requirements and commercial practices in foreign markets. It is a strange feature of those conflicts that the most significant of them often arise from the application of the most highly detailed, arcane, and seemingly trivial regulations – for example, those regarding the limitations on the trading activities of participants in an offering while a distribution of securities is under way in the US. Accordingly, in order to understand the nature of those conflicts, and to see how the regulators have attempted to resolve them, it is necessary to have a firm grasp of how the US regulations operate and the rationale for them.

A second reason for looking closely at the US regulatory regime is that its details reflect the solutions to problems that can be expected to arise in any sophisticated system of securities regulation. The effort to reduce transaction costs where appropriate by distinguishing between public offerings in which detailed disclosure requirements apply and private placements in which they do not, the regulations that are intended to ensure that investment decisions are made in a public offering on the basis of mandated disclosure rather than unwarranted publicity, the attempt to preserve the integrity of the secondary trading markets as a system for pricing securities that are being distributed, and the rules that are designed to ensure that the benefits of a distribution flow to the investing public and are not retained by the participants in a distribution (or shared only with large institutions), to name but a few of the matters dealt with here, all represent the endeavors of one important regulatory regime to solve problems that are universal in character. It is hoped that viewing the system in this light will not only be enlightening in itself but will also make intelligible, if not in all cases acceptable, the decision by US regulatory authorities to apply these solutions, even in certain cases outside the US, to the problems posed by global equity offerings.

Finally, a word should be said about what is not treated here. This chapter does not discuss the requirements for obtaining a listing on a major US stock exchange, such as the New York Stock Exchange or the American Stock Exchange, or a quotation on the National Association of Securities Dealers' Automated Quotation System (NASDAQ). These requirements are generally easy to meet in the context of a public offering since the information required by the relevant application will, for the most part, be contained in the filings made with the SEC under the Securities Act (and are irrelevant in private placements since the securities being offered will not be listed). As a technical matter, when securities are listed on a US exchange or quoted on NASDAQ, they are required to be registered under the Securities Exchange Act of 1934 (the Exchange Act) as well, but that also is a routine matter in the context of a public offering.

Nor does this chapter discuss American Depositary Shares (ADSs) or American Depositary Receipts (ADRs) which evidence them. Shares of foreign companies are usually offered to the public in the US in the form of ADSs and ADRs. An ADR is a negotiable certificate in registered form that evidences one or more ADSs, which in turn represent the underlying foreign shares on a share-for-share or multiple-share basis. ADRs are usually issued by a US commercial bank (the

Depositary) with which, or with whose foreign correspondent (the Custodian), the underlying shares have been deposited pursuant to a Deposit Agreement between the foreign company and the Depositary.[1]

Finally, this chapter does not discuss the securities laws of the fifty states – the so-called "blue sky" laws – which in many cases contain both registration requirements and anti-fraud protections. It is generally the task of US underwriters' counsel to ensure that all regulatory hurdles have been cleared in each state where shares are to be offered or sold. In a public offering, the registration requirements of most states can be avoided by ensuring that the shares are approved for listing on a US securities exchange before offers are made. Most blue sky laws also provide exemptions for private placements to institutional investors.

7.2.1 Public Offerings in the US

A public offering, with a stock exchange listing, is the route usually followed when a foreign private issuer wishes to gain the widest access to the US capital markets, to build a stable shareholder base in the United States, and to encourage the emergence of a secondary trading market there.[2] The US regulatory regime is, however, extremely rigorous when securities are being offered to the public. The most significant requirements are those imposed by the registration and related requirements of the Securities Act, which regulate disclosure and publicity; by Rules 10b-6 and 10b-7 under the Exchange Act, which regulate the market activities of the issuer and the underwriters while a distribution of securities is being made; and by the rules of the National Association of Securities Dealers, Inc. (the NASD), which are designed to ensure that members of the public are treated no less favorably than institutional participants in the US capital markets. Other restrictions, such as those imposed by section 7(d) of the Investment Company Act of 1940 (the Investment Company Act), which prevents a foreign "investment company" from offering its shares to the public in the US without registering with the SEC as an investment company, and by section 15(a) of the Exchange Act, which prevents any securities broker or dealer that has not registered as such with the SEC from offering securities in the US, are also relevant.

Registration and related requirements The purpose of the registration requirements of the Securities Act, broadly speaking, is to ensure that investment decisions in a US public offering are made on the basis of the disclosure mandated by the SEC and are not influenced by unwarranted publicity. Under section 5 of the Securities Act, it is unlawful *inter alia* for any person

- to offer to sell any security unless a registration statement in a prescribed form has first been filed with the SEC;[3]
- to use any prospectus – i.e. any communication in writing, or by radio or television, that offers any security for sale or confirms the sale of any security[4] – unless it is included in the registration statement and meets the disclosure requirements of the Securities Act;[5]
- to sell any security until the registration statement has been declared "effective" by the SEC;[6] and
- to deliver any security for sale until the prospectus included in the registration statement when it is declared effective has been furnished to the purchaser.[7]

The effect of these rules is to prohibit marketing efforts in connection with a public offering until a registration statement has been filed, to limit the use of written materials in connection with any marketing efforts to the preliminary prospectus that is included in the registration statement, and to prevent sales from being confirmed until the registration statement has been declared effective and the final prospectus printed, generally after review by the SEC to ensure that the disclosure requirements have been met. The underwriting agreement is generally signed, and the securities priced, close to the time when the registration statement is declared effective.

■ *Disclosure requirements.* The disclosure requirements for the prospectus included in a registration statement are set out in detailed regulations and forms provided by the SEC. The information called for is exhaustive – going well beyond what is required by regulators in other countries – and only those requirements which are generally thought to be most significant for foreign issuers can be touched on here.

The relevant forms for a foreign company wishing to offer its shares to the public are Forms F-1, F-2, and F-3 under the Securities Act.[8] Form F-1 is for an issuer that has not previously offered securities to the US public or arranged to have its securities quoted on a US securities exchange or on NASDAQ. Forms F-2 and F-3 are available to an issuer that has already taken such steps, and therefore has become subject to the periodic reporting requirements of the Exchange Act.[9] A foreign issuer will be eligible to use Form F-3 if

- it has been subject to such periodic reporting requirements for at least thirty-six months and has filed all required reports in the last twelve months on a timely basis;[10]

- its voting stock held by non-affiliates has an aggregate worldwide market value (the so-called "float") of at least $300 million;[11] and
- it has not defaulted on certain payments.[12]

An issuer that satisfies all the foregoing requirements except the float requirement will be eligible to use Form F-2, as will an issuer that satisfies the float requirement but has been subject to the reporting requirements for only twelve months.[13] The forms differ mainly in the extent to which they permit the information about the issuer that is required to be included in the prospectus to be incorporated by reference to previous reports filed under the Exchange Act, Form F-3 being the most permissive in this regard. Each of the forms refers to Regulation S-X for the requirements regarding financial statements and to Form 20-F for the other disclosure requirements.

The prospectus to be used in a public offering must contain financial statements that have been audited on the basis of auditing standards that are generally accepted in the US.[14] While these standards are in certain respects more rigorous than those applicable elsewhere,[15] audits conducted by major international accounting firms generally will meet the US requirements, as will audits conducted in accordance with the auditing standards of the UK.[16] The financial statements may be presented in accordance with accounting principles that are generally accepted in the issuer's jurisdiction of incorporation, so long as the main differences between those principles and generally accepted accounting principles in the US (US GAAP) are explained and numerical reconciliations to US GAAP of the principal income statement and balance sheet items are provided.[17]

Although the financial statements may be prepared on the basis of other principles, they must be similar in scope to those prepared in accordance with US GAAP and therefore must include audited balance sheets as of the end of each of the issuer's two most recent financial years and audited statements of income and cash flows for each of its three most recent financial years.[18] The balance sheets, statements of income, and statements of cash flows must have an informational content substantially similar to that required by US GAAP;[19] accordingly, "segment" financial data must be provided – i.e. information with respect to revenues, operating profits, assets, and capital expenditures broken down by industry segment and geographic area.[20] If a registration statement is filed more than six months after the end of the issuer's most recent financial year, the prospectus must also include financial statements, which may be unaudited, as of an interim date not more than six months prior to the effective date of the registration statement.[21] Moreover, certain selected financial data must be provided for each of the last five financial years, showing significant trends relating to revenues, income, liquidity, assets, liabilities, capital resources, and dividends per common share.[22]

In addition to the financial data, the prospectus must include a complete description of the issuer's business and an analysis by management of the issuer's financial condition and results of operations. The description of the business must highlight *inter alia* any special characteristics of the issuer's operations or industry that could have a material impact on future performance and must identify any material country risks.[23] Examples of factors which might be discussed include dependence on one or a few major customers or suppliers (including suppliers of raw materials or financing); existing or probable governmental regulation; expiration of material labor contracts, patents, trademarks, licenses, franchises, concessions, or royalty agreements; unusual competitive conditions in the industry; the cyclicality of the industry; and anticipated raw material or energy shortages to the extent management may not be able to secure a continuing source of supply.[24] The description must also explain any material variations between the percentage of revenues contributed by each industry segment and geographic area on the one hand and the corresponding percentages of operating profit contributed by the same segments on the other.[25]

The management's discussion and analysis of financial condition and results of operations (MD&A) is intended to help investors understand the financial statements contained in the prospectus and to assess the sources, and probability of recurrence, of earnings or losses.[26] The discussion is generally divided into two parts. In the first, the issuer must describe any unusual events or significant economic changes that materially affected the level of income, and any trends or uncertainties that have had, or that the issuer reasonably expects will have, a material impact on net sales or revenues or on income from continuing operations.[27] To the extent that the financial statements disclose material changes in net sales or revenues, the issuer must indicate the extent to which such changes are attributable to changes in prices or to changes in the quantities of goods or services being sold. The issuer also must discuss the impact of inflation on its sales, revenues, and income for the three most recent financial years. Where its consolidated financial statements reveal material changes from one year to the next in any line item, the issuer must describe the causes of the changes to the extent necessary to an understanding of its business as a whole. In the second part, the issuer is required to describe material commitments for capital expenditures and any material trends in such expenditures, and to identify its financial resources (and any deficiencies in them).[28] Any trends that are reasonably likely to result in material changes in the issuer's ability to finance its operations and capital expenditures also must be discussed.

For an issuer that has not previously offered securities to the US public, at least two months should be allowed for the preparation of a registration statement for filing with the SEC. The SEC staff will generally take one month to review the filing and to comment on the disclosure. During this period, offers may be made on the basis of the preliminary prospectus. Unless the SEC's comments are unusually extensive, one week should be allowed to prepare a response, and after that the registration statement can be declared effective, the underwriting agreement signed, the securities priced on the basis of indications of interest (or "circles") obtained from investors during the marketing period, and sales confirmed. There is usually a period of five business days between pricing and closing, so approximately three and a half months should be allowed from the time preparation of a registration statement begins to the closing date. Significantly less time is required for issuers that have previously offered securities to the public in the US and have been filing periodic reports with the SEC under the Exchange Act. The registration fee is 1/32 of 1 percent of the aggregate public offering price of the shares.[29]

■ *Civil liability and due diligence.* The disclosure requirements are given their sting by the civil liabilities imposed by the securities laws. Section 11 of the Securities Act imposes strict liability on issuers for material misstatements or omissions in registration statements, and liability, subject to a "due diligence" defense, on the directors and certain executive officers of the issuer and on the underwriters. (Certain others, including auditors, also have section 11 liability.)[30] In addition, section 12(2) of the Securities Act imposes liability, subject to a "reasonable care" defense, on anyone who sells a security through any written or oral communication containing a material misstatement or omission. Finally, Rule 10b-5 under the Exchange Act imposes liability on anyone who knowingly or recklessly makes an untrue statement of a material fact or omits to state a material fact in connection with the purchase or sale of a security. The litigious nature of American society, the relative ease with which class actions can be brought on behalf of similarly situated shareholders, and the prevalence of contingent-fee arrangements all combine to ensure that the threat of civil liability is an effective means of keeping disclosure standards high.

In order to establish a defense to claims under these liability provisions, the underwriters in a US public offering engage in a "due diligence" exercise, with the assistance of their legal advisers. Among other things, this involves (1) meetings with the principal executive and financial officers of the issuer to assess operating and financial results, identify any vulnerabilities, and discuss prospects, and (2) a review of all the issuer's significant documents, including minutes of the meetings of its shareholders and of its board of directors (and the board's more significant committees) for the past five years, and the issuer's material contracts. It is generally a condition to the closing of a US public offering that the legal advisers to the issuer and to the underwriters give letters to the underwriters confirming that nothing has come to their attention to cause them to believe that the registration statement or final prospectus contains a material misstatement or omission. In order to be in a position to give these letters, the legal advisers participate closely in the preparation of the prospectus and in the due diligence meetings with top management, and of course do the bulk of the review of the issuer's significant documents.

The due diligence process is generally considered to be burdensome, intrusive, time-consuming, and expensive, but it is also acknowledged to be thorough and, perhaps, more likely to identify areas of business risk than the comparable exercises in other countries.

■ *Restrictions on publicity.* The registration process and disclosure requirements are intended to ensure that potential investors are provided complete and accurate information about the issuer, and to ensure that investment decisions are made on the basis of that information and are not influenced by advertising campaigns or other forms of publicity. The requirement that no "offer to sell" can be made until a registration statement has been filed prevents so-called "gun-jumping" – efforts to "condition the market" in anticipation of an offering – and the prohibition on the use of written materials other than the preliminary prospectus after a registration statement has been filed precludes most forms of advertising, including newspaper, radio, and television campaigns, which are common in some countries. The only marketing efforts permitted in connection with a US public offering, other than the distribution of the preliminary prospectus, are so-called "road shows", in which executive officers of the issuer and representatives of the underwriters meet potential investors and give oral presentations, perhaps with slides, about the issuer and the offering, and respond to questions.

The restrictions on publicity apply to the issuer at least from the time it "reaches an understanding" with the managing underwriter with respect to the offering, and may reach back to the time the issuer decides to proceed with a public offering. The investment bank selected to be the managing underwriter becomes subject to the restrictions when it begins to participate in the preparation of a registration statement or otherwise "reaches an understanding" with the issuer that it will become the managing underwriter. Other investment banks become subject to the restrictions when they are invited by the issuer or managing underwriter to participate or when they seek to participate. The restrictions on the issuer fall away when both the distribution is over and securities dealers, whether or not they are participating in the distribution, are no longer required to deliver prospectuses to purchasers; the restrictions on a securities dealer fall away when it has sold its allotment and is no longer required to deliver a prospectus.[31] The period during which a prospectus is required to be delivered by securities dealers varies depending on a number of factors. If the issuer was subject to the periodic reporting requirements of the Exchange Act prior to the filing of the registration statement, the period lasts until the dealer has distributed its allotment. If not, the period lasts until the later of when the dealer has disposed of its allotment and a time that varies as follows:

- if arrangements are made to have the shares quoted on a US securities exchange or on NASDAQ when the offering commences, twenty-five days thereafter;
- if the shares are not so quoted when the offering commences, ninety days thereafter in the case of an issuer's first US public offering, and forty days thereafter in other offerings.[32]

The SEC has recognized that conservative interpretations of the restrictions on publicity in connection with a US public offering could have adverse effects on the quality of information that flows into the market, since the issuer and the underwriters may fear that press releases and research reports could be viewed as unlawful "offers to sell" the securities being distributed, or as "prospectuses" that do not meet the disclosure requirements. To reconcile the conflicting objectives of restricting the "hype" surrounding an offering while at the same time encouraging the flow of important information into the market, the SEC has issued a number of releases and rules providing guidance.

In the releases, the SEC encouraged issuers to continue to make factual information available to the public. The SEC stated that issuers should:

- continue to advertise products and services;
- continue to send out customary quarterly, annual, and other periodic reports to security holders;

- continue to publish proxy statements and send out dividend notices;
- continue to make announcements to the press with respect to factual business and financial developments; i.e. receipt of a contract, the settlement of a strike, the opening of a plant, or similar events of interest to the community in which the business operates;
- answer unsolicited telephone inquiries from security holders, financial analysts, the press, and others concerning factual information;
- observe an "open door" policy in responding to unsolicited inquiries concerning factual matters from securities analysts, financial analysts, security holders, and participants in the communications field who have a legitimate interest in the corporation's affairs;
- continue to hold shareholder meetings as scheduled and to answer shareholders' inquiries at shareholder meetings relating to factual matters.

The SEC warned, however, that the issuance of forecasts, projections, predictions, or opinions concerning value should be avoided.[33]

While the releases generally deal with corporate communications that are not related to an offering, the SEC has also recognized that the intention to make an offering is itself an important item of information which the issuer should be permitted to make available to the market. Accordingly, Rule 135 under the Securities Act provides that a pre-filing notice of an intention to make a public offering is not deemed to be an offer of any security for sale if it is limited to certain specified information, which includes the name of the issuer, the title, amount, and basic terms of the securities, the anticipated time of the offering, and a brief statement of the manner and purpose of the offering, but does not include a description of the issuer's business or the names of the underwriters. Rule 134 under the Securities Act provides that a post-filing communication is not deemed to be a "prospectus" if the communication is limited to certain specified information, which includes the name of the issuer, the title and amount of the securities being offered, a brief description of the general nature of the issuer's business, and the names of the managing underwriters, but does not include the purpose of the offering or earnings information.

Research reports published by a broker–dealer that is a participant in an offering are dealt with in Rules 138 and 139 under the Securities Act. Rule 138 excludes from the term "offer for sale" – and thus from the definition of "prospectus" – and from the term "offer to sell" the distribution by a broker–dealer in the regular course of its business of information, opinions, or recommendations as to an issuer's common stock if non-convertible preferred stock or debt securities are being offered and *vice versa*, but only if the issuer is eligible to file a registration statement on Form F-2 or Form F-3.

Rule 139(b) excludes from the terms "offer for sale" and "offer to sell" the distribution by a broker–dealer of any information, opinion, or recommendation about an issuer that is subject to the periodic reporting requirements of the Exchange Act if

- it is contained in a publication which is distributed with reasonable regularity in the normal course of business and includes similar information, opinions, or recommendations with respect to a substantial number of companies in the issuer's industry, or contains a comprehensive list of securities currently recommended by such broker or dealer;
- it is given no materially greater space or prominence in such publication than that given to other securities or issuers; and
- in the case of an opinion or recommendation, it is not more favorable with respect to the issuer or any class of its securities than the opinion or recommendation published by the broker or dealer in its last publication relating to the issuer or its securities prior to the commencement of its participation in the distribution.[34]

Rule 139 (a) excludes from the terms "offer for sale" and "offer to sell" the distribution by a broker–dealer of any information, opinion, or recommendation about an issuer that is eligible to file a registration statement on Form F-3, so long as it is contained in a publication which is distributed with reasonable regularity in the ordinary course of the broker–dealer's business.[35]

Restrictions on market activities The SEC has promulgated a number of detailed rules which are intended to prevent those with an interest in the success of a distribution from manipulating, through their activities in the market, the price of the securities being distributed. Rules 10b-6 and 10b-7 under the Exchange Act are the most significant of these rules when the effect of US laws and regulations on the structure and conduct of a global equity offering is being considered.[36]

- *Rule 10b-6.* Under Rule 10b-6, it is unlawful for an issuer, an underwriter, or a prospective underwriter in a distribution, or a broker, dealer, or other person who has agreed to participate or is participating in the distribution (or certain of their affiliates), to bid for or purchase any security which is the subject of the distribution, or any security of the same class and series, or any right to purchase any such security, or to attempt to induce any person to purchase any such security or right, until after it has completed its participation in the distribution. In order to obviate the need to engage in difficult line-drawing exercises on a case-by-case basis, Rule 10b-6 prohibits all bids for and purchases of the securities in question by participants in the distribution (and certain of their affiliates), without regard to whether such bids or purchases were made for the purpose of creating actual, or apparent, active trading in such securities (or raising their price) or for legitimate market-making purposes. The flexibility to continue ordinary trading activities, to the extent considered appropriate by the SEC, is provided by a number of exceptions to these restrictions.

The prohibition of Rule 10b-6 on attempts to induce purchases of securities also has the effect of restricting publicity in connection with a distribution, including the dissemination of information by issuers and the publishing of research reports by broker–dealers. However, although the matter is not free from doubt, the activities permitted by the SEC's releases on corporate communications, by Rules 134 and 135, and, in most cases, by Rules 138 and 139 under the Securities Act, should not be considered to be "attempts to induce" for purposes of Rule 10b-6, and thus should not be subject to the limitations.[37]

The period during which the restrictions of Rule 10b-6 will apply is set out, somewhat obliquely, in the definitions. A person becomes an "underwriter" for purposes of Rule 10b-6 – thereby becoming subject to the restrictions – when it has agreed with the issuer to purchase securities for distribution, to distribute securities for or on behalf of the issuer, or to manage or supervise a distribution for or on behalf of the issuer.[38] A person becomes a "prospective underwriter" when it has decided to submit a bid to become an underwriter (pursuant to an invitation for bids) or when it has reached an understanding with an issuer that it will become an underwriter.[39] The issuer becomes subject to the restrictions when it decides to go forward with the distribution, notwithstanding that it has yet to retain underwriters.[40] The restrictions fall away when the person in question has completed its participation in the distribution: in the case of the issuer, this is deemed to occur when the distribution as a whole has been completed; in the case of an underwriter, when it has distributed its allotment, including all other securities of the same class acquired in connection with the distribution, and any stabilization arrangements and trading restrictions with respect to the distribution have been terminated; and in the case of any other person (such as a securities dealer in a selling group), when it has distributed its allotment.[41] The period during which publicity and other activities are restricted under Rule 10b-6 is thus not quite coextensive with the period during which publicity is restricted by virtue of the registration requirements.

Rule 10b-6 recognizes a number of exceptions for activities that are not engaged in for the purpose of creating actual, or apparent, active trading in any security (or raising its price). Of these, the most significant is the exception that permits an underwriter, prospective underwriter, or dealer to bid for or purchase shares, or rights to acquire shares, prior to a "cooling-off" period that begins two (or in some cases nine) business days before the commencement of offers or sales of the securities being distributed.[42] For this purpose, the commencement of offers or sales is considered to occur when the underwriters are permitted to confirm sales (i.e. after the registration statement is declared effective, the underwriting agreement signed, and the securities priced). The rationale for this exception is that any effect of bids or purchases on the price of the security being distributed will be dissipated during the cooling-off period. A similar exception exists for bids and purchases by the issuer.[43] It is important to recognize that this exception applies only to bids and purchases and not to attempts to induce purchases, since the effect of publicity cannot be expected to dissipate during the cooling-off period.

Other significant exceptions include:

- offers to sell or the solicitations of offers to buy the securities being distributed, or securities or rights offered as principal by the person making the offer to sell or the solicitation of the offers to buy;[44]
- transactions with the issuer or among participants in the distribution effected otherwise than on a securities exchange;[45]
- unsolicited privately negotiated purchases, each involving at least a block of the securities in question, that are not effected from or through a broker or dealer;[46] and
- brokerage transactions not involving solicitation of the customer's order (or involving the solicitation of the customer's order prior to the commencement of the applicable cooling-off period).[47]

These exceptions are designed either to facilitate transactions that are essential to the smooth conduct of the offering, or to permit transactions that, in the absence of wilful misconduct, cannot be expected to affect the price of the security being distributed.

■ *Rule 10b-7.* Another important exception to the restrictions of Rule 10b-6 is the one permitting stabilizing transactions that are conducted in accordance with Rule 10b-7. Stabilization means placing a bid, or making a purchase, for the purpose of pegging, fixing, or stabilizing the price of any security.[48] The purpose of stabilization is to give comfort to potential purchasers in an offering that the price of the security in the after-market will not be significantly below the public offering price, thereby facilitating a smooth transition from the primary phase of the distribution to orderly secondary trading. Since stabilization involves almost by definition the creation of a somewhat false market, it is subject to detailed regulation.

The general requirement of Rule 10b-7 is that no stabilizing bid or purchase may be made except for the purpose of preventing or retarding a decline in the open market price of a security.[49] This general requirement is implemented through a number of detailed rules, as follows:

1 Except as provided in (2), (3), and (4) below, no person may (a) begin to stabilize a security at a price higher than the highest current independent bid price for such security or (b) raise the price at which such person is stabilizing. If no *bona fide* market for the security being distributed exists at the time stabilizing is initiated, stabilizing may be initiated at a price not in excess of the public offering price.[50]
2 If the principal market for a security is a securities exchange and stabilizing is initiated on such exchange the initial stabilizing bid or purchase may, subject to certain conditions, be made at a price up to the last independent sale price on such exchange, even if it is above the highest current independent bid price.[51]
3 If a stabilizing bid or purchase is made before the initial public offering price of the security to be distributed is determined, and such offering price is higher than such stabilizing bid or purchase price, then stabilizing may be resumed after determination of such public offering price at the price at which it could then be initiated.[52]
4 A stabilizing bid lawful when made may be continuously maintained or reduced irrespective of changes in the independent bid, asked or sale price of such security.[53]
5 No person may stabilize a security at a price above the price at which such security is then being distributed.[54]

Two other, highly technical, rules are of particular significance in the context of a global equity offering. The first provides that when a security is traded in more than one market, stabilizing may not be initiated at a price that would be unlawful in the market which is the principal market for the security in the US open for trading when stabilizing is initiated. If, however, the principal market for the security in the United States is a securities exchange, stabilizing may be initiated in any market after the close of such exchange at the price at which stabilizing could have been initiated on such exchange when it closed.[55]

The second rule provides that a stabilizing bid may not be placed on a securities exchange before the opening quotations for the security on such exchange are available, unless stabilizing is already being conducted lawfully on such exchange at that price. A stabilizing bid may, however, be placed immediately prior to the opening of a securities exchange at a price no higher than the price at which stabilizing could have been initiated on such exchange at its previous close.[56]

The general effect of these rules is to permit stabilizing bids to be initiated at a price no higher than the last independent bid or sale price. Once entered, a stabilizing bid may be maintained regardless of market developments but (subject to several limited exceptions) may not be raised, and must be reduced if the price at which the security is then being distributed is lower. When determining the level at which stabilizing bids may be initiated, reference must be made to the latest prices quoted in the principal market for the securities in the US.[57]

It is customary in US public offerings of shares to facilitate stabilization through "over-allotments." The managing underwriter in a US public offering is typically given the authority to over-allot – i.e. to offer and sell more shares than the underwriters have contracted to purchase from the issuer on a "firm" basis. By over-allotting shares, the managing underwriter can ensure that there are purchasers ready to accept resales of shares that the underwriters purchase in the market as a result of stabilization. In order to protect the underwriters in circumstances where the shares purchased as a result of stabilization are not sufficient to cover the short position created through over-allotments, the issuer typically will grant them a so-called "over-allotment option." The over-allotment option generally allows the underwriters, for a period beginning with the execution of the underwriting agreement and ending thirty days after the closing date, to purchase from the issuer, at the public offering price less the commissions provided for in the underwriting agreement, up to 15 percent of the shares being offered, but solely for the purpose of covering any over-allotments that are made on behalf of the syndicate by the managing underwriter. If the offering is a success, and there are no stabilizing purchases in the market, the managing underwriter will exercise the option on behalf of the syndicate for that number of shares which have been over-allotted, and the syndicate will earn the same commissions on the additional shares as it earned on the so-called "firm shares." If, however, stabilizing activities result in purchases in the market, the over-allotment option will be exercised, if at all, only to cover the syndicate's short position that remains after the shares purchased through stabilization have first been applied for that purpose. Of course, when shares purchased through stabilization are used to cover over-allotments, the commissions associated with the exercise of the over-allotment option are forgone since in most cases the shares will have been purchased in the market at, or slightly below, the public offering price and not, as would be the case if the over-allotment option were exercised, at the public offering price less the commissions. Any profits and losses arising out of stabilization activities are typically allocated among the underwriters *pro rata* to their underwriting commitments, subject to agreed limits.

The NASD Rules The Rules of Fair Practice of the NASD, and interpretations of these Rules by its Board of Governors, represent an attempt to codify the "high standards of commercial honor and just and equitable principles of trade" that are required of all securities dealers comprising its membership.[58] Two sets of rules are of particular importance in the context of a global equity offering. The first requires in effect that all potential investors in a public offering be offered the securities at the same public offering price, and the second ensures that the benefits of any rise in the price of a publicly offered security in the after-market flow to the investing community and are not retained by participants in the distribution.

The so-called "Papilsky" rules, requiring that all investors be offered securities at the same price, operate by limiting the scope of permissible discounts. Section 24 of the Rules of Fair Practice, as interpreted by the Board of Governors, requires that selling concessions, discounts, or other allowances in connection with a public offering of securities be paid only to brokers or dealers engaged in the investment banking or securities business and only as consideration for services rendered in distribution. Services will be considered to be rendered in distribution if the dealer in question is an underwriter of part of the offering, has made some selling effort with respect to the sale or has provided or agreed to provide *bona fide* research to the person to whom or at whose direction the sale is made. A broker or dealer who has received or retained a selling commission, discount, or other allowance may not grant or otherwise reallow all or part of it to anyone other than a broker or dealer that is itself engaged in the investment banking or securities business and, again, only as consideration for services rendered in distribution.[59]

The interpretation of the Board of Governors of the NASD on "Free Riding and Withholding" is based upon the premise that members of the NASD have an obligation in a public offering to make a *bona fide* public distribution at the public offering price of securities that trade at a premium in the secondary market (a so-called "hot issue"). Moreover, the Board considers that the failure to make a *bona fide* public distribution when there is demand for an issue can itself be a factor in artificially raising the price. Accordingly, the interpretation prohibits any member of the NASD from continuing to hold any security that is part of a hot issue or to sell any such security to related parties or to certain accounts where reciprocal benefits could be provided, except in accordance with previous investment practice and in immaterial amounts.[60]

The Rules of Fair Practice require in certain circumstances that the foreign underwriters in a global equity offering agree to abide by these and related requirements of the NASD. This is considered in the section on "The NASD rules" in 7.3.1 below.

Other restrictions Both the Investment Company Act and the Exchange Act contain additional requirements that are relevant to a US public offering of shares in a foreign company.

Section 7(d) of the Investment Company Act requires any foreign "investment company" that offers securities to the public in the United States to register as an investment company with the SEC; as a practical matter, this prohibits the securities of any foreign "investment company" from being offered to the US public unless an exemption is obtained. The definition of "investment company" is broader than might be expected, covering not only companies that engage primarily in the business of investing, reinvesting, or trading in securities,[61] but also in certain circumstances companies primarily engaged in other businesses if they own less than majority interests in their operating subsidiaries.[62] Because industrial companies in Europe often control their subsidiaries through minority interests they can become "inadvertent" investment companies, and thus be denied access to the public capital markets in the US.

Until recently, foreign banks and insurance companies were considered investment companies as well, but Rule 3a-6, adopted by the SEC in the fall of 1991, excepts them from the definition, provided among other things that they are regulated as commercial banks or insurance companies by the authorities in their home countries.[63] Rule 3a-6 also has the effect of excepting most bank holding companies from the definition of investment company.

Section 15(a) of the Exchange Act makes it unlawful for any securities broker or dealer to effect any transaction in, or to induce or attempt to induce the purchase or sale of, any security through the use of the US mails or of any means or instrumentality of interstate (i.e. US) commerce, unless the broker or dealer is registered with the SEC. In order for a foreign broker–dealer to register, its employees, including senior management, are required to pass examinations and register with the NASD, and the broker–dealer is required to comply throughout the world with US net capital and other rules (which are not consistent with the rules of a number of other countries). As a practical matter, therefore, section 15(a) has the effect of precluding foreign brokers or dealers from offering or selling securities in the US except through their US affiliates which have so registered. Accordingly, foreign brokers and dealers may not participate as underwriters in a US public offering.[64]

The impact of section 7(d) of the Investment Company Act and section 15(a) of the Exchange Act is less severe in the context of a US private placement, and this is discussed in the section entitled "Other considerations" in 7.2.2 below.

7.2.2 Private Placements in the US

With the adoption by the SEC of Rule 144A under the Securities Act in April of 1990, a significant impetus was given to the underwritten private placement as an effective way of including the US capital markets in global equity offerings.[65] As of September 30, 1991, there had been some thirty-three global equity offerings with placements in the US under Rule 144A. The global offerings raised approximately $23.1 billion in aggregate, with the US accounting for about $1.4 billion. The shares of issuers from seventeen different countries were involved.[66]

Rule 144A Rule 144A provides that an offer or sale of eligible securities to a qualified institutional buyer, or a person reasonably believed by the seller to be a qualified institutional buyer, is exempt from the registration requirements of the Securities Act,[67] provided only that the seller takes reasonable steps to make the buyer aware that the offer or sale is being made pursuant to the rule.[68] Any security sold under Rule 144A becomes a "restricted security" (as defined in Rule 144(a) (3) under the Securities Act), which means that resales are subject to limitations, discussed below, for a period of three years.[69] The assumption underlying Rule 144A is that qualified institutional buyers can be expected to know, and abide by, the restrictions on resale that apply to restricted securities.

A "qualified institutional buyer" is, in general, any institutional investor that owns and invests on a discretionary basis at least $100 million in securities of issuers that are not affiliated with that investor.[70] In the case of securities dealers, the threshold amount is reduced to $10 million,[71] and any bank or savings and loan association must also have an audited net worth of at least $25 million.[72] In forming a view as to whether a purchaser is a qualified institutional buyer, the seller is entitled to rely on certain publicly available information, or on a certificate of the chief financial officer (or other executive officer) of the purchaser specifying the amount of securities owned and invested on a discretionary basis as of a specified date at or since the close of the purchaser's most recent financial year.[73]

Shares of a foreign company are eligible to be sold under Rule 144A unless they are of the same class as shares that are listed on a securities exchange in the United States or quoted on NASDAQ.[74] If the issuer is not subject to the periodic reporting requirements of the Exchange Act and has not obtained an exemption from those requirements under Rule 12g3-2(b) under the Exchange Act, which requires that significant information made public in the issuer's home market, furnished to a securities exchange, or distributed to its security holders be furnished to the SEC, it must agree, for the benefit of holders and prospective purchasers of the shares, to provide certain reasonably current general information upon request, including a brief statement of the nature of its business and the products and services it offers, and its most recent balance sheet and profit and loss and retained earnings statements, and similar financial statements for the two preceding financial years.[75] Information will be considered to be "reasonably current" if it meets the timing requirements of the issuer's home country or principal trading markets.[76]

The requirement to furnish information applies for so long as the shares being sold are "restricted securities," and are thus subject to resale restrictions. Under Rule 144, the restricted period is three years.[77] During the first two years, restricted securities cannot be offered or sold in the secondary trading markets in the US,[78] and during the third year they may only be offered or sold in those markets in accordance with certain limitations regarding volume and manner of sale.[79] Throughout the three-year period, however, the securities may be offered and sold in the US on a private basis, for example to other qualified institutional buyers under Rule 144A (or in any other transaction that does not constitute a "distribution" for purposes of the Securities Act), or outside the US in accordance with Regulation S, which is discussed in the section on "Regulation S" in 7.2.3 below. A security lawfully sold into the secondary trading markets in the US, or outside the US, during the three-year restricted period ceases to be a restricted security.

Offers and sales of shares will be exempt from the registration requirements of the Securities Act under Rule 144A only if they are made without any form of "general solicitation or general advertising," which is the third source of restrictions on publicity we have encountered thus far. Rule 502(c) under the Securities Act states that this includes, but is not limited to, any advertisement, article, notice, or other communication published in any newspaper, magazine, or similar media, or broadcast over television or radio, and any seminar or meeting to which participants have been invited by any general solicitation or general advertising. Although the weight of authority may be to the contrary, the better view is that the kind of corporate communications contemplated by the SEC releases discussed earlier and, if the private placement is so material that failure to notify the market of its occurrence could subject the issuer to liability under Rule 10b-5 under the Exchange Act (or otherwise violate applicable law), notices of the kind contemplated by Rule 135 under the Securities Act should not be general solicitation or general advertising, nor should the publishing by a broker or dealer participating in the placement of a research report of the kind contemplated by Rules 138 or 139 under the Securities Act (so long as the private placement is not mentioned).[80] Moreover, it is clearly consistent with the prohibition on general solicitation and general advertising to conduct "road shows" in connection with the placement to which qualified institutional buyers are invited by letter or telephone, and these meetings can be held in several locations over an extended period of time and involve large numbers of potential investors. The road shows that have been conducted in large Rule 144A placements have been indistinguishable in many respects from those conducted in registered public offerings.[81]

Traditional private placements If Rule 144A is not available, or if it is not attractive,[82] in the context of a particular global equity offering, a private placement can still be made on the basis of traditional procedures. These procedures, developed over decades of practice, are designed *inter alia* to ensure that the initial offers and sales are not made to the public[83] and to demonstrate that the issuer has exercised "reasonable care" to ensure that the purchasers of the privately placed securities are not buying them with a view to their public distribution, or for reoffer or resale in connection with a public distribution, since buying for those purposes could jeopardize the exemption from the registration requirements of the Securities Act.[84]

In a traditional private placement, shares are usually offered to a limited number of sophisticated institutional investors – generally not more than 100 – and in minimum amounts, generally having a purchase price of at least $500,000; and there can be no general solicitation or general advertising. Each purchaser is required to provide a so-called "non-distribution letter" in which, among other things, it confirms its status and that it is not buying the shares with a view to their distribution, and agrees to abide by certain restrictions on resale for so long as the shares are restricted securities. These restrictions generally preclude resales except

- to other sophisticated institutional investors who also provide non-distribution letters (or to qualified institutional buyers without such letters if the shares are eligible for resale under Rule 144A);
- outside the US under Regulation S; or
- in other circumstances with an opinion of counsel that registration under the Securities Act is not required.

Finally, the shares are stamped with a legend notifying purchasers of the restrictions on resale (or custodial arrangements are imposed if stamping the shares in this way is not feasible), and "stop-transfer" procedures are put in place in order to enforce the resale restrictions.

Other considerations Many of the laws and regulations that apply in a US public offering do not apply, or are of less significance, in a private placement. Since the placement is by definition exempt from the registration requirements of the Securities Act, a registration statement need not be filed with the SEC, offers can be made at any time, written offers may be made through a variety of different media, and the detailed disclosure requirements outlined above, including in particular those regarding financial statements, need not be followed. None the less, since the liability provisions of section 12(2) of the Securities Act and Rule 10b-5 under the Exchange Act apply to private placements as well as public offerings, offers in writing are generally made by way of a prospectus that is prepared to a high standard. It is not, however, a *sine qua non* of avoiding liability under these provisions that the financial statements contained in the prospectus be reconciled to US GAAP, and none of the financial statements contained in the offering documents used in the US in the thirty-three global offerings involving Rule 144A included such reconciliations, although a number of them contained narrative discussions of the principal differences between US GAAP and the accounting principles actually used.[85]

The risk that a US court will conclude that there is a misstatement or omission in the prospectus is generally thought to be higher the more the prospectus departs from the SEC's detailed disclosure requirements set out in the forms used in public offerings. While section 12(2) of the Securities Act affords a defense to the underwriters if they have exercised reasonable care to ensure that the prospectus is accurate, the review process that typically takes place with regard to foreign offering documents may not satisfy the requirements of reasonable care, since it is generally less likely than US-style due diligence to identify business risks. Accordingly, the US underwriters in this situation have to decide early on whether they wish to engage in US-style due diligence – which might well be resisted by the issuer – or whether they are willing to accept the risks of proceeding on the basis of the practices that are customary in the issuer's country, relying on the representations and indemnities given by the issuer with respect to the accuracy of the offering document. This decision will vary depending on a number of factors, including the size of the placement in the US, the review process that is customary in the issuer's jurisdiction, the creditworthiness of the issuer, and the legality and enforceability of the issuer's indemnity.

The situation with regard to the restrictions on market activities imposed by Rules 10b-6 and 10b-7 under the Exchange Act is complicated in the case of a private placement, and is dealt with in the section on "Restrictions on Market Activities" in 7.3.2 below, where the question whether the rules apply at all is discussed together with the exemptions that are available, if they do apply, for market activities conducted outside the US. The Rules of Fair Practice of the NASD regarding limitations on discounts and free riding and withholding clearly do not apply.

While section 7(d) of the Investment Company Act would seem to be irrelevant to a private placement in the US by a foreign investment company, since that section applies by its terms only to "public offerings," the SEC staff has concluded that the Investment Company Act prevents a foreign investment company from making a private placement as well, if "as a result" of the placement there would be more than 100 beneficial owners of any of the issuer's securities (other than short-term debt) in the US.[86] In the release adopting Rule 144A, the SEC appeared to endorse the position of its staff, raising the question whether the resale under Rule 144A of securities of a foreign investment company that resulted in there being more than 100 owners of the company's securities in the US would constitute a violation of the Investment Company Act.[87]

This doctrine has created enormous practical difficulties. Firstly, it is unclear what the 100-owner test really means. Take, for example, the case of an issuer that has never sold securities in the US but finds that there are fifty holders of its securities there when a private placement is to be made, the securities having flowed into the US from foreign markets in secondary trading. It seems fair to conclude that a placement with up to another fifty US investors can be made, and let us assume that a placement to twenty-five US investors is in fact made. What happens if the privately placed shares are resold in the US, resulting in there being more than 100 owners? What if the privately placed shares are not sold, but other securities in the US at the time of the placement are, resulting in there being more than 100 owners? What if, after that, some of the privately placed shares are sold, increasing the number still further? What if, in that situation, the number of private placees is still below 100? What if additional securities flow into the US from foreign markets after the placement? What if a combination of all these possibilities occurs? The SEC has provided no guidance here, and it is very difficult for US legal advisers to give definitive advice in this area. Secondly, because many foreign companies issue securities in bearer form, it is often difficult to decide whether there is "room" for a US placement, since the number of existing US holders cannot be ascertained. Finally, the transfer restrictions that would have to be imposed on private placees in order to ensure that resales in the US do not breach the 100-owner limitation could add complexity and impair liquidity to a degree that would affect the marketability of the shares. It is worth noting that in a 1990 release requesting comment on how the Investment Company Act should be amended, the SEC raised for consideration the possibility of exempting from the definition of investment company any entity that sold its securities in the US only to institutional investors.[88] If this sensible position were to be adopted, a foreign investment company would not be subject to limitations under the Investment Company Act when making a private placement of its shares in the US.

Rule 15a-6 under the Exchange Act, adopted in the summer of 1989, softens the impact of section 15(a) when a US private placement is being made. Among other things, Rule 15a-6 permits a foreign broker or dealer to induce or attempt to induce the purchase or sale of any security by a US institutional investor without registering with the SEC, so long as any resulting transaction with the institutional investor is effected through a registered broker or dealer (the "intermediary") with whom the foreign broker–dealer has a relationship, and a number of other conditions are met.[89] The employees of a foreign broker–dealer must conduct their securities activities from outside the US, except for promotional visits to US institutional investors where they are accompanied by an employee of a registered broker–dealer that accepts responsibility for the foreign person's activities.[90] The employees of a foreign broker–dealer may call so-called "major US institutional investors" (i.e. institutional investors with total assets of $100 million) on the telephone, but an employee of a registered broker–dealer must participate if a call is made to any other kind of institutional investor.[91]

The foreign broker–dealer and each of its employees who participates in the solicitation of a US institutional investor must consent in writing to service of process in any civil action involving the SEC or a self-regulatory organization, and this consent must be obtained by the registered broker–dealer acting as intermediary.[92] The foreign broker–dealer must also provide to the SEC on request information that relates to transactions by or through an intermediary.[93] In addition to being responsible for effecting transactions, the intermediary is responsible for issuing all required confirmations and related reports, maintaining adequate capital, receiving, delivering, and safeguarding funds and securities on behalf of the US institutional investor, and maintaining in the US all required books and records relating to the transactions.[94] In addition, as between the foreign broker–dealer and the intermediary, the intermediary is responsible for the extension of any credit to the US institutional investor in connection with the transactions.[95]

7.2.3 Offerings Outside the US

Before turning to the effect on the structure and conduct of a global equity offering of the US laws and regulations outlined above, a word should be said about Regulation S under the Securities Act, which provides that offers and sales of securities outside the US are not subject to the registration requirements of the Securities Act. The limitations imposed by section 4(3) of the Securities Act on the ability of foreign securities dealers to resell into the US shares that they purchase in foreign offerings are also relevant.

Regulation S Regulation S was adopted by the SEC in April of 1990 to codify and rationalize the so-called "foreign offering exemption" from the registration requirements that had evolved out of the seminal Release 33-4708 and the no-action letters issued under it, initially in connection with Eurobond offerings by US companies.[96] Regulation S, and the earlier release and no-action letters, were considered necessary because there is no exemption in the Securities Act itself for offerings outside the US that make use in any way of US means of communication, including the US telecommunications and postal systems. It is important to recognize that the exemption afforded by Regulation S relates only to the registration requirements of the Securities Act, and not to the various provisions of the securities laws that impose liability for misstatements or omissions in offering materials.

Regulation S consists of a general statement and two safe harbors. The general statement provides simply that any offer or sale that is made outside the US is not subject to the registration requirements of the Securities Act.[97] While this standard seems clear, it is in fact fraught with uncertainty when important participants in an offering are in the US, negotiations or other activities relating to an offering take place there, some of the securities being distributed are sold in the US, or securities initially sold outside the US are resold there within a short period of time. The safe harbors of Regulation S are intended to eliminate this uncertainty. The first applies to initial distributions,[98] the second to resales.[99]

■ *Initial distributions.* There are two conditions to the availability of the safe harbor for an initial distribution outside the US of shares in most foreign companies.[100] First, no "directed selling efforts" can be made in the US by the issuer or any underwriter, dealer, or other person participating in the distribution pursuant to a contractual arrangement (each such person being referred to as a "distributor") or by any of their affiliates, or on behalf of any of them.[101] This prohibition on "directed selling efforts," the fourth (and happily the last) source of limitations on publicity discussed in this chapter, applies to the issuer until the distribution is completed and to each distributor until it has disposed of its allotment.[102] The failure by the issuer or any distributor to abide by this restriction will result in the loss of the safe harbor for all the participants in the distribution.[103]

"Directed selling efforts" are defined to mean any activity undertaken for the purpose of, or that could reasonably be expected to have the effect of, conditioning the market in the US for any of the shares being offered under Regulation S.[104] The release adopting Regulation S states that mailing printed material to US investors, conducting promotional seminars in the US, or placing advertisements with radio or television stations broadcasting into the US or in publications with a general circulation in the US, would constitute directed selling efforts, as could the publishing in the US of a research report containing information, opinions, or recommendations concerning the issuer or any class of its securities.[105] A publication has a general circulation in the US if it is printed primarily for distribution there or if it had, during the preceding twelve months, an average circulation there of 15,000 copies or more per issue. If a publication has both a US and a foreign edition, the foreign edition may be disregarded entirely.[106]

Regulation S and the adopting release specify a number of activities that do not constitute directed selling efforts. An advertisement will not be deemed to be a directed selling effort if it is required to be published under US or foreign laws or regulations, contains no more information than is legally required, and includes a statement to the effect that the shares have not been registered under the Securities Act and may not be offered or sold in the US unless an exemption is available.[107] This should permit an issuer whose shares are quoted on a US securities exchange or on NASDAQ to publish a notice in the US containing limited information about the offering being made outside the US if, in the judgment of the issuer's US legal advisers, such information is "material" for purposes of the US securities laws. Nor will a "tombstone" advertisement in a publication with a general circulation in the US be deemed to be a directed selling effort provided that the publication has less than 20 percent of its circulation in the US (aggregating for this purpose the circulation of its US and similar non-US editions), the information is limited to certain basic facts about the issuer and the offering, and a statement of the kind referred to above is included.[108]

The publishing in the US of a research report containing information, opinions, or recommendations concerning an issuer that is subject to the periodic reporting requirements of the Exchange Act (or any class of its securities) will not be deemed to be a directed selling effort if the publication meets requirements that are similar to those of Rule 139(b) outlined above.[109] It is noteworthy in this regard that the publishing of a research report that meets the more relaxed requirements of Rule 139(a) where they apply – i.e. to the publishing of reports about certain issuers which have been subject to the periodic reporting requirements of the Exchange Act for thirty-six months – is not excluded from the meaning of "directed selling efforts," nor is the publishing of a report that meets the requirements of Rule 138. This lacuna, which the SEC has not explained, appears to have no rationale, and US legal advisers ought to be able to conclude in most circumstances that the publishing in the US of a research report that meets the requirements of Rule 138 or Rule 139(a) should not be deemed to be a directed selling effort.[110]

The dissemination by an issuer of routine corporate communications of the kind normally published by companies, such as press releases regarding financial results or the occurrence of material events, will also not be deemed to be a directed selling effort.[111] Similarly, the prohibition on directed selling efforts is not intended to interfere with news stories about foreign companies or other *bona fide* journalistic activities, so access by journalists to press conferences and meetings with company spokesmen, and to notices released to the press, need not be limited, even when the journalists work for publications with a general circulation in the US and when the foreign offering is being discussed, so long as the press conference or meeting is held, and the notice is released, outside the US.[112] In general, Regulation S is not intended to interfere with any lawful and customary activities, selling or otherwise, that are conducted outside the US;[113] it is therefore consistent with Regulation S for there to be advertising campaigns for an offering outside the US, including on television and radio, as occurred regularly in the UK privatizations.

Limited contacts with the US, including limited activities directed at prospective investors which may even be unlawful offers under the Securities Act or unlawful solicitations under section 15(a) of the Exchange Act, generally will not constitute directed selling efforts for purposes of Regulation S, and accordingly will not result in the loss of the safe harbor for all participants in the offering.[114] Moreover, legitimate selling efforts in the US in connection with a US public offering that is registered under the Securities Act or in connection with an offering that is exempt from registration will not constitute directed selling efforts with respect to a contemporaneous offering being made outside the US under Regulation S.[115] Accordingly, the non-US portions of a global equity offering can have the benefit of the safe harbor of Regulation S even when major selling efforts are made in the US in connection with the US tranche, whether it be public or private.

The second condition to the availability of this safe harbor is that the initial offers and sales be made in "offshore transactions."[116] This means that

1 the offer may not be made to a person in the US, and
2 either
- at the time the buy order is originated the buyer must be outside the US (or the seller must reasonably believe that the buyer is outside the US), or
- the transaction must be executed on the physical trading floor of an established foreign securities exchange.[117]

A violation of the offshore transaction requirement will result in the safe harbor being lost for the person involved, but not for the other participants in the distribution.[118]

The release adopting Regulation S sets out certain guidelines for determining whether a buyer is outside the US when the buy order is originated. The general rule is that the buyer itself, rather than its agent, must be outside the US. If, however, the buyer is a corporation, partnership, or investment company, it is sufficient that an authorized employee of that entity, or, in the case of an investment company, an authorized employee of its investment adviser, be outside the US, and there is no need to consider where the investment decision is taken.[119] The release does not, however, provide any specific guidance as to whether US pension funds, which are typically organized as trusts, fall within the general or the specific rule. The question comes up when a distributor wishes to sell securities to accounts of US pension funds that are managed by fiduciaries outside the US. There seems to be little reason to distinguish for this purpose between the relationship an investment company has with its investment adviser on the one hand and the relationship a pension fund has with its fiduciary on the other, so when a fiduciary buys outside the US for the account of a US pension fund the requirement that the buyer be outside the US ought to be satisfied without regard to where, or by whom, the investment decision is taken. None the less, in the absence of guidance from the SEC on the question, it may be prudent to limit sales to circumstances in which the offshore fiduciary for the US pension fund is acting on a discretionary basis and is thus taking the decisions.

■ *Resales*. The second safe harbor of Regulation S is for resales. As in the case of an initial distribution, a resale will fall within the safe harbor if it is made without directed selling efforts and in an offshore transaction.[120] However, in contrast to the rules regarding directed selling efforts in an initial distribution, a violation of the requirement by one seller will not result in the resale safe harbor being lost for others.[121] The offshore transaction requirement is cast somewhat differently as well, in that the provision regarding sales on the physical trading floor of a foreign securities exchange is replaced by a provision permitting resales in a number of offshore securities markets, including most of the major European and Asian securities exchanges, without regard to whether they have a physical trading floor.[122]

The resale safe harbor of Regulation S is of particular significance in a global equity offering where a US placement is made under Rule 144A or on the basis of traditional private placement procedures, since it permits the US purchasers to resell the shares immediately into the principal trading market even though they are restricted securities (as that term is used in Rule 144). This ability to resell the shares immediately enhances their liquidity, and effectively integrates the US private placement market with the capital markets of the rest of the world.

Section 4(3) of the Securities Act Section 4(3) of the Securities Act affords an exemption from the registration requirements for offers and sales of securities by securities dealers, subject to certain limitations. These limitations have the effect of prohibiting all US and foreign securities dealers (whether or not they are participants in a distribution) from offering or selling unsold allotments in the US at any time, and other securities included in the offering that they acquire in the market until forty days after the commencement of the offering. Thus, securities initially offered and sold outside the US under Regulation S may not be resold into the US by a foreign securities dealer until forty days after the offering commenced.

7.3 The Impact on a Global Equity Offering

Having outlined the relevant US laws and regulations, we now turn to their effect on the structure and conduct of a global equity offering. The analysis begins with what is from the US perspective the standard situation: a public offering in the US combined with an international offering being made in the Euromarkets on the basis of the so-called "professionals exemption" that applies in one form or another in most countries.[123] The standard is then modified, first to show the reduced level of complexity when the US tranche is offered and sold on a private rather than a public basis, and secondly to demonstrate, by way of example, the increased level of complexity when a public offering in the US is combined with a regulated public offering in another country, such as the UK, France, or Japan.

7.3.1 Standard Global Equity Offering

In the standard situation, the US laws and regulations have a significant impact on the structure and conduct of the offering.

Underwriting arrangements Generally the global distribution is divided in two, with one underwriting syndicate being formed for the public offering in the US and a second for the international tranche. Each syndicate is responsible for the conduct of the offering in its market, and the underwriters in the international syndicate often allocate among themselves, sometimes in consultation with the issuer, the responsibility for making offers and sales in particular regions or countries. Each syndicate is led by one or more managing underwriters, and the offering as a whole is supervised by a global coordinator.

These arrangements are typically documented in underwriting agreements between each syndicate and the issuer, an orderly marketing agreement between the syndicates, and separate agreements among the underwriters in each syndicate. Each underwriting agreement sets out the representations and covenants of the issuer, the indemnities given by the issuer to the underwriters as to the offering documents, the conditions to the offering, the number of shares to be sold, and the combined managing, underwriting, and selling commissions. The orderly marketing agreement divides up the markets between the syndicates, and generally gives the global coordinator responsibility for over-allotments, stabilization, and publicity, and for determining when sales of shares between syndicates should be permitted in response to the varying levels of demand in different markets, any sales that take place generally being made at the public offering price less the applicable selling concession. Each agreement among underwriters provides among other things for the allocation of selling commissions. The closings for the US and international offerings generally occur at the same time, with each being conditioned on the other.

Registration and related requirements The registration requirements of the Securities Act, including the prohibition on offers before a registration statement is filed, the limitation of written offers thereafter to the preliminary prospectus included in the registration statement, the requirements that no sale be made until the registration statement is declared effective and that a copy of the final prospectus be delivered to each purchaser at or prior to the confirmation of sale, and the associated restrictions on publicity (as well as the restrictions on publicity imposed by Rule 10b-6) will, of course, apply to the public offering in the US. They will not, however, apply to the international offering so long as it is made outside the US in accordance with Regulation S.[124] None the less, for combined commercial and legal reasons, the registration requirements have a major influence on how the global offering is conducted.

First, as to timing, the US syndicate is likely to insist that the international underwriters be prohibited from making offers or confirming sales until offers and sales are permitted in the US. If offers could be made earlier outside the US, the US underwriters would be at some disadvantage since they would have less time to generate demand in their market, and this could have an adverse effect on their ability to compete with the international syndicate for the allocation of shares from the issuer and on their relative ability to dispose of the shares allocated to them. Permitting sales to be made outside the US before the registration statement is declared effective could be even more damaging, since "grey-market" trading of "when-issued" shares could occur at prices below the public offering price, which could have a disruptive effect on the marketing effort in the US as US investors would reach out to the foreign market to buy the shares at the lower price. In light of these considerations, the timing of offers and sales in the international offering is generally made subject to the constraints imposed by the registration process.

Secondly, the US syndicate has an interest in restricting the offering materials that are to be used by the international underwriters to a prospectus that is substantially identical to the one required to be used in the US in order, once again, to prevent the international syndicate from obtaining any marketing advantage. The issuer will generally insist on this as well, and the international underwriters are usually willing to go along, because the liability provisions of the US securities laws may apply on an extraterritorial basis and discrepancies in disclosure attract attention and create risks that are best avoided.[125]

The situation regarding research reports is more complicated, since it is common practice for the underwriters of a Euro-equity offering to publish research reports shortly before, and even during, a distribution. The US syndicate may, in order to preserve a level playing field, wish to prevent the international underwriters from publishing research reports other than those that meet the requirements of Rule 138 or Rule 139 under the Securities Act, but they do not always prevail in this. It is important, however, that steps be taken to ensure that any research report that does not comply with Rules 138 or 139 is not mailed into the US, since distributing any such report there could constitute

- an offer, or a non-complying prospectus, in violation of section 5 of the Securities Act, which could result among other things in the SEC requiring that the offering be delayed to allow the effect of the unlawful publicity to dissipate;
- an attempt to induce purchases in violation of Rule 10b-6 which could have similar consequences; or
- a directed selling effort which could result in the safe harbor of Regulation S being lost for the issuer and the other participants in the international offering.

It should, however, be sufficient in this regard to limit the mailing of the research report to addresses outside the US and to place on the cover a restrictive legend prohibiting the distribution of the report in the US.

Finally, while the shares being offered and sold outside the US are not required to be registered with the SEC, it is usually the case that up to 10 percent of such shares are so registered. This is done in order to permit transfers of shares from the international syndicate to the US syndicate, and their subsequent sale in the US by the US underwriters, pursuant to the orderly marketing arrangements, and to permit immediate resales into the US of shares initially sold abroad by securities dealers who purchase them in the market but would otherwise be subject to the forty-day restricted period of section 4(3)(a) of the Securities Act.[126]

Restrictions on market activities The restrictions on the market activities of participants in a US distribution set forth in Rules 10b-6 and 10b-7 apply in a global equity offering not only to the trading activities of the US underwriters in the US but also to the trading activities outside the US of all participants in the offering, including the international underwriters. The rationale for the extraterritorial application of these US regulations is that when shares of a foreign company are being distributed in the US, trading activities in the principal markets for the shares outside the US can be expected to have an effect on the US investment community, since the attractiveness of the price at which the securities are being offered in the US will be assessed in the light of the prices quoted in the foreign markets. The restrictions of Rules 10b-6 and 10b-7 are thought appropriate in order to ensure that the US investment community is not deceived by a false market, or confused about the significance of price fluctuations in foreign markets as a result of a lack of familiarity with the trading rules and practices there. The extraterritorial application of these regulations can cause significant difficulties, since the US rules often conflict with the trading rules and customary practices in the foreign markets. These difficulties, and the steps the SEC has taken to ameliorate them, are outlined below. For convenience, the discussion covers global equity offerings that involve a public offering in a national market outside the US as well as the standard situation.

■ *Rule 10b-6.* The most significant difficulty created by the extraterritorial application of Rule 10b-6 results from the requirement that participants in the foreign distribution and their affiliates refrain not only from activities engaged in for the purpose of creating actual, or apparent, active trading in the securities being distributed in the US (or of raising their price), but from entirely legitimate trading activities as well, including those in connection with market-making. Since, in many cases, the principal market-makers in the shares of a foreign company, or their affiliates, will be participating as underwriters in the global offerings of shares in that company, the strict application of Rule 10b-6 in the principal trading market would be severely disruptive. Moreover, in those circumstances where a market-maker is required by the rules of the trading market where it operates to hold itself out as a buyer of securities at all times, compliance with Rule

10b-6 could subject it to penalties. These problems are exacerbated by the view of the SEC staff that the exceptions permitting participants in a distribution to bid for or purchase securities until the beginning of the two-day or nine-day "cooling-off" period are not automatically available when the principal trading market for the securities being distributed is outside the US.[127]

The SEC staff has recognized these difficulties and has gone a long way toward resolving many of the most severe conflicts, both by granting relief of a general nature and by adopting no-action positions on a case-by-case basis. The most significant form of general relief granted thus far has been that permitting so-called "passive" market-making on the International Stock Exchange of the United Kingdom and the Republic of Ireland (the London Stock Exchange).[128] In granting this relief, the SEC staff recognized that Rule 10b-6 would interfere with the rules of the London Stock Exchange intended to preserve the integrity of London's trading market. These rules were designed to prohibit "fair-weather" market-making by preventing a member firm from resuming market-making activities in a security for three months after the firm ceased to make a market in that security. Market-makers in London would thus be penalized if they were to withdraw from the market when they or their affiliates participated in an offering, as would be required by Rule 10b-6.[129]

The passive market-making exemption permits participants in a distribution (and their affiliates) who are members of the London Stock Exchange to continue to make a market in shares of the same class as those being distributed, so long as they do not lead the market in terms of price or size. Specifically, they are permitted to enter bids for, and make purchases of, shares of a UK issuer classified as "alpha" or "beta" by the London Stock Exchange,[130] but only at a price no higher than the highest bid currently being displayed on the Stock Exchange Automated Quotation (SEAQ) system by an independent member of the London Stock Exchange, and subject to the additional requirement that no bid may be entered for a quantity of shares that is greater than the largest quoted size currently being so displayed. Prior notice to the London Stock Exchange and the SEC must be given by the firm that intends to avail itself of the exemption, and that firm must keep records of its trading activities during the distribution, and make such records and its personnel available to the SEC. A similar general exemption has been granted to market-makers on the Toronto Stock Exchange in connection with offerings of securities eligible for the multijurisdictional disclosure system between the US and Canada.[131]

The second kind of general relief granted by the SEC staff confirms that the two-day or nine-day "cooling-off" period may be determined by reference to the principal trading market for the shares outside the US, but only if that market is the London, Montreal, Paris, Tokyo, or Toronto stock exchange, each of which is covered by a memorandum of understanding with the SEC providing among other things for the sharing of information.[132] In other cases, US legal advisers will have to decide whether it is prudent to seek specific relief before advising that trading may continue up to a cooling-off period.[133]

The SEC staff has granted case-by-case relief in a number of different areas. Among other things, it has permitted market-making to continue on a passive basis on SEAQ International[134] and the Copenhagen,[135] Montreal,[136] and Oslo[137] stock exchanges; permitted the "cooling-off" period to be determined by reference to the principal foreign trading market for the securities (and allowed a two-day cooling-off period where a nine-day period would otherwise apply);[138] accommodated the market-making activities of affiliates of certain issuers;[139] permitted affiliates of the UK underwriters in a UK public offering (and the UK sub-underwriters) to continue their ordinary market-making activities on the London Stock Exchange;[140] and, in an unprecedented step taken in the context of the recent global offering of shares of British Telecommunications plc (BT), permitted ordinary market-making by affiliates of all the underwriters in a global offering to continue on the London Stock Exchange without regard to the passive market-making rules.[141]

■ *Rule 10b-7.* The SEC has also taken a number of steps to mitigate the effect of the extraterritorial application of the US rules on stabilization, as well as to adapt the rules to the requirements of a global equity offering where the principal trading market for the shares is outside the US.

Difficulties have arisen in this area for two principal reasons. First, the extraterritorial application of Rule 10b-7 requires the stabilizing underwriter to abide by at least two sets of regulations, those of the US and those of the market in which stabilizing takes place, and this has proved to be difficult.[142] Secondly, the requirement that stabilizing levels be determined by reference to prices in the principal market for the shares in the US and, once set, that they not be raised, created technical problems. If the principal market in the US for the security was a securities exchange and that exchange was closed when stabilizing was to commence, the price would have to be set by reference to the closing price on that exchange. For example, if the underwriters in an international offering for a security that was traded on both the London and New York stock exchanges wished to commence stabilizing during the day in London but before the New York Stock Exchange opened, the underwriters would have to commence stabilizing at a price based on the prior closing price on the New York Stock Exchange, which is likely to have become stale as a result of morning and early afternoon trading in London. Moreover, once the US stabilizing price was set in dollars, the rules prevented it from being raised if the dollar depreciated against the currency of the principal market where the shares were traded.

To overcome the difficulties resulting from the conflicts with local rules, the SEC proposed in January 1991 an amendment to Rule 10b-7 permitting stabilization to be conducted in compliance with foreign regulations that are determined by the SEC to be comparable to Rule 10b-7, so long as

- no stabilization takes place in the US;
- procedures exist to enable the SEC to obtain information concerning foreign stabilizing transactions; and
- no stabilizing transactions are effected at a price higher than the price at which the shares are then being distributed in the US.

The SEC has preliminarily determined that the stabilization rules of the UK Securities Investment Board (SIB) are comparable to Rule 10b-7 for these purposes.[143]

To deal with the technical problems that arise in a global offering in connection with stabilization levels, the SEC issued a second set of proposed amendments at the same time. If adopted, these would allow

- stabilization to be initiated at a price determined by reference to the principal foreign market for the securities rather than a US market;
- a stabilizing bid to be placed in any market at the current exchange rate equivalent of a stabilizing bid entered in the principal foreign trading market for the securities; and
- a stabilizing bid in a market other than the principal trading market to be adjusted in response to exchange rate fluctuations in the currencies in which the securities trade in such subsidiary markets against the currency in which the securities trade in the principal market.

These proposed amendments would apply only where the principal trading market was on a "specified foreign securities market" – i.e. the London, Montreal, Paris, Tokyo, or Toronto stock exchanges (or such other securities exchanges as the SEC may designate).[144]

Pending the adoption of the proposed amendments, the SEC staff has indicated that it will not take any enforcement action against any participant in a distribution that complies with the proposed rules.[145] Both sets of proposed amendments are codifications of no-action positions taken by the SEC staff in the context of particular offerings and in response to specific requests for relief. Application will still have to be made to the SEC staff on a case-by-case basis in circumstances where the proposed amendments do not apply.

The NASD rules Section 24(c) of the Rules of Fair Practice of the NASD obliges any member of the NASD who grants a selling concession, discount, or other allowance to a non-member broker, dealer, or other person in a foreign country in connection with a sale of shares that are registered with the SEC in a US public offering to obtain from such person an agreement that it will comply with the requirement that the shares be offered at the public offering price, even outside the US, subject to such selling concessions, discounts, or other allowances as would be permitted to NASD members. Similarly, paragraph 8(a) of the interpretation of the Board of Governors of the NASD regarding free riding and withholding obliges a member of the NASD who sells shares to a foreign broker, dealer, or bank who is participating in the distribution as an underwriter to obtain an agreement from such underwriter that it will abide by the rules requiring the benefits of "hot issues" to flow to the investing public.

These obligations to obtain agreements from the foreign participants in a distribution will apply in a global equity offering whenever sales of shares are made from the US syndicate to the international syndicate pursuant to the orderly marketing agreement. Since it is impossible to know in advance whether any such sales will be made (or in many cases when they are made, whether any particular offer and sale to the public outside the US is of shares that were part of the international syndicate's initial allocation from the issuer or of shares that were transferred to it pursuant to the orderly marketing arrangements), the relevant NASD rules are generally applied across the board. While abiding by these rules does not impose significant burdens on the international underwriters, it may require them to comply with obligations to which they are not accustomed and which are not imposed on them by the rules of the national markets in which they operate.

Other considerations The restrictions imposed by the Investment Company Act on the ability of a foreign investment company to offer shares to the public in the US are discussed in the section on "Other restrictions" in 7.2.1 above, as are the limitations that apply to the US activities of foreign broker–dealers.

7.3.2 *Global Equity Offering Involving a US Private Placement*

When a global equity offering involves a US private placement instead of a public offering, the impact of the US laws and regulations is far less pervasive. Moreover, the syndicate structure is often simplified, the private placement in the United States being made by US affiliates of one or more of the underwriters in the international syndicate, or by such underwriters themselves in accordance with the requirements of Rule 15a-6.

Registration and related requirements Since the registration requirements of the Securities Act do not apply, the structure and conduct of the US placement are likely to conform in a number of important aspects to the needs of the foreign participants in the offering, which will be influenced principally by the commercial and legal requirements of foreign markets. What is perhaps of most importance, the timing of offers and sales, no longer driven by the registration process, will generally be determined by foreign rather than US considerations, with a corresponding increase in flexibility. Moreover, because the extensive disclosure requirements of the SEC's regulations and forms do not apply, the private placement memorandum to be used in the US will generally be the foreign offering circular, with a US "wrap-around" containing:

- appropriate securities law legends and a recital of the restrictions on resale;
- a discussion of the US tax consequences of an investment in the shares;
- a discussion in some cases of the material differences between US GAAP and the accounting principles used in the preparation of the issuer's financial statements; and
- where the placement is being made on the basis of traditional procedures as opposed to Rule 144A, the form of non-distribution letter to be executed by each US purchaser.

The level of "due diligence" is also likely to reflect foreign rather than US standards. Finally, the international underwriters are even less likely than they would be when a US public offering is involved to limit the research reports they distribute outside the US to those that would be permitted by Rules 138 or 139 under the Securities Act. However, the prohibition on general solicitation and general advertising, and on directed selling efforts, in the US will still require that steps be taken to ensure that research reports published abroad that do not comply with Rule 138 or Rule 139 do not flow into the US.[146]

Restrictions on market activities The restrictions of Rule 10b-6 apply only when a "distribution" is being made. The term "distribution" means an offering of securities, whether or not subject to the registration requirements of the Securities Act of 1933, that is distinguished from ordinary trading transactions by the magnitude of the offering and the presence of special selling efforts and selling methods.[147] While a registered public offering of shares will constitute a distribution for purposes of Rule 10b-6 in all cases, a private placement will be a distribution only in certain circumstances. Because the meaning of "distribution" is unclear, US legal advisers in a global offering have often been unable to conclude that a particular private placement in the US is outside its scope, and they have considered it necessary to approach the SEC in order to obtain assurances that the restrictions of Rule 10b-6 will not apply to the activities outside the US of participants in the offering or to negotiate the terms of any passive market-making or other exemption. This need to approach the SEC staff obviates one of the principal benefits of the private placement route, which is the freedom to conduct the global offering without consulting US regulators, and, what is more important, may jeopardize the timing of the offering, which will have been dictated principally by commercial realities and legal requirements outside the US. Moreover, the kind of relief that is ultimately obtained may be viewed by the issuer and other foreign participants in the offering as still leaving them with unacceptable burdens on ordinary secondary market trading in the principal markets outside the US, given that the only distribution in the US is being made on a private basis to institutional investors and that no US listing is being obtained.[148]

In January 1991, the US Securities Industries Association (SIA), with the assistance of six major law firms in New York having expertise in the international application of the US securities laws, articulated these concerns to the SEC with a view to obtaining relief from the application outside the US of the restrictions of Rules 10b-6 and 10b-7 in circumstances where securities were being privately placed in the US to institutional investors. While the exemption requested by the SIA would have applied regardless of whether the placement was being made to qualified institutional buyers under Rule 144A or to a broader category of institutional investors on the basis of traditional private placement procedures, the SEC chose to grant a more limited exemption, providing that the restrictions of Rules 10b-6 and 10b-7 do not apply to trading by underwriters and their affiliates on the London, Montreal, Paris, Tokyo, and Toronto stock exchanges and on SEAQ International when shares that are eligible to be sold under Rule 144A are being privately placed in the US to qualified institutional buyers. The exemption is not available unless the voting stock of the issuer held world-wide by non-affiliates has an aggregate market value of at least $150 million and the issuer has an operating history of at least three years. The managing underwriter is also required to notify the SEC that the syndicate is relying on the exemption, and to provide to the SEC certain basic information about the offering.[149]

In circumstances where this exemption is not available, the US legal advisers to the offering will, in the case of Rule 10b-6, either have to conclude that the selling efforts in the US do not rise to the level of a distribution or seek specific relief from the SEC. The factors to consider when deciding whether a particular placement in the US constitutes a distribution include:

- the size of the offering in the US, both in absolute terms and in relation to the value of the issuer's publicly traded shares;
- whether there is an identifiable US underwriting syndicate and, if so, its size;
- whether shares are earmarked for sale in the US;
- the number of investors contacted in the US; and
- the nature of the selling efforts, including in particular whether a road show involving directors and officers of the issuer is being conducted.

While this area is murky in the extreme, it would not be unwarranted, perhaps, for the participants in a global offering to proceed on the assumption that a US placement will not be a distribution, regardless of its size, if:

- it is limited to qualified institutional buyers;
- there is no identifiable US syndicate;
- no shares are earmarked for sale in the US;
- the number of offerees is limited to 100;
- the underwriters contact investors either by telephone or in very small groups; and
- directors and officers of the issuer do not participate in the marketing efforts.

If these conditions are not met, all the relevant facts and circumstances will have to be considered including the size of the placement, and in many cases the US legal advisers may find themselves unable to reach a definitive conclusion. In those instances, the SEC's general relief regarding passive market-making, and the determination of the appropriate cooling-off period, may be relied on if they apply, and if they do not specific relief will have to be obtained.

In the case of Rule 10b-7, if the exemption granted by the SEC in response to the request of the SIA is not available, the no-action position regarding stabilization in accordance with the rules of the SIB can be relied on if it applies, but if it does not specific exemptions will have to be sought, including exemptions regarding stabilizing levels (at least until the technical amendments to Rule 10b-7 outlined above are adopted).

Other considerations Members of the NASD are not obliged to obtain agreements from the international underwriters of the kind outlined above, since the rules in question do not apply in a private placement. The restrictions regarding a private placement of shares of a foreign investment company are outlined in the section "Other considerations" in 7.2.2 above, as are the limitations on the ability of foreign brokers or dealers to offer and sell securities to US institutional investors.

7.3.3 *Global Equity Offering Involving Public Offerings in the US and in other Countries*

The potential for conflict between the US and foreign regulatory regimes is greatest when a global equity offering combines a public offering in the US with a public offering in one or more regulated national markets abroad. Reconciling the various requirements in these circumstances, and obtaining relief from the appropriate regulatory authorities when the rules are irreconcilable, is a subtle and delicate task. While it is beyond the scope of this chapter to analyze the laws and regulations of countries other than the US, it is hoped that some of the issues involved will be conveyed by the following discussion of global equity offerings in which US public offerings were combined with public offerings in the UK, France, and Japan.[150]

The United Kingdom The UK privatizations of the 1980s and early 1990s combined public offerings in the UK and elsewhere with traditional US private placements (e.g. the UK water companies), US private placements under Rule 144A (e.g. the UK electricity industry), and US public offerings (e.g. British Airways plc, British Petroleum plc, and BT). The structure and conduct of these global offerings were dictated in large measure by the commercial practices and legal requirements of the UK.

Until the BT offering in late 1991, the UK privatizations followed a broadly similar pattern. Marketing would begin in the UK on "pathfinder day" with the publishing of the so-called "pathfinder prospectus." Several weeks later, on "impact day," the shares would be priced, the underwriting agreements would be signed, the UK prospectus in final form would be made available, and the subscription period would begin. Several weeks after that, on "allotment day," the shares would be purchased and dealings on the London Stock Exchange would commence. In the earliest privatizations, UK underwriters and sub-underwriters would be paid commissions for agreeing to take up any shares allocated to the UK offering for which subscribers were not found; over time, as HM Treasury gained confidence, the UK underwriters and sub-underwriters were gradually eliminated.

It was considered essential in these privatizations that offers be made at the same time in all markets so as to prevent any underwriting syndicate from gaining a marketing advantage. It was also considered necessary to preclude "grey market" trading of "when issued" shares during the subscription period, since such trading could disrupt the UK marketing efforts. Moreover, the offering documents to be used in all markets were required to conform in substance to the UK pathfinder prospectus and final prospectus, and no changes in the substantive disclosure about the issuer or its business were permitted once the pathfinder prospectus was published. Finally, HM Treasury wished to retain complete discretion to decide whether the offering would proceed once the underwriting arrangements were put in place.

These *desiderata* had significant implications for the registration process in the US. First, while a registration statement could not be publicly filed with the SEC before pathfinder day, it was necessary to clear the preliminary prospectus with the SEC before then since no changes would be allowed thereafter, even in response to SEC comments. In order to ensure that the disclosure in the preliminary prospectus would not change, a confidential filing with the SEC was made sufficiently well in advance of pathfinder day to ensure that comments could be obtained, and any required amendments could be reflected in all the offering documents, by pathfinder day.

Secondly, in order to prevent flow-back into the UK, during the UK subscription period, of shares sold elsewhere, the underwriters were prohibited from confirming sales until allotment day. In the US, this prohibition was strengthened by having the issuer refuse to request the registration statement to be declared effective until allotment day, thus making it unlawful under section 5(a) of the Securities Act for the US underwriters to confirm sales in the US before then.

Finally, in order for HM Treasury to preserve discretion to decide whether the global offering would proceed, all conditions to the underwriters' obligations, including the effectiveness of the registration statement, and all termination rights, including customary *force majeure* provisions, were eliminated. This, combined with the long underwriting period covering the several weeks between impact day and allotment day, resulted in the underwriters having to assume significant risks. In the UK, these risks could be shifted to sub-underwriters or institutional investors, who would give commitments on impact day in return for a share of the commissions. This option was not available to the US underwriters, however, since obtaining commitments from sub-underwriters or institutional investors would be analyzed under the Securities Act as the equivalent of confirming sales, which would be unlawful until the registration statement was declared effective. Accordingly, when the market crash of October 1987 occurred after impact day but before allotment day in the second British Petroleum plc offering, the US underwriters took substantial losses.

Two additional peculiarities of the standard UK privatization are worth noting. First, an over-allotment option generally was not provided and stabilizing activities were not contemplated. Secondly, inter-syndicate transfers of shares were not permitted, except with the permission of HM Treasury.

In the second BT offering, which was made in late 1991, HM Treasury introduced a number of significant innovations. For the purposes of this chapter, the most significant was the tender system, which was used by HM Treasury as a basis for pricing and allocating the shares. The system was designed to obtain three principal benefits:

- to increase the "transparency" of the offering – i.e. to allow HM Treasury to look through the underwriters to see the actual interest in the shares of end-investors;
- to allow pricing to occur just before allotment day rather than on impact day, thus permitting market developments that would otherwise be ignored to be taken into account; and
- to shorten the underwriting period with a view to reducing commissions.

Expanded from its somewhat peripheral role in the later stages of the privatization of the electricity industry where it was first tested, the tender system worked as follows:

1 On November 13, pathfinder day, the underwriters and HM Treasury executed the orderly marketing agreement, the pathfinder prospectus and other preliminary offering documents were published, and marketing began.
2 On November 21, impact day, the underwriters and HM Treasury executed the international tender offer agreement, HM Treasury determined the size of the discount from the tender offer price (to

be decided later) that would be made available to UK individuals who subscribed for the shares, and the final UK prospectus was published. The international tender offer agreement obliged the underwriters to solicit indications of interest from investors in their markets, but did not oblige them to purchase any shares.
3 At the end of the day in London on Friday, December 6, the underwriters, through the managing underwriters in each of the ten syndicates, submitted bids on behalf of investors, indicating how many shares each investor wished to purchase and at what price.
4 Over the weekend of December 7–8, HM Treasury determined the number of shares to be allocated to each syndicate, with no syndicate being asked to purchase a number of shares in excess of the bids submitted on its behalf by its managing underwriter. If the managing underwriter for a syndicate accepted the number of shares that HM Treasury wished to allocate to it, and the price per share (which was to be the same for all syndicates), it would execute a purchase memorandum committing the syndicate to underwrite those shares. The purchase memoranda were held in escrow until the morning of Monday, December 9, when dealings commenced in London.

In this framework, the US preliminary prospectus was cleared with the SEC on a confidential basis in advance, the registration statement containing the preliminary prospectus was filed on pathfinder day, an interim amendment to the registration statement was filed on impact day, and an amended registration statement was filed and declared effective on Thursday, December 5, allowing the US underwriters to confirm sales promptly after the price was set, and their underwriting obligations crystallized, on December 8. Thus, because the US underwriters were free to sell the shares promptly after assuming their underwriting obligations, the risks they accepted in the offering were little different from those encountered in a standard US underwriting. However, because the risks were much reduced from earlier privatizations – even to the point where there was some loose talk of the "elimination of underwriting" – the commissions were lowered to unprecedented levels, well below what is customary in the US.

There were two other innovative features in the BT offering which were significant for our purposes. First, an over-allotment option was provided and stabilization was contemplated for the first time in a global equity offering involving a public offering in the UK (the stabilizing activities being conducted under the SIB rules in accordance with the no-action position outlined above). Secondly, the SEC staff was persuaded to allow market-making by all the underwriters and their affiliates to continue on the London Stock Exchange in the ordinary course, without regard to the restrictions of Rule 10b-6 or the passive market-making requirements.[151]

France A global equity offering of shares in a French company also raises difficult questions of coordination, and there is less experience than in the UK in reconciling the conflicting commercial and legal requirements.

A public offering in France typically involves offers to existing shareholders through priority subscription rights. Under French law, the terms of the offering, including in particular the price of the shares, cannot be made public until they are announced in the *Bulletin des Annonces Légales Obligatoires* (*BALO*) at about the time the offering is launched. If this limitation were to apply to the offering being made in the US, there would be no opportunity for marketing to commence on the basis of a preliminary prospectus, as is customary in a US public offering. Moreover, it is unlikely that the participants in the French offering would allow sales to be confirmed in the US until the end of the subscription period in France, since grey-market trading of shares bought in the US on a "when issued" basis could prove disruptive. Thus, the risks for the US underwriters would be similar to those in a UK privatization before BT.

These issues were identified, and resolved in a highly satisfactory way, in the global offering of shares in Société Nationale Elf Acquitaine (Elf) in the early summer of 1991. In that offering, the Commission des Opérations de Bourse (COB) permitted marketing in the offerings outside France, including in the public offering in the US, to begin in advance of the pricing announcement in the *BALO* on the basis of a preliminary prospectus that, as is customary, would leave out pricing information. What is perhaps more important, the COB permitted the offering to proceed without any priority subscription rights for existing shareholders, which allowed sales to be confirmed in the US immediately after pricing since there was no need to wait for the end of a subscription period in France. Finally, simultaneous trading in Paris and New York was facilitated by quoting *promesses d'actions* (rights to acquire shares, akin to "when issued" shares) on the Paris Stock Exchange at the same time as trading began on the New York Stock Exchange. This resolved the inconsistency between US and French practices deriving from the fact that trading in the US normally begins immediately after pricing while in France it would not commence until closing.

Japan Until recently, a non-Japanese company wishing to offer shares to the Japanese public was required, as a practical matter, to obtain a listing on the Tokyo Stock Exchange. Since that exchange's listing criteria are stringent, and the listing process is time-consuming and expensive, many foreign issuers had been deterred from raising capital in Japan's public markets and had relied instead on "private placement" procedures or "secondary" sales when offering securities to Japanese investors.[152]

In 1989, new procedures doing away with the Tokyo listing requirement were put into effect. These new procedures make it easier for foreign companies to offer shares in a public offering in Japan, particularly in connection with a global offering involving a public offering in the US or in another national market. For a company to be able to use the new procedures, its stock must be listed on its home stock exchange (which must be an exchange approved by the Japanese Securities Dealers Association) and its earnings per share must be at least 20 percent of the shares' par value prior to the offering.

Under the new procedures, the precise number of shares to be offered in Japan must be registered before sales can be confirmed, and a securities registration statement in Japanese must be declared effective by the Ministry of Finance pursuant to the Securities Exchange Law of Japan. In terms of substance, a US registration statement or UK listing particulars can easily be converted into a Japanese registration statement. However, the registration statement cannot be declared effective and sales may not be confirmed until the second Tokyo business day after the day when an executed underwriting agreement fixing the price of the shares is filed.[153] As a consequence, the Japanese syndicate generally has to wait two days after pricing of the issue before it can sell the shares to its customers in Japan, and is obliged to sell the shares at the original fixed price even if in other jurisdictions the distribution has been completed, the underwriting syndicates have been dissolved, and prices have changed. The Japanese underwriters have been persuaded to accept these risks in most global offerings.

Because the precise number of shares to be offered in Japan must be registered, the orderly marketing agreement generally will not provide for intersyndicate transfers to or from the Japanese underwriters, or for the Japanese underwriters to participate if the over-allotment option is exercised. Since the US syndicate will not be selling shares to the Japanese underwriters, the rules of the NASD need not be imposed on the Japanese syndicate.

7.4 Conclusion

As the world's capital markets grow ever more integrated in the 1990s, global offerings of shares are likely to become the preferred way for governments to privatize their state-owned companies and industries, and for world-class private issuers to raise equity capital. Two kinds of developments can be anticipated:

- commercial innovations, which among other things may involve efforts to increase "transparency," improve pricing mechanisms, and reduce commissions, perhaps following the path broken by HM Treasury in the recent UK privatizations; and
- coordination among regulatory authorities, which will harmonize many of the conflicting requirements of the legal regimes of the principal countries where offerings are generally made.

While commercial innovations are difficult to anticipate, the main lines of regulatory coordination, at least in so far as the US authorities are concerned, can now be seen.

First, the SEC can be expected to continue to refine its thinking about the application of Rules 10b-6 and 10b-7 to foreign trading activities. When, for example, in April 1991 it granted the exemption from the application of these rules to trading activities in certain markets outside the US in circumstances where a US placement was being made to qualified institutional buyers alone, the SEC requested its staff to report back within a year on the desirability of extending the exemption to offerings where other US institutional investors were involved as well, and it is hoped that this report will be favorable and that a further exemptive order will follow. In addition, as the SEC reaches understandings with more foreign regulatory authorities with respect to the sharing of information and other matters, it is likely to confirm that the "cooling-off" period of Rule 10b-6 may be determined by reference to the foreign markets supervised by those authorities and to allow "passive" (and perhaps ordinary) market-making in those markets after the cooling-off period begins. It is also likely that the SEC will determine, over time, that the stabilization rules of authorities other than the SIB afford protections comparable to those of Rule 10b-7, and will permit stabilizing activities outside the US in accordance with those rules, subject to certain conditions.

Secondly, the SEC is moving in the direction of permitting certain kinds of offerings – i.e. exchange offers and rights offerings when only a small proportion of the shares in the company in question is held in the US – to be made in the US on the basis of the offering documents that are used in the issuer's home market, without requiring additional disclosures (including in particular with regard to the issuer's financial statements). Recent proposals on these matters have been made, and they are expected to be adopted soon.[154] The principal purpose of relaxing the US requirements in these kinds of offerings is to allow US shareholders to take advantage of opportunities they would otherwise be denied; in many cases, US shareholders are excluded because of the issuer's unwillingness to comply with SEC requirements, since doing so could require additional disclosure, involve additional costs and potential liabilities, and subordinate the timing of the offering to the SEC registration process.

Finally, the SEC is exploring ways in which other kinds of public offerings can be made in the US on the basis of "home country disclosure." The most fruitful approach thus far has been to establish reciprocal arrangements with foreign regulatory authorities whereby certain classes of companies in each country are permitted to offer securities in the other country on the basis of the disclosure requirements of the home market. As noted above, these arrangements have been established with Canada, and comparable arrangements are now being considered for other countries. Significant movement along these lines can be expected in the 1990s.

Notes

1 An ADR is a substitute trading certificate similar in form to a standard US registered stock certificate. The underlying shares remain at the office of the foreign bank acting as Custodian. ADRs can be submitted by the ADR holder to the Depositary for cancellation and delivery by the Custodian of the underlying shares. Similarly, underlying shares can be deposited with the Custodian against issuance by the Depositary of ADRs.

   ADRs facilitate the transfer of ownership between US investors, since they may be transferred on the books of the Depositary in the same manner as US stock certificates and are eligible for clearing through The Depository Trust Company; accordingly, US investors are not required to follow foreign transfer procedures or send their certificates abroad. It is generally the case that ADSs, rather than the underlying foreign shares, are listed for trading on a US securities exchange or on NASDAQ so as to provide a US dollar market once the offering is complete. ADRs also permit US investors to receive in dollars dividends paid in a foreign currency; dividends on the underlying shares are collected by the Custodian, converted into dollars, and transmitted by the Depositary to the ADR holders.

   For purposes of the Securities Act, an ADS is a separate security the offer or sale of which must be registered with the SEC, as must the underlying shares, unless an exemption is available. A simple registration form – Form F-6 under the Securities Act – can be used to register the ADSs.

2 A foreign private issuer is any company incorporated under the laws of a foreign country, except for a company that meets the following conditions: (1) more than 50 percent of its outstanding voting securities are held of

record by US residents; and (2) any of the following: (a) the majority of its executive officers or directors are US citizens or residents, (b) more than 50 percent of its assets are located in the US or (c) it is administered principally in the US (Rule 3b-4 under the Exchange Act). If a company is not a foreign private issuer, it is treated as a US issuer and certain of the disclosure and other requirements discussed below are more rigorous.
3   S. 5(c) of the Securities Act.
4   The definition of "prospectus" is contained in s. 2(10) of the Securities Act.
5   S. 5(b) of the Securities Act.
6   S. 5(a) of the Securities Act.
7   S. 5(b) (2) of the Securities Act.
8   These forms, adopted in 1982, represent an effort by the SEC to tailor the disclosure requirements for a US public offering more closely to the requirements of the issuer's home country. The accommodations, however, are rather limited in scope. For a discussion of these forms, see Edward F. Greene and Eric D. Ram, "Securities Law Developments Affecting Foreign Private Issuers," *International Financial Law Review* (February 1983).
9   General Instruction I.A of Form F-2 and I.A.1 of Form F-3. A foreign company can become subject to the periodic reporting requirements of the Exchange Act, set out in s. 13 of that Act, by making a public offering in the US (s. 15(d) of the Exchange Act) or by registering a class of its securities under the Exchange Act. A foreign company is required to register a class of its securities under the Exchange Act if it obtains a listing or quotation for that class on a US securities exchange or on NASDAQ (s. 12(b) of the Exchange Act) or, in the case of a class of equity securities, if there are 300 or more US resident holders of that class (Rule 12g3-2(a) under the Exchange Act). Rule 12g3-2(b) under the Exchange Act provides an exemption from Rule 12g3-2(a)'s requirement to register so long as the issuer agrees to furnish to the SEC the significant information it makes public in its home country, files with a stock exchange on which its securities are listed, or distributes to its security holders.

   A foreign company that is subject to the periodic reporting requirements of the Exchange Act must file an Annual Report on Form 20-F within six months of the end of its financial year, including audited financial statements reconciled to US generally accepted accounting principles along the lines discussed below, and Reports on Form 6-K, which must contain the significant information the company makes public in its home country, files with a securities exchange, or distributes to security holders.
10 General Instruction I.A.2 of Form F-3.
11 General Instruction I.A.4 of Form F-3.
12 General Instruction I.A.3 of Form F-3.
13 General Instructions I.A, I.B, and I.C of Form F-2.
14 Rule 2-02(b) of Regulation S-X requires the audit report to state that the audit was conducted in accordance with generally accepted auditing standards. While the rule contemplates that exceptions may be taken, it goes on to state that "nothing in this rule shall be construed to imply authority for the omission of any procedure which independent accountants would

ordinarily employ in the course of an audit," and the SEC has taken a hard line on this.

15 Some procedures required by US auditing standards, such as observation of physical inventory and other fieldwork, may not be customary in certain countries.

16 The audit report contained in a registration statement for a UK company would typically state that the audit was "conducted in accordance with auditing standards generally accepted in the United Kingdom, which do not differ in any material respect from those in the United States."

17 Item 18(c) of Form 20-F. The numerical reconciliations can reveal significant variations: for one UK company, net income attributable to ordinary shareholders for the financial year ended March 31, 1991 was £150.0 million under generally accepted accounting principles in the UK (UK GAAP), but only £77.4 million under US GAAP, while shareholders' equity at the financial year-end was only £472.8 million under UK GAAP, but £1,585.4 million under US GAAP; and for the first six months of the financial year ending March 31, 1992, net income attributable to ordinary shareholders under UK GAAP was £65.2 million, while there was a *loss* of £306.7 million under US GAAP. The differences in these results were attributable principally to the treatment of goodwill arising as a result of acquisitions, which is written off against shareholders' reserves in the year of acquisition under UK GAAP, but is recorded on the balance sheet as an intangible asset and amortized over its estimated useful life (at most forty years) under US GAAP.

18 Rule 3-19(a) of Regulation S-X. Rule 3-19(b) allows an issuer to provide audited financial statements as of the end of the two financial years preceding the most recent financial year if (1) the audited balance sheet for the most recent financial year is not yet available, (2) interim financial statements, which may be unaudited, as of a date within six months of the effective date are provided, and (3) the registration statement is not declared effective more than five months after the end of the most recent financial year. The SEC has proposed a rule that would not require inclusion of the most recent year's audited financial statements unless the registration statement were declared effective more than *six* months after the end of that year. See Securities Act Release no. 6895, 56 Fed. Reg. 27562 (June 5, 1991).

19 Item 18(b) of Form 20-F.

20 Item 18(c) (3) of Form 20-F and Federal Accounting Standards Board, Statement of Financial Accounting Standards no. 14 (December 1976).

21 Rule 3-19(c) of Regulation S-X. The SEC has proposed a rule that would require interim financial statements only if the registration statement is filed more than ten full months after the end of the most recent financial year, in which case interim financial statements, which may be unaudited, would have to be provided for the most recently completed semi-annual period. See Securities Act Release no. 6895, 56 Fed. Reg. 27562 (June 5, 1991).

22 Item 8 of Form 20-F.

23 Item 1 of Form 20-F.

24 Item 1(b) of Form 20-F.
25 Item 1(a) (4) of Form 20-F.
26 Item 9 of Form 20-F.
27 Item 9(c) of Form 20-F.
28 Items 9(a) and (b) of Form 20-F.
29 S. 6(b) of the Securities Act.
30 In addition, controlling shareholders (or other controlling persons) of anyone liable under section 11 have similar liability under section 15 of the Securities Act, subject to a defense similar to, but more easily established than, the "due diligence" defense under section 11. S. 11(a) of the Securities Act states that any person who acquired a registered security may bring an action claiming that "any part of the registration statement, when such part became effective, contained an untrue statement of a material fact or omitted to state a material fact required to be stated therein or necessary to make the statements therein not misleading." The plaintiff need not prove reliance (or even that he had received or read the prospectus) unless he bought the security after the issuer had made generally available to its security holders an earning statement covering a period of at least a year beginning after the effective date; but even then "reliance may be established without proof of the reading of the registration statement by such person."

The standard for establishing the "due diligence" defense varies depending on whether the information that is the subject of the claim was prepared or certified by an expert, such as an accountant or lawyer.
31 Securities Act Release no. 5009, 34 Fed. Reg. 16870 at 16870–1 (October 7, 1969).
32 The general requirement that securities dealers, whether or not they are participating in the offering, deliver prospectuses to purchasers for a certain period is contained in ss. 5(b) and 4(3) of the Securities Act. Rule 174 under the Securities Act contains the specific rules regarding the length of the period. The requirement that securities dealers deliver prospectuses even after a distribution is completed derives from a Congressional desire to draw a bright and certain line between distributions and secondary trading and to prevent securities dealers from claiming that securities acquired in the process of distribution were acquired after such process had ended. See Louis Loss and Joel Seligman, *Securities Regulation*, 3rd edn (Boston, Little, Brown, 1989), vol. 1, pp. 388–9.

An offering is deemed to commence for purposes of determining the period in question when sales can be confirmed (i.e. after the registration statement is declared effective, the securities priced, and the underwriting agreement signed).

It must be kept in mind that the restrictions on publicity of Rule 10b-6 under the Exchange Act also apply, but for a slightly different period. See section on "Rule 10b-6" in 7.2.1.
33 Securities Act Release no. 5180, 36 Fed. Reg. 16506 at 16507 (August 16, 1971). Other releases covering similar ground include Securities Act Release no. 3844, 22 Fed. Reg. 8359 (October 8, 1957), Securities Act Release

no. 4697, 29 Fed. Reg. 7317 (May 28, 1964), and Securities Act Release no. 5009, 34 Fed. Reg. 16870 (October 7, 1969).

34 Special rules apply to projections for purposes of Rule 139(b). For projections to be included in a publication, they must have been published previously on a regular basis, they must be included with respect to either a substantial number of companies in the issuer's industry or all companies in a comprehensive list which is contained in the publication (and must cover the same periods with respect to such companies as with respect to the issuer), and they must be no more favorable to the issuer than those contained in the most recent publication in which projections were included. See Instruction 2 to Rule 139.

35 For purposes of Rule 139(a), a research report has not been distributed with "reasonable regularity" if it contains information, an opinion, or a recommendation concerning a company with respect to which a broker or dealer currently is not publishing research. See Instruction 1 to Rule 139. No similar caveat is made with respect to Rule 139(b).

The SEC has indicated that for purposes of Rule 10b-6 under the Exchange Act a research report that otherwise meets the requirements of Rule 139(a) will not be permitted if it contains an opinion or recommendation more favorable to the issuer (or the securities in question) than the one contained in the broker or dealer's previous report. See note 37 below.

36 Rule 10b-8 under the Exchange Act is also significant when shares of a foreign company are being distributed through a rights offering. The rule aims to maintain the integrity of the offering by setting an upper limit on the price at which the shares being offered may be sold and the price at which the rights themselves may be purchased, in either case by any person participating in the distribution.

37 Although one would expect that the rules applicable to public offerings of securities under the Securities Act would be carried over into Rule 10b-6, which was designed mainly for public offerings, that is not entirely the case.

When the SEC adopted amendments to Rule 139 in 1984, it stated that

> Rule 139 and Rule 10b-6 are designed to serve different purposes. Rule 139 provides a safe harbor from the strict liability provisions of the Securities Act, which assure that investors receive prospectus disclosure. In contrast, Rule 10b-6 is intended to assure that distributions of securities are free of the market effects of bids, purchases, or inducements to purchase by those who have an interest in the success of a distribution. The prohibition on inducements to purchase is an essential element of Rule 10b-6. Because inducements to purchase, such as improved recommendations, can be an effective and inexpensive method of facilitating the distribution of securities, the [SEC] staff is taking a no-action position that . . . is narrower than the safe harbor provided by Rule 139.

Accordingly, the SEC staff announced that it would not recommend that the SEC take enforcement action under Rule 10b-6 "with respect to a research report that is (1) within Rule ... 138 or paragraph (b) of Rule 139 or (2) within paragraph (a) of Rule 139 and does not contain a recommendation or earnings forecast more favorable than that previously disseminated by the firm" (Securities Exchange Act Release no. 21332, 49 Fed. Reg. 37569 at 37572: September 19, 1984). Moreover, when the SEC adopted amendments to Rule 10b-6 in 1987 it stated that even these permissible research reports could constitute solicitations of brokerage transactions (e.g. if the research report is focused on the issuer whose securities are being distributed and is directed at particular customers by a broker–dealer's sales personnel) and concluded that the distribution of such reports by a broker, if made after the "cooling-off" period discussed below, could violate Rule 10b-6 (Securities Exchange Act Release no. 24003, 52 Fed. Reg. 2994 at 2995 n. 17: January 16, 1987).

These arcane distinctions seem rather forced – indeed perhaps even overintellectualized – in character, and do not appear to be supported by empirical evidence; accordingly, US legal advisers may be able to conclude that what is permitted by the Securities Act is permitted by Rule 10b-6.

38 Rule 10b-6(c) (1) under the Exchange Act.
39 Rule 10b-6(c) (2) under the Exchange Act.
40 Securities Exchange Act Release no. 22510, 50 Fed. Reg. 42716 at 42721 n. 44 (October 10, 1985).
41 Rule 10b-6(c) (3) under the Exchange Act.
42 Rule 10b-6(a) (xi) under the Exchange Act. The "cooling-off" period will be two business days if the shares in question have a price of $5.00 per share or more and if there is a public float of 400,000 or more shares; in other cases the cooling-off period will be nine days.
43 Rule 10b-6(a) (xii) under the Exchange Act.
44 Rule 10b-6(a) (vi) under the Exchange Act. This permits the underwriters to offer the securities being distributed, and also allows them to offer any securities they own, or acquire, as principal.
45 Rule 10b-6(a) (i) under the Exchange Act. This allows the underwriters to transfer shares among themselves, for example pursuant to the orderly marketing arrangements discussed in the section "Underwriting arrangements" in 7.3.1, and to purchase shares from the issuer pursuant to the underwriting agreement (including pursuant to the exercise of any "overallotment option" discussed in the section "Rule 10b-7" in 7.2.1).
46 Rule 10b-6(a) (ii) under the Exchange Act.
47 Rule 10b-6(a) (v) under the Exchange Act.
48 Rule 10b-7(b) (3) under the Exchange Act.
49 Rule 10b-7(c) under the Exchange Act.
50 Rule 10b-7(j) (1) under the Exchange Act. The stabilizing price can, however, be raised if no stabilizing purchases are made for three consecutive business days, in which case a stabilizing bid may be entered at the price at which stabilizing could then be initiated, even if it is higher than that of the last stabilizing bid. See Rule 10b-7(j) (4).
51 Rule 10b-7(j) (2) under the Exchange Act.
52 Rule 10b-7(j) (3) under the Exchange Act.

53 Rule 10b-7(j) (4) under the Exchange Act. No stabilizing may be conducted, however, at a price higher than the price at which stabilizing is being conducted in the principal market for the security.
54 Rule 10b-7(j) (5) under the Exchange Act.
55 Rule 10b-7(h) under the Exchange Act.
56 Rule 10b-7(i) under the Exchange Act.
57 This general statement of the effect of the stabilization rules, and indeed the detailed description of the rules set forth above, is subject to a number of exceptions that are beyond the scope of this chapter. In addition, there are a number of disclosure and record-keeping requirements. See Rules 10b-7(k) and (1) under the Exchange Act.
58 S. 1 of the Rules of Fair Practice of the NASD.
59 Interpretation of the Board of Governors of the NASD on "Services in Distribution."
60 Interpretation of the Board of Governors of the NASD on "Free Riding and Withholding."
61 S. 3(a) (1) of the Investment Company Act.
62 S. 3(a) (3) of the Investment Company Act. See also Rule 3a-1 under the Investment Company Act.
63 Rule 3a-6(b) (1) (i) (B) under the Investment Company Act (in the case of banks) and Rule 3a-6(b) (3) (i) under the Investment Company Act (in the case of insurance companies). Trust or loan companies in Canada and building societies in the UK are also excepted from the definition of "investment company" by Rule 3a-6: Rule 3a-6(b) (1) (ii).
64 Foreign brokers or dealers may, however, join US houses in a single underwriting syndicate in a global offering, so long as the right to offer and sell the shares in the US is reserved to US registered brokers or dealers.
65 For a detailed discussion of Rule 144A, as well as of traditional private placement procedures, see Edward F. Greene and Alan L. Beller, "Rule 144A: Keeping the US Competitive in the International Financial Markets," *Insights*, vol. 4, no. 6 (June 1990) and Edward F. Greene, Alan L. Beller, George M. Cohen, Manley O. Hudson, Jr, and Edward J. Rosen, "Private Offerings in the US by Foreign Issuers," *US Regulation of the International Securities Markets* (Prentice-Hall, 1992), ch. 4.
66 Securities and Exchange Commission, "Staff Report on Rule 144A," September 30, 1991.
67 Rule 144A(d) (1) under the Securities Act. Rule 144A applies only to *resales* of securities; accordingly, for a placement by an issuer to be made under Rule 144A the shares must be sold through an underwriter acting as principal. It should be sufficient, however, for the underwriting commitment to be formulated as an obligation to procure investors to purchase and pay for the securities, failing which the underwriters themselves will be obliged to purchase and pay for them.
68 Rule 144A(d) (2) under the Securities Act.
69 Rule 144A(a) (3) under the Securities Act.
70 Rule 144A(a) (i) under the Securities Act. Special rules apply to families of investment companies. See Rule 144A(a) (iv) under the Securities Act.

71 Rule 144A(a) (ii) under the Securities Act.
72 Rule 144A(a) (vi) under the Securities Act.
73 Rule 144(d) (1) (i)–(iv) under the Securities Act. Most of the major US investment banks have now compiled lists of qualified institutional buyers based on certificates of the buyers' chief financial officers (or other executive officers). Standard & Poor's Corporation has begun publishing a list of qualified institutional buyers, and the SEC has stated that such a list could be relied on by sellers. *Standard & Poor's Corporation*, SEC No-Action Letter (July 8, 1991).
74 Rule 144A(d) (3) (i) under the Securities Act. ADRs and the underlying shares are considered to be the same class for this purpose.
75 Rule 144A(d) (4) (i) under the Securities Act.
76 Rule 144A(d) (4) (ii) (c) under the Securities Act.
77 Rule 144(k) under the Securities Act. In the case of affiliates of the issuer, resales remain subject to the volume and manner of sale limitations referred to below even after the three-year period.
78 Rule 144(d) (1) under the Securities Act.
79 See Rule 144(e) and (f) under the Securities Act.
80 The issue here is whether the policy objective of ensuring that privately placed securities do not flow into the public trading markets in the US requires that ordinary corporate communications and research reports that comply with the limitations already contained in the relevant rules and releases must cease while the placement is under way. So long as the shares are offered and sold only to qualified institutional buyers, who are presumed to know and to act in compliance with the rules regarding resales of restricted securities, or to other institutional investors on the basis of the traditional private placement procedures outlined below, which are designed to ensure that only certain limited kinds of resales can occur, the risk that the shares will be resold unlawfully to the US public is relatively small and would be reduced only marginally, if at all, if ordinary corporate communications and research were prohibited. What is at best only a marginal reduction in a risk already remote does not justify cutting off the normal flow of information about an issuer for the duration of a placement, which could deprive the market at large of information that would be useful in making investment decisions.

In an analogous context, where there is concern that securities initially offered and sold abroad would flow immediately into the US as a result of secondary trading, the SEC has stated that ordinary corporate communications and research reports permitted by Rule 139(b) need not cease during the offering. See the discussion in the section "Initial distributions" in 7.2.3 of "directed selling efforts" as that term is used in Regulation S under the Securities Act.

The question whether research reports meeting the requirements of Rules 138 or 139 constitute general solicitation or general advertising is not likely to arise very often, since a reporting issuer (the only kind of issuer about which such research reports could be published) generally will choose to offer its shares to the US public rather than to make a private placement.

This is especially true when the issuer has become subject to the reporting requirements of the Exchange Act through a securities exchange listing or NASDAQ quotation for its shares, since Rule 144A would not then be available to it, leaving only the more restrictive traditional private placement option.

While notices of the kind contemplated by Rule 135 under the Securities Act should be permitted in circumstances where the failure to publish could constitute a violation of law, notices of the kind contemplated by Rule 134 under the Securities Act, which may include the names of the underwriters, are harder to justify, and more likely to be viewed as a general solicitation, since the information contained in them in most circumstances would go beyond what is likely to be required to be published under applicable law, and naming the underwriters could be viewed as a general invitation to enquire about the possibility of purchasing the securities in question.

81 The conduct of road shows can, however, cause a private placement to rise to the level of a "distribution" for purposes of Rule 10b-6 under the Exchange Act, which could have the effect of subjecting the foreign market activities of the foreign underwriters in a global offering to the restrictions of Rule 10b-6. See the section "Restrictions on market activities" in 7.3.2.

82 Rule 144A might not be attractive if it is desired to expand the market for the shares to institutional investors other than qualified institutional buyers.

83 See section 4(2) of the Securities Act.

84 See Rule 502(d) under the Securities Act, which contains the "reasonable care" requirement.

85 Securities and Exchange Commission, "Staff Report on Rule 144A," September 30, 1991.

86 See *Touche Remnant*, SEC No-Action Letter (August 27, 1984).

87 Securities Act Release no. 6862, 55 Fed. Reg. 17933 at 17940–1 (April 23, 1990).

88 Investment Company Act Release no. 17534, 55 Fed. Reg. 25322 at 25337 (June 15, 1990).

89 Rule 15a-6(a) (3) (i) under the Exchange Act.

90 Rule 15a-6(a) (3) (ii) under the Exchange Act.

91 Rule 15a-6(a) (3) (iii) (B) under the Exchange Act.

92 Rule 15a-6(a) (3) (iii) (D) under the Exchange Act.

93 Rule 15a-6(a) (3) (i) (B) under the Exchange Act.

94 Rule 15a-6(a) (3) (iii) under the Exchange Act.

95 Rule 15a-6(a) (3) (iii) (A) (3) under the Exchange Act.

96 Securities Act Release no. 4708, 29 Fed. Reg. 9828 (July 9, 1964). For a discussion of the practices developed on the basis of that release, see Beller and Berney, "Eurobonds," *The Review of Securities & Commodities Regulation*, vol. 19, no. 4 (February 19, 1986).

97 Rule 901 under the Securities Act.

98 Rule 903 under the Securities Act.

99 Rule 904 under the Securities Act.

100 Rule 903(a) and (b) under the Securities Act. There are additional restrictions if there is a "substantial US market interest" in the class of shares being distributed. In the case of equity securities, "substantial US market interest" means that in the issuer's last financial year, (1) the securities exchanges and inter-dealer quotation systems in the US in the aggregate constituted the single largest market for the class of securities being offered, or (2) 20 percent or more of all trading in such class of securities took place on securities exchanges and inter-dealer quotation systems in the US and less than 55 percent of such trading took place in the securities markets of a single foreign country (Rule 902(a) under the Securities Act).

If the issuer reasonably believes at the commencement of the offering that this condition has not been met, as will be the case with most foreign issuers, there are no additional requirements (Rule 903(c)(1) under the Securities Act). If, however, the issuer does not have such a reasonable belief, there are three additional requirements. The first has the effect of prohibiting distributors from offering or selling in the US or to US persons, until the expiration of a forty-day "restricted period" commencing with the closing date for the offering, any shares that are sold initially outside the US and reacquired in foreign markets (Rule 903(c)(2)(ii) under the Securities Act). The second requires that "offering restrictions" be adopted, which means that each distributor must agree that all offers and sales during the restricted period will be made either pursuant to Regulation S or pursuant to another exemption from the registration requirements of the Securities Act, and that the offering materials used during the restricted period, including advertisements relating to the offering, must contain statements to the effect that the securities have not been registered under the Securities Act and may not be sold in the US or to US persons unless an exemption from the registration requirements is available (Rule 903(c)(2)(ii) and Rule 902(b) under the Securities Act). The final requirement is that each distributor selling securities during the restricted period to a securities dealer or a person receiving a selling concession, fee, or other remuneration send a confirmation or other notice to the purchaser stating that the purchaser is subject to the same restrictions on offers and sales that apply to a distributor (Rule 903(c) (2) (iv) under the Securities Act).

A breach of the "offering restrictions" requirement will cause the safe harbor to be lost for all participants in the distribution, but a breach of either of the other requirements will result in the safe harbor being lost only for the person who fails to comply (Securities Act Release no. 6863, 55 Fed. Reg. 18306 at 18319–20: April 24, 1990).

The "restricted period" and confirmation requirements should not be relevant when the "flow back" of an appropriate number of shares is registered with the SEC, either as part of a global offering or otherwise. See note 126 below.

101 Rule 903(b) under the Securities Act. The definition of "distributor" is contained in Rule 902(a) under the Securities Act.

102 Securities Act Release no. 6863, 55 Fed. Reg. 18306 at 18311 (April 24,

1990). If there is a "substantial US market interest" in the issuer's shares, the prohibition on directed selling efforts applies for the "restricted period" as well. See note 100 above.
103 Securities Act Release no. 6863, 55 Fed. Reg. 18306 at 18319–20.
104 Rule 902(b) under the Securities Act.
105 Securities Act Release no. 6863, 55 Fed. Reg. 18306 at 18311 (April 24, 1990) and Rule 902(b) (1) under the Securities Act.
106 Rule 902(k) under the Securities Act.
107 Rule 902(b) (2) under the Securities Act.
108 Rule 902(d) (4) under the Securities Act. The information permitted to be included is similar to that allowed by Rule 134 under the Securities Act.
109 Securities Act Release no. 6863, 55 Fed. Reg. 18306 at 18311–12 (April 24, 1990).
110 For a discussion of this question, see Joseph McLaughlin, " 'Directed Selling Efforts' and the U.S. Securities Analyst," *The Review of Securities and Commodities Regulation*, vol. 24, no. 11 (June 12, 1991).
111 Securities Act Release no. 6863, 55 Fed. Reg. 18306 at 18312 (April 24, 1990).
112 Preliminary Note 7 to Regulation S and Securities Act Release no. 6863, 55 Fed. Reg. 18306 at 18312 (April 24, 1990). The information, however, must be made available to the foreign and US press generally and must not be intended to induce purchases of securities by persons in the United States (ibid).
113 Securities Act Release no. 6863, 55 Fed. Reg. 18306 at 18312 (April 24, 1990).
114 Ibid.
115 Ibid. This is consistent with the SEC's view that offers and sales under Regulation S will not be integrated with contemporaneous SEC-registered public offerings or exempt private placements (ibid. at 18320).
116 Rule 903(a) under the Securities Act.
117 Rule 902(i) under the Securities Act. Not all foreign securities exchanges have, or make significant use of, a physical trading floor. A noteworthy example of one that does not is The International Stock Exchange of the United Kingdom and the Republic of Ireland. The SEC has not explained the rationale for the "physical trading floor" requirement and chose not to apply it for purposes of the resale safe harbor discussed in the section on "Resales" in 7.2.3.
118 Securities Act Release no. 6863, 55 Fed. Reg. 18306 at 18319–20 (April 24, 1990).
119 Ibid. at 18310.
120 Rule 904(b) and (a) under the Securities Act. Certain additional requirements apply to resales by a securities dealer or other person receiving a selling concession, fee, or other remuneration if there is a "substantial US market interest" in the issuer's shares. See note 100 above and Rule 904(c) (1) under the Securities Act.
121 Rule 904(b) under the Securities Act and Securities Act Release no. 6863, 55 Fed. Reg. 18306 at 18320 (April 24, 1990).

GLOBAL OFFERINGS OF SHARES   233

122 Rule 904(a) under the Securities Act. Regulation S specifies that resales may be made on the Eurobond market regulated by the Association of International Bond Dealers, the Amsterdam Stock Exchange, the Australian Stock Exchange Limited, the Bourse de Bruxelles, the Frankfurt Stock Exchange, the Stock Exchange of Hong Kong Limited, the International Stock Exchange of the United Kingdom and the Republic of Ireland, the Johannesburg Stock Exchange, the Bourse de Luxembourg, the Borsa Valori di Milano, the Montreal Stock Exchange, the Bourse de Paris, the Stockholm Stock Exchange, the Tokyo Stock Exchange, the Toronto Stock Exchange, the Vancouver Stock Exchange, and the Zurich Stock Exchange (Rule 902(a) (1) under the Securities Act).

Regulation S also confers authority on the SEC to designate such other offshore securities markets for this purpose as it considers appropriate. The attributes to be considered by the SEC when deciding whether to designate a market include organization under foreign law, association with a generally recognized community of financial intermediaries, oversight by a governmental or self-regulatory body, oversight standards set by an existing body of law, reporting of securities transactions on a regular basis to a governmental or self-regulatory body, a system for exchange of price quotations through common communications media, and an organized clearance and settlement system (Rule 902(a) (2) under the Securities Act). Thus far, the SEC has designated the Helsinki Stock Exchange (see *Shearson Lehman Hutton Inc.*, SEC No-Action Letter, July 7, 1990), SEAQ International (see *First Boston Corporation*, SEC No-Action Letter, June 14, 1990), and the Mexican Stock Exchange (see *Mexican Stock Exchange*, SEC No-Action Letter, February 15, 1990).

123 A survey of relevant requirements was conducted in connection with the global offering of shares in British Telecommunications plc, completed in the late fall of 1991. In that offering, shares were offered and sold to the public in the UK, Japan, the US, and Canada. Offers and sales in other countries were required to be made in compliance with the sales restrictions contained in Part 2 of the Eleventh Schedule to the Orderly Marketing Agreement dated November 13, 1991. That schedule set out the requirements for offering securities to professionals (or otherwise in a manner exempt from detailed regulation) in some forty countries, including all the major European, South American, and Asian capital markets.

124 The position is slightly less certain in so far as the extraterritorial application of the restrictions on publicity of Rule 10b-6 is concerned. A consensus among US legal advisers does seem to be emerging, however, that at least in so far as foreign issuers are concerned the distribution of research reports outside the United States should not raise Rule 10b-6 problems.

125 For one of a number of cases considering the extraterritorial application of the liability provisions of the US securities laws, see *Bersch v. Drexel Firestone*, 519 F.2d 974 (2d Cir. 1975). Although the possibility cannot be ruled out, it is unlikely that a US court would find subject matter jurisdiction over a claim brought against a foreign issuer or underwriter

by a foreign person who purchased shares of the foreign issuer outside the US, even if the US telecommunications or postal systems were used in the offering (or another basis of jurisdiction could be established). In those circumstances, as Judge Friendly articulated the issue in *Bersch*, "when . . . a court is confronted with transactions that on any view are predominantly foreign, it must seek to determine whether Congress would have wished the precious resources of United States courts and law enforcement agencies to be directed to them rather than leave the problem to foreign countries" (ibid. at 985). There is also some doubt as to whether a federal court is permitted by article III of the US Constitution to assert jurisdiction over a claim involving two non-US parties.

126 If there is a "substantial US market interest" in the issuer's shares (see note 100 above), it would be prudent to register all the shares offered and sold abroad in light of the likelihood that they will trade immediately into the US.

127 See *Rule 10b-6: Interpretation of "Business Day"*, SEC No-Action Letter (July 29, 1991) (hereinafter the *Business Day Letter*), which restates the staff's position on this.

128 *International Stock Exchange of the United Kingdom and the Republic of Ireland*, SEC No-Action Letters (September 29, 1987 and October 14, 1988).

129 Ibid.

130 These designations were replaced in January 1991 with a new system in which each security is allocated a "Normal Market Size" (NMS) calculated on the basis of trading volume in the preceding twelve months, and recalculated each quarter. There are twelve bands of NMS, ranging from 500 to 200,000 shares. See *British Telecommunications public limited company*, SEC No-Action Letter (December 3, 1991). Under the prior system, for a stock to be classified as "alpha" there had to be ten or more market-makers, the issuer was required to have a market capitalization of £500 million or more, and the volume of trading in the preceding quarter had to be £100 million or more. For a stock to be classified as "beta" there had to be six or more market-makers, the issuer was required to have a market capitalization of £50 million or more and the volume of trading in the preceding quarter had to be £10 million or more. It is unclear how the requirement that a stock be "alpha" or "beta" is being applied in the light of NMS.

131 *Distribution of Certain Canadian Securities*, SEC No-Action Letter (August 22, 1991). The multijurisdictional disclosure system is discussed in James G. Dannis and Douglas L. Poling, "The New US/Canadian Multijurisdictional Disclosure System," *Insights*, vol. 5, no. 9 (September 1991).

132 See the *Business Day Letter* (July 29, 1991). The SEC staff also clarified in the *Business Day Letter* that the two-day or nine-day period must include two or nine full trading days in the foreign market before the commencement of offers and sales in the US.

133 A consensus appears to be forming that reliance on a nine-day cooling-off period without approaching the SEC staff is not likely to create a signi-

ficant risk of enforcement action unless the issuer or any of its affiliates is substantially involved in trading in the shares being distributed (or the principal market for the shares exhibits other unusual trading characteristics).
134 *Atlas Copco AB*, SEC No-Action Letter (May 22, 1990).
135 *Novo Nordisk A/S*, SEC No-Action Letter (June 18, 1991).
136 *TransCanada Pipeline Limited Equity Offering*, SEC No-Action Letter (June 10, 1991).
137 *Norsk Hydro AS*, SEC No-Action Letter (May 5, 1988)
138 *Telefonos de Mexico SA de CV*, SEC No-Action Letter (May 13, 1991).
139 *Banco de Santander, SA*, SEC No-Action Letter (July 28, 1987).
140 *British Petroleum Company plc*, SEC No-Action Letter (October 14, 1989).
141 *British Telecommunications plc*, SEC No-Action Letter (December 3, 1991).
142 For example, the rules on stabilization of the UK Securities Investment Board also provide that a stabilization bid may not exceed the offering price, but they afford greater latitude than does Rule 10b-7 in permitting a stabilizing bid to be adjusted upward in response to market movements (Securities Exchange Act Release no. 28732, 56 Fed. Reg. 814 at 818: January 3, 1991). In France, article 7 of Regulation no. 90–04 of the Commission des Opérations de Bourse (July 5, 1990) provides that stabilization may be conducted only for the purpose of ensuring liquidity or smoothing excessive variations in the market price. Stabilization will be presumptively valid if it is conducted opposite to the trend of the last quoted price – i.e. if the market price of the shares is going up, the person conducting stabilization may sell (and vice versa) – and certain conditions regarding volume and other matters are met. Reconciling these various requirements can be a complex task.
143 Securities Exchange Act Release no. 28732, 56 Fed. Reg. 814 (January 3, 1991).
144 Ibid. The proposed definition of "specified foreign securities market" is discussed in Securities Exchange Act Release no. 28733, 56 Fed. Reg. 820 (January 3, 1991). Factors that the SEC will consider in deciding whether to designate a particular market are whether it has an established operating history, is subject to oversight by an authority that has a written understanding with the SEC that provides for cooperation and enforcement coordination in regulatory and enforcement matters, requires securities transactions to be reported on a regular basis to a governmental or self-regulatory body, has a system for public dissemination of price quotations, has sufficient trading volume to indicate liquidity, and has adequately capitalized financial intermediaries (ibid. at 821).
145 Securities Exchange Act Release no. 28732, 56 Fed. Reg. 814 at 819. For further discussion of the proposed amendments, see Richard J. Bauerfeld, "SEC Eases Up on Applying US Rules to Global Deals," *Investment Dealers' Digest* (March 11, 1991).
146 The prohibition on general solicitation and general advertising may

require that all research reports be excluded from the US, and the prohibition on directed selling efforts may require that research reports other than those permitted by Rule 139(b) be excluded. See note 80 above and the discussion of directed selling efforts and research reports in the section on "Initial distributions" in 7.2.3.
147 Rule 10b-6(c) (5) under the Exchange Act.
148 The restrictions of Rule 10b-6 on the distribution of research reports could also apply, making it necessary for this reason as well to take steps to ensure that research reports that do not comply with Rules 138 or 139 are not mailed into the US. See note 37 above.
149 *Securities Industry Association*, SEC Exemptive Order (April 25, 1991). The exemption also deals specifically with rights offerings, making the restrictions of Rules 10b-6 and 10b-7 inapplicable to concurrent trading anywhere outside the US in connection with a rights offering of foreign securities to US institutional investors, provided that the subscription price is discounted at the time the offering commences by at least 8 percent from the market price of the underlying shares and the voting stock of the issuer held world-wide by non-affiliates has an aggregate market value of at least $150 million. This element of the exemption is available only during the period when the rights or underlying shares are being offered and sold in the US and does not apply to the distribution of any underlying shares remaining unsubscribed upon expiration of the rights (but does apply to such sales to sub-underwriters who agreed prior to the expiration of the rights to be sub-underwriters).

For a further discussion of the exemption, see Richard J. Bauerfeld, "SEC Relaxes Application of Rules 10b-6, 10b-7 and 10b-8 Abroad," *Insights*, vol. 5, no. 7 (July 1991).
150 The discussions of public offerings in France and Japan in section 7.3.3 are based closely on Greene et al., "Global Offerings," *US Regulation of the International Securities Markets*, ch. 6.
151 In addition, the US underwriters were able to preserve in their agreement among underwriters the customary method of allocating selling commissions in the US, which is to give the lead underwriter the authority to make sales for the accounts of the other underwriters and to allocate the selling commissions with respect to those sales as requested by the purchasers. This contrasted with the system that applied to most of the other syndicates, which required in effect that selling commissions be allocated among the underwriters *pro rata* to their underwriting commitments.
152 Secondary sales include sales of shares that are purchased by underwriters in primary offerings outside Japan and then resold in Japan through Japanese brokers on the day after the closing.
153 In the global offering of shares in Telefonos de Mexico SA de CV in the spring of 1991, this waiting period was reduced to one business day.
154 Securities Exchange Act Release no. 29275, 56 Fed. Reg. 27382 (June 6, 1991) deals with exchange offers, while Securities Act Release no. 6896, 56 Fed. Reg. 27564 (June 4, 1991) covers rights offerings.

Part III

Trade-Related Financings

8

Forfaiting

HOWARD J. WATERMAN

Chapter Outline

8.1 Introduction
    8.1.1 General
    8.1.2 Motives of Exporter
    8.1.3 Comparison with Factoring

8.2 Features of Forfaiting
    8.2.1 Definition
    8.2.2 Guarantee
    8.2.3 Autonomy of Obligations

8.3 Legal Issues Involved in Forfaiting
    8.3.1 Sources of Law
    8.3.2 Types of debt Instrument
    8.3.3 Instruments Denominated in European Currency Units
    8.3.4 Forms of Guarantee
    8.3.5 Applicable Law
    8.3.6 "Without Recourse" Endorsement

8.4 Documentation

8.5 Syndication

Appendix 1 Definition of Negotiable Instruments

Appendix 2 Avals

This paper reflects the author's presentation at the 1990 Centre for Commercial Law Studies Summer School, Queen Mary and Westfield College, London, and speaks as of that date (June 1990).

8.1 Introduction

8.1.1 General

Since the early 1980s there has been an increase in the financing of trade by means of a technique called "forfaiting." Although several specialist institutions have been recently wound down, to a large extent due to the losses they have suffered from the increase in interest rates in all the major financing currencies (specialist institutions have tended not to match their medium-term investments in trade paper in the interbank market), trade and exports still need to be financed and banks and other financial institutions are offering forfaiting as a service to established customers. Those specialist institutions that remain are now funding their investments with matching deposits or entering into hedging arrangements to minimize foreign exchange risk. Trade obligations are rarely rescheduled (although it now appears that trade debt will be included in the future rescheduling of the debt of the former Soviet Union) and also it seems that trade financing can still be accomplished for the ever-increasing number of countries which nowadays are unable to raise finance on a voluntary basis. After all, if trade debts were rescheduled, trade with the debtor country (except on a cash basis) would probably stop, with disastrous consequences for both the country and the creditors of the country.

The purpose of this chapter is to review broadly the mechanics of this market and the associated legal issues, structures, and documentation involved. A discussion on the financing of trade paper would exclude the kind of paper which is taken by banks pursuant to note issuance facilities, Euro-commercial paper programmes, and acceptance credit facilities – this tends to be short-term paper and in any event financial paper in that it does not necessarily represent an underlying export trade transaction, which is the particular characteristic of the subject of this chapter.

8.1.2 Motives of Exporter

If it had ever been the case that the buyer or importer in a large export trade transaction paid the exporter in cash, this by and large ceased to happen some time ago. The buyer or importer in a substantial deal expects to pay on generous credit terms and the exporter could well be wasting his time if the package he offered to the importer failed to include them. So in an export trade transaction, the most common scenario is where the importer makes a downpayment for the goods or project in question, after which the remaining portion will be payable on deferred terms. This would probably be over five to seven years although increasingly over a longer period of time as competition among exporters and exporting countries becomes more fierce. In many transactions the obligations of the importer to pay the deferred portion of the contract price will be evidenced by bills of exchange or promissory notes.

Banks and other financial institutions can purchase these bills or notes from the exporter, so the exporter does not suffer a cash flow disadvantage from having to deliver goods without being paid for a number of years. Thus the exporter generally can "wash its hands" entirely of the risk of the importer not meeting his obligations on the bills or notes. In other words, the bills or notes are purchased by the bank without recourse to the exporter. This feature has resulted in the financing technique being entitled "forfaiting." It comes from the French word *forfait* and conveys the idea of surrendering or forfeiting rights – in this case, rights against the previous holder of the obligation (the exporter). This is of fundamental importance in forfaiting.

8.1.3 Comparison with Factoring

The broad principle of forfaiting is nothing new. It is comparable with the discounting of traders' receivables which is nearly as old as the City of London itself. It is similar to factoring, although factoring differs in the following respects:

- factoring will more often entitle the factor to have recourse against the exporter in the event that the debts are unpaid. In factoring the exporter is looking to improve its cash flow and not necessarily to divest itself of the risk of non-payment; in forfaiting, on the other hand, divesting the performance risk is very much the motive of the exporter;
- factoring does not involve negotiable instruments, so there tends to be a "one-off" sale of debt obligations to the factor with no secondary market; and
- factoring usually involves the purchase of all debts or all of a class of debts owing to the customer, while forfaiting is generally transaction- or project-based.

8.2 Features of Forfaiting

8.2.1 Definition

Forfaiting is the purchase of bills of exchange or promissory notes falling due at some future date arising from the export of goods (or, sometimes, services) without recourse to any previous holder of the bills or notes. In other words the forfaiter (the bank or financial institution which purchases the bills or notes from the exporter or in the secondary market) purchases bills or notes that have been issued by an importer to represent the deferred portion of the payments due under the relevant supply contract. Usually the bills or notes will form part of a series maturing at six-monthly intervals for a period of around five to seven years and will bear interest at a fixed rate, which often bears no relation to the market rate of interest prevailing in the currency concerned (and is sometimes linked to the "consensus rate" as agreed by the OECD member countries). The price that the bank or financial institution pays for the bills or notes will take account of the interest payable by the importer and the forfaiter's considered view of the likely trends in interest rates over the life of these bills or notes. The price is in fact usually calculated on a discounted basis – there is deducted from the face amount of the bills or notes an amount to represent interest and also the bank's fees and commissions and profit margin for taking on the risk.

8.2.2 Guarantee

Unless the acceptor of the bill (or issuer of the note) is a first-class company or institution or a governmental entity, the debt instrument will invariably be guaranteed by a bank or state organization acceptable to the forfaiter. So far as the forfaiter is concerned, this will be its credit risk.

8.2.3 Autonomy of Obligations

Finally on the subject of definition, notwithstanding that the debt instruments (and any guarantee) will represent an underlying trade transaction, they will be abstract obligations that a forfaiter can rely upon absolutely. There will be no reference at all to the underlying trade contract in the bills or notes themselves and there will certainly be no suggestion that payment is in any way contingent upon the performance by the exporter of his obligations in relation to the delivery of the goods or services, their quality, and so forth. If any dispute on the underlying contract should arise, the importer will have to rely on its contractual rights against the exporter.

What is attractive to the exporter is that it does not have to wait for its money. The exporter offers the bills or notes to its bank at a discount and receives a discounted sum immediately. A credit sale is thus transformed into a cash sale. No doubt the cost to the exporter of the forfaiting transaction will be built into the contract price. The exporter has no further involvement and it is for the forfaiter to collect payment of the bills or notes at maturity and to take the risk, that is, the credit risk, of non-payment.

8.3 Legal Issues Involved in Forfaiting

8.3.1 Sources of Law

One of the features of basic forfaiting is that the legal documentation is notable for its brevity and simplicity and there is no comparison to the length of loan documentation usually encountered in commercial lending. The documentation is limited, usually, to a brief list of the commercial terms of the transaction (that is, the forfaiting contract between the exporter and its bank, dealing with the interest or discount rate to apply, fees, commissions, and so forth), together with the bills or notes themselves and the guarantee.

On the other hand this does mean that the forfaiter should be fully aware of the legal issues involved so that adequate checks can be carried out before the bills or notes are actually purchased or a commitment to do so is undertaken. Forfaiters have tended to become experts in considering the right questions and have also built up a library of experience to which they can refer when they are offered debt instruments emanating from a particular country.

It should be noted that there does not appear to be any UK case law arising from transactions in the forfaiting market itself. Therefore the materials that a financial institution will look at in relation to the bills or notes themselves are restricted to the UK Bills of Exchange Act 1882 for negotiable instruments issued under English law, the Geneva Conventions on Bills of Exchange of 1932 (often called the "Uniform Law") for negotiable instruments issued under the laws of countries which are party to these conventions (which cover a large number of countries but notably not the UK), and finally basic market practice.

Following the Report of the Review Committee on Banking Services Law and Practice (commonly known as the Jack Committee) in February 1989, the UK government considered a number of recommendations for change in the English law of negotiable instruments and checks. However, the government subsequently appeared to have shelved all the recommendations regarding negotiable instruments, except for a relatively minor change to the law on checks.

A number of specific legal issues invariably arise, which are analyzed below.

8.3.2 Types of Debt Instrument

Although there are other types of debt instrument, the vast majority of transactions involve either bills of exchange or promissory notes. A bill of exchange will be drawn by the exporter on the importer and accepted by the importer. A promissory note will be simply issued by the importer in favor of the exporter. In general, the forfaiting financial institution will not have any particular preference provided that there is, as mentioned above, an absolute right of repayment without reference to the underlying commercial contract. Both instruments are usually straightforward and readily transferable by endorsement.

8.3.3 Instruments Denominated in European Currency Units

The subject of instruments denominated in European Currency Units (ECUs) has become particularly important during recent years. There is quite a large amount of this paper in circulation in the market, which is not surprising since the ECU has apparently become the fourth most popular financing currency in the world, following the US dollar, the Deutschmark, and the Japanese yen. Therefore the contract price of export transactions is often denominated in ECUs, especially where the domestic currency of the exporter is traditionally weak; and it follows from this that any associated bills or notes would also be denominated in ECUs.

Unfortunately legal problems arise as a result of the respective definitions of bills and notes in sections 3(1) and 83(1) of the UK Bills of Exchange Act 1882 and articles 1 and 75 of the Geneva Conventions on Bills of Exchange of 1932 (see appendix 1). To come within these definitions, the bill or note has to have (among other things) a promise to pay "a sum certain in money" – which is the Bills of Exchange Act definition – or "a determinate sum of money" – which is the definition in the Geneva Conventions. It is submitted that the ECU fails to satisfy this requirement. The Jack Committee certainly analyzed the position in this way and recommended a change in UK law.

It is not possible to say that the ECU is a currency. It is defined as the sum of the amounts of its components; that is, it is a "basket" of specified amounts of the currencies of the member states of the European Community. The actual composition of this basket changes every five years and, in fact, was changed on September 21, 1989 to bring Spanish pesetas and Portuguese escudos into the basket. When a bill or note matures, technically speaking the buyer would have to put the paying bank in funds in all the component currencies in the relevant proportions. The currencies and currency amounts in question may well not be the same as were applicable on the date when the bill or note was drawn or issued. Therefore the obligation would not even be said to have been an obligation to pay fixed amounts of specified currencies. Many bills and notes in circulation actually describe on their face what the ECU was at the date of issue and then go on to say that if the components change before the maturity date, the new components will be relevant for the purpose of calculating the value of the ECU and what must be paid on maturity. Accordingly, it is impossible to ascertain the sums payable without referring to the latest EC Council Regulation. For example, bills drawn early in 1989 are likely to have an out-of-date list of components on them.

The definitions in the current law ("a sum certain in money" or "a determinate sum of money") almost certainly mean that the amount payable must be readily ascertainable by reference only to the bill or note itself. There cannot be any reference to any extraneous factors in order to establish the precise amount payable.

If this analysis is correct, a bill or note denominated in ECUs would not be a negotiable instrument. This does not mean that it is unenforceable or not a valid contractual promise to pay, but it will not have all the advantages that negotiable instruments have. The most important advantage of negotiable instruments is that they can be transferred by simple endorsement. So if the ECU instrument is not negotiable, under English law it would be necessary to take a formal assignment which satisfies the requirements set out in section 136 of the UK Law of Property Act, 1925. Broadly these requirements are:

- the assignment must be in writing;
- the assignment must be in respect of the whole debt; and
- notice of assignment must be given to all parties liable on the bill or note in question.

It would be quite sufficient to have a very simple written assignment along the lines of "we hereby assign to you without recourse all our rights, title and interest in the following bill of exchange [or promissory note]" followed by a brief description of the parties to the bill or note, the date of issue, the maturity date, and the amount.

Unfortunately, it is possible that this assignment will be subject to the payment of stamp duty if it is executed in, or brought into, the UK. This would be necessary if, for example, any party wished to enforce it in the courts.

Another problem is that if an ECU bill or note is not a negotiable instrument, the holder does not become a "holder in due course."

Broadly this means that a *bona fide* purchaser without notice of anything adverse purchases the bill or note free from any adverse rights that may have affected previous holders (e.g. set-off).

The UK government in a White Paper had said that the statutory expression "a sum certain in money" should be modified to include "a monetary unit of account established by an inter-governmental institution" or by agreement between two or more states, which will include ECUs; although this will not, of course, assist where the Geneva Conventions apply.

8.3.4 *Forms of Guarantee*

As mentioned above, a guarantee will invariably be required to be given by a first-class bank (often the importer's bank) or, possibly, a state institution in the country of the importer. Quite apart from the credit risk itself, this eases the task of the forfaiter in its credit analysis as it is likely to know more about the guarantor than about the importer.

The associated guarantee will generally take the form of either an aval or a separate letter of guarantee.

An aval will appear on the bill or note itself and is constituted by the guarantor signing and adding the words "per aval" or similar such wording. The guarantor or avalizer then becomes liable to the forfaiter and all subsequent holders of the bill or note. The aval will automatically be transferred whenever the bill or note is transferred by negotiation and therefore the main advantage of this method of guarantee is that the forfaiter does not have to look into questions of transferability and transfer procedures (such as notice to the guarantor), which will confront it if the guarantee is constituted by a separate document.

The aval originates from the civil law jurisdictions and it is not a concept specifically recognized by English law. Where what purports to be an aval is used on a UK bill or note, it has generally been looked at as a "with recourse" endorsement of the instrument. This would make the endorser liable as a surety to all *subsequent* parties and holders of the instrument. Justification for this can be found in sections 28 and 56 of the UK Bills of Exchange Act 1882 (see appendix 2). In practice, this will satisfy a financial institution purchasing the instrument; and, since it is so much easier to pass the benefit of a guarantee by aval than of a guarantee constituted by a separate document, forfaiters even in the UK have a slight preference for guarantees by aval.

Unfortunately, no definitive ruling on the meaning of sections 28 and 56 in this context was given by the Court of Appeal in the recent case of *Irvani* v. *G. & H. Montage* [1990] 1 Lloyds Rep. 14, when an aval governed by German law came before the English courts on a procedural matter. The court avoided the question of whether an aval would be treated as an endorsement if English law applied, saying instead that on the facts German law applied so there was no need to consider the aval as an endorsement as understood by the Bills of Exchange Act 1882. (A similar judgment was given by the Court of Appeal in *Banco Atlantico SA* v. *British Bank of the Middle East* a year later, where Spanish law was considered to be the proper law. However, it was strongly implied that the aval would be treated as an endorsement under English law.)

The government proposed in a White Paper that avals will be specifically recognized by new UK legislation. This would mainly assist the exporter as drawer of a bill of exchange. Since the exporter would be a prior party – in other words, it draws the bill before the bill is accepted and avalized – the exporter would not be able to take advantage of sections 28 and 56. As mentioned above, this makes the endorser liable to subsequent parties and holders only and, therefore, would not assist an exporter who chooses not to discount the instrument but to hold it until maturity. A situation could be manufactured whereby the exporter became a subsequent party to the instrument by selling it to another party (perhaps even the guarantor) and then further negotiating it back to the exporter. However, this kind of arrangement is not ideal.

The subject of applicable law is dealt with below, but it should be mentioned that the question of whether an aval works or how it is given effect will be decided under the law applicable where the aval takes place. So in a UK export transaction English law is unlikely to be relevant anyway (this was the case in *Irvani* v. *G. & H. Montage* referred to above).

If the guarantee is a separate document it must, of course, be an abstract and absolute obligation to pay without any reference to the underlying supply contract and the forfaiter should ensure that the guarantor is stated to be a primary debtor so that it cannot resort to any defenses that the importer may wish to raise.

Again, if the guarantee is a separate document it should state that it is fully transferable and assignable to facilitate the sale of the bills or notes in the secondary market. However there will be procedures involved for the assignment in accordance with the guarantee's governing law. Under English law a guarantee would be construed as a chose in action, that is, a right of which the beneficiary cannot obtain physical possession and which, therefore, is enforceable only in the courts. The appropriate way to transfer it would be by legal assignment and a legal assignment must again satisfy the requirements set out in section 136 of the Law of Property Act 1925 referred to above in section 8.3.3.

The guarantee should be in favor of the exporter who will have formally to assign it to the forfaiter in accordance with these procedures. Additional assignments will probably be required if the bills or notes are sold on in the secondary market. There is a further drawback in that a single guarantee will often cover the whole of a series of bills or notes and the forfaiter may wish to sell only some of them, or to sell them all separately. Since in practice the guarantee will not be divisible it may be necessary to resort to some kind of trustee arrangement whereby the forfaiter holds the guarantee on behalf of all the banks which have purchased one or more of the bills or notes.

8.3.5 *Applicable Law*

Several different relationships arise from a forfaiting transaction and different laws may govern each of them or aspects of them. It is very important that the forfaiter is broadly aware of the answers to certain key legal questions under the laws which are commonly involved in forfaiting transactions. It is rarely practicable, except in the largest of transactions, to seek legal advice from lawyers in several jurisdictions each and every time a new transaction is contemplated.

First the forfaiter has to know which laws are relevant to a particular transaction, especially when he is purchasing bills or notes which are in a slightly unconventional form. Because this question of which laws apply to a transaction does not have a simple and straightforward answer, it may be helpful to consider the following hypothetical example:

Example

> An Italian exporter draws a bill of exchange in Italy on an Indian buyer. The Indian buyer accepts the bill in India and procures his local bank to avalize it. The Italian exporter takes the bill to Geneva where he endorses it in favor of a Swiss forfaiter. The bill is denominated in US dollars and is payable in New York.

Several different legal questions arise here and possibly the legal answers will be inconsistent. Certainly no single law applies to all the aspects of this transaction.

First, it is necessary to look at the sources of law. These are section 72 of the Bills of Exchange Act 1882 and articles 2, 3, and 4 of the

Geneva Convention on Conflicts of Laws. Where neither of these applies in a particular jurisdiction, the local rules on conflicts of laws will have to be considered. Broadly, the general rules are as follows:

Form The validity of the form of an instrument is decided under the provisions of the law of the place of issue. Under UK law this will be the place of delivery (usually to the exporter) but under the Geneva Convention it will be the place of signature. In practice a bill or note will generally state the place of issue and the forfaiter will have to know what the requirements are for an instrument to be valid under the law of that place. Applying these rules to the above example, Italian law will be relevant and if Italian law states that a bill must be printed on gold leaf, it will be invalid if it is not.

Interpretation The interpretation of the drawing, endorsement, or acceptance of an instrument will be determined by the law where the act takes place – again the place of delivery under UK law or the place of signature under the Geneva Convention. Accordingly in the above example it must be clear under Indian law that our Indian buyer is accepting the bill and that the Indian bank is adding its aval and what that means under Indian law.

Power and authority The question of whether a party to an instrument had power and was authorized to become a party, and whether its officers who actually signed the instrument had power and were authorized to do so, are matters decided under the laws of the place where that party is incorporated or established or is deemed to have his domicile. It would be necessary, in the above example, to look at the powers and authorities of the Italian drawer under Italian law, the Indian acceptor under Indian law, and the Indian avalizing bank also under Indian law.

Non-payment The law governing the position if the instrument is not paid on its due date will be the law of the place of payment. The forfaiter will look at these legal rules when establishing what steps should be taken: on the one hand the formal steps of noting and protesting in order to preserve all rights of recourse against the parties liable, and on the other hand the procedural steps which have to be taken to enforce payment in the local courts. In the above example the New York law requirements are relevant.

So far as presentation for payment is concerned it is prudent to present an unpaid instrument for payment to all parties liable, even though this may not be necessary under the law of the place of payment, as the law of the relevant contract (that is, the contract made by the drawing, endorsement, or acceptance) may apply to this particular aspect; it does under UK law (see further *Irvani* v. *Montage*, referred to above).

Illegality The law of the place of payment will also govern the question of whether or not a transaction is illegal or against public policy, and therefore unenforceable. However, a contract contained in the instrument will be illegal if it is illegal according to its governing law even though it may be legal in the place of payment – so there is a dual test here. The legality of the guarantee in the above example must satisfy both New York law and Indian law. Applicable foreign exchange authorizations will be crucial as it may be illegal for a party residing in a particular country to commit himself to make a payment in a foreign currency without certain consents being obtained in advance.

8.3.6 *"Without Recourse" Endorsement*

The exporter, as original beneficiary of the bill or note, will endorse without recourse to the forfaiter. If the paper is sold on in the secondary market, each subsequent forfaiter will also endorse the paper without recourse to the next holder. It is a feature of forfaiting that once the forfaiter buys the bills or notes from the exporter, it will be the forfaiter who will take the risk (that is, the *credit or commercial risk* that the importer and the guarantor may fail to pay without any valid reason), the *political risk* (the importer and the guarantor may not pay for example because of war or supervening governmental action), and the *transfer risk* (non-payment because of exchange controls or other restrictions imposed in the country of the importer and the guarantor). Accordingly, the exporter need not concern himself about cash flows or whether the importer will pay – there is no contingent liability on the exporter's books at all.

"With recourse" sales do take place, usually where certain details relating to the documentation still have to be resolved. Often the recourse to the exporter is only temporary. In slightly different types of financing, namely supplier credits (in essence, bill or note purchase transactions linked to a government export credit scheme), there is often recourse to the exporter and possibly also to an export credit institution. But this is not mainstream forfaiting and apart from transactions having the benefit of export credit guarantees, "with recourse" transactions are not desirable as they inhibit secondary market activity.

Reverting to the subject of the "without recourse" endorsement, under English law section 16 of the Bills of Exchange Act 1882 states that the drawer of a bill and any endorser may insert an express stipulation negating or limiting its own liability to the holder. Where the Geneva Conventions apply, article 9 interestingly allows an endorser to exclude liability but states that any attempt by a drawer to do so is deemed "not to be written." Therefore the drawer of a bill of exchange will, legally speaking, always be liable on the bill. However, in practice, it is extremely unlikely that any respectable forfaiter would sue an exporter as drawer having accepted the exporter's without recourse endorsement. Often a careful exporter will ask for a specific undertaking from the forfaiter in this respect and the forfaiter will usually give it. Of course, the problem does not arise with promissory notes as the exporter will only be the endorser.

The next question is whether an endorser without recourse has succeeded in stepping out of the picture in relation to all potential risks. As mentioned above, the forfaiter will take the credit or commercial risk, the political risk, and the transfer risk. However, the forfaiter does not wish to take the risk of the bills or notes not constituting a valid claim against the importer and the guarantor. If the exporter fails to provide a valid claim relating to a *bona fide* transaction, the forfaiter could base an action against the exporter on a fundamental breach of contract or breach of implied warranty. Indeed, section 58 of the Bills of Exchange Act 1882 specifically imputes such a warranty where English law applies. The entire purpose was to purchase a valid claim, and not financial or accommodation paper. There are bills and notes circulating that do not represent underlying trade transactions (e.g. commercial paper), but it is not the business of the forfaiter to deal in this kind of paper. As stated above, an attraction of trade paper is that it tends to be paid even where the debtor has stopped paying its other borrowings. Another avenue of claim for the forfaiter is that there may have been a material misrepresentation by the exporter in any discussions that preceded completion of the transaction.

8.4 Documentation

As stated above, a forfaiting transaction is effected with a minimum of documentation. Nevertheless general contract law still applies; and, if any untrue statements of fact are made during negotiations or in the documents themselves, an action for misrepresentation or a breach of warranty or, indeed, both may be available. In syndicated loans and other similar financings, the extent of the responsibilities of the agent, arrangers, or lead managers is defined in great detail and any other responsibilities are expressly excluded. However, in such transactions the syndicate members usually have more information on which to base their credit decision. In forfaiting, on the other hand, there is much more dependence on the primary forfaiter.

Another point on documentation is that when a forfaiter purchases a series of bills or notes and one is dishonored, there is no possibility of accelerating the payment of bills or notes which have yet to mature. This is not necessarily a disadvantage in practice as the bill or note will probably have been guaranteed by a bank or a state organization and if there really is a default that cannot be remedied fairly quickly it is unlikely that acceleration would obtain any better results.

Simplicity of documentation will not, however, necessarily apply if a transaction is syndicated.

8.5 Syndication

Forfaiting transactions tend to be of a relatively high value, usually dealing with exports of over $1 million in value. If a transaction is very large it is likely that the bank approached by the exporter will wish to organize the finance on a syndicated basis. This can be arranged in several ways.

- Different series of bills or notes could be purchased by different forfaiters, either direct from the exporter or through the original bank involved. This may not always be convenient, especially if the aggregate face amount of a series of bills or notes is itself very high. It is unlikely that individual bills or notes in the same series could be divided up among the banks because it may involve finding banks prepared to take later maturities without the earlier ones.
- The original bank could continue to hold the bills or notes and participations could be taken by the other banks. This is similar to a syndicated loan transaction where the agent deals directly with a borrower and then distributes the payments to the other banks in accordance with their respective entitlements.
- A third possibility that is often encountered is where the original bank purchases all the bills or notes but obtains indemnities or guarantees from other banks to cover its position should the bills or notes be dishonored. In this way, each bank in the syndicate takes a specified proportion of the risk but will not actually advance any money unless or until the bills or notes are dishonored. The disadvantage of this is, of course, that one bank has to fund the entire amount. It may, however, be advantageous to the other banks as the transaction will

appear differently on their balance sheets only as a contingent liability. On the other hand, the funding bank has a performance risk on the participating banks and apart from the credit risk, this will also have risk asset weighting implications for capital adequacy purposes. If the participating banks are all in the OECD there will be a 0.2 multiple weighting on the amount guaranteed.

It is also important to recognize the difference between a syndicated transaction and a series of transactions in the secondary market. In a syndicated transaction, where the duties and responsibilities of a lead manager will tend to be more akin to other types of syndicated financing, the documentation may well have similar extensive agency clauses with lists of exclusions and declarations by the syndicate that the syndicate members have made their own assessment of the underlying risk and documentation.

These syndicated arrangements have the appearance of more conventional medium-term financings and it may be that a bank wishing to introduce itself into this area will choose such a transaction as a place to start. Often the original bank involved will deal with collection at maturity and will carry out the various procedures necessary to enforce payment. It also enables a bank to commit a smaller amount of money to a single transaction, so a bank can obtain a wider geographical diversification of assets.

It is interesting to note that certain state banks have not been overjoyed about bills or notes which they have guaranteed being widely traded in the market. As a result they have employed various mechanisms, usually aimed at the negotiability of the bills or notes themselves. For example the Bank for Foreign Economic Affairs of the USSR often inserts pre-emption rights, which it would waive for selected transactions. Algerian state banks, on the other hand, usually state specifically that endorsements in favor of persons outside the banking system of the country of the exporter are prohibited. Forfaiters employ various devices to enable them to deal with this kind of instrument, such as silent participations, guarantee agreements, and trustee agreements that do not involve actual sale by endorsement.

However, there is always the risk that the guarantor may say that the spirit of the contract has still been broken and refuse to pay. It may be that its local courts would uphold its arguments. Unless, therefore, the forfaiter had some other way of enforcing a judgment (if for example the judgment were obtained in the English courts and there were available assets within the jurisdiction or in another jurisdiction which will recognize and enforce the English judgment) it may prefer to avoid this kind of transaction.

Appendix 1

Definition of Negotiable Instruments

Section 3(1) of the Bills of Exchange Act 1882:

> A bill of exchange is an unconditional order in writing, addressed by one person to another, signed by the person giving it, requiring the person to whom it is addressed to pay on demand at a fixed or determinable future time *a sum certain in money* to or to the order of a specified person, or to bearer. (emphasis added)

Section 83(1) of the Bills of Exchange Act 1882:

> A promissory note is an unconditional promise in writing made by one person to another signed by the maker, engaging to pay, on demand at a fixed or determinable future time, *a sum certain in money*, to, or to the order of, a specified person or to bearer. (emphasis added)

N.B. The Uniform Law on Bills of Exchange and Promissory Notes (Geneva Conventions on Bills of Exchange of 1932) provides (Articles 1 and 75): "A bill of exchange/promissory note contains ... an unconditional order/promise to pay *a determinate sum of money*." (emphasis added)

Appendix 2

Avals

Section 28(1) of the Bills of Exchange Act 1882:

> An accommodation party to a bill is a person who has signed a bill as drawer, acceptor, or endorser, without receiving value therefor, and for the purpose of lending his name to some other person.

Section 56 of the Bills of Exchange Act 1882:

> Where a person signs a bill otherwise than as drawer or acceptor, he thereby incurs the liabilities of an endorser to a holder in due course.

N.B. The Uniform Law on Bills of Exchange and Promissory Notes provides:

> [Article 30:] Payment of a bill of exchange may be guaranteed by an "aval" as to the whole or part of its amount. This guarantee may be given by a third person or even by a person who has signed as a party to the bill.

[Article 31:] The "aval" is given either on the bill itself or on an "allonge." It is expressed by the words "good as aval" or by any other equivalent formula. It is signed by the giver of the "aval." It is deemed to be constituted by the mere signature of the giver of the "aval" placed on the face of the bill, except in the case of the signature of the drawee or of the drawer. An "aval" must specify for whose account it is given. In default of this, it is deemed to be given for the drawer.

[Article 32:] The giver of an "aval" is bound in the same manner as the person to whom he has become guarantor. His undertaking is valid even when the liability which he has guaranteed is inoperative for any reason other than defect of form. He has, when he pays a bill of exchange, the rights arising out of the bill of exchange against the person guaranteed and against those who are liable to the latter on the bill of exchange.

9

Official Export Financing and Arrangements: US, UK, EC, and OECD

GRANT D. ALDONAS

Chapter Outline

9.1 Introduction

9.2 US Export Assistance
    9.2.1 Eximbank
    9.2.2 Private Export Funding Corporation
    9.2.3 Foreign Credit Insurance Association
    9.2.4 Small Business Administration
    9.2.5 Other Potential Sources
    9.2.6 Legislative Initiatives on "Tied" Aid

9.3 UK Export Assistance
    9.3.1 Export Credits Guarantee Department
    9.3.2 Effect of Privatization

9.4 European Community Export Financing Arrangements
    9.4.1 Origins of the Program
    9.4.2 Current Developments

9.5 OECD Guidelines
    9.5.1 Current Rules
    9.5.2 Continuing Negotiations

The author would like to thank Robert Crick of the Export Credits Guarantee Department (London) for his assistance in the preparation of this outline, which is based on a joint presentation given at the Conference. The views, however, are the author's own and he takes sole responsibility for any errors or omissions.

9.6 Searching for Alternatives
    9.6.1 World Bank
    9.6.2 International Finance Corporation
9.7 Financing Exports to Eastern Europe and the former Soviet Union: Official Export Financing at Work

9.1 Introduction

The world of trade finance and official export financing programs has undergone significant changes since the early 1980s. The pace of that change, due to the enduring debt crisis in the developing world and a more circumspect attitude on the part of governments providing official export credits, is accelerating. Apart from agriculture, where international agreement on limiting subsidies remains elusive, governments have drawn back from what their critics have deemed the "profligacy" of the past, and reconsidered the role and scope of their official export financing arrangements.

Within that context, this chapter provides a survey of current developments affecting official export financing arrangements in the US, the UK, and the European Community. The survey discusses the effect on these various official export financing programs of the guidelines developed by members of the OECD. The survey underscores how changes in official export financing programs have led exporters to search for alternative means to lower the cost of trade finance, particularly lending by the multilateral development banks and their various affiliates. Finally, the survey looks at the US as one example of the response of official credit agencies to the recent opening of the Eastern European and former Soviet markets to Western exports.

9.2 US Export Assistance

Although the activities of the US Export-Import Bank (Eximbank) are the most widely recognized US export financing program, the US government provides assistance to US exporters through a variety of other avenues as well. There are a number of export assistance programs available that are less widely publicized.

The various programs discussed below are available for financing most export sales of US capital equipment. Due to the nature of the commodities and the differing public policy goals that the programs are designed to achieve, the following discussion does not address two major sources of trade finance available from the US government: export credits for agricultural commodities extended by the US Commodity Credit Corporation and loans for purchases of military equipment provided under the US Defense Department's Foreign Military Sales program.

9.2.1 Eximbank

The most significant source of official export financing in the US is the Eximbank. In contrast to certain other governments' programs, Eximbank financing is, by statutory mandate, enjoined from supplanting private sources of export financing. Eximbank's role is to assist US exporters when such private financing is unavailable, and the bank's programs are largely defined by that policy constraint on its operations.

Existing programs Eximbank assistance takes four forms: direct loans to foreign buyers, foreign buyer intermediary loans, foreign buyer guarantees, and working capital guarantees.

- *Direct loans*. Under its direct loan program, the Eximbank offers fixed-rate loans directly to foreign buyers of US goods to help US exporters enter markets where financing might not otherwise be available, particularly when necessary to compete with exporters from other countries that benefit from government-subsidized trade financing. Like all Eximbank loan and guarantee programs, direct loans can cover up to 85 percent of the US export value of the sale. The foreign buyer must make a cash payment to the US exporter of at least 15 percent of the US export value.

Loans under this program generally involve amounts over $10 million or a repayment term of more than seven years (loans for lesser amounts or shorter terms are usually financed by an intermediary loan or guarantee: see below). Interest rates on direct loans are fixed for the life of the loan at the minimum rate applicable to the category of the importing country under the export credit guidelines established by the OECD.

- *Intermediary loans*. The bulk of Eximbank financing is in the form of "intermediary loans," which provide fixed-rate funding for intermediary financial institutions or other qualifying "responsible parties" – including exporters – that have themselves made fixed-rate loans to foreign buyers. Intermediary loans typically involve medium-term commitments (seven years or less) of up to $10 million. As with direct loans, the Eximbank will ask, when appropriate, for evidence of foreign competitors with subsidized official financing before it grants an intermediary loan.

Intermediary loans are structured as standby commitments that the intermediary can draw upon at any time during the term of the underlying loan. Assuming the underlying loan to the foreign borrower is made at the minimum OECD fixed rate, the rate charged by the Eximbank to intermediary financial institutions will be discounted 50–150 basis points from the OECD rate, depending upon the amount of the total loan commitment. Loans to other responsible party intermediaries are made at the OECD rate. Eximbank intermediary loans may be combined with Eximbank guarantees: see below.

■ *Foreign buyer guarantees.* Eximbank guarantees provide repayment protection for private sector loans to creditworthy buyers of US exports. These guarantees may be combined with Eximbank intermediary loans, but are also available separately for both fixed or floating market-rate loans. Two types of guarantees are available: comprehensive, and political risk only. Eximbank's comprehensive guarantee covers all types of risk of non-payment of principal, including both commercial and political risks. Commercial risks covered include those typically covered by such programs – currency devaluation, buyer insolvency, deterioration of the buyer's market, and natural disasters. Political risk coverage protects against expropriation, war, cancellation of an existing import or business license, and other forms of intervention in the buyer's business. In the case of common ownership between the exporter and the foreign buyer, only political risk guarantees are available.

All Eximbank guarantees commit the "full faith and credit" of the US government. Guaranteed notes are freely transferable.

■ *Working capital guarantees.* The working capital guarantee program provides repayment guarantees to lenders on secured (by inventory or accounts receivable), short-term working capital loans to qualified exporters that otherwise would not be made. The guarantee can apply either to a single export-related loan or to a revolving line of credit. If the exporter defaults, the Eximbank covers up to 90 percent of the loan's principal and interest. This program protects only the lender from default by the exporter. It does not cover the exporter if the buyer defaults. That type of risk must be covered by the Eximbank's comprehensive guarantee (discussed above) or by FCIA insurance (discussed below).

General conditions on Eximbank financing Eximbank loans and guarantees are subject to various conditions and limitations. Eximbank programs may, for example, cover only 85 percent of the US export value of a transaction. The Eximbank must find "reasonable assurance" of repayment in each transaction that it assists. In making this case-by-case determination, an Eximbank reviewing officer will consider the financial position of a foreign buyer, as well as the reliability of that buyer's financial statements.

Perhaps the most significant general limitation on Eximbank financing is the requirement that the goods involved must be over 50 percent US content. Foreign content of 15–49 percent will proportionately limit the amount of financing available.

Eximbank assistance is not available for military goods. As a result, exports of manufacturing equipment may be examined to determine the extent to which the items to be produced by the exported equipment are ultimately sold to military entities. If the Eximbank were to conclude that the exported equipment would be used in significant part to produce tires for military vehicles, for example, the Bank could refuse to provide assistance.

The Eximbank's policy of not supporting defense-related sales is, however, currently under review. Various federal departments and agencies, most notably the Departments of Commerce and Defense, are advocating changing this policy to allow the Eximbank to guarantee US defense exports as a means of preserving the US industrial base and improving the US trade balance. The Eximbank itself is resisting such change. Arms export sales from the US already benefit from export financing assistance under the Foreign Military Sales (FMS) program.

9.2.2 Private Export Funding Corporation

The Private Export Funding Corporation (PEFCO) is a private corporation owned by a group of fifty-one banks and seven industrial corporations. PEFCO was created by the Bankers Association for Foreign Trade in conjunction with the US government. It serves as a supplementary source of long-term financing for foreign buyers of US goods and services the high cost and long economic lives of which require large amounts of money for extended terms. PEFCO assists such sales by making long-term, fixed-rate loans with repayment terms that would be unacceptable to commercial banks.

All PEFCO loans must have the Eximbank's guarantee. After the Eximbank has issued a Preliminary Commitment making available its guarantee of the financing needed on a particular transaction, the lender involved with that sale will usually contact PEFCO on behalf of the borrower or the exporter to discuss that portion of the financing that the lender chooses not to keep in its own portfolio. The buyer or exporter may, however, contact PEFCO directly.

9.2.3 Foreign Credit Insurance Association

The Foreign Credit Insurance Association (FCIA) was created by the Eximbank and a group of private insurance companies in 1961 to help US exporters develop and expand their overseas sales by protecting them against loss should a foreign buyer default for political or commercial reasons. Eximbank insures the political risks under the policies and either insures or reinsures all the commercial risks.

FCIA, as Eximbank's agent, is responsible for marketing, servicing, and administering the insurance program. FCIA policies assist exporters in obtaining export financing more easily because, with prior approval, the proceeds of the policy can be assigned to a financial institution as collateral. FCIA offers a variety of policies tailored to the different needs of exporters, including single- and multi-buyer policies for both short- and medium-term sales. The terms and conditions of a single-buyer policy will depend upon the particulars of the insured's transaction with the buyer. The terms for multi-buyer policies are based on the applicant's terms of sale, experience with export sales, its historical and anticipated export volume, foreign markets, and the credit history of its buyers.

Exporters interested in FCIA insurance must complete an "Application for Quotation" and attach the following documentation:

- the exporter's most recent annual report or signed interim financial statement;
- a credit agency report that is no more than six months old; and
- brochures or other literature describing the exporter's products.

After the exporter itself is approved, it must obtain FCIA approval of its foreign buyers, generally by submitting an application for a Special Buyer Credit Limit (SBCL) for each buyer. An SBCL establishes a dollar limit on the amount of insured credit an exporter may have outstanding with that buyer. SBCL applications typically require at least two current credit reports from different sources, but SBCL requests above $100,000 also require financial statements for the current fiscal year.

9.2.4 Small Business Administration

For eligible small businesses, the US Small Business Administration (SBA) provides three useful financing mechanisms. First, for small businesses considering exporting into overseas markets, SBA will provide a guarantee of up to 85 percent of a private lending institution's loan to an eligible small business, provided that SBA's guarantee does not exceed the $500,000 statutory limit.

Second, SBA has established an Export Revolving Line of Credit loan guarantee program. Any number of withdrawals and repayments can be made as long as the exporter does not exceed the specified credit limit and disbursements are made within a stated maturity period. Proceeds must be used to finance labor and materials needed for manufacturing or wholesaling for export, or otherwise entering or developing foreign markets.

Third, SBA will serve as a co-guarantor with the Eximbank for trade credits to small businesses for export or for financing the activities of certain export trading companies. The co-guarantees cover loans in principal amounts ranging from $200,000 to $1 million per borrower. The co-guarantees will cover 85 percent of the amount of the loan.

Eligibility for SBA programs varies by industry. The rules generally set limits in terms of annual sales or number of employees. Whether a particular entity is eligible may depend on its affiliation with other corporate entities as well.

9.2.5 Other Potential Sources

Due to the continuing debt service problems experienced in the developing world, exporters and their intermediaries have been forced to pursue creative alternatives to traditional export financing mechanisms. The increase in offsets, countertrade, and forfaiting over the last decade are all evidence of that trend. The following discussion focuses on how US exporters can, in addition, benefit from project assistance offered by the US government.

Overseas Private Investment Corporation The focus of the Overseas Private Investment Corporation (OPIC) is on investment, not sales. The only sales explicitly eligible for OPIC assistance are long-term (more than three years) sales to government agencies. A government agency for this purpose is an entity supported by the full faith and credit of the central government. Such sales are eligible for an OPIC guarantee of performance on advance payment terms.

OPIC more traditionally insures and/or finances US investment abroad. OPIC insures US foreign investment against a wide variety of risk, including expropriation, inconvertibility of earnings, and the failure of a foreign subsidiary or joint venture to return principal and interest to its US parent.

As holds true for a number of the programs discussed below, however, the investment funds offered by OPIC can provide a channel for low-cost export financing. For example, a US investor eligible for financing under OPIC programs will likely use some portion of those funds on purchases of capital equipment. An exporter working closely with the US investor may in turn see those funds flowing through the US investor as a source of export financing. Alternatively, OPIC financing and insurance can be viewed as a means of reducing and spreading the risk associated with a particular project sufficiently to encourage commercial financing of export sales to the project managers abroad.

Agency for International Development The Agency for International Development (AID) administers US foreign economic assistance programs throughout the developing world. Development assistance is provided in the form of loans and grants. The intent is to encourage, particularly through the development of a viable private sector, the long-term economic growth of countries in various stages of economic development.

While not a direct export assistance program, the projects financed by AID development assistance funds often involve funds for purchases of significant amounts of capital equipment and materials not available in the local economy. Congress has increasingly pressured AID to ensure that its funds go toward financing exports of US goods and services. Thus, exporters and financial intermediaries can, by working with the AID project cycle, potentially gain access to development assistance funds as an additional source of financing for exports to developing country markets.

Trade and Development Agency The US Trade and Development Agency (TDA) is designed to assist exporters in penetrating or expanding markets for US goods in developing countries. TDA provides financing for feasibility studies and other planning services. TDA co-finances, on a reimbursable grant basis, planning services for projects in which a private US investor intends to have an equity participation. TDA also has statutory authority to assist in the development of foreign sources of supply of strategic minerals and metals, which often involves assistance to US exporters of equipment needed to complete such projects.

The TDA can serve, in effect, as a source of direct export assistance to firms providing a variety of consulting services in the planning stages of export projects. It also serves as an indirect source of financing for US exporters by freeing other sources of capital for direct export assistance through reductions in the cost of planning and feasibility studies.

9.2.6 Legislative Initiatives on "Tied" Aid

While the US has pressed its trading partners in the OECD to eliminate the concessional element of official export credits, particularly the practice of "tied" aid, the US Congress appears to be headed in exactly the opposite direction. A bill introduced in Congress recently – the Aid for Trade Act – is intended to assist US exports of capital goods by increasing tied aid within the US foreign aid program and promoting tied aid credits within the US export financing system.

Under the legislation, a substantial portion of all US bilateral economic assistance would have to be used for the construction, design, and servicing of capital products. The bill would also authorize a 15 percent increase in the Eximbank's direct loan ceiling for each of the next five years, with a substantial share of new funds – $400 million – dedicated to Eximbank's Tied Aid Credit Fund.

Significantly, in introducing the legislation, the bill's sponsors noted that the practice of tying aid to trade was widely used by America's major competitors in the international market place. The legislation was described as a further supplement to the seemingly endless round of trade legislation recently introduced in the US to improve the country's international competitiveness.

Needless to say, the legislation conflicts directly with the US initiative in the OECD. For that reason, President Bush opposed the measure and his veto threat proved sufficient to scuttle such proposals in successive appropriation bills.

That policy, however, may change with the election of Governor Clinton in late 1992. The President-Elect has made no specific statement regarding tied aid, but his general trade policy pronouncements evince a greater willingness to intervene in the market in favor of US industry and support for a policy of tied aid would be consistent with that approach.

9.3 UK Export Assistance

The United Kingdom's official export credit agency is the Export Credits Guarantee Department (ECGD). The ECGD is officially a government department, responsible to the British Secretary of State for Trade and Industry. The ECGD, as part of its statutory mandate, is also answerable to the Export Guarantees Advisory Council – made up of leading bankers and businessmen – with which the ECGD must consult prior to offering certain types of guarantees.

The ECGD's statutory mandate includes the provision of guarantees to UK exporters against non-payment by overseas buyers for specified risks and the provision of similar guarantees to banks intended to mobilize export financing. In addition to its financing activities, the ECGD represents the UK in negotiations with other European Community countries designed to develop a uniform position on export credit guarantees.

As the discussion below will explore, the ECGD's nature, organization, and responsibilities are the subject of continuing debate within the United Kingdom. There is a significant effort underway to privatize the agency, which would ultimately require a substantial change in its current operations.

9.3.1 Export Credits Guarantee Department

The ECGD offers two basic types of programs for exporters, taking the form either of comprehensive short-term policies or of specific guarantees.[1] The comprehensive short-term policies are designed for all types of export businesses that sell on credit of up to 180 days. There is a preference to cover the whole of a company's export turnover, but the ECGD will tailor comprehensive short-term policies to meet the individual policyholder's needs.

The preference is based on the diversity of buyers and a greater spread of the consequent risks to the ECGD when covering a company's entire export output. That spread is reflected in more favorable premium rates.

Under comprehensive short-term policies, the ECGD normally covers 90 percent of the loss for commercial risks and 95 percent for political risks. Commercial risks include buyer's insolvency, default by the buyer, and the buyer's refusal to accept goods tendered under the export contract. Political risks cover such items as war, insurrection, and, importantly, currency inconvertibility.

Under comprehensive policies, the ECGD does not offer separate commercial and political risk insurance. Effectively, the only variation offered is between pre-shipment and post-shipment coverage. ECGD policies normally cover only post-shipment risks, although the exporter may opt for pre-shipment coverage as well.

In contrast to comprehensive short-term policies, specific guarantees offered by the ECGD are provided for single contracts for capital goods or projects that do not fit the comprehensive pattern. The variation on when coverage begins (pre-shipment or post-shipment) is the same under specific guarantees as under comprehensive policies. The coverage, however, is limited to 90 percent on all risks. ECGD will also consider separate political risk coverage on its specific guarantees.

Eligibility for coverage on ECGD's programs for exporters is based largely on the risks associated with the transactions. The ECGD does assess projects in all overseas markets; at times it will set limits on the total amount ECGD will insure and may introduce certain conditions, such as stipulations about the method and timing of payment.

There are percentage limits on the non-UK content permitted in exports covered by the ECGD. They vary depending on whether there is some bilateral or multilateral agreement with regard to the inclusion of components from certain markets. For example, European Community subcontracts may form up to 30 or 40 percent of the export contract issued by ECGD, depending on the circumstances.

A slightly different regime applies to ECGD insurance of credits offered by financing banks, although the eligibility rules are the same. On supplier credits, the ECGD may offer a 100 percent guarantee. Such policies are available, however, only for business on credit of longer than two years. ECGD retains a right of recourse to the exporter, in certain circumstances, under its supplier credit program.

The ECGD will also provide buyer's credit in the form of guarantees to the lending bank insuring the repayment of loans to overseas borrowers. The ECGD offers such coverage on purchases of major UK capital goods worth £1 million or more. The guarantees are normally for 100 percent of the interest and principal.

In addition, the ECGD offers project financing for project loans of £20 million or more. The coverage is for certain defined political risks and, in some cases, commercial risks as well. The basic structure for project finance is the same as other ECGD-guaranteed buyer credits, but the lending bank may not be offered 100 percent coverage, depending on the selected risks covered by the ECGD guarantee.

Lastly, the ECGD offers guarantees on lines of credit provided by banks to certain buyers to facilitate the placing of orders for British goods. The guarantees are for 100 percent of the principal and interest on loans repayable over a two- to five-year period.

9.3.2 *Effect of Privatization*

The ECGD appears to be following an increasing trend away from governments themselves being involved in the export credit business, toward using some private or quasi-public entity to act as the government's "agent" in providing export credit financing. A move is underway to privatize the ECGD.

The precise contours and the consequences of that move are not yet clear. It is ECGD's short-term portfolio that has attracted the greatest interest, from both British and foreign bidders. The intent behind the privatization is to permit a recast ECGD to compete more aggressively for business after the EC insurance market is liberalized as part of the single market program.

Conversely, the bidding on ECGD's short-term business reflects an industry-wide recognition that ECGD's long-term business may not be commercially viable without continuing government support. That has led to further questions as to how the ECGD may lay off some of the risk associated with its long-term portfolio on to a reinsurance market, which has, in turn, led some to suggest the creation of an EC-wide export credit reinsurance facility. ECGD's future hangs in the balance.

9.4 European Community Export Financing Arrangements

Due to the nature of the activities of official export credit agencies, their supervision falls within the province of the European Community under article 113 of the Treaty of Rome and the EC's Common Commercial Policy. Accordingly, it is the EC that represents the member countries in negotiations with other countries on export credit matters – the prime example being the OECD export credit guidelines. The following discussion examines the existing arrangement among EC member countries and continuing negotiations designed to develop a common approach for upcoming discussions in the OECD.

9.4.1 Origins of the Program

The EC member countries meet monthly in Brussels to formulate a common policy on export credits. Those discussions focus on two principal topics: adopting a common position for OECD talks and developing a consensus on the structure of trade finance in EC member country programs.

No specific legislation establishes a mandate for these discussions and no legislation to regulate the activities of export credit agencies is being considered. Rather, the existing informal arrangement draws its authority directly from the Treaty of Rome, under which the EC was established.

9.4.2 Current Developments

Current discussions among the EC countries have focused on the "segmentation" of the trade finance market. The talks have recognized the separation of short-term from medium-term and long-term markets.

The short-term market is dominated by financing of exports within the EC and to other OECD countries – a market for which there is already substantial private sector competition. The medium- to long-term market, on the other hand, largely involves insurance against political risks associated with exporting to the developing world.

The net effect – exemplified by the experience of the UK's ECGD discussed above – is to segment the market and have official export credit agencies to respond accordingly. This has led to a number of governments' interest in privatizing their existing short-term programs, and retaining only the medium- to long-term business in which continuing government involvement may be required.

The EC discussions have also led EC member countries to attempt to achieve a consensus on basic principles of coverage (risks covered, percentage of loss, and date of payment of claims). The effort is designed to avoid any possible distortion of competition among EC member countries due to differences in coverage available from individual members' export credit facilities.

9.5 OECD Guidelines

The origins of the OECD guidelines lay in the rapid expansion in the early 1970s of project finance that involved some official support as a means of making an individual company's bid more competitive. The dangers of a potential "credit race" led the members of the OECD to initiate discussions aimed at introducing certain rules to govern the use of official credits.

The result is formally known as the Arrangement on Guidelines for Officially Supported Export Credits. The guidelines do not constitute a formal international accord. They represent, instead, a "gentlemen's agreement."

9.5.1 Current Rules

The OECD guidelines apply to "officially supported export credits with a repayment term of two years or more relating to contracts for sales of goods and/or services or to leases equivalent in effect to such sales contracts."[2] The guidelines provide special rules for four sectors: ships, nuclear power plants, other power-generating facilities, and aircraft.[3] The guidelines expressly exclude export credits relating to exports of military equipment and agricultural commodities.[4]

The guidelines introduced four basic disciplines, governing

- minimum down-payments;
- length of time for which credits could be extended;
- minimum interest rates; and
- elements of development assistance or tied aid that could be combined with official export credits on a given project.

The current rules require, for example, that all officially supported credits call for a 15 percent downpayment at the time of delivery. The maximum length of the credit (i.e. the time allowed for repayment) varies according to categories that are based on the relative economic development of the recipient country. The guidelines include a matrix of repayment terms and interest rates that apply to all export credits subject to the Arrangement. Finally, participants in the Arrangement have agreed not to provide tied aid unless it involves a "concessional" element of 35 percent or more outright grant.

The last landmark change in the consensus came in 1987, although current talks in the OECD may introduce significant further changes. The 1987 changes raised the requisite concessional element in tied aid financing from 25 percent to its current 35 percent level. The 1987 changes also effectively eliminated matrix financing for the Category I or relatively rich countries.

9.5.2 Continuing Negotiations

There is widespread disagreement about the future role of official export credit agencies in general. The pattern will necessarily vary by country, but renewed discussions within the OECD to eliminate the subsidy element associated with official credits are likely to diminish their importance in financing exports.

The main issue for OECD governments is the question of sovereign debt. That issue has been joined squarely by the significant losses and continued reschedulings of official debt, particularly export credits provided to a number of Latin American and African countries. There are both political and economic incentives for official export credit agencies to continue lending in such risky markets, but the renewed discussions on limiting official export credits in the OECD suggest that some governments, particularly the US, have at last gagged on such requests, arguing that the suppliant industries already benefit enough from government largesse.

The proposed changes in the OECD guidelines governing export credits could radically alter the structure of such financing, and the contours of such an agreement could be in place within one year. A plan proposed by the US and Canada would introduce further cutbacks in routine interest rate subsidies for middle-income countries under the OECD guidelines and would include cutbacks for even the poorest countries.

That proposal would also involve restraints on governments' ability to increase the subsidy element associated with official export credits by adding them to a package that includes development aid provided at concessional rates (i.e. tied aid). Under such a proposal, officially backed fixed rate financing would, in most cases, be permitted only at market rates of interest as defined by the OECD through the Commercial Interest Reference Rate formula, which is linked to the interest rates on government bonds.

There is also a continuing debate about whether to permit the extension of maturities on official export credits. The current limit stands at ten years. The UK has suggested that, if all lending is to be at market rates in the future, there is no justification for imposing any limit on the maturity of such financing other than that which the market would introduce. The US, which has traditionally balked at any attempt to extend maturities on official export credit financing, has indicated it is willing to consider extending maturities on credits lent at market rates of interest, but only if the extension of permissible maturities is not artificially long. That policy stance, however, has not prevented the US from proposing the lengthening of the special maturity rate on export financing for commercial sales of aircraft from twelve to eighteen years – a market where the extension of maturities would significantly benefit US commercial interests.

The current OECD discussions have been intertwined with the US proposal to ban all tied aid in certain sectors. The example most often cited is that of the telecommunications sector, where official export financing could, in effect, provide certain producers with an effective monopoly on a developing country's entire communications sector. Other industries often cited include the transportation and power generation sectors, and, for different reasons, the steel industry, where the US has opposed any concessional lending that would exacerbate the already substantial excess capacity in world-wide steel production.

The net effect of the US initiatives within the OECD is again to reduce the effect and significance of official export credit agencies as a tool for gaining access to new markets. Should a compromise be reached, as seems likely, the final arrangement is likely to alter not only the role of official export credit agencies, but the activities of commercial banks as well. Commercial banks will no longer have the opportunity to follow an official export credit agency into a new market. It is not clear that commercial banks are in a position, absent such support, to provide adequate financing.

9.6 Searching for Alternatives

The gradual trend toward eliminating official export credit financing has led exporters to seek alternative means for lowering the financing costs associated with exports, particularly to markets in the developing world. That search has led exporters to turn, in part, to the multilateral development banks as one means of providing a secure source of financing at the lowest cost possible. Of the various lending agencies, the two primary alternatives used to date have been the World Bank and its affiliate, the International Finance Corporation.

9.6.1 World Bank

The World Bank provides development assistance to its member nations. World Bank assistance is available only to member nations, and must be requested by an agency of the member government. Most World Bank programs take the form of project loans.

Applying for and receiving World Bank assistance involves a process lasting several years, and procurement under the resulting loan must be competitive. None the less, for exporters willing to work with the Bank's project cycle, World Bank funds can be a significant source of financing for exports, particularly for large-scale projects.

The World Bank has separately developed an export financing program for certain limited markets. The Bank's Export Credit Enhanced Leverage or EXCEL program is designed as a co-financing scheme to provide export assistance for sales to markets where such financing would otherwise be unavailable even from official export credit agencies.

9.6.2 International Finance Corporation

The World Bank's investment affiliate, the International Finance Corporation (IFC) can also provide a potential source of funding. The mandate of the IFC is to promote private sector development in its member countries. The IFC does this by financing private sector projects, mobilizing funds from other investors and lenders for projects, and providing technical assistance and advisory services to both governments and private enterprises. Given its focus on private sector development, the IFC emphasizes assistance to private entities or those facing imminent privatization, although the IFC will allow minority government investment in a project.

IFC projects must be economically viable and generally involve more than $15 million. The IFC takes a flexible approach in its assistance, and will consider equity shares of up to 25 percent and assistance in the form of loans. Unlike finance from other lenders, IFC financing can cover all project costs, including not just construction costs and work-in-progress financing, but also the cost of permanent working capital. In addition, the IFC is willing to be the lead financier on a project, providing a portion of the needed assistance from its own resources and then forming a syndicate to supply the rest.

As noted above with respect to OPIC, IFC funding can provide a source of low-cost export financing. Again, it requires a willingness on the part of exporters and their intermediaries to work with the IFC and the investor, but the reward can be worth the effort as an essentially risk-free avenue of entering new markets, such as those developing in Eastern Europe.

9.7 Financing Exports to Eastern Europe and the Former Soviet Union: Official Export Financing at Work

In the wake of recent changes in Eastern Europe and the former Soviet Union, Western exporters are once again returning cautiously to markets that were largely cut off by the general cooling of relations between East and West in the late 1970s and early 1980s. Western exporters have, as they did during the heyday of "detente" in the early 1970s, sought significant commitments from official export credit agencies to permit competitive access to the East European and former Soviet markets.

That has been no less true for US exporters than for those of Western Europe. Of the US export financing programs discussed above, virtually all are open to Eastern Europe and the former Soviet Union. For example, Eximbank assistance is currently available for US export sales to Czechoslovakia, Hungary, Poland and certain other East European states.[5]

In the case of East European countries, Eximbank has, however, often found that financial statements and accounting records maintained by government entities under the earlier non-market economies were inadequate to ascertain the creditworthiness of those entities. Thus, in Czechoslovakia and Hungary – where there are still relatively few private buyers – the Eximbank will usually require that would-be buyers be guaranteed by a national bank or other entity supported by the full faith and credit of the national government.

FCIA insurance is currently available for Czechoslovakia and Hungary. In Poland, the FCIA will currently insure only letters of credit. No insurance is currently available to Bulgaria. In Eastern Europe,

OPIC coverage is currently available only in Poland, Hungary, and Czechoslovakia.

In addition, the US has recently authorized new sources of funding dedicated specifically to Eastern Europe. On November 28, 1989, Congress enacted the Support for East European Democracy Act of 1989 (SEED Act), which comprises a variety of undertakings to assist those East European countries that are "institutionalizing political democracy and economic pluralism." Besides its investment, political, and humanitarian initiatives, the SEED Act also

> grants Poland and Hungary eligibility for OPIC and Eximbank programs, and provides guarantees to AID of 200 million for loans to Hungary to import U.S. products [guarantees are actually made to Eximbank, which in turns provides the guarantees to the U.S. exporter; AID has already transferred the appropriation to Eximbank and does not play a role in private commercial activity].

A similar piece of legislation, called "SEED II," was introduced earlier this year and is currently pending before Congress. SEED II, as proposed, would further increase US assistance to East Europe, but would not directly affect US export sales to those countries.

At the time of this writing, previous limits on Eximbank export financing for the newly independent states of the former Soviet Union have been lifted. The Eximbank had almost $200 million in approved loans pending the lifting of the credit limits and the naming by Russia of a foreign trade bank to act as an official guarantor of the Eximbank credits.

With those obstacles removed, Eximbank financing is now available throughout the former Soviet Union, as is FCIA insurance. OPIC programs are available in most of the newly independent states as well, although OPIC investment insurance and project financing are still blocked in some parts of the former Soviet Union by the failure to sign certain investment agreements. At the time of writing in late 1992, OPIC expects those agreements to be signed shortly and for its programs to be available throughout the region in 1993.

Notes

1 Organization for Economic Cooperation and Development, *The Export Credit Financing Systems in OECD Member Countries* (4th edn, 1990).
2 Arrangement on Guidelines for Officially Supported Export Credits

("Arrangement"), article (1) (a), reprinted in *Export Credit Financing Systems*, p. 267.
3 Ibid., article (1) (b).
4 Ibid., article (1) (c).
5 Until recently, Eximbank assistance to Poland was limited to short-term credit insurance only (repayable within one year from the date of arrival at entry port). On May 12, 1990, however, the President announced that medium-term loans would also be available. According to Eximbank staff, the Bank will consider intermediary and direct loans to private sector entities or to state institutions preparing for imminent privatization in amounts up to $15 million, with a maximum repayment term of five years. The new policy officially took effect June 1, 1990.

10

The Increasing Importance of Countertrade

ADRIAN A. MONTAGUE

Chapter Outline

10.1 Introduction
10.2 A Definition?
10.3 Objectives of the Importing Country
10.4 Traditional Structure
    10.4.1 Barter Transactions
    10.4.2 Counterpurchase Arrangements
    10.4.3 Variants of Counterpurchase
    10.4.4 Buy-back Arrangements
10.5 Increasing Usage of Offset Arrangements
10.6 Concluding Observations

10.1 Introduction

The Project and Export Policy Division of the UK Department of Trade and Industry issues a booklet that contains valuable guidance for exporters on the general topic of "Countertrade." The booklet summarizes the difficulties of dealing with countertrade transactions in the following terms: "Countertrade is not a game for amateurs. Even experienced specialists expect, at best, only about one deal in ten to succeed, and even the successful transactions can prove more expensive and difficult than foreseen." There is only a limited body of experience in dealing with countertrade transactions, and this lack of familiarity has caused them to attain at best something of a mystique and at worst an altogether unmerited reputation for being slightly shady. The purpose of this chapter is to provide an introduction to the subject of countertrade by outlining the various forms that a countertrade transaction may take and the roles of the various participants in a countertrade deal, by looking briefly at the problems that can arise from such transactions, and by assessing the importance of the role countertrade plays in world trade.

10.2 A Definition?

Where better to start, then, than with a definition of the term "countertrade"? In 1988 the Secretary-General of the United Nations Commission on International Trade Law (UNCITRAL) presented a report to the Twenty-First session of the Commission in New York. His report contained a preliminary study of the legal issues in international countertrade. It started with the following definition of countertrade transactions:

> A countertrade transaction, as it is normally understood, is an economic transaction in which one party supplies, or procures the supply of goods or other economic value to the second party, and, in return, the first party agrees to purchase or procures to be purchased from the second party, or from a party designated by the second party, goods or other economic value, so as to achieve an agreed ratio between the reciprocal performances.

This definition is more comprehensive than clear. The problem is that there is no one single form of countertrade transaction: "countertrade" is an umbrella term for a whole range of commercial mechanisms for reciprocal trade. The financial press has the habit of referring to countertrade as involving "trading goods for goods, not money." Although the suggestion that money is not used as a medium of exchange in countertrade transactions is both incorrect and unnecessarily alarmist to the uninitiated, none the less there is more than a grain of truth in this tag. And, although not as accurate as UNCITRAL's definition, it does have the merit of conciseness.

10.3 Objectives of the Importing Country

In order to set the scene, it may be helpful to identify the principal commercial objectives that an importing country sets itself by engaging in countertrade:

- Countertrade may be used as a financing mechanism in cases where proceeds realized from the export of countertrade goods are used to finance an import. This is particularly the case in the developing world when goods have to be paid for in convertible currencies and the importer's country is short of foreign exchange that can be used for these purposes.
- Even where there is no shortage of foreign exchange, exports of countertrade goods may be used as a means of facilitating the marketing of goods for which the importing country is seeking to develop its own export markets.
- In other cases, countertrade may be used as an instrument of industrial development, for example when countertrade is made part of an industrial cooperation arrangement or if it attracts foreign investment or technology into areas where the importing country is concerned to develop its own technological capability.

The first two of these objectives, earning the foreign exchange to pay for imports and developing export markets, are clearly sales-related. In the importing country's financial accounts they are typically current account transactions, the parties deal entirely at arm's length, and no enduring cooperation is required between them. On the other hand, the considerations underlying transactions that are intended to secure the third type of objective are rather different: often they are, for the importing countries, transactions of strategic importance, they may take place on capital account, and tend to be characterized by the need for continual cooperation between the parties, especially where a transfer of technology is involved. They are in essence investment-related, and they require different techniques in drafting the contractual arrangements. In many ways the investment-related countertrade deals resemble joint ventures and many of the same considerations in balancing the parties' mutual rights of control over the venture and reconciling possibly conflicting interests must be employed. It is no coincidence, for example, that many transactions that are known as "joint ventures" in the People's Republic of China take a form similar to "buy-back" deals as they are known in Western countries.

10.4 Traditional Structure

Before considering the various structures of countertrade transactions that are encountered in practice, a note of caution must be sounded: the descriptions adopted in this chapter are by no means "terms of art." There is no uniform terminology to describe particular types of countertrade: for example, particularly in the context of East European countertrade transactions, the term "compensation" is used either generically to describe the whole range of possible structures for countertrade transactions or, more particularly, to describe what English usage has come to refer to as "counterpurchase" transactions. English usage, in contrast, treats the term "compensation" as a synonym for "buy-back" which is commonly known in Eastern Europe as "coproduction," and "coproduction" in its turn is often identified in the West as a type of "offset" arrangement. If care is not exercised in relation to the terminology employed in describing the different structures of transactions total confusion may easily result. UNCITRAL has been making a most welcome attempt to promote a common terminology in international countertrade transactions. The draft chapters for the legal guide on countertrade presented to the Twenty-Third session of the Commission in New York in June 1990 contained a helpful glossary of terms which broadly endorsed English usage, and this is the usage adopted in this chapter.

10.4.1 *Barter Transactions*

The first type of transaction to be considered is the simplest form of countertrade – a barter or exchange transaction.

Barter is, of course, the oldest form of commercial transaction known to man. It involves simply the exchange of goods for goods without the medium of cash payments. For all its ancestry, however, the very simplicity of the structure of barter rendered it ill-adapted to the sophisticated needs of modern trade and finance, as is evidenced by the basic elements of barter transactions:

- bilateral arrangement usually contained in a single contract;
- goods specified in quantity and quality without monetary valuation;

Figure 10.1 Structure of barter

- consideration consisting entirely of counterdelivery with no cash payments; and
- deliveries typically concurrent.

Barter deals are by definition bilateral arrangements and are usually contained in a single contract. This is unusual in itself since, for good reason, much attention is usually given to separating the export and countertrade elements of a transaction into separate documents.

The goods are specified in quantity and quality without monetary valuation. The absence of provision for valuation of the goods gives rise to a major difficulty: if one party delivers goods that are not in accordance with the requirements of the contract as regards either quantity or quality, monetary relief is difficult to calculate since there is no benchmark for calculating the shortfall in value to the receiving party that the deficiency in quantity or quality may produce.

The consideration given by both parties to the arrangement consists entirely of their respective counterdelivery obligations; there are no cash payments. Since there is no provision for monetary adjustments, the value of the goods to be exchanged must be strictly comparable, and this in turn implies that both quantity and quality of the goods have to be precisely defined at the time the contract is entered into. This is never easy and may not be possible at all.

Deliveries are typically concurrent. A moment's thought will show that a fundamental difficulty of pure barter is to decide which party is going to deliver its goods first. Much negotiation in barter deals is directed to just this point, since the party who delivers first is exposed to the defective performance of the other party. This is particularly so since the absence of monetary valuation limits the use of instruments such as documentary letters of credit that are otherwise often used in international sales of goods to ensure that one obligation has been performed as condition to the performance of the counterobligation. Of course, letters of credit are not the only security that can be called for in these circumstances and some barter transactions envisage that the parties' obligations to deliver will be secured by the provision of bank guarantees. Usually, however, each of the parties requires the other to provide a bank guarantee of its performance: if both guarantees are on demand guarantees, a party not faithful to the contract could effectively deter the other party from calling one guarantee by itself threatening to call the other guarantee.

As a result of these difficulties barter contracts are relatively seldom used as the legal form for international countertrade.

10.4.2 Counterpurchase Arrangements

Next to be considered are counterpurchase arrangements. Figure 10.2 illustrates an elementary form of this kind of transaction.

The simple form of counterpurchase transaction involves delivery and counterdelivery obligations contained in two legally self-contained contracts. The basic elements are:

- two separate contracts;
- separate and often quite different payment terms;
- extent of counterpurchase commitment;
- penalties for non-performance of counterpurchase undertaking; and
- availability of financing and credit insurance support.

Generally the exporter will undertake to purchase goods and services from the importing country, concurrently with and as a condition of securing the sales order. The two contracts are parallel but, generally, legally entirely distinct: there is one contract for the sale of the export goods, and another separate arrangement for the counterpurchase. The payment terms, too, are separate and may be quite different: the exporter may provide supplier credit or buyer credit arrangements for the benefit of the importing country, and yet the sale of the countertrade goods may require payment in cash. Practice varies both in relation to the value of the counterpurchase undertaking and also as regards the extent of the commitment undertaken by the exporter to proceed with the countertrade transactions. The value of the counterpurchase undertaking may well vary in value between 10 percent and 100 percent (or even more) of the original export order according to the particular country concerned. The exporter's undertakings, too, can vary from a general declaration of intent to a binding contract

Figure 10.2 Simple counterpurchase

specifying in detail the goods and services to be supplied, the markets in which they may be sold, and the penalties for non-performance. The penalties are a significant item for negotiation to which we will return below. However, the separation of the two contracts does have one advantage, and that is that export credit agencies in particular are less reluctant to offer credit and political risk insurance in such cases, although that does not mean to say that obtaining such insurance is by any means plain sailing.

We should now turn to the more elaborate form of countertrade often encountered in East European transactions. In this case the exporter may employ the services of a countertrade house to satisfy its countertrade obligation and, on the side of the importing country, the foreign trade organization with which the exporter deals in its contract for purchase of the export goods may provide internal switching facilities between the various state enterprises for which it is responsible.

Only a few large exporting firms which regularly encounter countertrade demands (for example, those regularly trading with certain non-market economies) maintain an in-house capability to handle countertrading goods on their own account. For the vast majority of exporters, there is no practical alternative to obtaining the assistance of outside specialists.

The simplest method of handling counterpurchase undertakings is to assign the obligation – for a fee – to a third party trading house or broker. Sometimes the third party trader can be an open signatory to the counterpurchase agreement, but more often the importing country will insist on dealing only with the exporter itself.

As a practical matter, the exporter need have no further involvement in the countertrade transaction after its obligations have been

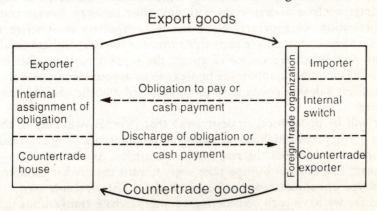

Figure 10.3 Countertrade with assignment

delegated to the trading house, but it is important to note that, as a legal matter, the delegation of the counterpurchase obligation to the countertrade house is usually purely an internal matter. For legal purposes, the exporter remains obligated as against the importer and therefore assumes the risk of non-performance by the countertrade house. Similarly, too, it is the exporter who will be liable for the penalties for any failure to comply with the countertrade obligation; and in practice it is not uncommon to find that the obligations of the countertrade house to fulfill the countertrade obligation are expressed only in terms of best efforts while the exporter's obligations are absolute. Often, too, the countertrade house will accept liability for any penalties only to a very limited extent, and in any event only to the extent of the fee or subsidy paid to the countertrade house. A good deal of residual risk may, therefore, remain with the exporter.

The other clearing mechanism which is commonly encountered in counterpurchase transactions is that practiced by importing countries. In some East European countries, in particular, the choice of counterpurchase goods is often restricted: most foreign trade with Eastern Europe has been conducted with the state foreign trade organizations, and depending on the country, the choice of goods may be limited to goods emanating from the industries over which the foreign trade corporation has jurisdiction. The practicality of securing access to a list of countertrade goods that extends beyond the areas of influence of the particular trade organization varies from country to country. Sometimes internal switching between foreign trade organizations is possible and access can be given to a wide range of goods but in other, less developed countries where access to foreign currency is highly prized by foreign trade corporations there may be a good deal of resistance to sharing the benefit of foreign currency generated through counterpurchase undertakings with any other ministry, foreign trade organization, or province. None the less, exporters must strive to retain as much free choice as possible over the counterpurchase goods. With an unrestricted choice of goods, the support payment that has to be made to the countertrade houses can be appreciably smaller than when less saleable goods have to be accepted and the choice is narrower.

It will be understood straight away that internal switching of this sort presupposes a high degree of central economic planning and ready cooperation between the responsible ministries. As the countries of Central and Eastern Europe take steps toward the market economy, this type of countertrade has become only of historical interest.

So far we have been considering counterpurchase transactions that are essentially bilateral in their nature. The countertrade transactions can, however, become multilateral, setting enormous challenges both for the commercial negotiators responsible for structuring the transactions and also for the luckless lawyers who have to follow in their wake and try to document the relationships which the negotiators create. It would be wrong to spend too long discussing these types of transaction in this short introduction, but there are two variations on the basic counterpurchase theme that should be described in order to illustrate the complexity which can be involved.

10.4.3 Variants of Counterpurchase

Triangular arrangements One variant on the simple counterpurchase arrangement is triangular counterpurchase, where the counterpurchase contracts are concluded between more than two parties (see figure 10.4). Triangular counterpurchase may arise, for example, if the countertrade goods are not taken by the Western exporter, but are passed on to a buyer in another country. The buyer in the third country will then pay the Western exporter.

Switch trading Counterpurchase deals also can be structured to involve "switch trading." Before we look at the structure of a switch deal, it will help to describe the sort of circumstances in which such deals can arise. Long-term bilateral trading agreements are relatively unusual in Western economies, but they are a more common feature of trade between the centrally planned economies and the developing countries. Sometimes imbalances can occur in these long-term bilateral trading agreements that may lead to the accumulation of uncleared credit surpluses in one or other country: for example, at one time Brazil had large credit surpluses under its agreement with Poland. These surpluses can sometimes be tapped by third parties, so that (for

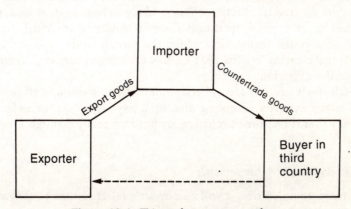

Figure 10.4 Triangular counterpurchase

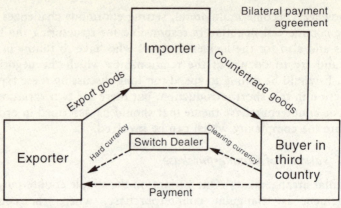

Figure 10.5 Switch deals

example) UK exports to Brazil might be financed from the sale of Polish goods to the UK or elsewhere.

Switch deals can be extremely complicated, involving a chain of buyers, sellers, and brokers in different markets. In the case outlined schematically in figure 10.5 the importer pays for the export goods by delivering goods to the third country, which thereby enters into a commitment to pay the exporter in hard currency, in the same way as it would under a "simple" triangular counterpurchase. The switch dealer acquires the clearing currency (that is, the currency in which the surpluses under the bilateral trading agreement have arisen) and passes on hard currency to the exporter after deducting his own commission, the size of which is likely to be determined by the negotiability of the clearing currency. It goes without saying, of course, that the dealer is only likely to accept clearing credits that he can either use for his own purposes, or sell on. It follows, therefore, that this fairly complicated transaction chain is likely to represent, at best, only one half of an overall operation since it would be matched, on the other side, by the transaction which the switch dealer will set up to absorb the clearing credits that he has exchanged for hard currency paid to the exporter.

Switch deals are not always triangular: there is nothing to prevent the Western exporter accepting directly a payment claim in a clearing currency that it can then exchange for hard currency through a switch dealer.

10.4.4 Buy-back Arrangements

After these complexities, it will be almost a relief to turn to the rather simpler structure of "buy-back."

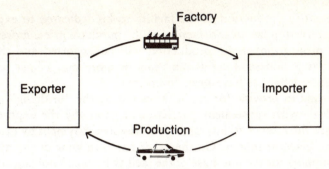

Figure 10.6 Buy-back

As will be seen from figure 10.6, the essence of buy-back is that the exporter supplies some sort of productive capacity to the importer and receives in return all or part of the production from the completed facility. The types of plant that may be supplied on buy-back arrangements vary enormously: they include the supply of mineral extraction equipment in return for ore, the supply of petrochemical facilities in return for refined product, the supply of pulp mills in return for paper, and many others besides.

The most important features of buy-back arrangements are as follows:

- delivery and counterdelivery linked through the production process;
- transactions denominated in single reference currency of account;
- long counterdelivery schedule;
- credit terms generally applicable;
- buy-back sometimes in excess of 100 percent of plant value.

Delivery and counterdelivery are linked through the production process. The buy-back goods are usually produced or processed by the installation that the Western exporter has supplied. Occasionally, because of long installation and production periods, similar products from an existing plant in the importing country may be supplied, either instead of the direct product or for a limited period until the new facility has been fully commissioned.

All buy-back transactions are denominated in a single reference currency of account.

A long period elapses between the delivery of the manufacturing facility and the first counterdelivery. Many process plants take three or four years to complete from the date of placing the contract to the date of commissioning. Unless there is provision for interim deliveries of the same product from another source, counterdeliveries will not start until commissioning has been completed. Thereafter, it is unusual for the entire production of the facility to be dedicated to export to the Western supplier in satisfaction of the purchase price: more often, only a proportion of the production will be exported and this can mean that periods as long as ten years or more may elapse until all the counterdeliveries have been completed.

It is usual to provide for credit terms during the "bridging" period. Cash deals with subsequent purchases of goods by the exporter are rare since the essence of buy-back deals involves payment by produced goods in place of money. On the other hand, in view of the need for credit support for the purchase of the facility by the importing country, separate contracts are generally drawn up for the purchase of the production facility and the supply of the buy-back goods. In addition, there may be other agreements dealing with the provision of continuing technical assistance and operating management services.

The proportion of the purchase price of the Western goods for which the buy-back has to account varies considerably. The buy-back product may simply constitute a proportion of the supply value of the production facility, may equal it, or may even amount to more than 100 percent of the value of the exporter's contract, in order to cover financing costs and local currency costs connected with the installation of the plant.

10.5 Increasing Usage of Offset Arrangements

So far this chapter has addressed the classic forms of countertrade. Many of these forms came to be practiced first in trade with the centrally planned economies of Eastern Europe, although they have been adopted as government policy in developing countries elsewhere in the world. It is worth re-emphasizing that, with the economic and political upheavals in Eastern Europe, the centralized control over currency and goods essential to the types of counterpurchase that involve switches of one form or another is disappearing, and it is not hard to predict that these types of countertrade are likely to diminish in importance fairly rapidly. Given a basic degree of political stability, buy-back deals are likely to flourish and grow in number but, increasingly, the type of countertrade that is becoming of very substantial importance is "offset." This is the last type of countertrade arrangements to be considered here.

Types of offset include:

- co-production;
- licensed production;

- subcontractor production;
- overseas investment; and
- technology transfer.

The origins of offset are to be found in military trade, although the term is now also used for large civilian procurements. Initially military offset consisted mainly of co-production arrangements but, in the last few years, the objectives of importing countries have changed and offsets are increasingly being used as vehicles for employment, industrial development, and export development. The structure of offset trade has also been changing and the original orientation of offset as government-to-government deals has been changing to come to include also private-sector-to-government transactions.

The more common military offset arrangements made by the US exporting companies which are leaders in this field include:

- *co-production*: these are overseas production arrangements usually based on a government-to-government agreement that permits a foreign government or foreign producers to acquire the technical information needed to manufacture all or part of defense equipment originating in the exporting country;
- *licensed production*: these cases involve the overseas production of defense equipment based upon transfer of technical information under direct commercial arrangements between a manufacturer in the exporting country and a foreign government or foreign producers;
- *subcontractor production*: here, too, overseas production of defense equipment is envisaged, but in this case the subcontract does not necessarily involve the license of technical information and will usually be a direct commercial arrangement between the manufacturer in the exporting country and a foreign producer;
- *overseas investment*: in these cases we are concerned with investment arising under an offset agreement, taking the form of capital invested to establish or expand a subsidiary or joint venture in the foreign country;
- *technology transfer*: these are cases of the transfer of technology occurring as a result of an offset agreement, often taking the form of research and development conducted abroad, technical assistance provided to the subsidiary, or a joint venture established under the offset arrangements.

Offset arrangements are particularly prominent in the international sale of civil and military aircraft. Two of the best known examples involve Saudi Arabia: the arrangements between the UK government and the Saudi Arabian government for the supply of Tornado aircraft and the Boeing Company's supply to Saudi Arabia of AWACS aircraft have both involved extensive offset programs.

In the case of the AWACS program (known as the Saudi Arabian Peace Shield) the value of the total contract was about $1.3 billion and the required offset proportion was 35 percent, or roughly $450 million. Boeing was required to enter into an agreement with the Saudi government to invest and participate in joint venture industries that would involve hi-tech related processes and products. The size of the Boeing contract required a very formal structure for the offset program and, although not many other contracts will involve commitments of the extent or formality of those accepted by Boeing, offset requirements have been introduced by a number of other countries and are clearly an established feature of international projects of this type. The Boeing program has successfully spawned a number of joint ventures in Saudi Arabia. Not all programs are this popular: they involve contractors in much trouble and require a lot of experience, there is frequently a great deal of bureaucracy in getting projects approved for offset, and government-to-government deals may not create the right degree of commitment or incentive in contractors to live up to their offset commitment.

10.6 Concluding Observations

This chapter started with the salutary warning that countertrade is not a game for amateurs. Structuring the transactions to contain the risks that countertrade involves is an essential part of the lawyer's role in this area of practice. Therefore, it is appropriate to conclude this chapter by identifying some of those risks:

■ *Cost.* Countertrade transactions are invariably costly. They involve both direct and indirect cost. The direct cost usually arises because the exporter or countertrade house who receives the countertrade goods may need to seek a significant discount in order to be able to dispose of the goods in export markets. In addition, countertrade transactions are complex and slow and expensive to negotiate: large amounts of management time are likely to be involved that will account for a good deal of indirect cost.

■ *Selection of countertrade goods.* In pure buy-back the selection of the goods is not a problem: they will simply be the production of the facility supplied by the exporter. In counterpurchase arrangements where there is no connection between the goods supplied by the exporter and those received in exchange, selection can make all the difference between profit and loss. More often than not, parties to a countertrade transaction do not commit themselves to a particular type of counter-export goods, and the guidelines concerning the goods available for counter-export are frequently expressed in the form of a list attached to the countertrade agreement indicating the goods that may be purchased to fulfill the countertrade commitment. The list may be out of date, however, or some of the goods on the list may not be available.

■ *Price of countertrade goods.* Whether or not the goods to be delivered under the countertrade arrangements are identified at the time of contract, it is unusual for their price to be specified. If no procedure for determining the price is identified, the exporter is at risk of a commitment to purchase countertrade goods at a price that may inhibit their profitable sale on external markets. Much work is therefore required, on most countertrade transactions, to include standards or procedures capable of being used to determine the price at which the counter-export goods are to be taken by the exporter.

■ *Availability and delivery.* Much the same uncertainty applies in relation to the delivery of the counter-export goods. One particular point to be watched concerns the basis on which any penalties are payable by the exporter: it is obviously crucial to ensure that penalties are extinguished simply by the act of contracting for the purchase of counter-export goods rather than their delivery, otherwise the exporter may find that it is unwittingly underwriting the performance of the other party to the countertrade commitment.

■ *Quality.* Concern over the quality of goods to be offered for counter-export is one of the major problems in countertrade transactions. If the goods are not known when the countertrade agreement is concluded, or are known only by broad categories, precise statements of quality cannot be made. Contractual requirements regarding quality may therefore have to be limited to broad generalizations, and yet such a generalized description of quality may not provide an adequate means of measuring whether the counter-exporter is offering goods in conformity with its countertrade commitments.

■ *Security for performance.* There are two aspects to this risk. First, the Western exporter will generally be required to obtain a bank guarantee providing for the payment of penalties in the event that the Western exporter does not perform its countertrade obligations. The risk of unfair call of these guarantees is just the same as in relation to other bonds which contractors can be called upon to issue in different types of transactions. The second point is more problematic. It concerns the effect of the breach of either the export contract on the one side or the countertrade commitment on the other. Although the two contracts are separate, does breach of one of the contracts affect the non-defaulting party's obligations under the other?

■ *Penalties.* Penalties have come to be a normal feature of countertrade commitments. The penalty will vary from country to country and depend on the circumstances of the individual case but is often in the range of 10–15 percent of the unfulfilled portion of the counterpurchase obligation. Is it, however, the sole remedy available to the importing country in respect of a failure to attain full performance of the counterpurchase obligations?

These are a few of the risks that countertrade involves. Clearly, it is not a straightforward business. Perhaps the best summary of the difficulties of countertrade comes from the conclusion to the UNCITRAL report:

> The conduct of countertrade often requires the ability to resolve difficult problems of a commercial nature and to coordinate the undertaking and performance of obligations that are disparate in nature and in time and that must often be undertaken by parties who are not parties to the countertrade agreement. This calls first of all for commercial skill in conducting these transactions. It also calls for skill in drafting the contractual agreements that structure the transactions, whether or not those contractual agreements are fully enforceable through the use of the usual legal means.

Part IV

Niche Financings

11

Asset Securitization Developments: US and UK

DAVID BARBOUR AND R. E. PARSONS

> **Chapter Outline**
>
> Part A: Asset Securitization in the US
>
> 11.1   Introduction: What is Securitization?
>
> 11.2   Purposes of Securitization in the US
>
> 11.3   Characteristics of Assets Subject to Securitization
>
> 11.4   Types and Transactions of Asset-backed Securities in the US
>
> 11.5   Securitization Structures in the US
>
> 11.6   US Securities Law Considerations
>
> 11.7   US Bankruptcy and Insolvency Considerations
>
> 11.8   US Federal Tax Law Considerations
>
> 11.9   Special Considerations of Risk-based Capital Requirements in the US
>
> Part B: Securitization Developments in the UK
>
> 11.10 Introduction to the UK Situation

Part A of this paper was written by David Barbour and Part B by R. E. Parsons. David Barbour wishes to thank Michael B. Thimmig of Winstead Sechrest & Minick PC for his assistance in preparing the paper.

  For more detailed discussion of this topic, see J. Norton and P. Spellman (eds), *Asset Securitization: International and Financial Perspectives* (Blackwell, 1991).

> 11.11 Exposure Draft 42 – March 1988 (1)
>
> 11.12 Off-balance-sheet Treatment of Accounts of Institutions Regulated by the Bank of England
>
> 11.13 Companies Act 1989
>
> 11.14 Exposure Draft 42 – March 1988 (2)
>
> 11.15 Exposure Draft 49 – May 1990
>
> 11.16 Conclusion

PART A: ASSET SECURITIZATION IN THE US

11.1 Introduction: What Is Securitization?

"Asset securitization" refers to the process of raising funds through the issuance of marketable securities backed by future cash flow from revenue-producing assets. Conceptually, asset securitization is the "conversion" or repackaging of cash flows from a pool of revenue-producing assets into marketable securities. The resulting asset-backed securities differ from other types of securities in that the creditworthiness of these securities depends primarily on the assurance of a stream of cash flow from the asset collateral rather than on the credit strength of the issuer or the market value of such collateral.

Asset-backed securities are a superior source of funding in comparison to the traditional asset-based lending transactions such as loan participations, loan syndications, or discounted loan or receivable sales. In fact, asset-backed securities are liquid, fixed rate, investment grade obligations which trade at rates 50 to 100 "basis points" over US Treasury obligations of comparable maturity. Generally, the structure of an asset-backed security with an investment grade rating will utilize a bankruptcy remote issuer in order to insulate these securities from the credit risk of the company selling or transferring the assets to such issuer. In addition, an asset pool having a greater degree of diversification and a larger number of assets will diffuse the credit risk of each individual obligor of the respective asset within the pool collateralizing an asset-backed security.

Typically, the company originating the assets will sell or transfer a pool of assets to an issuer which is either a grantor trust or a special-purpose corporation and such originating company will retain the rights to service the pooled assets for a fee. The pool of assets will collateralize the issuance of the asset-backed securities by the trust or corporation. The servicer will remit the cash flows from the assets to the trustee, which pays scheduled interest and principal payments to the holders of the asset-backed securities along with any principal prepayments on the assets. Assuming no delinquencies or defaults with respect to the scheduled payments from the assets, the aggregate cash flow from assets will always equal or exceed the required payments on the asset-backed securities. The excess cash flow, or spread, may be paid to the originating company as excess servicing compensation, or to the person investing in the residual interest in the pooled assets; or all or a portion of such spread may be retained for credit enhancement purposes and deposited into a reserve fund.

11.2 Purposes of Securitization in the US

11.2.1 Improvement of Capital Structure

If a securitization transaction is structured and accounted for as a sale of the underlying assets, the transaction results in a reduction in both assets and liabilities, the effect of which is to increase the ratio of equity to debt. Improvement of capital ratios may provide relief with respect to any corporate debt covenants, and more importantly (for a financial institution) may assist the institution in meeting its regulatory capital adequacy requirements and reduce loss reserves with respect to such assets. Also, if the transaction qualifies as a sale under applicable financial institution regulatory accounting principles, the effect of a sale is to release capital for the generation of new assets and may provide relief with respect to applicable growth restrictions.

The accounting treatment for securitized sales under generally accepted accounting principles (GAAP) is governed primarily by the Financial Accounting Standards Board Statement of Financial Accounting Standards no. 77.[1] Under FASB 77 a transfer of receivables which purports to be a sale may be recognized as a sale for financial accounting purposes. In determining whether the transfer will be recognized as a sale the three conditions set forth in FASB 77 focus on whether

- the transferor surrenders control of future economic benefits;
- the transferor's recourse obligation can be reasonably estimated; and
- the transferor can be required to repurchase the receivables (other than pursuant to its recourse obligation).

With respect to regulatory accounting principles for US banks, the Federal Financial Institutions Examination Council has declined to follow FASB 77 and has provided, in the instructions to the "Call Report" for banks, that a transfer of loans or receivables, or participations therein, must be reported as a borrowing if the transferring bank retains any risk of loss or has any obligations for the payment of principal or interest (except in cases of incomplete documentation or fraud) resulting from default of the original debtor, from changes in market value, or from any other cause.[2] Nevertheless, numerous securitizations by banks have achieved sale treatment through structures whereby there is no direct recourse to the banks.

11.2.2 Asset–Liability Matching

Regardless of the accounting treatment of a transaction, securitization can improve the matching of duration of an enterprise's assets and liabilities which, in turn, may achieve significant benefits in reduction of interest rate risk.

11.2.3 Improved Liquidity

The ability to convert assets into marketable securities can improve an enterprise's ability to raise needed funds on a timely basis and provide a source of funding for new assets. The creation of a secondary mortgage market by the Federal National Mortgage Association provided the basis for creation of an entire industry, mortgage banking.

11.2.4 Alternative Funding Source

Securitization can provide a mechanism for an enterprise to raise funds at an investment-grade cost of funds that would not otherwise be available.

11.2.5 Source of Fee Income

Generally, the selling entity continues to service the securitized assets in return for a retained portion of the yield on the assets.

11.2.6 Compliance by Financial Institutions with Capital Standards

The Financial Institutions Reform, Recovery, and Enforcement Act of 1989 (FIRREA) was enacted on August 9, 1989, and provided for a restructuring of the US regulation of federally insured depository institutions and the establishment of new capital standards for such financial institutions.[3] Under FIRREA the new capital standards for thrift institutions are required to be no less stringent than the capital standards for national banks and include similar risk-based capital requirements, which impose a minimum ratio of an institution's regulatory capital to the risk-weighted values of such institution's assets and off-balance-sheet items.

Generally, with respect to financial institutions (including both banks and thrifts) which are subject to federal regulation, the risk-based capital regulations place obligations of issuers and other investment assets into different specified credit risk-weighted categories based primarily on the nature of the underlying obligor. These regulations require financial institutions to maintain greater amounts of capital in order to support investments classified in higher risk-weighted categories, which in turn increases the effective financing costs associated with securities and other assets classified in the higher risk-weighted categories. Thus, these regulations provide an incentive for financial institutions to invest their funds in assets assigned to lower risk-weighted categories. The risk-based capital regulations generally place mortgage-related securities in the lower risk-weighted categories, while residential mortgage loans (including first-lien, single-family mortgages), commercial mortgage loans, and consumer loans are classified in the higher risk-weighted categories. Accordingly, financial institutions have an increased incentive to securitize and sell their higher risk-weighted assets, which include mortgage loans and consumer loans, and to invest in lower risk-weighted assets, which include certain mortgage-related securities (see section 11.9 below).

11.3 Characteristics of Assets Subject to Securitization

11.3.1 Characteristics that Facilitate Securitization

The most readily securitizable assets have the following characteristics:

- predictable cash flows;
- consistently low delinquency, default, and loss history;
- fully amortized payment stream;
- demographic and geographic diversity of asset obligors;
- seasoning of assets;
- underlying collateral with high liquidation value and utility to the obligor; and
- standardized, high-quality underwriting and collection policies.

With respect to financial institutions, most of the financial assets included on the financial institution's balance sheet are susceptible to securitization.

11.3.2 Negative Characteristics

Characteristics that cause difficulties in securitizing assets are as follows:

- inexperienced or undercapitalized servicer;
- small number of assets in the collateral pool and a high ratio of the largest asset to the average asset;
- balloon maturity;
- infrequent payment dates; and
- ability of asset obligors to modify payment terms.

11.4 Types and Transactions of Asset-backed Securities in the US

11.4.1 Mortgage Loans

Asset securitization in the US started with residential mortgage loans in the late 1970s. Residential mortgage loans have been the most frequently securitized assets, because of the interest rate risk inherent in holding long-term fixed rate assets. In addition, residential mortgage loans have the characteristics which facilitate securitization, including uniform underwriting documentation, historical prepayment information, and full amortization of principal. Many mortgage-backed securitization structures have involved the creation of debt securities collateralized by a pool of mortgage loan assets (see section 11.5.1 below).

The securitization of mortgage loans is expected to increase as a result of the adoption of risk-based capital requirements and the funding and disposition of insolvent savings associations under FIRREA. For example, the risk-based capital requirements assign a lower risk weight to mortgage-backed securities issued by the Federal Home Loan Mortgage Corporation (FHLMC) and Federal National Mortgage Association (FNMA) than to the mortgages themselves that underlie such securities. Accordingly, FHLMC and FNMA are anticipating increased demand for each of them to purchase conventional mortgages and, in turn, to issue mortgage-backed securities representing interests in the mortgages previously purchased by FHLMC or FNMA.

11.4.2 Consumer Loan and Trade Receivables

In recent years, automobile loans, boat and recreational vehicle loans, mobile home loans, and other types of consumer loans have been securitized utilizing the grantor trust, or "pass-through" structure.

Automobile loans typically exhibit maturities of two to six years with predictable prepayment patterns. Light and heavy truck installment loans have been securitized utilizing structures identical to those used for automobile loans, because they have similar characteristics to automobile loans.

In September 1988 Chemical Bank structured the first asset-backed security collateralized by boat loans through Chemical Bank Grantor Trust 1988-B. While recreational vehicle loans had been securitized through private placements since 1986, First Boston in late 1988 structured the first public pass-through issuance of asset-backed securities collateralized by recreational vehicle loans which were originated by a subsidiary of Fleetwood Enterprises, Inc.

Boat and recreational vehicle loans have been securitized using pass-through structures similar to those used for automobile loans. However, the structure for boat and recreational vehicle loans typically requires a third-party buy-out to restrict the final maturity of the securitized pool of loans, because such loans usually have five- to fifteen-year maturities.

Trade receivables have been securitized through a commercial paper structure, where a non-affiliated, special-purpose issuer acquires the trade receivables and issues commercial paper secured by such receivables (see section 11.5.4 below). Credit card receivables, utility lease receivables, insurance premium loans, railroad receivables, and hospital medical insurance receivables are some of the different types of trade receivables which have been securitized through commercial paper structures.

11.4.3 Credit Card Receivables

In January 1987 RepublicBank Delaware publicly issued the first asset-backed securities collateralized by credit card receivables. Credit card receivables have been securitized by lending institutions or their subsidiaries in order to reduce assets and obtain funds for new lending while retaining significant servicing fees for such institutions or their subsidiaries.

The unique characteristics of credit card receivables include short and irregular paydown periods and relatively low individual loan balances. The pool of credit card receivables collateralizing an asset-backed security generally is comprised of a large number of asset obligors with a wide geographic dispersion.

Credit card receivables have been securitized utilizing a "revolving structure" in which principal payments are used to purchase new credit card balances; at the end of a predetermined period such purchases cease and principal is paid to investors as received. This revolving structure has been developed to extend the average life of the asset-backed securities issued, because of the unique character of the credit card receivables including the short and irregular paydown periods and relatively low individual loan balances. This revolving structure also includes two separate classes of securities to accommodate the aggregate principal balance fluctuations of the credit card receivables such that a larger principal portion with a fixed percentage is sold to third party investors and a smaller principal portion with a floating percentage is retained by the seller of the credit card receivables.

Recent innovations in the structures of credit card receivable securitizations have included bullet maturities, senior-subordinated structures, and the combined issuance of long-term and commercial paper obligations. The bullet maturity for credit card securitization structures has been accomplished by incorporating into these structures a principal accumulation period, a guaranteed rate agreement, and, in some transactions, a maturity guarantee. During such principal accumulation period, principal payments on the receivables that would otherwise be paid to security holders during the amortization period are retained and reinvested in qualified investments. The Security Pacific Credit Card Trust 1989A is an example of what the rating agencies refer to as a "soft bullet," and the Euro Credit Card Trust 1989–2 is a so-called "hard bullet' transaction. In addition to these innovations, credit-card-backed securities were recently marketed for the first time to European investors and retail investors in the US.

11.4.4 *Lease-backed Securities*

In March 1985 Sperry Lease Finance Corporation publicly issued asset-backed securities collateralized by leases on data processing equipment. Various types of leases have collateralized asset-backed securities, including leases of retail automobiles, computer equipment, hospital equipment, utility equipment, and airplanes. Lease-backed securities utilize a structure having credit enhancement in order to minimize the risk of default on rental payments and losses from the residual value realized at lease termination.

11.4.5 *Junk Bonds and HLT Loans*

Asset-backed securities have recently been collateralized by high-yield corporate debt including junk bonds and highly leveraged transactions

(HLT) loans, which include leveraged buyout (LBO) loans. In 1987, Imperial Savings Association offered three junk-bond-backed issuances which utilized a structure with substantial over-collateralization. Continental Bank completed an overseas offering of senior and subordinate floating rate notes collateralized by LBO loans. Banque Nationale de Paris packaged HLT loans purchased from other commercial bank portfolios into the first public offering by Afer BV of these asset-backed bonds. Since the junk bonds and HLT loans are subject to substantial default and price volatility risks, the securitization structures of these types of high-yield corporate debt have focused on

- over-collateralization or discount factors, which increase as the credit rating on the underlying corporate debt declines, and
- diversification parameters for the underlying pool relating to the underlying obligors of the corporate debt and their respective industry concentrations.

11.4.6 Non-performing Loans

The Grant Street National Bank offering in 1988 of extendible pay-through notes was the first rated transaction of securities backed by cash flows from the workout of non-performing loans and repossessed assets. The Grant Street National Bank transaction is an alternative vehicle for financial institutions to liquidate and limit loan loss exposure by the spin-off of bad assets to a securitized liquidating bank. The redeployment of failed thrift assets by the Resolution Trust Corporation, together with the number of thrifts to be brought under conservatorship and the capital funding pressures in the thrift and banking industries, according to the rating agencies, may accelerate use of these non-performing loan securitization structures.

11.4.7 Tax-exempt Bonds

Another form of pooled collateral for asset-backed securities is tax-exempt bonds. An institution with a significant portfolio of tax-exempt bonds can securitize these assets in order to liquefy them and hedge against interest rate fluctuations.[4]

11.5 Securitization Structures in the US

11.5.1 Pass-through Structures

Generally speaking, pass-through structures consist of instruments in which payments on the instruments flow through directly from payments on the underlying assets, which are deposited to a grantor trust created for the benefit of investors. (See section 11.8.2 below for federal tax law considerations relating to such grantor trusts.) A typical example is a mortgage pass-through security in which all principal payments received on the mortgages are passed through to investors and interest payments up to a fixed yield are also passed through to investors, with interest above the fixed yield retained by the mortgage servicer as servicing compensation.

Variations on the pass-through structure include senior subordinated pass-throughs in which investors receive certificates representing senior fractional undivided interests in the assets and the seller retains the remaining interest. The remainder retained by the seller is subordinated in payment and acts as a form of credit support for the investors in a manner similar to over-collateralization. Other pass-through structures include "strips" in which multiple classes of securities are issued backed by the same pool of assets, with some classes receiving only principal payments or principal payments plus a portion of interest payments and other classes receiving the remainder of the interest payments. Pass-through structures may also include structures involving revolving credit in which investors receive an undivided interest equal to a fixed dollar amount and the seller retains the remaining interest in the assets which floats as a percentage as the underlying debts are paid down or reborrowed.

11.5.2 *Participation Structures*

A participation security is similar to a pass-through security except that the investors directly own the underlying assets, no trust is created, and no trustee acts on behalf of the investors. In the case of assets consisting of negotiable instruments, such as mortgage notes, the instruments representing the assets may be placed with an independent custodian in order to perfect the ownership interest of investors. However, enforcement of the rights against the servicer of the assets or the seller must be undertaken directly by the investors. Therefore, investors must be capable of servicing the assets themselves in the event of termination of the servicer if no substitute servicer can be found, and generally must be more willing to deal directly with the assets and the servicers than in the case of a pass-through structure. Section 541(d) of the US Bankruptcy Code[5] (which does not apply to banks or thrifts, but would apply to finance subsidiaries of banks and thrifts and to bank and thrift holding companies and their non-bank subsidiaries) affords some protection to participants that do not perfect transfer of the assets. However, application of this section in connection with section 544(a) of the Bankruptcy Code is unclear, and some cases indicate that this section only applies in *"bona fide* secondary mortgage market transactions."[6] The use of these bankruptcy provisions in a bank or thrift insolvency would only be applicable if, by analogy, the receiver (in its discretion) referred to such provisions for guidance.

11.5.3 Secured Debt

Secured debt offerings avoid some of the tax limitations that are applicable to pass-through structures and, in some cases, provide for more flexibility with respect to forms of credit enhancement. However, secured debt offerings, unlike some pass-through and participation structures, do not result in sale treatment for accounting or regulatory purposes. Secured debt structures may include direct offerings by the originating company, which in the case of a financial institution may provide the benefits of certain exemptions under securities laws (see section 11.6.1 below), or participation through conduits or special purpose subsidiaries.

Debt structures include typical debt arrangements with fixed interest rates and fixed maturities and more complex structures such as the collateralized mortgage obligation or CMO, and recently with respect to junk bond and HLT loan collateral, collateralized bond obligations (CBOs) and market value securitized notes.

CMOs typically provide for multiple classes of securities backed by the same underlying pool of assets, with principal payments being allocated unevenly among the classes. The traditional CMO involves a sequential payment structure in which no payments of principal are made on any class until all classes having an earlier stated maturity are retired in full. Prepayments on the underlying pool of assets are "paid through" to security holders such that the remaining principal amount of the securities can be supported by the scheduled future payments on the remaining asset collateral. As a result, the amount and timing of principal payments to the security holders of a CMO are determined by reference to the amount and timing of principal payments on the underlying pool of assets. CMOs may include "compound interest bonds" which pay neither principal nor interest until earlier classes are retired, with accrued but unpaid interest being compounded and added to principal. More recent offerings include

- floating rate bonds, typically providing for an interest rate based on LIBOR or another index;
- "strips," structures in which two or more classes of bonds pay principal simultaneously and ratably but bear different coupon rates of interest; and

- "planned amortization" or "targeted amortization" classes to which principal payments are allocated in a manner designed to create more predictable rates of payment.

The purpose, and the advantage, of devising multiple classes of securities backed by the same pool of assets is expansion of the class of investors willing to invest in such assets. For example, the introduction of floating rate CMOs greatly increased the market among European investors, who traditionally have been hesitant to invest in fixed rate securities with uncertain maturity, such as mortgage-backed securities. The different types of securities outlined above may vary in one or more of the following respects that are important to investors: maturity, rate of change of price with respect to yield ("duration"), and the relative ability of the security to decrease slowly in price as interest rates rise and increase rapidly in price as interest rates fall ("convexity").

CBOs, first issued in 1988, are collateralized primarily by HLT loans from banks' commercial loan portfolios. The CBO security holders look to both the cash flow and the over-collateralization from the HLT loan collateral to provide debt service payments on a continuing basis and to insulate them from defaults by the underlying HLT loan obligors.

The market value securitized notes collateralized by junk bonds and HLT loans have been issued as the single class of senior debt of closed-end mutual funds registered under the Investment Company Act of 1940. The structure of the market value securitized notes focuses on the liquidity and price volatility of the underlying junk bond and HLT loan collateral in the secondary bond market, and features a regular mark-to-market of the underlying collateral, substantial over-collateralization for credit enhancement, and diversification restrictions on the underlying collateral pool. The market value securitized note structure also includes a liquid asset provision or LAP which requires on an ongoing basis the deposit of sufficient cash or creditworthy deposit securities in advance of scheduled payments on the notes so that collateral can be liquidated in the event of a default in the underlying collateral. If the market value of the underlying collateral falls below a specific level and additional collateral is not pledged to cure such deficiency, then the collateral is liquidated and principal payments are made to redeem all or a proportion of the notes.

11.5.4 Commercial Paper

Assets, primarily receivables, have been securitized through "special purpose issuers," i.e. corporations or other entities not legally affiliated with the originator of the assets. The business of such special-purpose issuers is limited to the acquisition of assets to be securitized and the issuance of commercial paper collateralized by such assets. Generally, the issuer will retire maturing commercial paper through the issuance of new commercial paper. In the event of a disruption of the market impeding such new issuance, a maturity guarantee, such as a refunding loan commitment from a bank consortium, is normally required in order to assure that sufficient funds will be available to retire maturing commercial paper. Additional credit enhancement may be obtained to cover defaults on the asset collateral. The commercial paper structure enables the originator of the receivables to obtain the desired amount of funding from time to time by selling varying amounts of outstanding receivable balances.

11.5.5 Credit Enhancement for Asset-backed Securities

Nearly all publicly issued sale and debt structured asset-backed securities transactions have utilized a form of credit enhancement to obtain one of the two highest ratings available. The rating agencies determine the level of loss coverage on the asset pool that is required to obtain the desired rating by analyzing the following factors:

- the structure of the security;
- historical delinquency;
- charge-off experience of the asset portfolio;
- the originator's underwriting standards and account solicitation methods;
- cash-flow analysis using worst-case scenarios for charge-offs and late payments;
- legal opinions regarding the perfection of a security interest in the collateral; and
- the servicer's ability to continue to service the assets.

Credit enhancement is determined by projecting the anticipated losses on the pooled assets, based upon historical figures from the originator's entire portfolio of these assets, and, in certain instances, by projecting the anticipated expenses in administering the assets and securities. The credit enhancement utilized for an asset-backed security structure may consist of one or a combination of the following:

- reserve fund, which may be funded by an initial up-front deposit or out of excess cash flow on the underlying collateral up to a specific level;

- letter of credit, insurance, or comparable guaranty, which may be obtained from a banking institution or insurance company rated at least as high as the securities, and which typically covers a certain percentage of the first losses on the total pool at a level comparable to historical losses plus an extra margin of loss;
- over-collateralization, which may be referred to as a senior subordinated or class A/B structure (the class B security being the interest retained by the issuer) for pass-through certificates in a sale transaction, or which may be simply a required level of additional asset collateral typically for debt structures.

If a financial institution uses over-collateralization as the method of credit enhancement, the decision on whether to sell the assets or issue debt financing should be carefully considered, because over-collateralization may jeopardize the treatment of the transaction as a sale of assets.

11.6 US Securities Law Considerations

11.6.1 Securities Act of 1933

Generally If a "security" exists then its offer and sale are subject to the relevant federal and state registration requirements unless a specific exemption (e.g. the private placement exemption) can be established. Even if there is an exemption, the purchase or sale of such security will generally be subject to securities anti-fraud liability provisions such as the Securities and Exchange Commission (SEC) Rule 10b-5. Thus, the issuer is required to disclose material information relating to the issuance of the security.

Definition of security A "security," for purposes of the Securities Act of 1933, as amended, and most state securities laws, includes any "note" and any "investment contract." While traditional commercial loan participations have often been held not to constitute "securities," the reasoning of such cases is not applicable to offerings of pass-through certificates which evidence fractional undivided interests in the underlying pool of loan assets and which are freely transferable and are issued in circumstances where investors are not expected to underwrite the individual loans themselves.[7]

Financial institutions With respect to banks and thrifts, sections 3(a)(2) and 3(a)(5) of the Securities Act of 1933 provide exemptions for securities issued by banks and thrifts, respectively (subject to certain fee limitations in the case of section 3(a)(5)). Section 3(a)(2) also exempts securities "guaranteed" by a bank. The section 3(a)(2) and 3(a)(5) exemptions apply only to the financial institution itself, and not to its subsidiaries. Furthermore, each exemption is not available unless the investor has recourse to the bank or thrift, respectively, for payment. Thus, a pass-through security sponsored by a bank or thrift will not generally be subject to the exemption unless the bank or thrift guarantees all of the pass-through payments.[8] In addition, section 4(5) of the 1933 Act provides a limited exemption for certain mortgage-backed securities transactions.

Even where a national bank is specifically exempt from registering its securities with the SEC, it may (if there is a public distribution) still have to file a prescribed offering circular with, provide disclosure required by, and have the Offering declared effective by the Comptroller of the Currency.[9]

Non-bank subsidiaries of banks, and bank holding companies and their non-bank subsidiaries, are subject to the SEC registration requirements, while a subsidiary which is a non-bank bank would remain subject to the Office of the Comptroller of Currency requirements.

Likewise, the issuance of securities by a thrift institution which are exempt from registration under the Securities Act of 1933 is subject to the Federal Home Loan Bank Board (FHLBB) regulations which impose filing and disclosure requirements similar to those required of other entities under the Securities Act of 1933.[10] Generally, the FHLBB regulations provide that a federally insured thrift institution may not offer or sell, directly or indirectly, any security issued by it, unless the offer or sale is accompanied or preceded by an offering circular which includes the information required by these regulations and which has been filed and declared effective pursuant to these regulations, or unless the offer or sale is exempt under these regulations.[11] Under FIRREA, which abolished the FHLBB, the FHLBB regulations then in effect are to remain in effect until modified, terminated, or superseded by the appropriate successor regulatory agency.

11.6.2 State Securities Laws

Any offering of securities must comply with the state securities laws ("blue sky laws") of each jurisdiction in which such securities are offered or sold, or must be exempt from such laws. The Secondary Mortgage Market Enhancement Act of 1984 (SMMEA)[12] generally exempts the offer and sale of "mortgage-related securities" from state securities laws to the same extent as obligations of the US government are exempt from such laws. The definition of a "mortgage-related security" is set forth in section 3(a)(41) of the Securities Exchange Act of 1934, as amended. States could override such pre-exemption by legislative action up to October 3, 1991. SMMEA exemption is generally available in a mortgage-backed offering, but is usually not available in other types of asset securitization.

11.6.3 Legal Investment Laws

The legality of investment in asset-backed securities for state-chartered institutional investors is generally governed by state law. Ordinarily debt securities rated investment grade by a nationally recognized rating agency qualify as a legal investment for most institutions in the majority of jurisdictions. Furthermore, under SMMEA "mortgage-related securities" are eligible investments for institutional investors under the laws of any state to the same extent that US government securities are eligible investments for such investors. States could override such pre-exemption by legislative action up to October 3, 1991.

11.6.4 Disclosure

In a structured financing in which there is minimal or no recourse to the originator of the security, but only to the underlying assets, or to a partial extent from credit enhancement sources, disclosure (for securities law and marketing purposes) focuses more on the underlying assets and less on the financial characteristics of the originator. The most important characteristics of the assets that must be disclosed are those characteristics that could affect default in payment on the asset or yield on the asset. Yield, in turn, depends on the price and the maturity of the asset. Maturity of the asset depends on

- stated maturity,
- rate of prepayment, and
- other factors, such as the presence of "due on sale" clauses.

Important factors that normally must be disclosed include

- interest rate,
- seasoning (i.e., how long the asset has been in existence),
- delinquency history,
- maturity of the assets,
- geographic diversity of the assets,
- underwriting and originating procedures with respect to the assets, and

- credit support, such as mortgage insurance or other insurance.

An important asset characteristic that can affect default is the quality of servicing of the assets. Disclosure should include the experience of the entity that will continue to deal with the underlying obligor, as well as information regarding its financial strength. Disclosure documents for asset-backed securities often include tables that demonstrate the effect of prepayment rates or other factors upon the rate of principal payments on the security offered. If the maturity of the security offered is extremely sensitive with respect to rate of prepayment, consideration should be given to disclosure of the effect of such prepayments on the yield of the security. For example, in the sale of "residuals" for CMOs (i.e. residual cash flow to equity owners after payments on the CMOs), disclosure documents often include a table that shows the internal rate of return on the investment as a function of various prepayment rates and various rates of reinvestment of funds held by the trustee.

11.6.5 Investment Company Act of 1940

The Investment Company Act of 1940 (the 1940 Act), by its terms, requires registration with the Securities and Exchange Commission of almost any "asset-backed arrangement." The definition of "security" under the 1940 Act is not coextensive with the definition of "security" under other securities laws, and had been construed broadly by the SEC to effectuate the purposes of the 1940 Act.[13] The definition of "company" (which in turn controls the definition of "person" and "issuer") includes any "trust" or "fund." Therefore, an "issuer" can include a passive pool of assets. Because regulation of investment companies under the 1940 Act is very restrictive, including restrictions on indebtedness and other conditions that may preclude any asset-backed securities offering, it is necessary in most asset securitization programs to ensure that the arrangement falls within one of the exemptions under the Act. The exemptions under the 1940 Act include the following:

- *Section 3(c)(1).* This section exempts issuers whose outstanding securities (other than short-term paper) are beneficially owned by not more than 100 persons and that are not involved in public offerings of securities. For purposes of the exemption, beneficial ownership by a company is deemed to be beneficial ownership by one person, except that if the company owns 10 percent or more of the outstanding voting securities of the issuer, the beneficial ownership shall be deemed to be that of holders of such company's outstanding securities unless certain conditions are satisfied.

▪ *Section 3(c)(3)*. This section exempts any bank or insurance company; any savings and loan association; certain similar institutions; and certain collective investment funds maintained by banks. For purposes of the 1940 Act, the term "bank" includes any national bank, any member bank of the Federal Reserve System, or any other banking institution or trust company doing business under the laws of any state or the US, a substantial portion of the business of which consists of receiving deposits or exercising fiduciary powers similar to those permitted by national banks under the authority of the Comptroller of the Currency, and which is supervised and examined by a state or federal authority having supervision over banks and which is not operated for the purpose of evading the provisions of the Act, or any receiver, conservator, or other liquidator of any such institution.

▪ *Section 3(c)(4)*. This section exempts any person substantially all of whose business is confined to making small loans, industrial banking, or similar businesses.

▪ *Section 3(c)(5)*. This section exempts "any person who is not engaged in the business of issuing redeemable securities, face-amount certificates of the installment type or periodic payment plan certificates, and who is primarily engaged in one or more of the following businesses:

A purchasing or otherwise acquiring notes, drafts, acceptances, open accounts receivables, and other obligations representing part or all of the sales price of merchandise, insurance, and services;
B making loans to manufacturers, wholesalers, and retailers of, and to prospective purchasers of, specified merchandise, insurance, and services; and
C purchasing or otherwise acquiring mortgages and other liens on and interests in real estate."

This exemption is particularly significant for asset-backed securities, and has been the subject of numerous no-action requests to the SEC. For purposes of the 3(c)(5)(C) exemption, the staff of the SEC, in its no-action letter responses, has indicated that (1) for purposes of determining whether an issuer is "primarily engaged" in purchasing or otherwise acquiring mortgages, where an issuer's only business is investing in real estate interests, at least 55 percent of the assets must consist of mortgages and other liens on and interests in real estate and the remaining 45 percent of such an issuer's assets must consist primarily of real estate related investments,[14] and (2) mortgage participation or pass-through certificates issued or guaranteed by the Government National Mortgage Association (GNMA), FNMA, or FHLMC will be considered "mortgages or other interests in real estate" if, and only if, the asset-backed arrangement contains certificates comprising an undivided interest in the entire pool of mortgages backing the certificates.[15]

■ *Section 6(c)*. This section allows the SEC to grant discretionary exemptions if and to the extent "that such exemption is necessary or appropriate in the public interest and consistent with the protection of investors and the purpose is fairly intended by the policy and provisions of this title." Because "partial-pool" GNMA, FNMA, and FHLMC certificates do not satisfy the definition of "interests in real estate" for purposes of the section 3(c)(5)(C) exemption, numerous applications have been submitted to the SEC for exemptions under section 6(c) for mortgage-related investments. The SEC has developed standardized categories of representations required in order to receive such an exemption.

11.7 US Bankruptcy and Insolvency Considerations

In order to assure timely payments to investors, and to satisfy rating agency requirements, asset-backed securities must be structured so that the bankruptcy or insolvency of a related party will not impair timely or ultimate payment under the securities. Certain provisions of the US Bankruptcy Code may impair the timeliness of payment or in some cases the ultimate payment with respect to the underlying assets that are subject to a bankruptcy proceeding, including sections 362 (automatic stay), 363 (ability of the bankruptcy trustee to use, sell, or lease property of the estate), 364 (ability of the bankruptcy trustee to obtain credit secured by a junior lien on property of the estate), 542 (requirement to turn over property of the estate), 547 (avoidance of preferential transfers), 548 (fraudulent conveyances), and 552 (limits on post-petition effect of security interests).

With respect to debt obligations of banks (but not their non-bank subsidiaries, or parent holding company and its non-bank subsidiaries), thrifts and other institutions that are ineligible to be "debtors" under the Bankruptcy Code, the foregoing provisions of the Bankruptcy Code do not apply.

The principal rating agency concerns relating to issuers in a securitization are that

- the collateral securing the debt be validly pledged and perfected under applicable law, and

- the pledge of such collateral and the proceeds thereof not be subject to avoidance or attack by a receiver of the institution in an insolvency proceeding.

With respect to issuers subject to the Bankruptcy Code, unless the issuer has a long-term debt rating as high as that sought for the asset-backed security, the asset-backed security must be issued by a special-purpose subsidiary or other entity whose business is confined to acquiring the assets and issuing the securities, and which is unlikely to incur any other liabilities that might result in a voluntary or involuntary petition under the Bankruptcy Code. If a special-purpose entity is used, assurance must be obtained that

- the transfer of assets to the entity is a true sale and not a pledge or other financing transaction and is not voidable as a fraudulent conveyance, and
- that, upon the bankruptcy of the seller or another affiliate of the issuer, the separate corporate nature of the asset-backed security issuer would not be ignored, resulting in "substantive consolidation" with the insolvent entity for purposes of the bankruptcy proceeding.

11.8 US Federal Tax Law Considerations

11.8.1 *Debt Securities*

In order to avoid unfavorable tax consequences, a debt offering of asset-backed securities by a special-purpose entity should be structured in such a manner that the securities are treated as debt for federal income tax purposes. For example, the offering of the debt securities under certain circumstances could be recharacterized as a sale of the underlying assets to the bond trustee, and in turn, the trust created under the bond indenture would be treated as an association taxable as a corporation and each investor would be treated as having an equity investment in such association, resulting in taxation at both the "corporate" level with respect to the trust and the "stockholder" level with respect to the investor. In addition, the offering of debt securities under certain circumstances could be recharacterized as an equity investment in the issuer, in which case the interest payments to the investors would be recharacterized as dividend payments, resulting in the loss of the interest deduction to the issuer. Characterization of the offering as indebtedness of the issuer for tax purposes requires (1) the issuer's retention of sufficient interest in the underlying assets to avoid sale treatment of the assets to the bond trustee and (2) the issuer's maintenance of sufficient equity to avoid recharacterization of the debt as equity investments in the issuer.

The structuring of mortgage-backed securities to achieve this debt characterization has historically led to certain inefficiencies in the issuance of mortgage-backed securities. Partial relief from these requirements for mortgage-backed instruments was obtained with the "real estate mortgage investment conduit" or "REMIC" legislation enacted in 1986 and included in the Internal Revenue Code of 1986, as amended. Election of REMIC status and compliance with the REMIC structure allows the issuer to treat the transaction as a sale of the assets for federal income tax purposes while allowing investors in "regular interests" to characterize their investment as debt for federal income tax purposes. However, in certain circumstances, an issuer may not wish to make a REMIC election because its sale of the mortgage loan assets may cause it to recognize gain or loss. In addition, a securitization of non-mortgage assets does not qualify for the REMIC election and treatment.

11.8.2 Grantor Trusts

A grantor trust, pass-through structure, allows sale treatment by the sponsor of the trust and purchase treatment by the investors. The trust is ignored for income tax purposes and investors are treated as owning an undivided interest in each of the trust's assets. Qualification as a grantor trust for tax purposes requires that (1) the trust be a "fixed investment trust" and (2) the trust have a single class or the proper type of multiple classes of ownership. A fixed investment trust is a trust that does not have any power under the trust agreement to vary the investment of the investors. Thus, such trust must not have any power to reinvest any income received by the trust (other than certain limited exceptions with respect to such income during the period between collection and the date of distribution). In order to qualify as a grantor trust the fixed investment trust generally must have only a single class of ownership interest (e.g. a CMO structure will not qualify as a grantor trust). However, a fixed investment trust with multiple classes of ownership interests will qualify as a grantor trust if the trust is formed to facilitate direct investment in the assets of the trust and the existence of multiple classes of ownership interests is incidental to that purpose (e.g. a senior/subordinated pass-through certificate). With respect to mortgage pass-through certificates, by electing REMIC status an issuer may utilize a multiple class structure without the above restrictions.

11.8.3 Accounting Treatment

While characterization of the transaction for accounting purposes is an important consideration in classification for tax purposes, it is not dispositive. Some transactions have been structured so that they are accounted for as sales, but treated as debt for tax purposes.

11.8.4 Original Issue Discount, Market Discount, and Amortizable Bond Premium

Original issue discount (OID) is the excess of the "stated redemption price at maturity" of an obligation over its issue price. Generally, holders of obligations issued with OID must include the OID in gross income as it accrues under a constant interest method over the entire life of the obligation using a yield that takes into account compounding of interest. Consequently, OID generally must be reported as taxable income before the receipt of cash attributable to such income. In the case of any debt instrument issued with OID under which payments may be accelerated by reason of prepayments of other obligations securing such debt instrument (e.g., an MO), the holder thereof must accrue the OID taking into account the prepayment assumption used in pricing the obligation.

Generally, when an obligation is purchased in the secondary market at a price less than its adjusted issue price (the original issue price plus OID accrued thereon to the date of purchase less payments of principal thereon), the difference is considered "market discount." The market discount must be accrued over the remaining life of the obligation, and unless an election is made to include accrued market discount in income on a current basis on all of the holder's "market discount obligations," market discount must be reported as ordinary income to the extent of any gain on disposition or retirement of the obligation. In the case of an instrument payable in installments, such as a mortgage, the accrued market discount is also treated as ordinary income to the extent of any principal payment received. A holder of an obligation acquired at a market discount may also be required to defer until disposition of the obligation the deduction of a portion of any interest expense on indebtedness incurred to purchase or carry the obligation.

If an obligation is purchased for more than its stated redemption price at maturity, such premium generally may be amortized over the life of the obligation under a constant interest method.

11.8.5 Coupon Stripping

For federal income tax purposes, the separation of ownership of the right to receive some or all of the interest payments on an obligation from the ownership of the right to receive some or all of the principal payments results in the creation of "stripped bonds" with respect to principal payments and "stripped coupons" with respect to interest payments. The person who strips an obligation and sells a stripped coupon or stripped bond must allocate his adjusted basis in the whole obligation between the interests retained and those sold to compute his gain on the portion sold. The seller is treated as having purchased on the date of the sale each interest retained for an amount equal to the basis allocated to that item. The seller would then report the difference between the stated redemption price at maturity of the retained interest and its deemed purchase price as it accrues under the OID rules. The purchaser of a stripped bond or stripped coupon is treated as acquiring an obligation issued on the purchase date and having an OID equal to the excess of the stated redemption price at maturity (or, in the case of a stripped coupon, the amount payable on the due date of each coupon), over such stripped bond's or stripped coupon's ratable share of the purchase price. Any subsequent purchaser of a stripped bond or stripped coupon is subject to the OID rules and is not subject to the market discount rules.

The coupon-stripping rules apply to pass-through "strips" and are often implicated in other asset-backed securities, including pass-through structures in which the coupon rates on the underlying assets exceed the pass-through rate to investors by more than a "reasonable servicing fee," in which case both the seller and the investors may be deemed to own stripped bonds or stripped coupons. Application of these rules may impose a significant administrative burden on the issuer because, in order to meet its requirement to report information to investors to enable them to complete their tax returns, the issuer must perform significant computations on each payment date.

11.8.6 Foreign Withholding Requirements

Payments in respect of interest or OID on an obligation to a non-US person will generally not be subject to US withholding tax if the obligation was issued on or after July 18, 1984. Such non-US person must not actually or constructively own 10 percent or more of the combined voting power of all classes of equity of the issuer and must not be a "controlled foreign corporation" related to the issuer. Furthermore, such non-US person must comply with certain identification and certification requirements. Payments in respect of interest or OID that are attributable to obligations issued before July 18, 1984 and paid to a foreign person are subject to a 30 percent US withholding tax, unless such tax is reduced or eliminated by an applicable tax treaty. If any such payments are effectively connected with a US trade or business conducted by a foreign person, such payments will be subject to regular US income tax, but ordinarily will be exempt from US withholding tax.

For the foregoing purposes, acquisition of an investment consisting of a pass-through or participation security backed by loans or other obligations is deemed to be acquisition of "obligations" consisting of the loans or obligations. If the underlying loans or obligations were originated prior to July 18, 1984, foreign persons will be subject to the 30 percent withholding requirement with respect to their *pro rata* ownership interest unless relief is provided by treaty.

11.9 Special Considerations of Risk-based Capital Requirements in the US

The risk-based capital regulations, which are similar in most respects, were adopted by the following federal regulatory agencies:

- the Board of Governors of the Federal Reserve System (FRB), which regulates bank holding companies and state-chartered banks that are members of the Federal Reserve System;[16]
- the Office of the Comptroller of the Currency (OCC), which regulates national banks;[17]
- the Federal Deposit Insurance Corporation (FDIC), which is responsible for state-chartered, federally insured banks that are not members of the Federal Reserve System;[18] and
- the Office of Thrift Supervision (OTS), which pursuant to FIRREA succeeded to the regulatory functions of the FHLBB pertaining to federally insured savings associations.[19]

11.9.1 Banks

Generally, under the federal banking regulations of the FRB, OCC, and FDIC, banks and bank holding companies are required to comply with new risk-based capital guidelines which impose a minimum ratio of capital to risk-weighted assets. The framework for these guidelines includes a definition of regulatory capital for risk-based purposes and a system for calculating the risk-weighted assets by assigning the bank's assets and off-balance-sheet items to one of four broad risk-weighted categories, each of which has a specific risk-weight percentage. Each off-balance-sheet item is converted to an on-balance-sheet credit equivalent amount and then assigned to a risk-weighted category according to its underlying characteristics.

Mortgage-backed securities may be assigned to any of the four risk-weighted categories depending upon the securitization structure including the issuer, underlying collateral, and the guarantor. Under the risk-based capital guidelines a bank may reduce its required regulatory capital by shrinking its higher risk-weighted assets through securitization structures treated as a sale for accounting purposes, assuming the bank does not recognize a significant loss. Likewise, a bank may reduce its required risk-based capital by swapping its mortgage loans for mortgage-backed securities issued or backed by US government agencies and US government-sponsored entities (i.e. FHLMC or FNMA).

11.9.2 Thrifts

Likewise, under the regulations of the OTS federally insured savings associations (thrift institutions) are required to comply with new risk-based capital guidelines which impose a minimum ratio of regulatory capital to risk-weighted assets. The framework for these guidelines is similar to the risk-based capital guidelines for banks set out above. In fact, FIRREA requires that the risk-based capital standards for thrifts be no less stringent than the standards applicable to national banks, with the exception that such standards may deviate to reflect interest rate risk or other risks. The OTS regulations calculate the risk-weighted asset values by assigning the thrift's assets and off-balance-sheet items to one of six risk-weighted categories, each of which has a specific risk-weight percentage including a 200 percent and 300 percent risk-weight percentage for the two highest categories, respectively.

Mortgage-backed securities and mortgage loans held by thrifts under the risk-based capital regulations are treated in a similar manner as set out above for banks, and accordingly, a thrift may reduce its required regulatory capital by swapping its mortgage loans for mortgage-backed securities issued or backed by US government agencies and US government-sponsored entities.

PART B: SECURITIZATION DEVELOPMENTS IN THE UK

11.10 Introduction to the UK Situation

In part A of this chapter David Barbour has already explained the concept of securitization, and given an overview of securitization structures. I do not propose to elaborate further on that topic other than to say that the basic structure of a securitization program in the UK will, generally, be little different from that in the US, save for structures based on grantor trusts, which do not exist in this country.

In this part B, however, the author wishes to concentrate on the motive which underlies all securitization programs, that is, the transfer of risk for purposes of balance sheet management. Through- out part A, the first author has identified a number of risk concerns, for example, the concern of the regulators in determining whether or not the risk of the assets of the regulated institution may properly be said to have been transferred, and the concern of investors that sufficient credit enhancement has been provided to minimize their risk in acquiring an interest in the assets. This part B considers the latest developments in the UK on the regulatory and accounting treatment of the transfer of risk. This author will confine his comments in the first instance, however, primarily to banking institutions, that is, institutions authorized by the Bank of England to carry on a banking business in the UK.

The concept of securitizing assets has evolved very much as a result of the LDC debt crisis of the early 1980s and the consequent internationalization and sophistication of banking regulatory and accounting requirements on the treatment of assets.[20] Before the LDC debt crisis, the primary objective of treasury departments within banking institutions was to promote balance sheet growth, and in so doing, to encourage relationship-oriented business. Assets were rarely traded down, much less repackaged and issued on public markets. There was relatively little analysis of the manner in which credit risk could be transferred. The LDC debt crisis highlighted the dangers of this approach, and its legacy has been to revolutionize the approach to balance sheet management within the banking institutions themselves.

These days, assets of banking institutions are seen not so much as static and immovable but as inherently tradeable. Profit is sought from administration and underwriting fees rather than on interest margins, and commercial banking has, in this way, encroached further and further into the province of the investment banks.

There are a number of ways of trading these assets, without embarking on a full securitization program, which enable the relationship which a bank has developed with its borrowers to be maintained, but which allow, in addition, the bank to transfer, without informing its borrowers, the risk associated in the loan asset derived from its borrowers. The most obvious ways of achieving this position are for the bank to sub-participate its commitment in a loan, or for it to assign the benefit of the loan. Securitization is a variation on this theme, but is capable of reaching a much broader spectrum of investors. Investors are attracted to the repackaged assets as they afford an opportunity to obtain the benefits of markets previously closed to all but specialist banks, for example, mortgage lending, credit card lending, and asset financing such as aircraft leasing. Historically these markets, because of their intricacies, have been limited to the larger banking institutions or to specialist players. The returns, however, have been consistently high. One of the more obvious results of the success of securitization, and other methods of disintermediation, has been the deepening of the secondary market in asset trading and, correspondingly, the redistribution of risk throughout the financial markets, enabling institutions to trade out of overexposure to certain types of asset and to trade into new kinds of assets offering attractive yields.

For the originator, securitization has enabled it to sell its assets to a far wider pool of investors than previously available, while retaining, at least superficially, its relationship with its borrowers and customers. In addition, securitization programs can be structured so that if a profit over funding costs is made by the program, this profit can be rechannelled to the originator. This does seem like a classic attempt to have one's cake and eat it, and indeed an ever-more ingenious approach is required, in these days of more vigilant and directed regulation, to achieve this result. Profit extraction, however, is a subject which should be at the forefront of any originator's mind.

The LDC debt crisis and the consequent liquidity crisis in banking institutions that were exposed to LDC debt caused the national regulators to reappraise the evaluation of risk of balance sheet assets and the capital adequacy of banking institutions in the context of such risks. In addition, there was concern among national regulators that banking institutions, in engaging in off-balance-sheet financing activities so as to improve their balance sheets, were failing to take on board the risks still inherent in these assets. Regulators were concerned that banking institutions were relying on a narrow legalistic approach to the transfer of risk rather than looking to the commercial reality. If the buyer was in fact no more than the seller's *alter ego* (albeit not a subsidiary of the seller for accounting purposes) no substantive transfer of risk had in fact taken place. Banking institutions were, therefore, "dressing up" their balance sheets through the purported removal of assets in which such institutions still held, for all practical purposes, an interest. Such interests might be as blatant as a right of recourse against the selling institution should the asset sold default after the sale, or, alternatively, as subtle as commercial pressure brought to bear on the selling institution by the underlying obligors to relieve or reschedule obligations due from them in respect of the assets sold.

In recent years, there has been concerted effort at an international level to provide a uniform basis for the measurement of capital against risk of banking institutions. This objective has become all the more important in the light of the globalization of the financial markets, which has provided more opportunities than ever before for regulatory arbitrage and, therefore, unfair and anti-competitive practices. The UK has seen the introduction of internationally based capital adequacy/risk asset requirements on two levels. First, the Bank of England has adopted the recommendations of the Basle Committee on Banking Regulation and Supervisory Practices, agreed by the Governors of the G10 central banks on July 11, 1988 (the Basle Convergence Agreement).[21] The Bank of England issued a notice in October 1988 to institutions authorized under the Banking Act 1987, advising of the manner in which it proposed to implement the Basle Convergence Agreement in the UK. Consequent on this paper, the Bank of England has now issued a new form of capital adequacy return which must be completed each year by institutions authorized by the Bank of England, in which the approach to capital adequacy and risk asset weighting adopted by the Basle Convergence Agreement is followed through into practical effect.

Secondly, at the end of 1989 the European Community Own Funds Directive[22] and Solvency Ratio Directive[23] came into effect. These measures provide for the measurement of capital and risk on terms similar, but not identical, to those put forward by the Basle Convergence Agreement.[24] At present, the Bank of England has made no changes to its calculation of capital adequacy and risk asset weightings so as to take into account those differences which do exist between the approach of the Basle Convergence Agreement and the criteria specified in the Own Funds Directive and the Solvency Ratio Directive nor, indeed, has it indicated that it sees the differences as being material.

The adoption by the Bank of England of the proposals set out in the Basle Convergence Agreement has undoubtedly prompted institutions authorized by the Bank of England to examine carefully their balance sheets, and to consider whether or not it will be possible for them to adjust their balance sheets so as to eject assets which have risk asset weightings of 100 percent (e.g. commercial loans) in favor of assets with low or relatively low risk asset weightings (for example, loans collateralized by residential mortgages, which are weighted at 50 percent).

The primary concern of the regulators, however, is the identification and attribution of risk. If, no matter in what form one purports to transfer an asset, the risk inherent in that asset remains with the transferor, then regulators and auditors alike will refuse to treat that asset as having been transferred so as to justify the removal of that asset and the capital supporting the investment in that asset from the asset and liability side of balance sheets. In part B this author wishes to consider this concept in particular in the light of the changes effected by the Companies Act 1989, and of the proposals of the Accounting Standards Committee (ASC) in their Exposure Draft 49, entitled "Reflecting the Substance of Transactions in Assets and Liabilities." These provisions and recommendations will affect all companies incorporated in the UK. Before considering these general aspects, however, the author will refer to the requirements which the Bank of England will impose upon an institution authorized under the Banking Act 1987 where that institution wishes to securitize its assets. The Bank of England's approach to such matters is to be found in its Notice of February 1989 entitled "Loan Transfers and Securitisation." A useful place to start, however, in the identification of risk is Exposure Draft 42 (ED42) published by the Accounting Standards Committee in March 1988.

11.11 Exposure Draft 42 – March 1988 (1)

Although ED42 has now been revised by ED49 (see section 11.15 below) many of the general requirements set out in ED42 remain unaltered. ED42 was directed specifically to the treatment of SPVs which sought to achieve off-balance-sheet status in respect of the originator's statutory accounts. The intention of ED42 was to provide a framework for statutory accounting purposes which recognized the economic and commercial reality of off-balance-sheet financing, primarily by consolidating the accounts of the SPV with those of the originator if the auditors of the originator determined that the reality of the SPV financing was that the risks involved in such financing either never left the originator or reverted to the originator in time of crisis. In presenting this framework, ED42 isolated five categories of risk associated with securitization programs involving, essentially, interest-bearing assets (these categories were later adopted by the Bank of England for the purposes of its paper on "Loan Transfers and Securitisation" in February 1989 – see section 11.12 below). The categories of risk are as follows.

11.11.1 Bad Debt Risk

This refers to the risk of default by the underlying debtor on its obligations in respect of the securitized asset. This should be covered to a large extent by the terms of the eligibility criteria which an asset must satisfy if it is to be offered for purchase to the SPV. It should be a *minimum* requirement that the originator represents and warrants to the SPV that assets which arise from a contract which is unenforceable for any reason, or which is affected by claims from third parties or the other party to which is insolvent or in receivership, *will not* be offered for purchase. The bad debt risk can be further insured against by the SPV acquiring more assets from the originator than is necessary to fund the payments due to its investors. In the case of a corporate receivables program, the receivables that constitute the subject of the program may be acquired by the SPV for less than their face value, in the same way ensuring that there is, or should be, excess liquidity in the program over that required to meet funding costs. So far as the originator is concerned, however, it should not otherwise cover bad debt risk, and in particular should only sell on non-recourse terms if it wishes to prove full transfer of this type of risk.

11.11.2 Liquidity Risk

This refers to the risk of income from the securitized assets not being received in sufficient time to fund payments of principal and interest due from the SPV to its investors. The obvious answer to this problem so far as the SPV is concerned is to ensure that the income stream and the payment obligations are not mismatched, but this in itself will not solve problems such as an unusually high default rate which precipitates a cash shortfall. In certain limited circumstances, the originator may cover such shortfalls without thereby reassuming the risk in the securitized assets and jeopardizing the off-balance-sheet nature of the SPV financing. Any indemnity to the SPV provided by the originator in these circumstances should relate only to shortfalls that do not arise by reason of default under the securitized assets. For example, the originator may make a one-off loan to the SPV at the commencement of the securitization program to cover liquidity crises, provided that such a loan is made on a long-term, subordinated basis, repayable only after all other creditors of the SPV have received payment in full and the securitization program has been wound up. The provision against shortfalls arising by reason of default under the securitized assets is, however, normally forthcoming from a third party credit enhancer.

11.11.3 Basis Risk

This represents the risk of the rate of interest accruing on the securitized assets or income falling below the rate of interest due from the SPV to the investors. The likelihood of this risk arising will depend on the type of asset securitized. In the case of pure receivables financing, there is no interest as such arising from the assets. If interest-bearing assets are securitized, then there is a much greater vulnerability to basis risk in the case of mortgage-backed securities than those based on car or credit card receivables which have, historically, borne far higher rates of interest than the LIBOR or base rate plus margin rates common in mortgage financing. Basis risk will also be a factor to consider if funding is acquired on a fixed rate basis, but the interest due on the interest-bearing assets is levied at a floating rate. One obvious solution is to engage in interest rate swaps and it is possible for the originator to enter into a swap agreement with the SPV without thereby reassuming the risks in the securitized assets, provided that the swap agreement is entered into on an arm's length basis and on normal commercial terms.

11.11.4 Reinvestment Risk

This type of risk is, again, particularly pertinent to securitizations of interest-bearing assets, and represents the risk which arises in cases of prepayment of high-interest-bearing assets at a time when similarly high interest rates are not available in the market place for the newly released capital to earn. If the funding to the SPV has been structured on the basis of a notional prepayment rate which in reality is far exceeded, and in the meantime the market rates chargeable on the securitized assets are falling, then clearly a risk arises that the interest payments due under the funding of the SPV, calculated on the basis of the notional prepayment rate, cannot be met. This risk can be absorbed in a number of ways, for example by interest rate swaps,[25] by arranging a guaranteed investment contract with a third party, or, in the case of an issue of debt securities, structuring the issue from the outset so that there is a multiple issue of fast-pay and slow-pay tranches. As well as absorbing the interest rate mismatch on reinvestment, a multiple issue may appeal to a broader spectrum of investors. Again, if the originator is a swap counterparty or provider of a guaranteed investment contract in such circumstances, the agreements evidencing these arrangements with the SPV should be concluded on an arm's length basis and on usual commercial terms.

11.11.5 Administration Risk

This type of risk is specific to an originator which is appointed administrator of the portfolio of securitized receivables sold to the SPV, and is a risk of a moral rather than a legal nature. The benefit to the originator of removing the risk of these assets without the underlying debtors being aware that this has happened is acquired only at the expense of the originator being subject to external pressures to ease the repayment burden in times of economic downturn or to alleviate payment difficulties experienced by particular borrowers. This is particularly so where the securitized assets are of an interest-bearing nature and are due from ordinary consumers, and where pressure is brought to bear for a moratorium on or reduction of interest payments. The risk on the originator in these circumstances is analogous to that identified by the Bank of England on banks which grant participations in their loans, but remain vulnerable to calls for debt rescheduling, and is perhaps the most difficult type of risk to confront satisfactorily because it is unquantifiable, unspecific, and divorced from the securitized assets themselves and the logical purity of the securitization structure.

Each of the five forms of risk referred to above will be encountered in most securitization structures, and must be addressed in each case to the satisfaction of the originator's auditors and, more pertinently, of any regulatory authority to whom the originator is accountable, if the securitized assets are to be removed from the originator's balance sheet. It should be remembered, however, that the five categories of risk identified in ED42 do not constitute an exhaustive list, but are merely examples of particular types of risk that may be encountered in a securitization program. The underlying principle of accounting practice in this area should always be borne in mind, that is, that the commercial and practical reality of an enterprise's transactions should be reflected in its financial statements. The approach is one of substance, not form. A seller does not divest himself of risk in an asset if the person to whom he sells is for all practical purposes the seller in a different guise. The type of risk to which the seller is prone may have changed, but risk remains none the less.

11.12 Off-balance-sheet Treatment of Accounts of Institutions Regulated by the Bank of England

In February 1989, the Bank of England issued a notice (the Notice) setting out its policy on the treatment of loan transfers and securitization for the accounting and regulatory purposes of institutions authorized by it. As stated above, the publication of the paper arose as a result of the increasingly sophisticated financial institutions finding more and more methods to transfer assets in a manner which relieved them from reporting liability for the assets concerned and thus from the liability to set (expensive) capital against such assets, without necessarily relieving them entirely of the risk associated with those assets. The result, in the regulators' eyes, was a potential destabilizing effect on the financial institutions as the capital adequacy/risk asset ratios previously determined were eroded by artificial and incomplete means. The Notice followed on from a consultative paper on the subject issued in December 1987 and subsequent to that, a draft paper sent to the British Bankers' Association in August 1988.

The Notice applies only to institutions authorized by the Bank of England and incorporated in the UK, and covers both the sale of single loans and the packaging, securitization, and sale of loan pools. It also covers the transfer of risk under sub-participation agreements, and although most references in the Notice are to sales of loans, the policy in principle applies also to sales of other forms of assets, and to the transfer of risk under contingent items such as letters of credit and acceptance credits. It also covers undrawn commitments. The Notice examines each method of transfer and specifies the treatment for accounting regulation purposes in each case. For present purposes, however, the author will refer only to those aspects of the Notice which concern securitization.

The Notice sets out the following particular conditions which must be satisfied where an authorized institution acts as a servicing agent of a loan packaging scheme. The requirements are particularly relevant to the situation in which the authorized institution which is appointed servicer is also the originator. A careful balance must be achieved which, although retaining the originator (in its capacity as servicer) as its primary point of contact and relationship with the underlying debtors, none the less satisfactorily divorces the risk associated with those assets from the originator. In order for an originator who is appointed servicing agent of a portfolio of assets transferred under a securitization program to ensure that its role is not seen as being more than acting as an agent or administrator:

- The Bank of England will expect the servicing agent to have evidence available in its records that its auditors and legal advisers are satisfied that the terms of the program protect it from any liability to investors in the program, save where it is proved to have been negligent.
- The servicing agent must be able to demonstrate that it has taken all reasonable precautions to ensure that it is not obliged, nor will feel compelled, to support any losses suffered by the program or investors in it. Any offering circular should contain a highly visible, unequivocal statement that the servicing agent does not

stand behind the program or the vehicle and will not make good any losses in the securitized portfolio.
- The servicing agent (or any other group entity covered by the Bank of England's consolidated supervision of a group of which the servicing agent is a part) may not own any share capital in any company used as a vehicle for the program, nor in any other form hold a proprietary interest in or control over that company, either directly or indirectly. For this purpose, "share capital" includes all classes of ordinary and preference share capital and so goes beyond the definition of "equity share capital" found in section 744 of the Companies Act 1985 (which would not, normally, encompass preference shares as these carry a right to participate which is limited to a specified amount in a distribution).
- The Board of a company used as a vehicle for the program must be independent of the servicing agent, although the latter may have one director representing it.
- The name of a company used as a vehicle for the program must not include the name of the servicing agent or imply any connection with it.
- The servicing agent must not bear any of the recurring expenses of the program. However, the agent may make a "one-off" contribution to enhance the creditworthiness of a vehicle. It may also lend on a long-term subordinated basis to the vehicle provided that the loan is only repayable following winding up of the program. Any transactions under these headings must be undertaken at the initiation of the scheme and disclosed in any offering circular. They will be deducted from capital for capital adequacy purposes.
- The servicing agent may not intentionally bear any losses arising from the effect of interest rate changes on the program. However the servicing agent may enter into interest rate swap agreements with the vehicle at market prices. There should be provision for unintended temporary losses arising from normal administrative delays in changing mortgage rates to be recovered by the servicing agent as soon as possible.
- A servicing agent may not fund a vehicle or program (except within the terms of the sixth condition listed above) and in particular may not provide temporary finance to a program to cover cash shortfalls arising from delayed payments on non-performance of loans which it administers.
- A servicing agent may not retain an option to repurchase (or refinance) loans except where the loan portfolio has fallen to less than 10 percent of its maximum value and the option extends to fully performing loans.

If any one of the above conditions is not satisfied, the assets administered by the servicing agent will be consolidated with the servicing agent's balance sheet for capital adequacy/risk asset ratio purposes.

The intention of the Bank of England in setting these requirements is evident. The transfer of risk means a clean transfer of all ownership interests and all ancillary rights and obligations whether of a legal or a moral nature. A total severance from the assets must be achieved, and in accomplishing this severance there should not be any connection or putative connection between the originator and the SPV save in a purely commercial context. If in any circumstances the risk of non-performance of assets sold can fall back on the selling institution, then a clean transfer has not been achieved. Even where the selling institution is under no legal obligation to cover losses in securitized assets, if the Bank of England is of the opinion that the selling institution, whether acting out of what it deems its moral obligations or in order to protect its relationship with an underlying defaulting obligor or its name in the marketplace, will in fact intercede to cover portfolio losses, then the assets comprised within the portfolio will be consolidated into the selling institution's accounts for Bank of England regulatory purposes. Similarly, any funding by the originator of the SPV can only be made in restricted circumstances and on terms which are not related to the performance of the assets sold.

There have been suggestions recently from regulators in the US that where an originator offers credit enhancement which provides protection against a default rate of the underlying assets far in excess of the historical default rate, then it is arguable that the originator, in providing such over-compensatory support, is in fact underwriting the whole securitization program, and its accounts should reflect this. No such similar mutterings have yet emanated from the Bank of England, other than that it is preferable, to prove full transfer of risk, for credit enhancement to be provided to the SPV by unconnected third parties. That course would, of course, diminish the profitability of the program to the originator.

The competing elements of control and risk are thus clearly identified in the Notice, and the problems of achieving a satisfactory compromise of these elements are evident.

11.13 Companies Act 1989

11.13.1 Introduction

On April 1, 1990 the provisions enacted in Part I of the Companies Act 1989 (the 1989 Act) came into force. I wish to concentrate in this section on the amendments made to the Companies Act 1985 (the 1985 Act) by sections 5, 21, and 22 of the 1989 Act. Section 5 of the 1989 Act introduces a new section 227 into the 1985 Act, the effect of which is to impose an obligation on a "parent company" to prepare annual consolidated accounts of the "parent company" and its "subsidiary undertakings." The concept of "subsidiary undertakings" is entirely new to English law, and is defined, in section 21 of the 1989 Act and Schedule 9 to that Act (which inserts a new Schedule 10A into the 1985 Act) in extremely wide terms. The basis for the definition of subsidiary undertaking is, however, that of control, whether control arises as a matter of fact or practice or as a matter of law.

Before the introduction of the concept of subsidiary undertakings, it was comparatively easy, from a Companies Act point of view, to structure a vehicle company to which the securitized assets could be sold, which would not constitute a subsidiary of the originator for the purposes of the 1985 Act, but which the originator might none the less control and obtain benefits from by way of dividend. The reason for this anomaly was the definition of subsidiary contained in section 736 of the 1985 Act, which is a definition which concentrates solely on the equity structure of the subsidiary, rather than factors evidencing control. Under section 736 of the 1985 Act, a company is deemed to be a subsidiary of another company if (but only if):

(a) that one [i.e., the other company] either
   (i) is a member of it and controls the composition of its board of directors; or
   (ii) holds more than half in nominal value of its equity share capital.

The phrase "equity share capital" is defined in section 744 of the 1985 Act as follows: "in relation to a company, its issued share capital excluding any part of that capital which, neither as respects dividends nor as respects capital, carries any right to participate beyond a specified amount in a distribution." Thus, for example, preference shares carrying a fixed dividend do not constitute equity share capital as that phrase is defined by the 1985 Act.

The first limb of the definition of "subsidiary" focused on control of the *composition* of the board of directors: this control was attributed only to shareholders (members) of the company in point. This appeared to refer simply to the *number* of directors which a person had a right, by its shareholding, to appoint, without regard to the voting power of such an appointee as against other directors. Thus it

ASSET SECURITIZATION DEVELOPMENTS

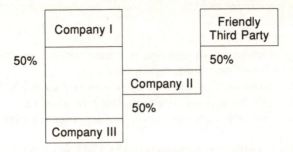

Figure 11.1 The 'diamond structure'

was possible to share equally with another shareholder the right to appoint directors to the board of the SPV, but to ensure that certain directors, e.g. in the case of securitization, the originator's appointees, carried weighted voting rights. Provided that the second limb of the test in s. 736(a) was not satisfied, the originator was not thereby deemed to be a holding company of the SPV.

One of the most common off-balance-sheet schemes was the so-called diamond structure, shown in figure 11.1. Under this scheme, Companies II and III had two shareholders, each owning half the shares and having the right to appoint an equal number of directors. But the directors appointed by Company I had, under the articles of each company, more votes than their counterparts appointed by the Friendly Third Party or by Company II. Neither Company II nor Company III was therefore a subsidiary of Company I under the old definition of subsidiary (although Company I controlled them) but because of the indirect holding of 75 percent in Company III, Company III would be grouped with Company I for tax purposes.

It will be apparent from the above that the test for determining whether or not one company is a subsidiary of another under the 1985 Act, before it was amended, was entirely formalistic, and the substantive questions of effective control, influence, or risk participation were not addressed.

11.13.2 Changes in the Requirements on a Parent Company to Present Consolidated Annual Accounts

The EC Seventh Company Law Directive sets out the situations in which it is perceived that accounts of different corporate entities should be consolidated for reporting purposes.[26] In the UK, these proposals were summarized in DTI Notice 88/602 published on August 16, 1988, which advised that the principal changes required in the UK to implement the Directive would be to alter the definition of subsidiary by:

- the replacement of the existing test based on equity share capital with one based on voting rights; and
- a new requirement to consolidate where one company has a certain interest by way of a shareholding in another and the first company actually exercises a dominating influence over the other.

The 1989 Act effects the changes in the 1985 Act required to implement the Seventh Company Law Directive in the UK, so far as consolidation of accounts is concerned. The main provisions of the 1989 Act, in the context of asset securitization structures, are as follows.

Duty to prepare group accounts If, at the end of a financial year, a company is a parent company then, subject to certain exceptions, the directors of that company, as well as preparing individual accounts for the year, are also required to prepare group accounts, comprising a consolidated balance sheet dealing with the state of affairs of the parent company and its subsidiary undertakings and a consolidated profit and loss account dealing with the profit and loss of the parent company and its subsidiary undertakings.[27] The "group" has been redefined, for accounting purposes only, as comprising the parent company and its subsidiary undertakings. The various accounts identified above must give a true and fair view of the state of affairs of the undertakings as at the end of the financial year in respect of which such accounts are prepared.

Definition of "parent undertaking" and "subsidiary undertaking" The expression "subsidiary undertaking" is defined in section 258(2) of the 1985 Act as follows:[28]

> An undertaking is a parent undertaking in relation to another undertaking, a subsidiary undertaking, if –
> (i) it holds a majority of the voting rights in the undertaking, or
> (ii) it is a member of the undertaking and has the right to appoint or remove a majority of its board of directors, or
> (iii) it has the right to exercise a dominant influence over the undertaking –
>   (1) by virtue of provisions contained in the undertaking's memorandum or articles, or
>   (2) by virtue of a control contract, or

(iv) it is a member of the undertaking and controls alone, pursuant to an agreement with other shareholders or members, a majority of the voting rights in the undertaking.

Each of these circumstances should be considered separately:

■ *(i) it holds a majority of the voting rights in the undertaking* "Voting rights" are defined as "the rights conferred on shareholders in respect of their shares or, in the case of an undertaking not having a share capital, on members, to vote at general meetings on all, or substantially all, matters."[29] In relation to an undertaking which does not have general meetings at which matters are decided by the exercise of voting rights, the reference to holding a majority of the voting rights in the undertaking is to be considered as a reference to having the right under the constitution of the undertaking to direct the overall policy of the undertaking or to alter the terms of its constitution.

The test of holding a majority of the voting rights under the 1989 Act is in contradistinction to the present test of a subsidiary in the 1985 Act, as voting rights are not necessarily identical or related to "equity share capital" as such term is defined in the 1985 Act. For example, an allotment of preference shares might carry a majority of voting rights in an undertaking, but as preference shares which carry a fixed dividend and confer no other rights except in the winding-up of the allotting company do not constitute equity share capital, the holder of such shares which carried weighted voting rights would not, under the old definition of subsidiary, be deemed the parent of the allotting company for accounting purposes. Such a shareholding would now, however, constitute the holder of such shares as the parent company of the allotting company. It will, therefore, be more difficult to create an equity structure for the SPV which, if the originator wishes to control it through voting equity rights, does not result in the originator being deemed the parent undertaking of the SPV. However, if the originator holds equity in the SPV which does not carry any voting rights, or does not carry the majority of voting rights, then the test laid down in section 258(2)(a) of the 1985 Act will not be satisfied, and consolidation under this head would be avoided. Consolidation would be avoided, however, at the expense of loss of control of the SPV.

■ *(ii) it is a member of the undertaking and has the right to appoint or remove a majority of its board of directors* The first point to note under the test is that the dominant undertaking must in any event be a "member" of the dependent undertaking. No definition is given for the word "member" although statutory explanation for the use of the word "share" is provided,[30] which explanation may affect any interpretation put on the word "member." The word "share" is widely defined so as to cover most situations in which a person has a proprietary interest in an undertaking of a nature which entitles such person to share in the profits of the undertaking or exposes it to its losses. The word "member" is therefore likely to include shareholders of whatever class in an undertaking, if the undertaking is a body corporate. The expression "member" will, by virtue of the definition of "undertaking,"[31] also include a partner in a partnership, or a beneficiary under a trust, or at least a person entitled to a share in the trust assets. The originator can avoid this head of consolidation altogether, therefore, if it is not a member of the SPV, in other words if it does not share in the profits of the SPV. However, if the originator is not a member of the SPV, the most tax-efficient manner used to date of passing back profit made by the SPV, that is, through declared dividends to shareholders, will not be available to the originator.

If the originator is a member of the SPV, the second limb of the test comes into focus, that is, the right to appoint or remove a majority of the board of directors. The right to appoint or remove a majority of the board of directors is defined as "the right to appoint or remove directors holding a majority of the *voting rights* at meetings of the board on all, or substantially all, matters."[32] For this purpose an undertaking shall be treated as having the right to appoint to a directorship if

"(1) a person's appointment to it follows necessarily from his appointment as director of the undertaking, or

(2) the directorship is held by the undertaking itself."

However, it should be noted that a right to appoint or remove which is exercisable only with the consent or concurrence of another person shall be left out of account unless no other person has a right to appoint or, as the case may be, remove in relation to that directorship.[33]

Again, the approach is one of substance, not form. It matters not if the originator has a minority in numbers of appointees to the board of the SPV if it has a majority in the ability to appoint or remove a majority of the board of directors. The power referred to is a power to appoint or remove – either power is sufficient to satisfy the test. The emphasis, again, is on executive control. However, if this power is exercisable by the originator only with the consent of a third party, then the element of control is missing and the existence of this power in the originator will not of itself result in the SPV amounting to the originator's subsidiary undertaking.

■ *(iii) it has the right to exercise a dominant influence over the undertaking, (1) by virtue of provisions contained in the undertaking's memorandum or articles, or (2) by virtue of a control contract* For the purposes of this test "an undertaking shall not be regarded as having the right to exercise a dominant influence over another undertaking unless it has a right to give directions with respect to the operating and financial policies of that other undertaking which its directors are obliged to comply with whether or not they are for the benefit of that other undertaking."[34] "Control contract" means "a contract in writing conferring such a right which (a) is of a kind authorised by the memorandum and articles of the undertaking in relation to which the right is exercisable, and (b) is permitted by the law under which that undertaking is established."[35]

In order to satisfy this test it is not necessary that the dominant undertaking be a shareholder or member of the dependent undertaking. Instead the question of who is in actual day-to-day control of the dependent undertaking and its decision-making processes is examined, without looking behind to its equity structure. The clarification provided in Schedule 9 of what is meant by the right to exercise a dominant influence over the dependent undertaking implies that the directors of the dependent undertaking have ceded all independent rights of direction on such issues to the dominant undertaking. This would in itself be a peculiar situation where the subsidiary undertaking is a body corporate, for, as a matter of general law, a director of a body corporate owes a fiduciary duty to that company to act at all times in the best interests of the company, and is obliged not to place himself in a position where his duty might be compromised. If the SPV is not a subsidiary of the originator, ceding control of all decision-making on major aspects of the SPV's business, where this cession is not made for the benefit of the SPV or is made in blanket terms without retention of any right to veto particular decisions, may cause any director of the SPV to be in breach of its duties to the SPV and liable, therefore, to an action brought by the SPV. If the directors of the dependent undertaking are obliged merely to take into account the views of the dominant undertaking, but ultimately the policies are determined by them, then presumably this test will not be satisfied.

In the case of a corporate receivables securitization program, if the originator is appointed servicing agent of the portfolio of assets, care must be taken when drafting the servicing contract lest it gives to the originator any rights to direct the SPV in the operation of the portfolio (as opposed to rights to make representations). Ultimate control must remain with the SPV and its board of directors. This requirement may be difficult to satisfy in the case of a mortgage securitization program where the originator will want to retain the right to vary the interest payable by the underlying debtors on the portfolio assets, but it should not pose a problem in corporate receivables securitization programs where factors such as interest changes are not present.

The phrase "by virtue of provisions contained in the undertaking's memorandum or articles" in section 258(2)(c) is somewhat obtuse. If what is meant is that the test is satisfied if the dominant undertaking may direct the operating and financial policies of the dependent undertaking provided that does not breach the *ultra vires* rule, so far as the dependent undertaking is concerned, the test will be satisfied on almost every occasion. Most memoranda and articles of association of modern companies are drafted in wide terms, and may well include a wide power for the company to delegate certain decision-making functions to third parties. Again, though, this power should always be exercised in the best interests of the SPV. If any action taken in reliance on this power is not in the best interests of the SPV, then such action will be *ultra vires* the directors of the SPV and voidable at the instance of the SPV. (The *ultra vires* rule itself, however, has been amended by the 1989 Act, again in a manner which is not entirely clear but which space constraints prevent me from considering.)

If the phrase means that there must be express and specific provisions in the memorandum and articles of association of the dependent undertaking which expressly provide for the dominant undertaking to have the right to direct operating and financial policies, then the test is more easily avoided by simply not including such express provisions. However, the test is sufficiently widely drafted to admit an interpretation somewhere between these two extremes, particularly given the overall intent of the changes proposed by the 1989 Act to concentrate on the substantive, rather than formalistic, issue of control. In particular (but subject to the operation of the *ultra vires* rule mentioned above), the courts could construe as satisfying this test a general power in the dependent undertaking's memorandum and articles to delegate certain functions or responsibilities to a third party, which is relied upon in practice, although nothing express is agreed in writing to bestow upon a particular third party the "right to direct" with regard to such functions.

■ *(iv) it is a member of the undertaking and controls alone, pursuant to an agreement with other shareholders or members, a majority of the voting rights in the undertaking* "Voting rights" refers to the right to vote at general meetings on all, or substantially all, matters[36] – see test (i) above. Test (iv) is in fact analogous to test (i), the difference being that test (i) requires the dominant undertaking to "hold" (i.e. to be entitled to legal or (presumably) beneficial ownership of, whether in its name or in the name of a nominee) a majority of voting rights in the dependent undertaking whereas test (iv) requires the dominant undertaking to be a member of the dependent undertaking and to "control" a majority of the voting rights pursuant to an agreement with other shareholders or members.

It would, therefore, be comparatively easy to avoid the requirement to consolidate the accounts of the originator and the SPV under tests (i) and (iv) by structuring the SPV such that the originator does not have any ownership interest in relation to voting rights (test (i)) and is not a member of the SPV (test (iv)). Such a route does not prevent the originator from "controlling" a majority of the voting rights in the SPV, as the fact of control is not, on these statutory tests, divorced from the requirement that the person having "control" be a member. Whether or not test (iii) can be avoided by this route is a more difficult question to answer.

Section 21 of the 1989 Act adds another test,[37] separate from those specified above and intended as a "catch-all." The provision states:

> An undertaking is also a parent undertaking in relation to another undertaking, a subsidiary undertaking, if it has a participating interest in the undertaking and –
> (a) it actually exercises a dominant influence over it, or
> (b) it and the subsidiary undertaking are managed on a unified basis.

A "participating interest" is defined as an interest held by an undertaking in the shares of another undertaking which it holds on a long-term basis for the purpose of securing a contribution to its activities by the exercise of control or influence arising from or related to that interest.[38] A holding of 20 percent or more of the shares is presumed to be a participating interest unless the contrary is shown. An interest in shares includes an interest which is convertible into an interest in shares, and an option to acquire shares or any such interest.

Again, therefore, an undertaking must own shares or an interest in shares in the dependent undertaking to fall within this category. As a deliberate policy, no definition of "dominant influence" has been included in the 1989 Act. The DTI's view is that this requirement to consolidate should depend upon the actual relationship between the dominant and dependent undertakings and not just the detailed formal structure. The interpretation of this phrase will, therefore, be entirely left to the judiciary to determine.

It is likely that, if the originator under a securitization program is appointed servicing agent of the portfolio of the assets, and therefore carries out substantially the whole of the business of the SPV, an accountant will regard the originator and the SPV as "managed on a unified basis." Thus, the originator should avoid as far as possible any share ownership in the SPV, although the absence of share ownership may severely circumscribe the number of methods available to pass up to the originator the profits made by the SPV. In any event, in order to ensure removal of securitized assets from an originator's balance sheet, an originator which is an authorized institution subject to regulation by the Bank of England is precluded from owning any shareholding in any vehicle company to which it sells assets under a securitization scheme, and is further precluded from holding a proprietary interest in or control over that SPV, either directly or indirectly (see the Bank of England Notice referred to in section 11.12 above). The effect of the amendments to the 1985 Act brought about by the 1989 Act is merely to expand this approach to accountability, in this context, from originators which are banking institutions to all originators.

Finally, section 5 of the 1989 Act contains a further "catch-all" provision which may prove particularly troublesome to those structuring off-balance-sheet securitization programs. As mentioned at the beginning of this section, a reporting enterprise is required to prepare group accounts, consolidating the accounts of parent companies and subsidiary undertakings in the form and manner specified in Schedule 4A to the 1985 Act (as amended).[39] The consolidated accounts should present a true and fair view of the state of affairs of the parent company and its subsidiary undertakings. Section 227(6), however, further provides that:

> If in special circumstances compliance with any of those provisions [i.e. those of Schedule 4A and other provisions of the 1985 Act, as amended] is inconsistent with the requirement to give a true and fair view, the directors [of the parent company] shall depart from that provision to the extent necessary to give a true and fair view. Particulars of any such departure, the reasons for it and its effect shall be given in a note to the accounts.

It is possible, therefore, that although an SPV may be structured such that it is not a "subsidiary undertaking" of the originator,[40] none the less the originator will be obliged to report its existence, assets, and liabilities in a note to the originator's annual accounts if to omit to do so would result in the originator's annual accounts failing to represent a true and fair view of the state of affairs and assets and liabilities of the originator. Auditors could, therefore, refuse to sign the directors' report and annual accounts of an originator if they were of the view that an originator had failed to divest itself of the risks associated with securitized assets packaged and sold off to an SPV, which SPV is not referred to in the originator's annual accounts or the notes thereto. The ASC refers to section 227(6) in Exposure Draft 49 (see section 11.15 below), and indeed introduces the term "quasi subsidiaries" to refer to undertakings which, although not within the definition of subsidiary undertakings, none the less represent entities in which, for all practical and commercial purposes, a reporting company has an interest and the risks of which entities may fall back on to the reporting company.

11.14 Exposure Draft 42 – March 1988 (2)

As a result of the concern felt within the accountancy profession, and, in the case of banking and financial institutions, among the regulators (particularly the Bank of England), that the old definition of a subsidiary under the Companies Act 1985 allowed a number of ventures to be engaged in by companies without the risks thereby incurred appearing on their balance sheets, the ASC issued Exposure Draft 42 to which reference has already been made.

ED42 deals specifically with the accounting practice to be adopted with regard to SPVs and also to securitized receivables, and states that the key question is whether any benefits and related risks remaining with the originator are of a kind that is best indicated by retaining the assets on its balance sheet. ED42 identifies five categories of risk associated with securitization programs, each of which was considered in section 11.11 above.

According to ED42, it is only if the combined effect of the five identified risks represents a significant risk or benefit to the originator that the securitized assets should be retained on its balance sheet with a corresponding liability for the amount due to the SPV.

11.15 Exposure Draft 49 – May 1990

The proposals contained in ED42 have been revised and amended by the ASC in Exposure Draft 49 (ED49) which takes account of the new and wider definition of "subsidiary undertaking" in the 1989 Act. As already mentioned in section 11.13 above, the new section 227 of the Companies Act 1985 imposes a duty on a parent company to prepare group accounts comprising consolidated balance sheet and consolidated profit and loss accounts of the parent company and its subsidiary undertakings. Section 227(3) provides that such accounts shall give a true and fair view of the state of affairs as at the end of the financial year and the profit and loss for the financial year of the undertakings included in the consolidation as a whole. In special circumstances where compliance with the provisions of section 227 will be inconsistent with the requirement to give a true and fair view, section 227(6) obliges the directors of the reporting institution to depart from the provisions to the extent necessary to give a true and fair view. No guidance is given by the Companies Act 1989 as to when such special circumstances shall exist, and this will be a matter, in each case, for the judgement of the directors of the reporting institution and its auditors.

Section 227(6), therefore, provides a statutory device which underlines the new approach to reporting requirements taken in the 1989 Act, in that it obliges a reporting institution to report, whether through its annual accounts themselves, if it has any subsidiary undertakings, or through the notes to its accounts, in the case of other undertakings in which the reporting company has an investment and whose commercial risks it assumes (either actually or contingently), all substantive transactions, interests, and matters in which the dependent undertaking is engaged or which the latter holds as at the date of the accounts or during the period which they represent.

As mentioned above, the ASC has introduced in ED49 a further refinement on the definition of subsidiary undertaking given in the 1989 Act, and that is the coining of a new term – "quasi subsidiary." "Quasi subsidiary" is defined in ED49 as

> a company, trust or other vehicle which, though not fulfilling the Companies Act definition of a subsidiary undertaking, is directly or indirectly controlled by and a source of benefits or risks for a reporting enterprise or its subsidiaries that are in substance no different from those that would arise were the vehicle a subsidiary.

This definition is clearly very wide and loosely worded, again to preserve the substantive over the formalistic approach.

It is stated in ED49 that the existence of a "quasi subsidiary" will often of itself constitute special circumstances (as referred to in section 227(6) of the 1985 Act, as amended) requiring the assets and liabilities of the quasi subsidiary to be included in the group accounts and for the heading to the accounts to state that they include assets and liabilities of a quasi subsidiary, in order to give a true and fair view of the reporting enterprise and its subsidiaries. This statement in ED49 would appear to require that the quasi subsidiary's accounts actually be consolidated with those of the reporting enterprise, rather than the existence of the quasi subsidiary being merely referred to in the notes to the reporting enterprise's accounts, as required by section 227(6).

The approach taken by the ASC in ED49 is more general than that taken in its predecessor, ED42, which was concerned with accounting for off-balance-sheet finance, with the emphasis on SPVs. The underlying premise is, however, identical, and that is that in preparing annual accounts, a true and fair view of the state of affairs of a reporting enterprise can be presented only if that enterprise discloses all concerns and transactions in which it has a participating interest and which are properly categorized as assets or liabilities of the reporting enterprise. In short, accounting for a transaction in accordance with the substance of ED49 requires that its accounting treatment should fairly reflect its commercial effect on the affairs of the reporting enterprise. ED49 addresses the problem of categorization by defining what it understands by the terms "asset" and "liability." An "asset" is defined as a resource controlled by an enterprise as a result of past events and from which future economic benefits are expected to flow to the enterprise. "Control of a resource" is defined as the ability to obtain the future economic benefits that are associated with that resource. A "liability" is defined as a present obligation of an enterprise arising from the past events the settlement of which is expected to result in an outflow from the enterprise of resources embodying economic benefits.

"Application Notes" are appended to ED49 to provide guidance as to how the proposals made in ED49 should be implemented in particular accounting situations. One such situation for which Application Notes are provided is that of securitizing mortgages (Application Note D). Application Note D5 notes that most securitization structures in the past have avoided creating the SPV as a subsidiary of the originator. Past structures, however, have been based on the definition of "subsidiary" in the 1989 Act, and not on the definition of "subsidiary undertakings." As seen above, it is now substantially more difficult to achieve an off-balance-sheet structure under the Companies Act requirements and yet to retain substantive control of the assets sold off-balance-sheet and an interest in their residual profits.

The question of whether the originator should consolidate the SPV in its annual accounts cannot, however, in the field of securitization, be determined by reference to control, in the sense of discretion over major issues of policy, since all such issues will normally be predetermined in the contractually binding administration and servicing agreement. (Following the implementation of the definition of "subsidiary undertaking," care will now need to be taken, in any event, to ensure that the administration and servicing agreement does not constitute a "control contract," so constituting the SPV a subsidiary undertaking of the originator.) Application Note D5 identifies, rather, that the relevance to the originator of the assets and liabilities of the SPV lies in the extent to which their associated benefits and risks continue to flow to the originator. Attention will be paid, therefore, to the terms of sale, which, clearly, should be without recourse to the originator, to the types of credit enhancement, if any, provided by the originator, and to the terms on which the originator extracts excess profits from the SPV. As stated earlier, the most favored method of profit extraction from a tax-avoidance point of view has in the past been by declaration of dividends by the SPV, from which the originator would benefit only if it were a shareholder in the SPV. The originator is, however, precluded from owning or controlling a majority interest in the SPV if it wishes to avoid the necessity of consolidating the SPV's accounts with its own. Further, if the originator is a banking institution, it is precluded from owning any shares in or participating in the profits of the SPV.

Possible ways of extracting profit are in administration fees, brokering fees, and swap transactions. The two former methods convert, as it were, profit into an expense of the SPV such that the SPV makes no profit. The swap method, which is perhaps the cleanest way to date of extracting profit, converts the profit arising from the underlying receivables into monies payable under a swap. The basic premise is that the income stream from the securitized assets is swapped through to the originator, as swap counterparty, as it arises and in return the swap counterparty swaps back, when required, the monies required by the SPV to meet its funding obligations in the securitization program, for example payment of principal and interest due to investors, payment of fees to providers of credit enhancement, and so on. Any excess over the monies swapped through by the SPV is then retained by the swap counterparty as profit arising under the swap. If there is a deficit between monies swapped through by the SPV and the monies which the SPV requires to meet payments at the end of the period in question, the swap counterparty swaps back only what it has received, less any fees due to it in its capacity as servicing agent, and the shortfall is made up from drawings under the various credit enhancement facilities available. Using this technique, the originator never assumes any of the risks of default in the assets, but obtains the benefit of the income stream produced by the assets during a collection period and can swap out profit under the program as it arises. The profit is swapped out under the terms of a commercial contract entered into on an arm's length basis.

To return to ED49, the Application Note then proceeds to consider whether or not the manner in which the originator obtains the residual benefit of the securitization program, that is, the profit made by the SPV after paying financing charges, servicing fees, and credit enhancement fees, should properly be represented in the originator's accounts on a net level, as an investment, or on a gross level by separate presentation of the assets which give rise to this profit and their supporting liabilities. If the latter approach applies, then a further determination should be made, that is, whether the gross presentation should be achieved by consolidating the accounts of the SPV with the originator, or by treating the transfer of mortgages as the provision of security rather than as a sale.

As stated above, the cleanest method of stripping profit out of a securitization program and back into the hands of an originator, however, would appear to be to convert the nature of the profit arising from the program from profit earned by the SPV on the underlying receivables to profit earned by the originator itself under a separate and distinct contract with the SPV. Although the originator is in this way obtaining a benefit from the success of a program, it is not necessarily in control of the assets producing this benefit and is clearly not assuming any risks of non-performance of the assets. The "liability" aspect of the assets is covered by third party credit enhancers. It should be remembered, however, that the fiscal treatment accorded to swap transactions by the Inland Revenue is vital to the viability of this method of profit extraction. At present, the treatment of swap fees by the Inland Revenue is made on a concessionary basis, and this may well change in the future.

Application Note D10 identifies further the requirements of insularity that an originator must display from the SPV, these requirements being substantially those identified by the Bank of England in its Notice of February 1989 on loan transfers and securitization, which was considered in section 11.12 above.

It should be noted that the revisions to ED42 introduced by ED49 are considered by the ASC to represent an innovation and require public comment before they can be issued as part of an accountancy standard.

11.16 Conclusion

To conclude, therefore, recent developments both on a statutory front and in the approach of regulators of banking institutions have combined to ensure that off-balance-sheet financing of schemes such as securitization programs will become much more difficult to structure successfully so as to ensure on the one hand an outright transfer of the assets but on the other hand an uninterrupted and unaffected relationship between the originator of the asset and its underlying obligor. The originator cannot both control the asset, whether directly or through its participating interest in the buyer of the asset, and still claim to have divested itself of all risks in the asset. Although, undoubtedly, subtle structures may still be set up (for one should never underestimate the ingenuity of bankers or their lawyers) which will circumvent these problems to an extent, and which will still allow for profit in securitization programs to be extracted on terms which are economically viable, the question of control will always be looming large in the minds of the regulators. The recent amendments to the Companies Act 1985, and the extensive powers of regulation bestowed on the Bank of England under the Banking Act 1987, allow regulators much more scope and flexibility in examining and insisting on the reporting of the commercial effect of transactions such as securitization programs. The question of control of the SPV is particularly important; it may be that from now on creatures such as deadlock joint ventures will constitute the majority of SPVs, with two friendly shareholders neither of which holds a controlling shareholding or weighted voting rights. The developments in securitization structures in the UK over the coming months will certainly be most interesting.

Notes

1 "Reporting by Transferors for Transfers of Receivables with Recourse," December 1983 (FASB 77).
2 See "Federal Financial Institutions Examination Council, Letter to Banks re Reports of Condition and Income – Revision of the Instruction for the Treatment of Sales of Assets" (October 10, 1985; reprinted in Practicing Law Institute, *Asset-backed Securities* 359–72 (1986).
3 Pub. L. No. 101–73, 103 Stat. 183 (1989).
4 The foregoing discussion regarding "Types And Transactions of Asset-backed Securities" was derived in part from the Standard & Poor's "Credit Review" publications on *Structured Finance* and *Asset-backed Securitization*.
5 11 USCA s. 541(a) (1978).
6 See *In re SOAW Enterprises, Inc.*, 32 Bankr. 279 (Bankr. WD Tex. 1983), *In re Executive Growth Investments, Inc.*, 4 Bankr. 279 (Bankr. WD Tex. 1983), *In re Executive Growth Investments, Inc.*, 40 Bankr. 417 (Bankr. CD Cal. 1984).
7 See SEC Release 33–3892, January 31, 1958.

8   See Bank of America National Trust and Savings Association (SEC no-action request) '77–'78 CCH Dec. para. 81,193 (1977).
9   See 12 CFR s. 16.
10 See 12 CFR 563g.
11 See 12 CFR 563g2.
12 P.L. 98–440, 98 Stat. 1689 (SMMEA).
13 See Bank of America Canada, SEC no-action request, publicly available July 25, 1984.
14 See e.g. Salomon Brothers, Inc. (publicly available June 6, 1985).
15 See e.g. Arlington Investment Company (publicly available August 31, 1974).
16 12 CFR Part 208, Appendix A and Part 225, Appendix A.
17 12 CFR Part 3, Appendix A.
18 12 CFR Part 325, Appendix B.
19 12 CFR Part 567.
20 See J. Norton (ed.), *Bank Regulation and Supervision in the 1990s* (1991), and chapter 3 in this volume.
21 See, *inter alia*, J. Norton, "The Work of the Basle Committee on Bank Capital Adequacy and the July 1988 Report on 'International Convergence of Capital Measurements and Capital Standards,'" *International Law*, 23 (1989), p. 245.
22 See EC Council Directive 89/229/EEC.
23 See EC Council Directive 89/647/EEC. For further discussion of EC Solvency's Own Funds and Second Directives, see R. Cranston (ed.), *The Single Market and the Law of Banking* (1991).
24 See Norton, "Basle Committee."
25 See chapter 12 in this volume.
26 See EC Council Directive 83/349/EEC.
27 S. 227 of the 1985 Act as inserted by s. 5 of the 1989 Act.
28 S. 258 of the 1985 Act as inserted by s. 21(1) of the 1989 Act.
29 Schedule 10A of the 1985 Act as substituted by Schedule 9 of the 1989 Act.
30 S. 22 of the 1989 Act.
31 S. 22 of the 1989 Act.
32 Schedule 9 to the 1989 Act; emphasis added.
33 Ibid., para. 3.
34 Ibid., para. 4(1).
35 Ibid., para. 4(2).
36 Schedule 9 of the 1989 Act.
37 By inserting a new s. 258(4) into the Companies Act 1985.
38 See s. 22 of the 1989 Act inserting a new s. 260 into the 1985 Act.
39 S. 227 of the 1985 Act as introduced by s. 5 of the 1989 Act.
40 S. 21 of the 1989 Act.

12

Swap Financing

SCHUYLER K. HENDERSON

Chapter Outline

12.1 Introduction

12.2 Description of Swaps
    12.2.1 Interest Rate Swaps
    12.2.2 Currency Swaps
    12.2.3 Variations
    12.2.4 Derivative Products

12.3 Uses of Swaps
    12.3.1 Reducing Borrowing Costs
    12.3.2 Asset and Liability Management
    12.3.3 As an Investment Device
    12.3.4 As a Financial Service and Dealing Instrument
    12.3.5 Interim Summary

12.4 Legality of Swaps

12.5 Swap Risk
    12.5.1 Rate Risk
    12.5.2 Credit Risk

12.6 Operation of the Swap Market

12.7 Description of ISDA Forms

12.8 Credit Provisions

12.9 Termination Provisions
    12.9.1 Termination Event
    12.9.2 Event of Default

12.10 Calculation of Cash Settlement

Copyright © 1990 Schuyler K. Henderson.

12.11   Settlement Provisions

12.12   A Final Note: Enforcement Issues

12.1 Introduction

At present, the combined total of outstanding interest rate and currency swaps (in an aggregate notional principal amount) is probably in excess of $2.5 trillion (up from a combined figure of $600 million in mid-1987 and $1.1 trillion in 1988.

The genesis of swaps lay in the "back-to-back" loan of the mid-1970s, and the cash flows of the early currency swaps were precisely those of that type of deal, but affording simplified documentation, greater credit protection, and off-balance-sheet treatment. In the early 1980s, the swap took on new meaning, first as a hedging instrument and then as a device for borrowers to obtain relatively cheap financing through arbitrage of different lending markets. Finally, swap financing has become a central tool of financial engineering, an instrument for which there exists a substantial trading market.

12.2 Description of Swaps

The underlying principle of any swap is an agreement between two parties to pay to each other a series of cash flows, based on fixed or floating interest rates, in the same or different currencies. At the outset, when the agreement is formed, the parties view as equal the present values of the respective cash flows at the current prevailing interest or exchange rates. This is true even with respect to those swaps (termed "off-market" swaps) that have unequal cash flows, usually in consideration of a front-end payment by one of the parties. The definition holds if that front-end payment is included in the cash flows. Virtually all common interest rate indices are regularly used in swaps. While the US dollar is the most commonly swapped currency, all major covertible currencies are swapped.

12.2.1 Interest Rate Swaps

A typical interest rate swap agreement obligates the first party to pay an amount equal to interest that would accrue on an agreed principal amount during a period at one type of interest rate. It obligates the

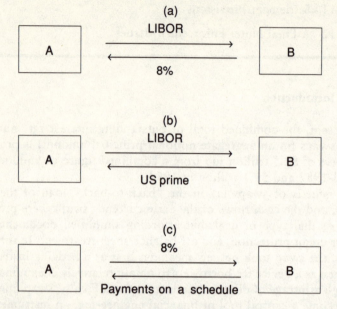

Figure 12.1 Swaps: (a) fixed to floating, (b) floating to floating, (c) fixed to fixed

second party to pay an amount equal to interest which would accrue on that agreed principal amount during that period at another type of interest rate. To the extent that payment dates are simultaneous, the parties typically net the payments, with the party owing the larger amount paying the difference to other party. The principal amount in an interest rate swap is not paid.

There are three basic types of interest rate swaps: fixed to floating, floating to floating, and fixed to fixed. For illustrative purposes, we will assume a notional principal amount of $50 million, by reference to which the two series of cash flows are determined.

First is the fixed to floating swap (see figure 12.1(a)). This type of swap is the single most common form. In this example, every six months the parties would calculate interest that would have accrued on $50 million at six-month London Interbank Offered Rate (LIBOR) as in effect at the beginning of that period and interest that would have accrued during that period at an annual rate equal to 8 percent. The two amounts would be compared, and the party owing the larger amount would pay the excess to the other. If the amounts by chance were the same, no payment would be made.

Second, the floating to floating swap (see figure 12.1(b)) would compare two floating rate indices, but in other respects the payments would be calculated as above. For instance, one party might pay the LIBOR rate and the other might pay a rate based on the US prime rate. This type of swap is referred to as a "basis swap."

Third is the fixed to fixed swap (see figure 12.1(c)). One party might agree to pay 8 percent over the term against payments based on a fixed schedule. In this situation, one party may have uneven cash flows, either a series of operational payments or estimated revenues, which it would like to level out over the term.

12.2.2 Currency Swaps

A typical currency swap involves an agreement under which the first party agrees to pay an amount in one currency, usually at periodic intervals, and the second party agrees to pay an amount in a different currency at the same or different intervals. These amounts may be expressed either as stated amounts (implicitly inclusive of interest and principal) due at stated times or as interest accruing on principal amounts in different currencies plus payment of those principal amounts at maturity. It is not uncommon to have the notional interest rates in a currency swap calculated on different bases so that effectively the interest rate swap and the currency swap are combined. Payments, even if due on the same date, are usually not netted but paid gross. Again, there are three types of currency swaps: fixed to floating, floating to floating, and fixed to fixed (see figure 12.2).

12.2.3 Variations

Numerous variations exist on these basic structures, including swaps with delayed effectiveness, periodic reduction ("amortization") of the notional principal, periodic increase ("step-up") of the notional principal, payment of the entire fixed amount at the inception of the swap on a present value basis ("accelerated" swap), payment of the entire fixed amount at termination of the swap on a rolled-up basis ("zero coupon" swap), and change in one or both of the rates throughout payment periods or at the end of payment periods.

12.2.4 Derivative Products

Swap principles can be extended to any product that can be readily priced, e.g. oil, gold, and stock indices. The variety of swaps is limited only by the imagination of swap specialists, the availability of financial markets with unique investment criteria, and the restraints of applicable law.

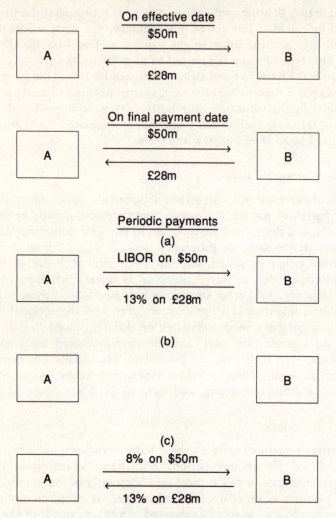

Figure 12.2 Currency swap: exchanges of principal

In addition, financial engineers have developed a number of so-called derivative products, which combine swap structures with elements similar to futures or options.

A "cap" (figure 12.3(a)) is an instrument under which the purchaser pays the seller, or "writer," of the cap a fee, generally when the deal is struck or at the beginning of the term of the cap. If the actual interest rate determined at the specified index (e.g. six-month LIBOR) for any of the agreed periods exceeds the agreed upon cap rate (or

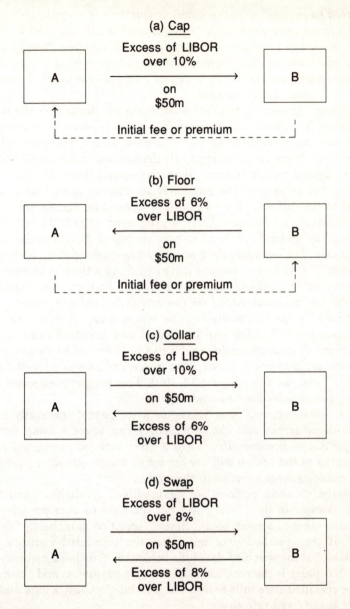

Figure 12.3 Swap derivatives (three-year term; semi-annual payments)

"strike level"), the seller of the cap pays the purchaser a sum equal to the amount of interest that would accrue on a notional amount at a rate equal to the differential for the relevant period. Caps are sometimes referred to as "ceiling" arrangements and limit the purchaser's exposure to rising interest rates. A "vertical cap" is a device used to reduce the cost of cap protection. This reduction is achieved through placement of a limit on the protection of the cap, by having the purchaser of the protection itself write a cap at a rate above which it does not believe it needs the protection.

A "floor" (figure 12.3(b)) is conceptually similar to, but the reverse of, a cap. It is attractive, for example, to the holder of a floating rate asset seeking protection against a decline in interest rates below a given level. If the actual interest rate determined at the specified index for an agreed period is lower than the agreed floor rate (or "strike level"), the seller pays the purchaser an amount computed at a rate equal to the differential on a notional amount for the period.

A "collar", or "floor/ceiling" arrangement (figure 12.3(c)), combines a cap and a floor so as to provide cap or floor protection at a lower cost. For example, the buyer of a cap might give up some of the benefits of a decline in interest rates by selling a floor to the writer of the cap, thereby reducing the cost of the cap by the value of the floor. Conversely, the purchaser of the floor might be willing to give up some benefits of a rise in interest rates by selling a cap to reduce the floor purchase price. A collar can be viewed as a standard cap and floor combined. It is worth noting that a cap or floor can be viewed as half a swap; or, conversely, a swap can be viewed as a combined "at the market" cap and floor (figure 12.3(d)). This perspective creates interesting possibilities for financial engineering.

In a "swap option," one party, for a fee payable generally on the trade date, agrees that the other party can cause a swap between the parties to become effective at a later date on pre-agreed terms. The seller of the option will use the fee to hedge against any potential loss resulting from exercise of the option.

Related to swap options are "extendible," "callable," and "puttable" swaps. In these, one party has the right to alter the scheduled maturity date of a swap to a different, specified date, being "extendible" if the specified date falls after the scheduled maturity date; "callable" if the specified date falls before the scheduled maturity date and that party is the recipient of fixed rate payments; and "puttable" if the specified date falls before the scheduled maturity date and that party is the fixed rate payer.

A "forward rate agreement" is a single payment agreement, also called a "future rate agreement," in which the parties select a period in the future (e.g. a six-month period commencing six months in the future) and one party agrees to pay a fixed rate in respect of the period and the other party agrees to pay LIBOR. A net payment is generally made when the relevant amount is determinable (generally the first day of the period), discounted from the last day of the period to its present value on the payment date, which is often called the "settlement date."

12.3 Uses of Swaps

Most major borrowers are aware of the benefits of swaps in decreasing their cost of borrowing. Most major treasury groups use swaps as asset and liability management tools. Virtually all major financial institutions have teams of swap specialists which deal in swaps as trading units and assist in providing sophisticated swap-related financing to the institutions' major customers. A number of institutions specialize in the brokerage of swaps.

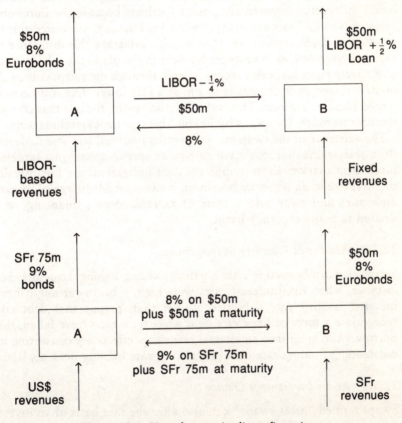

Figure 12.4 Use of swaps in direct financing

12.3.1 Reducing Borrowing Costs

The swap in figure 12.1(a) can be used to illustrate the use of swaps in direct financing (see figure 12.4). The basic principle is that each (or at least one) party has access to a particular financial market on relatively more favorable terms than does the other.

Assume Party A is a European bank, well known in the Euromarkets. Party A has not issued fixed rate Eurobonds because its revenues are based on fluctuating rates of interest (a LIBOR loan portfolio). Party B, less well known in the Euromarkets, cannot issue Eurobonds except at a rate at least 1 percent in excess of that at which Party A could issue the same bonds. However, Party B can obtain bank financing at a spread of 0.5 percent over LIBOR. Party A, if it accepted deposits in the London interbank market, would pay (for purposes of illustration) interest at LIBOR flat. Thus, the Eurobond market imposes a 1 percent credit differential and the bank lending market imposes a 0.5 percent credit differential between the parties (perhaps because the Eurobond investor is more "name-sensitive," while bank lenders are better able to conduct in-depth credit investigations). To arbitrage this difference in credit perceptions, each party incurs debt in the market in which it has a relatively more favorable reception and, through the swap, effectively obtains financing in the desired form at a rate lower than it otherwise would be able to obtain. This is the "classic" swap, the one that created the breakthrough for swaps by linking them to the capital markets.

The existence of the swap market permits financial advisers to devise debt obligations that may have narrow or special appeal in a targeted investment market. Even though the debt obligations are intrinsically unattractive to an issuer or borrower, it can take advantage of market anomalies and swap into a form of more favorable financing on a desired rate and currency basis.

12.3.2 Asset and Liability Management

Swaps also can be used to alter a party's existing liability structure. For instance, when fixed interest rates were high, a borrower might have incurred floating rate liabilities. Rather than prepay that debt and renegotiate a form of fixed rate debt when term rates have fallen, this borrower can enter into an interest rate swap, effectively converting its outstanding floating rate debt into a fixed rate liability on a net basis.

12.3.3 As an Investment Device

Swaps termed "asset swaps" can also alter the rate basis of an investment in the hands of an investor. For instance, for portfolio diversification reasons, an investor may be attracted to the credit of a particular issuer which has issued a fixed rate debt instrument. However, the investor, because of its funding sources or income requirements, desires a floating rate asset. The investor purchases the underlying fixed rate asset and enters into a swap with another entity pursuant to which the investor pays a fixed rate equal to that on the asset purchased and receives in exchange a floating rate from the swap counterparty (see figure 12.5).

12.3.4 *As a Financial Service and Dealing Instrument*

Parties engaged in the swaps described above are termed "end-users," i.e. they use the swap for a direct financing, asset/liability management, or investment purpose. Because these end-users might not have an established commercial relationship with each other, might not be in the business of making credit decisions, or might not be able directly to find counterparties, each would prefer to deal with a strong-credit financial institution. This institution would function as an intermediary

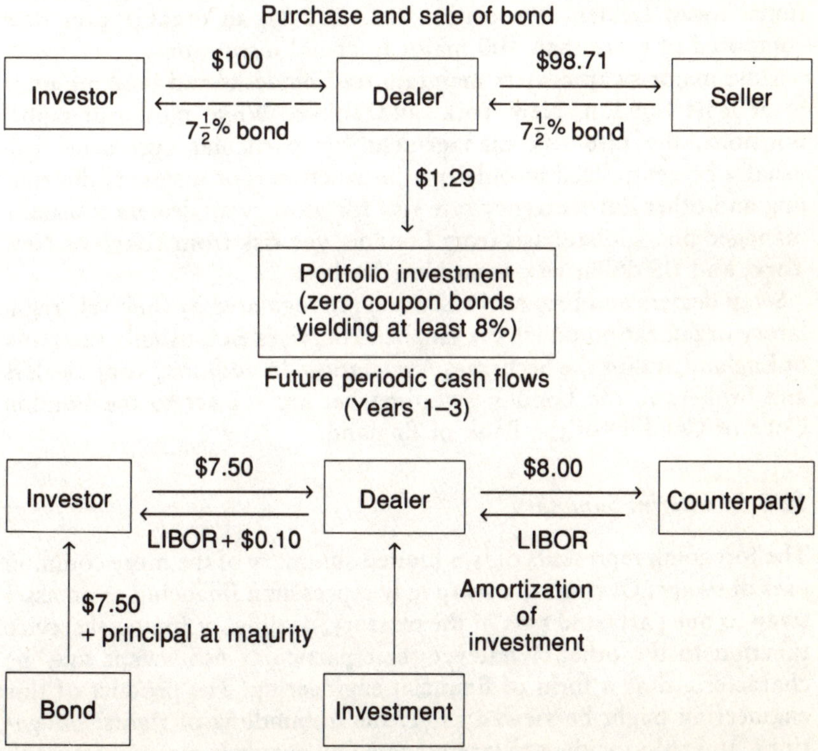

Figure 12.5 Asset swap

by entering into matching reverse agreements with each party. The intermediary would bear the credit risk of each end-user and, for its services and risk, would retain a spread in the transaction. Each agreement with the intermediary normally would be independent of, and not even refer to, the transaction with the other end-user. Indeed, the end-users normally would not know of the existence of their counterparties. Thus, the typical swap is not one of those illustrated in figures 12.1–4, but a swap in which one or more financial institutions act as intermediaries between end-users.

Historically, as intermediaries refined their swap funding capabilities, a critical mass of swaps developed until the swap contracts themselves became instruments which, while not tradable, developed many indicia of tradability. Trading indices were simulated by making, terminating, and assigning swaps and quoting swap prices, coupled with using sophisticated portfolio hedging activities. Many financial institutions began to view themselves as "dealers" in swaps, rather than extenders of corporate financial services or credit. The swap market began to take coherent form with the creation of the International Swap Dealers Association Inc. (ISDA), an organization now composed of more than 100 major financial institutions.

Most major swap dealers maintain trading desks and booking units in at least London, New York, and Tokyo. While most run global positions, the rate risk management for particular currencies will usually be centralized in only one jurisdiction. For instance, the sterling and other Eurocurrency rate risk for most swap dealers is usually managed on a global basis from London, yen risk from Tokyo or New York, and US dollar risk from New York.

Swap dealers and brokers in London are regulated by their self-regulatory organization under the Financial Services Act, usually the Bank of England and/or the Securities Association. In addition, swap dealers and brokers in the London swap market are subject to the London Code of Conduct of the Bank of England.

12.3.5 *Interim Summary*

The foregoing represents only a limited summary of the more common uses of swaps. Of course, a swap may represent a financing or an asset swap to one party and part of the treasury, dealing, or financial service function to the other. Whatever their particular use, swaps may be characterized as a form of financial engineering. The product of this engineering might be viewed as (1) the unbundling of rights, obligations, and risks incident to interest rate and currency movements, both in funding and investment, and (2) the transfer of the relevant rights

SWAP FINANCING   355

to those to whom the rights are most valuable and the assumption of specific risks by those who are best able to bear them. These often elaborate structures permit a degree of fine-tuning and targeting of financial packages which maximizes the efficiency of the markets, results in better pricing for borrowers, and provides an extended range of debt management tools for modern treasury departments.

12.4 Legality of Swaps

In analyzing the legality of swaps, there will be a number of issues one would wish to consider under the laws of one's jurisdiction.

Most jurisdictions have laws that either prohibit or render unenforceable gambling contracts. A gambling contract is often defined to include contracts for differences. Swaps are therefore, technically, often caught up within the terms of these laws. In jurisdictions where swaps are regularly transacted, the almost universal view is that swap transactions between commerical parties for a commercial purpose are not gambling contracts. The issue may not be entirely free from doubt, but the risk is regarded as sufficiently remote for the market to operate. In some jurisdictions, such as Germany, a specific statute was regarded as necessary.

Many jurisdictions have laws that regulate the conduct of futures business. In the US, for example, futures transactions can only lawfully be conducted on a recognized exchange. If a typical swap between two dealers was regarded as a futures contract, it would be illegal. There are substantial arguments that a swap is not a futures contract, and nobody in the US really focused on this issue. The swap market evolved despite the risk. When the regulators (the Commodity Futures Trading Commission) began to focus on commodity swaps, however, they also looked at financial swaps. Ultimately, after a great deal of industry pressure, the CFTC issued a policy statement in July 1989 providing a safe harbor exemption for individually tailored swaps between sophisticated commercial entities, with several other safeguards. While helpful, this was not regarded as entirely satisfactory by the industry, and legislation was passed in October 1992. The point to bear in mind is that, again, this issue must be looked at on a case-by-case basis.

Many jurisdictions have laws regulating the issuance of securities or investments. If swaps are deemed to be such securities or investments, they must comply with the national regulatory scheme. In the US, it is generally held that a typical swap is not a "security" because of the mutuality of performance in the swap, and thus it need not be registered under the securities laws. Unilateral instruments, such as a cap or a floor, might well constitute such a security and, in the absence of other exemptions, would require registration. Needless to say, registration would destroy the flexibility of the market, and, to the extent that in a particular transaction there is perceived to be a risk under the US securities laws, an exemption is usually found on the basis that the issuer is a bank (securities of which are exempted from the registration requirements) or that the instrument is issued in the context of a private placement with a sophisticated entity and is non-transferable. In the UK a swap, as a contract for differences, is included in the definition of "investment." Thus, an entity regularly entering into swaps or arranging swaps in the UK must be a member of one of the designated self-regulatory organizations.

As a swap provides for payment in the future based on a contingent event, some lawyers have expressed concern as to whether or not statutes regulating the insurance business applied to swaps. Most lawyers believe that they do not, but the issue is not definitively resolved.

If a jurisdiction imposes foreign exchange controls, those will of course need to be reviewed with respect to currency swaps and, perhaps, interest rate swaps.

12.5 Swap Risk

It should be noted in all cases that the swap does not in fact amend or change the rate basis of any related instrument: the swap is a separate contract independent of that instrument and the payments under the swap are simply used to offset or hedge the payments under the related instrument.

Swap risk has two components: rate risk and credit risk.

12.5.1 *Rate Risk*

Rate risk is the risk that rates will move in such a way that the party loses money. When the rates have moved such that the swap is unfavorable to a party, that party is said to be "out of the money." When rates have moved favorably, that party is "in the money." It should be noted that this risk is implicit in all rate-sensitive transactions, including every borrowing decision.

12.5.2 *Credit Risk*

Credit risk in a swap is a combination of rate risk and the ability of the counterparty to perform. If rates have moved such that the swap is favorable for a party, that is, it is in the money, *and* its counterparty fails to perform, the first party will incur a loss: the position for which

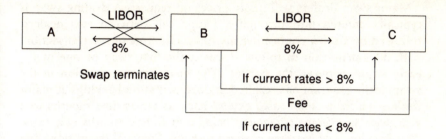

Figure 12.6 Quantification of loss; replacement of flows

it has bargained is lost and/or it may now be exposed on the original instrument that the swap was hedging. If rates have moved unfavorably for a party, that is, it is out of the money, and the counterparty fails to perform, the resulting termination of the swap will result in a gain to the first party.

Loss or gain will be determined by calculating the replacement of the swap given rates then current in the market. Thus, referring to the swap used in figure 12.1(a), if after a year one of the parties has defaulted, the swap terminates and fixed rates for the remaining two years have fallen to 7 percent, Party A will incur a loss on termination of the swap, since it would have to pay a third party (i.e. Party C) to incur a liability at the higher contract rate (8 percent); Party B will incur a gain on termination, since it is relieved of the obligation to pay the now higher rate of 8 percent. If rates have increased to, say, 9 percent the reverse would be true. If Party A had defaulted, Party B would thus ascertain its gain or loss caused by the termination. On default, the defaulting party would typically be obligated to pay over the non-defaulting party's loss.

Given the volume of swaps, parties often have multiple swaps with each other. A party can expect that it will be in the money on some of these swaps and out of the money on others. If it is possible to terminate all swaps simultaneously and net the termination gains against the termination losses, its credit exposure will be substantially reduced. Accordingly, parties almost invariably attempt to document swaps with a given counterparty under one master agreement, in the hope that, on default by that party, it can terminate and net out exposure.

12.6 Operation of the Swap Market

So far this chapter has discussed what swaps are, whether swaps are legal, and what swap credit risk is. This section will address how the market functions.

Major swap dealers will quote prices on request. A dealing swap is typically entered into through a phone call between two dealers, followed by a telex confirming the financial terms of the transaction, with documentation to follow if this is the first swap or one of the early swaps between the parties. The quantitative explosion in the swap dealing market has resulted in documentation backlogs at major dealers which in some cases extend back as far as nine months to a year, with an average agreement being four to five months in arrears. This backlog is of extreme concern to many financial institutions and their regulators.

The first risk is that, for a period, there may in fact be no binding agreement between the parties. The New York Statute of Frauds requires that a contract that by its terms cannot be performed within a year be evidenced by a sufficient writing signed by the party to be charged therewith. Therefore, until the parties confirm the content of their oral understanding through an exchange of confirmation telexes, there may well be no enforceable agreement. It is thus of primary importance for at least telexes to be promptly exchanged. Industry practice is for this to occur within a business day of oral agreement. Under English law, the Statute of Frauds does not apply. To avoid confusion or dispute as to the terms of an oral agreement (under English law) or as to whether or not the telexes conform to the oral understanding (under New York law), many dealers record the relevant phone conversations.

The confirmation telexes will usually contain all the essential financial provisions of the transaction (without, however, defining them). If a telex does not, in one party's view, reflect the oral commitment, if the parties dispute the meaning of the financial provisions in the telexes, or if clauses are inadvertently omitted from the telexes by one party (e.g. providing for exchange of principal on a delayed effective date of a currency swap), the question as to whether or not an agreement was reached becomes of fundamental importance. The party against whom the swap has moved is generally regarded as having the better negotiating position, since a breakdown of negotiations could result in it being relieved from a now unfavorable swap.

Assuming the individual executing and sending the confirmation telex has the authority to do so, an exchange of confirmation telexes setting forth the intent to be bound and the essential financial terms of the swap would generally constitute a binding agreement between the parties, despite the inclusion of an agreement to enter into definitive documentation at a later date. However, until the master agreement is executed, none of its protective provisions are available.

12.7 Description of ISDA Forms

In 1985, ISDA published a Swaps Code for US dollar interest rate swaps, amended in 1986. It also prepared a printed form master agreement to go along with it. In 1987, ISDA prepared a master agreement to accommodate single-currency rate swaps in any currency as well as currency swaps. Most master swap agreements are based on these printed form ISDA Agreements.

The currency master does not incorporate the Swaps Code, which contemplates only US dollar rate swaps. ISDA's "1987 Interest Rate and Currency Exchange Definitions" (the 1987 Definitions), however, is a companion to the currency master in the same way that the 1986 Swaps Code is a companion for the rate swap master. While the provisions in the two agreements are otherwise nearly identical in substance, the latter is almost the unanimous choice outside of the US and by now the most common choice for swaps within the US. In 1991 ISDA published revised definitions and in 1992 a revised master agreement. Each was based on its predecessor but provided for a broader range of products. The 1992 master agreement also reflected market developments in documentation preference over the preceding five years.

The ISDA Agreement consists of two basic parts, the first setting out the basic terms of the master and the second being a Schedule on which some of those terms may be completed, added to, or varied. The subjects dealt with in the body of the agreements are payments, representations, covenants, events of default and termination events, early termination and payments in connection therewith, transfer, and other standard contractual provisions for commercial agreements. Each of the agreements also contains a "Multibranch Party" provision designed to allow a party to designate any of its branches or offices specified in the Schedule as an office or branch through which that party may enter into swaps under the master, in order to gain the benefits of termination netting. Another provision, to be completed in the Schedule, facilitates the designation of third parties as entities that will be providing credit support (e.g. a guaranty or a letter of credit) or that will be relevant for purposes of the cross-default clause, if appropriate.

The ISDA Agreement provides for individual transactions to be completed through an exchange of documentation, the "confirmation" discussed earlier, setting out the particular financial provisions of each swap.

12.8 Credit Provisions

The credit provisions of the ISDA Agreement can be analyzed in the following categories:

- relating to delivery exposure:
    netting of same-day payments;
    conditionally;
- relating to term exposure:
    substantive credit controls;
    warranties and closing documents;
    covenants and events of default;
- change of legal assumptions:
    withholding tax;
    change in reserves or capital requirements;
    supervening illegality;
- enforcement:
    right to terminate if breach of credit controls (event of default) by a party (defaulting party) or change in legal assumptions (termination event) with respect to a party (affected party) and other remedies;
- allocation of gains and losses and enforcement expenses.

The key elements of enforcing the ISDA Agreement are ability to terminate and the right to settle gains and losses.

12.9 Termination Provisions

A swap transaction can be terminated on a date (the early termination date) before its scheduled termination date by one party acting alone on either of two bases: an occurrence of a termination event with respect to itself or, in some cases, the other party; or the occurrence of an event of default with respect to the other party.

12.9.1 Termination Event

A change in law rendering performance by a party illegal prior to execution of documentation, or under agreements not addressing the issue, exposes a party to the risk that its counterparty might be restricted from performing and become discharged from the agreement or that its own performance might become illegal and it would lose the benefit of the agreement. A withholding tax applicable to payments under a swap agreement would destroy the commercial benefits of the swaps thereunder. The ISDA Agreement provides for representations as to legality and the absence of withholding taxes.

Even if withholding taxes are not imposed at the inception of a transaction, there is a real risk that subsequent interpretation or change in law or treaty could alter the exemption. Governments do not always act with concern for the financial markets uppermost in their minds. The ISDA Agreement, therefore, includes a clause providing for "grossing-up" if withholding taxes are imposed on payments by one party to another, subject to certain exceptions based on misrepresentations, actions, or omissions by the payee.

To avoid the adverse effects of subsequent illegality or withholding taxes, the ISDA Agreement permits the party affected thereby to terminate the agreement after having made reasonable efforts to transfer the affected swaps to another office or affiliate.

12.9.2 *Event of Default*

Due to the credit risk in swaps described above, each party is usually concerned about the continuing creditworthiness of the other. Accordingly, there are a number of events of default included in the ISDA Agreement not too dissimilar to those basic events of default found in loan agreements: a breach of payment obligations, a breach of other covenants in the Agreement, a breach of warranty, a breach with respect to a guarantor, cross-default to other indebtedness, and certain bankruptcy events. If any of these events of default occurs, the other party would have the right to terminate the agreement. On the occurrence of a "Bankruptcy Event," the agreement is expressed to terminate automatically.

12.10 Calculation of Cash Settlement

If a swap transaction has become out of the money (i.e. unfavorable) for a party, the swap transaction has a negative value for the party and termination results in a gain to it. If the swap transaction is in the money (i.e. favorable) for a party, the swap transaction has a positive value for the party and termination results in a loss to it.

Cash settlement under the ISDA Agreements consists of two components: "unpaid amounts" and "settlement amounts."

A party's unpaid amounts are payments (plus interest) which were initially scheduled to have been made to it before the early termination date but which were never made. These payments may have not been made because of either a default by the payer or the deferral of payment as a result of, for instance, the payee being in default.

The settlement amount is the gain or loss to a party resulting from termination of the future cash flows of all terminated swap transactions, being the aggregate of market quotations for the individual terminated swap transactions. The ISDA Agreements provide for the non-defaulting party or the non-affected party, as the case may be, to calculate a market quotation for each terminated swap, being the average (after disregarding the highest and the lowest) of quotations from four leading dealers as to the amount each dealer would require from (a positive amount) – or would pay to (a negative amount) – the non-defaulting or non-affected party for the market-maker to enter into a new replacement swap with that party on substantially the same economic terms as those of each terminated swap transaction.

12.11 Settlement Provisions

Having made these calculations, the parties can choose one of several different settlement procedures.

Counterparties invariably provide in their agreements that, where early termination is based on a "termination event", "two-way payments" applies. Under this method, the non-affected party's settlement amount (positive or negative), being the aggregate of its market quotations, is aggregated with any unpaid amounts owing to the non-affected party and, from this sum (which may be positive or negative), any unpaid amounts owing to the affected party are subtracted. The resulting amount, if positive, is paid by the affected party to the non-affected party. If the amount is negative, the non-affected party would pay that amount to the affected party.

Where early termination occurs as a result of an event of default, some end-users and a growing number of dealers also use two-way payments, where the non-defaulting party would make the above calculations and would be entitled to claim from the defaulting party any resulting positive amount or be obligated to pay to the defaulting party any resulting negative amount. Because of concerns that payments to a defaulting party might be made under circumstances where the non-defaulting party would be at further risk, some agreements provide for conditions to such payment that contain important safeguards for the non-defaulting party.

Where early termination is based on an event of default, most dealers have, however, generally provided in their agreement that limited two-way payments (really one-way payments) applies. The non-defaulting party would calculate the aggregate of its settlement amount and unpaid amounts owing to it and subtract therefrom unpaid amounts owing to the defaulting party, as above. If the resulting amount is positive, the defaulting party is obligated to pay that amount to the non-defaulting party. If the resulting amount is negative, there is no obligation imposed on the non-defaulting party to make any payment to the defaulting party.

12.12 A Final Note: Enforcement Issues

The laws of any given jurisdiction must be looked at to determine enforceability of the termination and settlement provisions of the ISDA Agreement. English or New York law generally is selected to govern, and there are issues as to enforceability under these laws. Even when enforceable under English or New York law, there may be substantive policy issues and bankruptcy law considerations in the jurisdiction of incorporation of the counterparty and (if different) of enforcement that would override the provisions of the chosen contract law.

Particular issues to look at are the following. In some jurisdictions, the right to terminate an agreement might be limited by the equitable powers of the court. For instance, a breach that is regarded by a court as immaterial might not be upheld as a valid cause for a termination, particularly if the "breaching" party stood to lose substantial value in the agreement as a result of one-way payments. Alternatively, a court might enforce the termination provisions but depending on a number of circumstances, equitably impose an obligation on the non-defaulting party to pay over any gain on termination (being somewhat less than the loss to the defaulting party). Second, bankruptcy laws may render ineffective termination provisions and permit a trustee acting on behalf of the bankrupt party to choose among the swap transactions under the agreement, thereby destroying the hoped-for benefits of netting. This risk has basically been eliminated in the US through the passage of laws with respect to banks and amendments to the federal Bankruptcy Code. In other jurisdictions, the risk of "cherry-picking" may or may not be regarded as slight, but the possibility cannot in any jurisdiction be ignored.

13

Issues and Trends in Aircraft and Ship Financing from Current Methods

GORDON C. C. HALL AND IAN R. SIDDELL

Chapter Outline

13.1 Preface
13.2 Introduction
13.3 Issues
    13.3.1 Legal Issues
    13.3.2 Commercial Issues
13.4 Trends
    13.4.1 The Background
    13.4.2 The Methods
13.5 Concluding Summary

13.1 Preface

The chapter which follows was written in the summer of 1990 at a time when Pan Am and Air Europe were still flying, the future of both shipping and aviation looked stable, and the realities of world recession had yet to be felt. The concluding paragraph of the chapter, written at that time, has proved prophetically true. If written now, the content of the chapter would be radically different and its tone significantly less optimistic.

For neither shipping nor aviation has there been the continued growth anticipated in 1990. The aviation market has not recovered from the severe setbacks suffered by the effects of the Gulf War, although the reasons for this failure seem to be not so much a reluctance to fly as the unwillingness of people to afford flights and the lack of business reasons to fly. Shipping has been hit by low freight rates and falling second-hand prices which have meant that existing ships which carry debt cannot be sold and other resources are required to be employed in the servicing of existing debt. It is said that some shipowners are sitting on large cash reserves which they will spend when second-hand prices appear to have reached the bottom and freight rates appear to be turning upwards. This cash represents liquidity withdrawn from the market.

There is also a severe squeeze on funding which has affected both ships and aircraft. Equity financing has been hit by the reduced financial circumstances of individuals who would normally comprise the investing group and banks have found themselves with less funds available to lend. The funds which are available now seem to attract greater margins and the tendency toward lending only to the better risks seems even more marked.

An illustration of how things have changed can be found in the example of GPA. GPA, the largest aircraft leasing company in the world, successfully launched a publicly offered securitized note issue based on the credit of airlines to whom GPA has leased aircraft but shortly afterwards had to withdraw a public capital fund-raising exercise for lack of investor interest.

In the 1980s large numbers of ships were in lay-up without employment. More recently, large numbers of aircraft have been found in the same position. Confidence is very low; few shipowners and airlines are making profits. Those that are strongest have reacted to the adversity by seeking to strengthen themselves. The chapter notes the desire among airlines to seek alliances and worldwide access to markets. This trend has been highlighted recently by the series of discussions which British Airways has held with carriers such as Sabena of Belgium, KLM, and, most recently, US Air. Indeed, British Airways' appetite is not yet satisfied: it has expressed interest in gaining a share in Qantas of Australia and, closer to home, has pursued the ailing Dan Air.

There will always be a need for ships and a demand for aircraft and the issues facing aircraft and ship financing now are how to find the funds to finance investments which only recently have manifested a new fragility. The trends in aircraft and ship financing reflect the response to those issues: the relatively scarce funds which are available are offered only to the better credits and then only at higher margins to reflect higher risks.

Finally, there has been one significant legal development as far as transactions in England are concerned. This was the decision in *Ensign Tankers (Leasing) Ltd.* v. *Stokes (HMIT)* [1992] STC 226. Despite its name, the case related to film financing, but the decision affected all forms of structured financing, particularly those with a tax element. The effect of the decision has been to reduce the taxation-related benefits which can be derived from limited recourse financing, which has been a feature of ship and aircraft financing in recent years.

Despite such a complete change in the background against which the chapter was written, it is felt that much of the chapter still has validity in that, when matters begin to improve again, the natural starting point for the new era will be refinement of those aspects of the old order which were the best and which remain appropriate in the light of intervening changes in tax laws, asset value perceptions, trade prospects, and the host of other factors which impinge independently on the evolution of ship and aircraft financing techniques.

13.2 Introduction

In many people's minds ship and aircraft financing are probably regarded as somewhat self-contained and esoteric areas of legal practice, being neither pure banking work nor mainstream asset financing nor equipment leasing. Ship and aircraft financing is a distinct area of legal practice but it is one which, in the main, draws on developments in other spheres of law, banking, and commercial practice and molds them or adapts them to fit for ship and aircraft acquisitions.

This chapter will look briefly at some, but certainly not all, of the current issues and trends affecting the methods by which ships and aircraft are financed. Ship and aircraft financing arrangements are international transactions and it would hardly be possible to address or even note all the issues affecting this topic worldwide, but this chapter will have reference to the international nature of the business as it would be impossible to look at the topic without taking account of its nature.

Consideration will be given first to the issues affecting ship and aircraft financing which fall, broadly, into the two categories of legal issues and commercial issues and then to some of the trends that are discernible or that some consider as having potential for the future.

13.3 Issues

13.3.1 Legal Issues

By taking the view that ship and aircraft financing transactions draw from other areas of law and banking practice and then adapt the principles to meet the needs of ships and aircraft and their operators, it is possible to dispose of the first element of the subject of this chapter relatively quickly from a legal point of view. Quite simply, the basic legal issues affecting ship and aircraft financing at any time tend to be those that affect other areas of legal practice.

Recently, for the English lawyer, the issues have been the familiar ones of the problems arising out of the decisions in the *Slavenburg* and *Charge Card* cases and those cases which followed, with a "weather eye" on new legislation relating to the execution of documentation and the content of certain security documents.

The *Slavenburg* decision (relating to the registration of charges against foreign incorporated companies not known to have a place of business in England and Wales) is one of particular relevance as it is often the case that in a ship or aircraft finance transaction the mortgagor is a company not incorporated under English legislation. However, in case the mortgagor does, as a matter of fact, have, or at some later stage does establish, a place of business in England and Wales it is prudent to apply for registration of all charges at the English Companies House. A charge in respect of which no application for registration has been made may be void against a liquidator or creditors of the chargor.[1]

The *Charge Card* decision (relating to the ability of a deposit-holder to take a security assignment of the benefit of its own repayment obligation in respect of that deposit) clearly affects arrangements for collateral cash deposits and accounts for the collection of earnings and other proceeds in which a financier may require a security interest.

The recent legislation concerning execution of documentation is the Law of Property (Miscellaneous Provisions) Act 1989 and the Companies Act 1989. Section 36A(v) of the Companies Act 1985 was introduced by the Companies Act 1989 and came into effect on July 31, 1990; however, this section may in fact do no more than restate existing law as to the fact that a document executed as if it were a deed is treated as a deed. Section 130 of the Companies Act 1989 effectively removes the obligation on a company to have a Common Seal and introduces a new section 36A(iv) to the Companies Act 1985 which provides that documents signed by a director and the secretary of a company or any two directors and expressed to be executed by the company have the same effect as if they were executed under the Common Seal of the company. If a document executed by a company makes it clear on its face that it is intended by those making it to be a deed, that document has effect on delivery as a deed.

Of recent concern in other areas of law, but not so much that of ship and aircraft financing, was section 2 of the Law of Property

(Miscellaneous Provisions) Act 1989, which introduced the need to make reference in a land mortgage deed to all the terms concerning the transaction of which that mortgage is part. This provision can be of relevance in a ship or aircraft finance transaction however, where a floating charge over all the present and future assets of the mortgagor is involved, since such a charge will normally contain a charge or mortgage over all the mortgagor's real property interests.[2]

13.3.2 Commercial Issues

Moving away from the legal issues, there are some notable commercial issues that the ship or aircraft financier should consider.

Ship and (particularly) aircraft financing transactions, although they started by borrowing ideas from other spheres, have tended to become very innovative. Because the stakes are high, in that the subject of these transactions is a high-value asset with which the parties intend to live for an appreciable period of time and which the parties expect to be able to employ throughout that period in a competitive way, there are possibly greater incentives than in other types of asset-based transaction to reduce the costs that are associated with acquiring the asset as far as possible. Ships and aircraft operate in very competitive and inherently cyclical markets and generally it takes a long time and needs a fairly steady income stream to pay off the financing debt. To reduce the effect of the "up and down" cycles of the business (whether it be the ebb and flow of intercontinental trades or the seasonal nature of much air traffic) it is necessary to insulate the asset as far as possible; and the surest way to do this is to reduce the financial burdens it has to carry. For these reasons, operators are willing to enter into highly complex transactions that often follow untested routes and financiers must ensure that they adequately take account of the risks in such transactions in case the edifice they are supporting collapses.[3]

Deregulation, a matter of prominence in Europe in the run-up to 1993, affects the views taken by airlines as to their needs for the future. It has affected the activities of US carriers (who are seeking to have Europe treated as a single country so as to obtain preferential routing to and within Europe) as well as the decisions being taken by European airlines as to what opportunities deregulation will offer them and how best to position themselves to be ready to seize those opportunities. The financier must consider carefully the long-term viability of its borrower in times of enhanced competition. The lessons learned in the US from the great "shake-up" of the aviation industry following deregulation there should be heeded.

Another development of recent years has been the realization by airlines that if they are to maintain competitiveness, they need to have access to markets all round the world and to the facilities that are available at principal airports in strategic locations. This has led to a number of groupings developing and to strategic alliances being forged between airlines. The likely effect of this is to produce an increasing rationalization of such matters as aircraft acquisition programs (so that airlines in a grouping tend to acquire the same equipment), maintenance arrangements, and pooling agreements. One can speculate that the "knock-on" effect on aircraft finance transactions is that there is potential for such groupings to come to the financiers together for a "mixed bag" of facilities giving them flexibility in their financing arrangements so as, for example, to enable them to share domestic tax and financial benefits available to each of them. Thus, the financier may need to consider the credit of not just one but a number of airlines and to assess their relative strengths and weaknesses in relation to the facilities it will provide.

A further major issue coming to the fore recently has been the ability of a financier or lessor to go into possession or to repossess an aircraft from a defaulting owner or lessee. A particular element of this issue that has struck home has been the ability of government agencies and international bodies to arrest aircraft to recover outstanding air traffic control or landing fees. Possibly the most spectacular example arose in connection with an Air Canada aircraft arrested in London in 1987 because of a small quantity of cannabis found on board. The English Court of Appeal recently held that HM Customs and Excise were entitled to arrest and detain the aircraft and to forfeit the aircraft if the sum demanded by HM Customs and Excise in order to release the aircraft was not paid. This was in spite of the fact that the court accepted that none of the crew nor the airline had or could have had any knowledge of the illegal substance on board. The Court of Appeal held that English law entitled HM Customs and Excise to forfeit not only the illegal substance but also the aircraft on which the substance was found. Clearly this is a matter of some concern not only to an owner but also to a financier.

A matter more closely related to shipping arises out of the established policy (particularly of European states) to provide subsidies to the domestic shipbuilding industry to keep that industry going. There are a number of schemes offering "soft" financing to encourage owners to purchase vessels from domestic yards (for example in England, the home shipbuilding scheme operating under section 10 of the Industry Acts 1972 and 1975 and the similar terms available from the Export Credits Guarantee Department). With the advent of the

European Community, direct subsidies to the shipbuilding industry have been drastically reduced and most yards in Europe have now closed. There is the potential for the European Community to sanction some form of central subsidy arrangement; but if the domestic yards are not kept open, there will be little for the domestic soft financing arrangements to apply to and they too may disappear. The US is lobbying hard for the abolition of all subsidies and it may succeed in achieving its goal through economic and political pressure. On the other hand, there is little to suggest that subsidies to Far Eastern shipbuilders or other subsidizing arrangements available to buyers from those yards will be reduced at any time other than when the economics of shipbuilding make it viable for yards to stand alone.

13.4 Trends

13.4.1 The Background

When considering the trends in aircraft and ship financing it is useful to look back to see in broad terms how ship and aircraft financing transactions have developed to their current structures.

After the boom times of the 1970s when the shipbuilding industry flourished world-wide there was a dramatic slump in shipbuilding and the size of the world fleet. The world fleet is now said to have its highest ever average age, reflecting the reluctance among owners over the last few years to order new ships. However, it is now the case that yards' order books are filling up and new vessels are becoming ever more urgently required.

Almost contemporaneous with the downturn in the shipping industry was the upturn in the aviation industry, which continued through the 1980s and is projected to continue strongly in the 1990s and the next century.

In the boom times for shipping, financiers were keen to lend money by means of straight loans secured on the ship in the apparently safe belief that ship values would continue to rise and so the loan would become an ever safer asset. Once the downturn in ship values became a reality, many financiers with loans secured on ships became at best uneasy, or at worst unstuck, and much money was lost. Financiers became shipowners in some cases.

In trying to continue with ship financing, financiers began to regard the value of the asset as an uncertain security and the wiser financiers began to look only to more certain security and, in particular, the strength of the balance sheet of the company (or guarantor) against whose covenant to repay they were lending.

Clearly, not all who sought finance for their ships could obtain the finance they needed under these criteria and not all who could do so wanted to. Apart from anything else, straight borrowing was an expensive way to obtain finance, especially in connection with an asset of high value such as a new ship, which required a large loan. Furthermore, with world trade slumping the ability of a ship to earn enough to service a large loan was becoming ever less, particularly in a market with an oversupply of ships resulting in a sharp reduction in charter rates.

One way found to provide ships to those who were considered good risks was the tax-based lease. Typically, this provided the operator with use of a ship, effectively on a bareboat charterparty, but at a variable rate of hire reflecting a competitive financing cost reduced by tax benefits available to the lessor that may not have been available to the operator. Additionally, the operator had the opportunity to benefit from any increased value in the ship at the end of the lease period.

At about this time aircraft financing began to emerge as a new area of asset-related financing business. It emerged because of a combination of factors (deregulation in the US, growth in tourism, improvements in technology) which made it possible for smaller independent airlines to be set up to offer a service that could complement or challenge the business of the larger, established airlines. Up to this point the major airlines (but not all of them) had tended to have government backing and to purchase their aircraft more or less for cash without regard for financing alternatives available in the open market.

The independents financed their acquisitions by taking over the structures familiar to the ship financiers and applying them with appropriate modifications to aircraft. Through the 1980s the principal pioneers of international asset finance techniques have been airlines or their financiers, lessors, and transaction packagers.

The growth of independent competitors and more recently the phenomenon of airline privatization have driven all airlines into a frenzy of "cutting edge" financing arrangements. At first, taking the lead from their shipping experiences, financiers offered straightforward tax-based leases but that financing technique, although still used as an element in financing arrangements, soon came to be considered, by itself, not to offer sufficient advantages to the owner or operator. Thus, ever more complex financing structures emerged seeking to obtain as many benefits from as many sources as possible and building the necessary elements on to one another.

Such a transaction might, for example, provide the operator with an aircraft that would not appear on his balance sheet, at a rental taking into account tax benefits available against the outlay by a financier or investor of the capital cost of the aircraft, enhanced by the cost of repayment being reduced by virtue of tax benefits available to those providing some of the financing. This transaction would also involve arranging for funds (usually in the form of deposits or bonds) to be established in amounts which when interest accrued on them would be sufficient to repay the financing cost (both principal and interest) over the agreed repayment period. That "present value" interest benefit would often result in the operator receiving a substantial lump sum at the outset of the transaction.

The legal relationships involved in such transactions are complex and by some tests may be found to be verging on the artificial. Additionally, such structures carry significant risks since they are largely untried and innovative and require the airline or its parent to indemnify the parties involved in the transaction for losses arising by reason of the structure being prematurely dismantled, collapsing, or having to be adjusted. Furthermore, a fundamental feature of such transactions is often the need to exploit the tax regimes of countries not associated with the operation of the aircraft. Such exploitation is generally unpopular (although it may be useful politically) and recently the Japanese have severely restricted the possibilities for exploiting their tax regime in future transactions. These aspects can make the structures seem fragile and a little uncertain; but, so far, financiers have been found who are willing to be a part of them, which can only augur well for the future of innovation in financing.

13.4.2 *The Methods*

Despite the risks, the need for competitive financing remains. The aircraft market is buoyant and the market for new ships is improving with the price of both new buildings and secondhand ships rising dramatically. In these circumstances, if he is not willing to get involved in what is possibly a fragile structure, how will the shipowner or airline finance a new acquisition and remain competitive?

To meet this need a number of new, and some not so new, financing techniques are emerging. The common basis of them seems to be a willingness in financiers or investors to take a stake in the operation and capital value of the asset. It has to be said that currently few of the techniques seem to be used for both ships and aircraft; however, the history of these industries tends to suggest that they will continue to borrow ideas from each other.[4] With appropriate adaption to suit the different operational and regulatory requirements of ships and aircraft, all of the techniques that are now considered should work for both types of asset.

Joint venture In a straightforward joint venture, the parties usually set up a company to own the asset in question. The asset is acquired by use of shareholder funds and then leased on to the joint venture party which it is intended should operate the asset. Although this may not seem to be a particularly new arrangement, the novelty lies in the fact that banks and financiers are becoming joint venture parties themselves rather than, as before, financiers to the joint venture company. The benefits to the operator are the provision of the asset off-balance-sheet, probably under a tax-based leasing arrangement, supported by funds provided by a financier with a vested interest in the success of the venture, since, typically, the financier will be looking to take a share of the equity in the asset on its eventual sale.

From the financier's point of view, this may put him closer to the asset and the incidents of ownership than he might like to be, but careful choice of the joint venture partner and careful division of liabilities with suitable cross-indemnities, possibly reflected in the pricing and equity share ratios, should resolve this problem acceptably.

Mezzanine financing A technique in some ways similar to a joint venture is mezzanine financing. There are a variety of ways to structure a mezzanine financing transaction and some structures fall almost squarely into what has just been described as a pure joint venture.

An example of mezzanine financing involves a number of different lenders whose debt is layered in terms of priority and whose recourse is effectively limited to the value of the asset. In such a transaction, the asset might be subject to an operating lease and the loans of the lenders secured principally by mortgages over the asset, ranking in priority.

The rights of the junior lenders to recover their loans will be expressly subordinated to those of the senior lenders. The amounts of the loans could be set at a level such that the lease rental would pay off an agreed amount of the senior loan during the remaining life of the underlying operating lease and the conservatively estimated market value of the asset at the end of the lease would repay the second and third loans.

In such a structure, the first lender would normally be very well secured. The second lender would normally have some cause for concern if the value of the asset fell, although it would have to be a fairly substantial fall. Subsequent lenders would have greater concerns and might be given some additional security. However, the bottom-ranking lender also often takes an equity interest in the asset so that if the asset increases in value, that lender stands to benefit handsomely.

The direct commercial gain derived by each of the participants in such a transaction is clear. For the lenders, the benefit lies in the pricing of the various loans which reflects the risk each lender takes; the greater the risk, the greater the margin. The operator achieves a substantial benefit by arranging finance for virtually the full market value of the asset, at a spread of rates, and with little, if any, recourse personally (except in relation to passing on lease rentals, performing certain obligations as lessor, and the possible provision of some security to the junior lender). At the same time, the operator retains the potential of further equity profit when the asset is sold at the end of the lease term.

Despite its apparent simplicity, this structure is fraught with legal difficulties relating to such matters as ensuring that there is effective subordination of the junior loans, controlling the enforcement of security, ensuring that the priority of the security interests is properly recognized by third parties (e.g. the lessee, insurers, and the bank holding the account through which rental and sales proceeds are distributed). Furthermore, there is a need to protect and to balance the interests of the ultimate lessee and the operator of the asset against those of the lenders who have no direct contact with each other.

Limited partnerships/income funds The limited partnership is, effectively, the entity known sometimes in the US as the "income fund."

The limited partnership structure is quite well established, particularly in Norway, in relation to ship financing; and, although perhaps now waning in significance in that country, it is becoming prevalent elsewhere.

This structure involves establishing a legal entity in which there is at least one general partner with unlimited liability (to third parties) and a potentially large number of small investors who are liable to third parties only for their investment in the partnership and who take no part in the management of the partnership.

The benefits of these arrangements to the operator are principally a spread of risk and reduced financing cost. The investors obtain personal tax benefits on their investments.

The particular significance of limited partnerships here is that there is evidence that the US version of these (the "income fund") is coming into increasing prominence due to the fact that recent changes in US tax laws have made investment in the right fund tax efficient.

Funds Another type of fund is an altogether more sophisticated entity. It too involves a spread of risk among a large group of small investors who have no involvement in the day-to-day management of the business in which they have invested. Instead of tax advantages, the investors seek capital gains (quickly and in large amounts) or substantial dividends.

A number of these funds have been established. Broadly the principles are that the prime movers behind the scheme establish the fund typically to trade in assets in a rising market, but also to employ the assets in less bullish times. Normally the fund will have a limited life so that it is written into the fund's constitution that it is liable to be wound up at a predetermined time.

The promoters of the scheme will issue a prospectus inviting investment in the fund, and the shares or loan notes or certificates of the fund may be quoted on a recognized stock exchange.[5] Investors buy the stock and normally are able to trade it freely. Thus finance is raised cheaply (further finance, if needed, can be raised by more conventional methods) and the money invested is applied by a trustee in the purchase of the assets which are subsequently mortgaged back to the trustee for the benefit of the investors and then sold for profit or put out to work.

Operating leases In the aviation field perhaps the strongest trend that is discernible is toward greater use of operating leases. In shipping terms, an operating lease would equate with a bareboat charter; it will constitute an arrangement under which the operator takes the full risk of loss of the aircraft and of all liability claims while it is in its possession, but no interest in the equity. Such a lease may well be for a very short term.

A particular feature of the growth in operating leasing of aircraft has been the emergence of leasing companies which purchase fleets of various types of aircraft and put them to work with airlines around the world. They are able to conduct such a business because the operating lease is considered by many to be the tool of the future for airlines. It combines at once the flexibility to take on and offload capacity in emergencies or seasonally (which is crucial to most airlines), generally fixed rentals (usually with no attendant tax indemnities), the ability to upgrade the airline's fleet continually (with added marketing and reduced maintenance cost potential), and the provision of an off-balance-sheet fleet while distancing the airline from financing debt burdens.

The operating lease is a prime example of how the aviation market has refined a basic shipping concept to produce something really quite distinct in its commercial utility. However, it is unlikely that the operating lease as it is used for aircraft will break into the shipping industry due to the intrinsically different nature of the trade and operation of ships.

13.5 Concluding Summary

In order to remain competitive airlines and shipowners will always seek the edge that can be provided by taking the next step on the road of innovation and this stimulates the development of new and more effective methods of financing. As those methods are refined and developed, new issues arise and new trends are discernible.

For the lawyer, ship and aircraft financing is challenging because it is a constantly changing area of practice. The legal issues that arise require novel legal solutions and the commercial issues that arise need imaginative consideration. It is the merging of those legal solutions and commercial considerations in dealing with opportunities that arise which creates trends and new financing methods.

Those methods must be devised against an ever-changing background of tax laws and international trade cycles and the effect is to keep up the momentum of the development of ship and aircraft financing in the search for the best solution to fit each new set of circumstances. The result is that this chapter can represent little more than a snapshot of an evolutionary process and if it were written annually its contents would vary each year.

Notes

1 *NV Slavenburg's Bank* v *Intercontinental Natural Resources Ltd. and others*. [1980] 1 All ER 955.
2 *Re Charge Card Services Ltd*. [1986] 3 All ER 289.
3 Law of Property (Miscellaneous Provisions) Act 1989 c. 34; Companies Act 1989 c. 40.
4 Companies Act 1985 c. 6.
5 Industry Act 1972 c. 63; Industry Act 1975 c. 68.

Part V

Special Legal Concerns

Part V

Special Legal Concerns

14

Confidentiality of Bank Records, Money Laundering, and Transaction Reporting Requirements under US Law

STEPHEN K. HUBER

Chapter Outline

14.1 Introduction
14.2 General Provisions of the Bank Secrecy Act
14.3 Domestic Currency Transactions
14.4 Movement of Monetary Instruments across US Borders
14.5 Records of Customer Transactions
14.6 Successor Liability: Alamo Bank
14.7 Constitutionality of the Bank Secrecy Act
14.8 State Law Regarding Bank Disclosures
14.9 Enforcement of the Bank Secrecy Act
14.10 Structured Transactions
14.11 Administrative Rulings on BSA Issues
14.12 The Costs and Benefits of Disclosure Requirements
14.13 European Community Directive on Money Laundering

14.1 Introduction

The duty of banks and other providers of financial services to disclose information to the federal government about certain currency and other customer transactions is based on the grotesquely misnamed Bank Secrecy Act of 1970 (the BSA).[1] The title suggests that the BSA promotes bank secrecy, whereas it does quite the opposite. The common law position was, and still is to the extent that it is not superseded by a state or federal statute, that banks have an affirmative duty not to make voluntary disclosures concerning the financial affairs of their customers without the consent of the customer, except as incident to a normal business transaction. Thus a bank may refuse to honor a check because the customer's account contains insufficient funds, even though this conveys information about the customer, but the bank may not inform a third party (such as an employer) that the customer has "bounced" a check. As a leading case put the matter, "Inviolate secrecy is one of the inherent and fundamental precepts of the relationship of the bank and its customers or depositors."[2] The adoption of the BSA reflected an important retreat from the tradition of bank secrecy, rather than an affirmation of that principle.

There were some earlier exceptions to the non-disclosure principle. Banks were required to produce customer information in response to a court order or grand jury subpoena in the same manner as any other person. The most significant instance of legislation that granted the federal government power to coerce the disclosure of information from third party record-keepers was that granted to the Internal Revenue Service (IRS).[3] This power was granted for a specific situation, the enforcement of the tax laws, and to obtain disclosure the IRS was (and still is) required to demonstrate that:

- its investigation is pursuant to an authorized purpose;
- the requested information is relevant to that purpose;
- the information is not already available to IRS; and
- the statutory summons procedures were followed.[4]

This approach, where banks and other holders of relevant financial information may be required to disclose data about a particular customer when that information is not otherwise available to the government, is far more restrictive than the blanket disclosure requirements imposed by the BSA. A practical difference of great interest to bankers is that Congress made provision for the reimbursement of costs associated with compliance with IRS summonses, whereas the costs of BSA compliance are borne by the providers of the mandated disclosures.[5]

Fundamental to understanding the BSA is a recognition that the legislation reflects law enforcement concerns rather than a perceived need to regulate banking organizations. There is no pretense that the BSA promotes safety and soundness, or other goals of bank regulation. Banks are a central focus of the BSA because of their role in facilitating the movement of money. Congress was concerned about criminal activity in the US, and also sought to thwart the improper use by US taxpayers of foreign providers of financial services located in jurisdictions with highly restrictive financial privacy laws.[6] The initial concern was money laundering generally, but in recent years the focus has become drug money. The scope of the BSA was expanded by provisions of the Anti Drug Abuse Acts of 1986 and 1988.[7] The law enforcement focus of the BSA also is reflected in the placing of administrative authority for implementation as regards banks with the Department of the Treasury, an agency with extensive law enforcement responsibilities, rather than with the bank regulatory agencies.[8]

14.2 General Provisions of the Bank Secrecy Act

The BSA requires banking organizations and certain other entities to maintain extensive records relating to specified customer dealings. These dealings include deposit account activity, domestic currency transactions, and the movement of monetary instruments across US borders. The Secretary of the Treasury is authorized to require institutions to maintain and submit records that he determines have "a high degree of usefulness" in criminal, tax, or regulatory investigations or proceedings.[9] Congress gave the Secretary unfettered discretion to determine what records meet this test. The payment of rewards is authorized for information that results in the imposition of significant sanctions on violators.[10] The Treasury Department can require officials of depository institutions to personally appear, produce records, and testify under oath in connection with money laundering or compliance investigations.[11] Regulated institutions must establish internal controls to assure BSA compliance, monitor the implementation of compliance procedures, designate one or more individuals as responsible for supervising day-to-day compliance, and provide training for personnel.

The Treasury Department has adopted increasingly stringent regulations regarding the implementation of the BSA.[12] For example, the period for which depository institutions must maintain transaction records, which initially was two years, has been increased to five years.[13] The result was to vastly increase the total volume of records that must be retained, virtually all of which will never be looked at. The objective of this policy was to make it easier to document BSA violations and related financial crimes. No cost–benefit analysis was conducted, and the Treasury Department simply asserted that this rule would not have a major impact on small businesses.[14] This conclusion is patently wrong, because additional paperwork requirements are particularly burdensome for small institutions.

Credit unions have been especially hard hit by BSA reporting requirements, and the National Credit Union Administration (NCUA) has been forced to postpone the implementation of some BSA procedures.[15] A small credit union that mainly serves the Polish community in and around Lynn, Massachusetts, was convicted for failure to file currency transaction reports (CTRs).[16] Forms were completed, but never filed, by the credit union bookkeeper. Since most credit union officers are unpaid and serve on a part-time basis, it is unrealistic for them to expect them to discover even unsophisticated money laundering plans.

14.3 Domestic Currency Transactions

Reporting requirements are triggered when a financial institution participates in any domestic deposit, withdrawal, exchange, or other transfer of currency in excess of $10,000 ($3,000 in certain situations).[17] In a few instances, an individual has been treated as a financial institution for BSA purposes. A person who accepted cash in return for cashier's checks, and was paid a fee for the service, was held to be subject to the BSA reporting requirements,[18] but another federal court came to the opposite conclusion when faced with similar circumstances.[19] Even an individual who is not required to file a CTR can be convicted of the crime of willfully causing a financial institution to fail to file CTRs, by structuring cash transactions.[20] The transactions in this case took place in 1986, when it was unclear if there was a duty to aggregate transactions. The court ruled that the bank had such a duty, and by dividing the transactions the depositor willfully caused the bank to fail to report the transactions. This so-called reasoning is pretty weak.

"Currency" does not include checks and other instruments, but it does include legal tender from other countries.[21] Transactions between depository institutions or with Federal Reserve or Federal Home Loan banks, account activity by certain retail businesses, withdrawals for payroll purposes, and transfers by governmental entities are exempted, provided the amounts involved are commensurate with customary cash transactions. Other exemptions require the approval of the Treasury Department. An institution must maintain a centralized listing of its authorized exemptions.[22] This listing must indicate the dollar limit of each exemption, and whether it covers deposits, withdrawals, or both. The list is subject to administrative review, and reports can be required for customers exempted by the institution.

The Treasury Department is authorized to impose special reporting requirements on any bank or group of banks in a geographic area.[23] Targeting orders will not be published in the Federal Register, and institutions subject to such orders should not disclose the lower reporting threshold to their customers. (No advice is given about how institutions are to provide information needed to complete CTRs without disclosure of the special reporting requirements.) No minimum dollar amount is stated, so the Treasury has the power to establish any reporting floor. The American Bankers' Association estimates that a $3,000 floor would result in a tenfold increase in the number of CTRs a typical bank would be required to file.[24] The Treasury can order the use of a lower dollar reporting level whenever appropriate to carry out the purposes of the BSA. Orders can be renewed any number of times. These orders can target specific types of transactions. The Treasury has awarded itself essentially unlimited authority to reduce CTR requirements for any bank and to substitute any lower dollar level.

Domestic CTRs must be submitted on forms prescribed by the government, and submitted to the IRS within fifteen days after the transaction.[25] Reporting institutions must retain copies of reports about domestic currency transactions for five years. Reports and records about currency transactions are exempt from disclosure under the Freedom of Information Act.[26] In addition to these reporting requirements, institutions must collect information about customers who purchase over $3,000 in traveler's checks, cashier's checks, bank checks, or money orders on the same day.[27] The lower requirement was imposed because money launderers commonly purchased such instruments in amounts up to $10,000 without providing identification. A financial institution must maintain a register of sales over $3,000 up to $10,000, and provide the information to the Treasury upon request. Larger transactions continue to be subject to the regular BSA reporting requirements.

The information that must be collected is less extensive for holders of a deposit account at the selling institution, because the institution already has information about the person. An account-holder is easier to find, and is less likely to engage in money laundering. For account-holders, the institution must record:

- name of the purchaser;
- account number;
- purchase date;
- location of branch effecting the transaction; and
- type, serial number, and dollar amount of instruments.

The seller is responsible for verifying that the purchaser has a deposit account at the institution. For other purchasers, the financial institution must collect additional information:

- address of purchaser;
- birth date of purchaser;
- payee on instrument (bank and cashier's checks); and
- if the instrument is purchased on behalf of a third party, the identity of the real party in interest.

The financial institution need not investigate the response of the purchaser with regard to purchases on behalf of third parties. The name and address of the purchaser must be verified by suitable identification, such as a driver's license.

Financial institutions must retain these records for five years. Records can be maintained in a single transaction log for the institution, or separate logs can be kept for each office. Records must be maintained at a centralized location, and must be filed there within fifteen days after the record is created. A single log can be maintained for all instruments, or separate logs may be maintained for each type of instrument.

14.4 Movement of Monetary Instruments across US Borders

The physical transportation into or out of the US of cash or monetary instruments in an aggregate amount exceeding $10,000 must be reported by the party doing the transporting or by the party in the US that receives the funds.[28] Monetary instruments include currency, checks, money orders, investment securities in bearer form, and negotiable instruments.[29] Documents that represent goods rather than money (i.e. bills of lading and warehouse receipts) are not subject to reporting requirements.

Travelers checks (except for those that have been negotiated and are in the collection process) are included in the definition of monetary instruments, and therefore are subject to reporting when they are brought into or taken out of the US.[30] Several separate transactions can be treated as one, if the purpose was to evade the reporting requirements. This approach is easier to implement for the international movement of monetary instruments than for domestic reporting requirements, because in the former instance the duty to report is placed on the transferring party whereas with domestic transactions the duty to report is placed on a third party institution which usually does not know the intentions of its customer.

The duty to make a report is imposed on anyone who transports monetary instruments across a US border, without regard to that person's ownership interest, if any, in the instruments.[31] Transfers of funds through bank channels that do not involve the physical movement of currency or instruments are exempted, as are shipments sent through the mails or by common carrier. Most international transactions engaged in by depository institutions need not be reported because no monetary instrument is involved, or because an exemption is applicable. (These international transactions will, however, be subject to the customer transaction record requirements discussed in the next section.) Required reports must be filed with the Commissioner of Customs within thirty days after receipt of the currency or monetary instrument.[32]

Monetary instruments for which a materially accurate report has not been filed can be seized in the course of transportation, and subsequently forfeited to the US.[33] The full value of the instrument is subject to forfeiture, not just the amount by which it exceeds the reporting floor.[34] Forfeiture is permissible even though the property itself is not the object of a crime.[35]

Failure to file an accurate currency transaction report is a strict liability offense that can lead to forfeiture of the funds, notwithstanding that the under-reported amount was small, the error was inadvertent, and it was discovered only because of the honesty of the person involved. In an extraordinary case, a person bringing $173,081.04 into the country lost the entire amount for erroneously reporting that the amount was $1,000 lower.[36] The court that heard an appeal from the forfeiture decided that it had no discretion to reverse the action of the Customs Office because the applicable regulations state that discretion to remit forfeited funds rests exclusively with the Secretary of the Treasury. It was unsuccessfully argued that forfeiture of the funds amounted to a violation of due process because the law imposes no restriction on the movement of monetary instruments, but only imposes a reporting requirement. The court responded that forfeiture was reasonably related to the objective of deterring potential violators of the reporting requirements.

The disclosure rules apply equally to over-reporting, because the BSA requires accurate reports, but the cases nearly all involve under-reporting or a failure to file a required report at all. There is no ceiling on the amount of a forfeiture, and nearly $1.5 million has been forfeited for failure to make the requisite disclosures.[37]

14.5 Records of Customer Transactions

Reporting requirements relating to the movement of cash and monetary instruments are of minor consequence compared to the general record-keeping provisions of the BSA, in terms of both the impact on depository institution operations and potential intrusiveness into the affairs of individuals. Banks, savings associations, and credit unions are required to keep extensive records concerning their deposit account customers and transactions involving these accounts.[38] These requirements apply to uninsured depository institutions, all organizations chartered under the banking laws of any state, and certain nonbanking providers of financial services.

Depository institutions are required to obtain taxpayer identification numbers (TINs) for all new checking and savings accounts, and for certificates of deposit that are sold or redeemed.[39] Mortgage escrow accounts and credit card programs are not covered. Identification numbers are issued to businesses and other organizations by the IRS, while individuals use their Social Security numbers. Special provision is made for members of the Old Order Amish Sect, who decline to use identification numbers on religious grounds. Only one identifying number per customer is required, but a person (legal or individual) who holds accounts in different capacities may use separate numbers for each account. An institution must maintain a list that states the names, addresses, and account numbers of all customers for whom a TIN cannot be secured despite reasonable efforts. There are a number of exceptions to the identification number requirement, but their aggregate importance is not great.

The Secretary of the Treasury can require depository institutions to maintain account records and other information that he determines to have a high degree of usefulness in criminal, tax, and regulatory proceedings. Such a determination has been made for a wide variety of records, including:

- documents granting signature authority over deposit accounts;
- account statements (which reflect all transactions);
- checks, clean drafts, and money orders drawn for more than $100;
- records needed to reconstruct demand deposit accounts and to provide an audit trail for deposits in excess of $100; and
- transfers of more than $10,000 into or out of the United States.[40]

Securities brokers and dealers are also subject to important record-keeping requirements.[41]

Despite the exclusion for checks up to $100, which constitute the vast majority of checks, banks routinely microfilm all checks because it is cheaper to proceed in this manner than to segregate the larger items for copying. Both the front and back of instruments and other documents must be copied unless the back is entirely blank.[42] Records necessary to reconstruct demand deposit accounts and to trace checks of more than $100 must be retained for at least two years, while other required records must be retained for five years. The records must be accessible within a reasonable period of time. While the cost of copying a single instrument and storing information about one transaction is tiny, the aggregate cost of records maintenance is huge. By the absence of any reimbursement provisions, these costs were imposed on depository institutions, and ultimately on those who use their services.

Disclosure of the customer transaction information collected by banking organizations pursuant to the reporting requirements discussed in this section is not authorized, let alone required, even to the government. Rather, the institution must simply hold the records. These records are not automatically available for law enforcement purposes, but they can be obtained pursuant to regular legal process.

Electronic funds transfer (EFT) transactions are not presently subject to record-keeping requirements, but the rule-making authority of the Treasury Department is sufficiently broad to allow for their inclusion. Many electronically initiated transactions are reflected on account statements, but retention of the information that must presently be provided on customer receipts would cover more transactions and preserve more data about all electronic transfers. The National Automated Clearing House Association rules require clearing houses to retain a copy of each sent or received EFT transaction for at least six years.[43] The Chairman of the Banking Committee in the House of Representatives, Henry B. Gonzales (Democrat, Texas) has introduced legislation that would require financial institutions to keep records of all wire transfers sent or received, but adoption of such a requirement in the near future is unlikely.[44] Proposed legislation adopted by the House Banking Committee would permit the Treasury to adopt record-keeping rules for domestic and international wire transfers.[45]

14.6 Successor Liability: Alamo Bank

An acquiror bank in a merger has been held responsible for pre-acquisition BSA violations, specifically the failure to file CTRs for large cash transactions.⁴⁶ As long as a national bank is one of the parties to the merger, federal law applies. It does not matter whether the surviving institution has a state or a federal charter. In this case the violations took place some three years prior to the merger. Alamo argued that the BSA does not apply to successor banks, and that the requisite criminal intent cannot be attributed to it. These arguments were rejected, and Alamo was held criminally responsible for the BSA violations of the acquiree bank. The court placed the bank on probation for three years and fined the bank $750,000, of which $250,000 was suspended.

The policy that the acquiror is the acquiree for purposes of legal responsibility is sensible enough, at least in the context of a merger between two healthy institutions who have ample time to make an investment decision. The issue takes on significance now because of the vast number of failed or failing thrifts that must be merged into existing institutions. The specter of legal responsibility for unknown violations is a worrisome one that might discourage acquisitions that are in the public interest. The court did not address the issue of BSA liability in the context of a federally assisted acquisition, so it is possible that such mergers will be treated differently from unassisted mergers.

It should be noted that the fine levied against Alamo was not the greatest concern of the bank. The felon label on an institution subjects it to additional reporting requirements and increased scrutiny by regulators. The consequences of a subsequent violation of the BSA, or of other legal requirements, would be much greater than in the absence of the previous conviction.

14.7 Constitutionality of the Bank Secrecy Act

Constitutional challenges to the BSA were raised and rejected in two important cases decided by the US Supreme Court. In *California Bankers Association* v. *Schultz*, the plaintiffs sought a declaratory judgment to enjoin the enforcement of the BSA, but no specific dispute about the recording or disclosure of information was involved.⁴⁷ The Fifth Amendment privilege against self-incrimination was held to be inapplicable because of the well-established rule that the privilege is available only to natural persons, and not to corporations or other organizations.⁴⁸ Furthermore, the privilege is unavailable to an accused person to preclude the provision of incriminating information by a third party. The bankers, while conceding that their customers could be required to keep records, argued unsuccessfully that they were mere conduits, and that to compel them to keep records of customer transactions deprived them of due process. Presumably, the banks simply wanted to avoid the trouble and expense of keeping records.

The Fourth Amendment protection against unreasonable searches and seizures was deemed irrelevant with respect to international transactions because of the congressional authority over foreign commerce, and inapplicable to other records because disclosure of the bank records requires the use of existing legal process. (It is well established that corporations and other organizations are protected by the Fourth Amendment.[49]) Several arguments based on potential misuse of information were rejected as premature because no actual abuse was alleged.

The second major case regarding the constitutionality of the BSA is *United States* v. *Miller*, which involved access to the bank records of an individual convicted of illegal distilling and tax evasion.[50] The bank, without Miller's knowledge or consent, produced copies of checks and other documents retained pursuant to the BSA in response to a *subpoena duces tecum* (a summons to appear and bring documents or other evidence) issued by a grand jury. Miller was held to have no legitimate expectation of privacy in the records kept by the bank, and no Fourth Amendment right to challenge the manner in which papers were obtained from a third party. An analogy was drawn between this process and the well-established procedures by which the IRS obtained financial records from banks about taxpayers. Taken together, *California Bankers* and *Miller* firmly established the constitutionality of the BSA.[51]

14.8 State Law Regarding Bank Disclosures

The BSA requires that banks keep certain financial records, and in some circumstances report information to the US government, but the Act is silent regarding the disclosure of information by banks. The federal Right to Financial Privacy Act imposes procedural requirements for disclosures of financial information about consumers and small unincorporated businesses, but it does not place substantive limitations on disclosure.[52] In the absence of specific federal law, such as the Internal Revenue Code, bank disclosures are subject to the laws of the state where the bank or its customer is located.[53]

Some states have sought to provide greater protection for account records than is available under the BSA. As so often is the case in US law and in other aspects of life, California took the lead. In the case of *Burrows* v. *Superior Court* the California Supreme Court ruled that customers of depository institutions have a reasonable expectation of privacy in bank records about them, and that therefore records of their transactions could not be disclosed.[54] The *Burrows* litigation arose after the bank voluntarily gave law enforcement officials a copy of its customer's account statement. Despite the fact that this information was prepared and provided by a third party, the court held that this voluntary disclosure without the consent of the customer represented an unreasonable search and seizure, and therefore suppressed the evidence.

A California bank may respond to a law enforcement request about whether a person has an account with that institution, and if so, to provide the account number.[55] A bank that is the victim of a crime may disclose account information, even if monetary loss is only a possibility and there is no current loss, because the institution has a substantial interest in the matter, instead of being merely a third-party stakeholder.[56] Pennsylvania and Colorado have adopted the California position,[57] and a few other states can be expected to follow course, but the predominant position is that articulated by the Supreme Court in *California Bankers* and *Miller*.

The discussion of reasonable customer expectations in *Miller* and *Burrows* is circular, if not misleading. What is reasonable for the public to believe about the disclosure of information by banking organizations depends on what the law requires. To state that a bank may or may not disclose information because its customers do or do not have a reasonable expectation of privacy sounds like a reason, but it is merely a conclusion. Worse, it prevents serious examination of important issues relating to the circumstances in which disclosure should be authorized, and what procedural safeguards are appropriate.

This inability to obtain records from banks without a court order is inconvenient but not fatal for proper law enforcement efforts. The subpoena power is available to obtain financial records from a bank, particularly if the customer cannot or will not produce them. It is not even clear that the customer must be informed about the issuance of a subpoena of bank records, let alone be given an opportunity to object to a disclosure. Such a notice requirement has been imposed in a civil case, but the interests and potential objections in criminal cases are quite different from those in the civil area.[58] In the criminal context there is no basis for objection to a grand jury subpoena or a search warrant except that it was improperly issued, so there is little privacy to protect by notifying the customer.

Financial institutions are permitted, but not required, to inform their customers about disclosures made pursuant to the BSA.[59] This result should apply even in jurisdictions that afford greater financial privacy protection to bank customers than is provided under federal law. Since the BSA disclosure requirements are so extensive, a notification requirement would be quite burdensome. The disclosure provisions of the federal Right to Financial Privacy Act are inapplicable to disclosures about information collected in compliance with the BSA. People can determine when information about their transactions will be reported to the government by consulting the BSA and the implementing regulations.

In this confusing environment of sometimes inconsistent state and federal law, which is composed of common law as well as legislation, the sensible approach for banks is clear. A bank should never disclose information about a customer absent legal compulsion, even for the generally laudable purpose of assisting law enforcement officials. This point is best demonstrated by a cautionary tale (that did not involve disclosures covered by the BSA).[60] A bank received an $800 deposit of consecutively numbered $50 and $100 bills. First, the bank gave the FBI the serial numbers on the bills, without disclosing the identity of its customer. This conduct does not raise a problem. The FBI reported back that the bills had not been reported as stolen, whereupon the bank spoke with local police officials. Upon being told of a recent residential robbery in which $3,000 in $50 and $100 bills had been stolen, a bank official disclosed the name, address, and other identifying information about its customer. The victim of the crime identified the customer from pictures, whereupon the customer was arrested and charged with the crime. The victim subsequently retracted his identification and the charge was dropped. The bank was found liable for wrongful disclosure, and since that disclosure proximately caused the depositor's arrest, the damages were not insignificant. The Maryland court held that, absent compulsion by law, a depository institution is not entitled to make disclosure about a customer's account without the express or implied consent of the customer.

Even in complying with compulsory service, an institution should be certain that the period for protesting disclosure has expired. For example, a taxpayer has twenty days to file suit to challenge an IRS summons directed to a third-party record-keeper.[61] In the absence of such a challenge, the institution must disclose the requested information even if the customer has instructed it not to make the disclosure, but only after the expiration of the twenty-day protest period.[62]

14.9 Enforcement of the Bank Secrecy Act

The major BSA compliance issues for banks have involved the duty to make CTRs for domestic currency transactions in excess of $10,000.

The reporting requirements for the physical movement of monetary instruments across US borders have relatively little impact on banks. The copying of checks and other documents related to customer accounts is an economic burden, and retrieving copied checks is a labor-intensive and therefore expensive activity, but few compliance problems arise because the copying is done by machine as part of the check sorting process: batches of checks are microfilmed, and a trace number is sprayed on the back of each check. Accordingly, the discussion in this section is limited to the duty placed on banks to file CTRs.

Major firms in highly regulated industries such as banking are faced by a seemingly endless sea of regulations and requirements, and this body of law is subject to frequent changes.[63] It is inevitable and common that some rules are violated, either intentionally or by oversight. Bureaucrats and officials of regulated firms know that some rules are more important than others. Bank compliance with the CTR requirements imposed by the BSA presents a classic example of a set of rules that was often honored in the breach. Filling out CTR forms requires the bank to obtain information from customers making large deposits who might take their money elsewhere. Low-level staff must be trained in yet another compliance procedure. Scrupulous attention to currency transaction reporting means additional costs but produces no economic benefits for the bank. Compliance takes place in a reactive environment in which regulated firms adjust their behavior in response to cues from their regulators. Although industry compliance before 1985 was haphazard, little was made of this fact in the regular examinations to which all banks are subject. The natural response in the banking community was to treat BSA compliance as a low priority matter.

Upon occasion, a single event focuses attention on an issue in a manner that quite transcends the intrinsic importance of that event. An example of this phenomenon occurred in 1985 when the Bank of Boston pleaded guilty to charges of failing to file reports for transactions in excess of $1 billion, and agreed to pay a fine of $500,000.[64] The unreported transactions mostly involved international interbank transfers, but the bank also failed to report sales of over $7 million in cashier's checks to persons associated with an organized crime "family." The disclosure of these violations at a venerable institution, the twentieth largest in the country with the fourth-largest international division, far away from states traditionally associated with drug traffic and the laundering of money, came as a shock to the public and to government officials. The matter received front page coverage in the *New York Times*.[65]

In the wake of the Bank of Boston affair, banks and regulators began to treat BSA compliance as a much more serious matter, and numerous violations were uncovered. Review of exemption lists and the more rigorous examinations for BSA compliance by the banking agencies uncovered problems at many banks. Such major institutions as Chase Manhattan, Manufacturers Hanover, Irving Trust, and Chemical Bank were fined for failing to file reports.[66] A civil fine of almost $5 million was imposed on the Bank of America for failing to file CTRs in more than 17,000 instances. These banks had compliance procedures in place, but they were not followed. Although the applicable legislation and regulations have not changed substantially since 1985, the attitude of both regulatory bodies and financial institutions toward the importance of BSA compliance has altered dramatically.

The widespread publicity accompanying the sanctions imposed on the Bank of Boston and other major banks for failure to make reports as required by the BSA and the implementing regulations led to a dramatic increase in compliance with reporting requirements by depository institutions. The number of CTRs received by the IRS skyrocketed from 63,000 in February 1985 (the month the Bank of Boston situation became public) to 272,000 in January 1986.[67] Presently, the number of CTRs filed each month exceeds 500,000.

As a consequence of the BSA reporting requirements, and the monitoring of compliance by depository institutions, increasingly sophisticated schemes have been developed to "launder" money.[68] At the same time, the enormous amount of money involved in illegal activities, particularly the drug trade, has increased the potential rewards of evading reporting requirements. Sometimes it is possible to persuade bank officials simply not to report large transactions, but complicated chains of transactions often are employed to disguise money laundering. Foreign banks may be used, notably in tax havens such as the Cayman Islands. In one instance, an attorney paid local bank officials in the US not to report deposits of money obtained from the sale of drugs. The money was then wired to trust accounts in Bermuda that were controlled by Liberian corporations. The money returned in the form of loans to corporations established in the US by the lawyer on behalf of his drug dealer clients. These corporations then provided the dealers with seemingly legitimate salaries, expense accounts, automobiles, and pension plans.[69] Few prosecutions of those involved in these sophisticated schemes are undertaken because tracing the chain of transactions is a time-consuming and expensive process, and it is difficult to convince a jury beyond a reasonable doubt that indicted white-collar professionals were knowing participants in criminal activities.

14.10 Structured Transactions

After the adoption of the BSA reporting requirements, there was considerable debate over whether a depository institution was under an obligation to make a report where a person engaged in several transactions during a reporting period (normally, a calendar day) that, if undertaken as a single transaction, would be subject to the reporting requirements. (The structuring of transactions in this manner became widely known as "smurfing," after the characters in a children's television program.[70])

The courts divided on this issue. The decision by a federal court of appeals in *United States* v. *Bank of New England* illustrates the issues raised by structured transactions, and is representative of the cases that found banks liable for not detecting smurfing activities by their customers.[71] In over thirty separate instances, a particular customer withdrew amounts in excess of $10,000 from a single account by cashing several smaller checks. The bank was convicted of the felony of willfully failing to file currency transaction reports as part of a pattern of illegal activity involving more than $100,000 within a twelve-month period.[72] The court found that a duty existed to report these transactions, and that the bank knew of the inaction of its employees. In response to the argument that this approach permitted a finding of criminal liability for failing to maintain a proper communications network, the court responded that attributing the collective knowledge of employees to the organization was appropriate. The court also rejected the argument that repeated transactions with a single customer cannot constitute a pattern of wrongful activity by the bank. Finally, the court ruled that each of the separate transactions that constituted the pattern of CTR violations was a separate felony.

The question of whether a bank can be held responsible for "smurfing" by its customers was put to rest by the Anti Drug Abuse Act of 1986, which specified that the BSA applied to multiple same-day transactions of more than $10,000.[73] Congress considered lowering the reporting cut-off for cash purchases to transactions in excess of $3,000, and the Treasury Department considered a rule to the same effect, but neither proposal was adopted.[74]

To state that a bank can, in principle, be held responsible for failing to cumulate the transactions of a single customer for accounts held in the same capacity and to stop there, as Congress did, leaves the difficult issues unaddressed. It is easy enough to state that a banking organization is required to file CTRs for transactions about which it has knowledge, and that the willful failure to acquire information about customer transactions also constitutes a violation of the BSA, but this approach does not answer the hard questions about what efforts are to be required of banks. People can and commonly do have several accounts at a single bank. The capacity in which these accounts are held is of little moment unless the bank fails and the aggregate deposits exceed the maximum deposit insurance coverage of $100,000. There is much case law on this important subject, and the FDIC has adopted detailed regulations.[75]

Does BSA compliance now require banks to make determinations in all instances where customers have multiple accounts about whether the account is held in a separate capacity? What if a person places funds in the accounts of a spouse and several children? The relaxation of restrictions on branch banking and the increasing use of electronic banking facilities means that individual banks accept deposits from an increasing number of locations.[76] How do banks deal with aggregation requirements for transactions undertaken at separate locations? What of transactions at independent banks controlled by a single bank holding company? (Interstate banking laws commonly provide for the ownership of banks in several states, but restrict or prohibit a single bank from having offices in more than one state.[77]) None of the questions raised here is unanswerable, but if the "no smurfing" principle is pressed seriously banks could face large compliance costs.

Coverage of structured transactions means that banking organizations are required to collect more information about their customers. Such coverage raises serious privacy concerns. What a bank knows is largely a matter of programming computers. Smaller banks that do not own sophisticated hardware typically lease equipment or purchase computer services, often from larger banks. Still, complex regulatory requirements favor larger organizations over smaller ones, and undermine competitive goals. Banks must make full use of existing computer capacity and should consider BSA record-keeping and reporting requirements in the purchase of new equipment. The Treasury Department does not demand that banking organizations purchase new hardware or even software.[78] It is arguable, however, that the purchase of new equipment that does not have the capacity to monitor for BSA compliance could constitute a willful failure to acquire information, particularly if the additional costs are modest.

The BSA clearly does not apply to transactions structured over several days – for example, depositing $9,000 every day for an entire year. Because of the focus on reporting by individual institutions, the BSA is inapplicable to daily deposits of large sums by an individual, as long as the currency transaction at any one bank does not exceed $10,000. Since there are over 13,000 separate banks in America, this is not a trivial matter, but a different approach would require the aggregating of data from separate banking organizations. Such aggregation would be very costly, and probably could only be undertaken by the federal government. Even in the midst of the current hysteria about drug dealing, Americans are not yet willing to authorize this sort of an invasion of privacy by the government.

14.11 Administrative Rulings on BSA Issues

Financial institutions faced with specific BSA compliance issues can turn to the Treasury Department for assistance.[79] Requests for rulings must be in writing, state a clear and concise question, and explain the background facts that give rise to the inquiry. Requests may advocate a particular interpretation. The Department issues two types of rulings, which differ as to the form of publication and precedent value. Letter rulings are published in the Federal Register, and are binding on the Treasury Department in its dealings with all institutions. Private rulings are not officially published, and are binding only with respect to the party that requested the ruling. This system parallels that employed by the IRS for tax compliance questions.

14.12 The Costs and Benefits of Disclosure Requirements

Whether the requirements for disclosure of information to the government by banks about their customers constitute sound public policy depends largely on one's views about law enforcement needs, privacy, and related issues. That is a matter of political and social philosophy, about which readers can reach their own conclusions. If the issue is not one of principle, the remaining question is whether the costs associated with BSA requirements are worth the benefits obtained by society. Unfortunately, the evaluation of the BSA record-keeping and reporting requirements does not get addressed in this form because the costs and benefits accrue to different parties. Legislators benefit by getting credit for attacking evil, particularly when they can do so without spending government money. Law enforcement officials obtain access to sometimes useful information for use in prosecutions that often is not otherwise available. Reports of currency transactions are a major source of information on which federal drug and money laundering prosecutions are based. IRS uses information collected pursuant to various statutes, including the BSA, to verify the accuracy of tax returns, and in the prosecution of tax evasion cases.

Transaction reporting is of little assistance to law enforcement officials in uncovering wrongful activities. As Terrence Burke, a senior Drug Enforcement Administration (DEA) official admitted, the DEA receives "virtually no leads" from random screening of CTRs.[80] Instead, CTRs are used as evidence in cases that were built on information from other sources. In these circumstances, it might make sense to eliminate reporting requirements, but still require financial institutions to retain information for use by prosecutors in appropriate circumstances.

A study sponsored by the American Bankers Association (ABA) estimates that the annual cost of BSA compliance, based only on employee time, exceeded $26 million.[81] A more complete accounting might increase the cost of BSA compliance to $50 million per year. Barnett Banks of Florida estimates that it spends $2 million per year on training employees about how to file CTRs, and how to spot suspicious transactions.[82]

The ABA recommends two major changes in public policy with regard to disclosure about customer transactions. Banks should be compensated for compliance costs; and the focus of disclosure should be redirected by imposing direct reporting requirements on businesses that are likely recipients of illegally obtained money (e.g. sellers of automobiles and real estate). To put the matter kindly, this approach is unrealistic. Increasing the national debt to improve the balance sheets of banks, which would be the practical consequence of compensating banks for reporting costs, is inconceivable. Imposing additional reporting requirements on purveyors of luxury goods is an idea with little merit. One suspects the ABA likes this idea mainly because it would expand the base of economic interests that are opposed to reporting requirements.

The costs of BSA compliance are borne initially by the individuals and institutions that must file reports. The major cost burden is placed on banks (and ultimately on their customers). If a case is to be made that the economic and privacy costs associated with the BSA exceed the social benefits, it is incumbent on the banking industry to do so. Until a serious effort in that direction is made, banks that operate in America can expect to face continued, if not increased, BSA compliance costs.

14.13 European Community Directive on Money Laundering

The Council of the European Communities (EC) has adopted a Directive on the prevention of the use of financial systems for money laundering.[83] In addition to banking organizations, the Directive applies to non-bank credit and financial institutions, including insurance companies. Other groups that have extensive cash dealings, such as casinos and money changers, also should be covered. Compliance with the provisions of the Directive was required by January 1, 1992 at the latest.[84]

The Directive reflects concern about money laundering activities in general, and drug trafficking in particular. It represents the latest of several related international initiatives. The Group of Seven industrialized countries created a Financial Action Task Force in July 1989. It has issued a report, and collects statistics and information about laundering methods. The United Nations Convention against Illicit Traffic in Narcotic Drugs and Psychotropic Substances (commonly referred to as the Vienna Convention) was adopted in Vienna on December 19, 1988. It requires signatories, which include the EC countries, to criminalize certain activities related to drugs and money laundering. While these strictures on money laundering are limited to drug activities, the implementing legislation is likely to apply more generally. This is the approach taken by the EC Directive. Even if national legislation applied exclusively to drug activities, the impact on money laundering would be enormous. In practice, it is often difficult to determine the source of laundered funds, or the type of illegal activity in which the funds originated.

An argument for EC action was that if the Community did not take steps, individual member states would adopt inconsistent measures, which in turn could undermine the creation of a single market. Money laundering must be criminalized, it was argued, because bank secrecy laws commonly protect against civil but not criminal cases or investigations. (This statement is a vast oversimplification of a highly complex area of law.)

The Directive is addressed to the member states of the EC, which are instructed to treat the laundering of proceeds from serious crimes as a criminal offense.[85] In addition, member states should require financial institutions to know the identity of their customers.[86] Where the person conducting a transaction is acting as an agent, reasonable efforts must be made to identify the principal. A financial institution must give special attention to "unusual" transactions, and it should not enter into a transaction that it has "reason to suspect" has "any relation" to money laundering.[87] This amorphous standard reflects a general policy objective, and local law must provide detailed working guidelines for banking organizations to apply in their daily operations.

State law must require financial institutions to establish internal controls for the detection of money laundering, and to provide training for their employees.[88] Records relating to the identification of customers must be retained for at least five years.[89] Unlike the Bank Secrecy Act, the Directive does not require that records be made about specific transactions. Thus the burden of record creation and storage is vastly reduced. Another difference is that records made by a financial institution are not sent to the government, but are retained at the institution.

A striking level of cooperation with law enforcement and judicial authorities is required under the Directive. Member states are directed to require that financial institutions "cooperate fully" with the authorities responsible for enforcing the criminal laws.[90] In addition to furnishing all requested information for criminal inquiries, institutions must on their own initiative disclose facts that "could be related" to a money laundering offense.[91] Disclosure absent compulsion by the state is directly contrary to the principle of customer privacy that has been a hallmark of banking practice in the US and Europe. The disclosure threshold does not even embody a probable cause standard. Any unusual transaction by a customer is subject to being reported under a "could be related" standard. This due diligence principle requires financial institutions to carefully examine unusual activities, and to refrain from entering into suspect transactions. If applied with full force, this approach could result in banks being constant spies on their customers. Large banks all have sophisticated computer systems that can track customer transaction patterns and identify unusual ones.

The cooperation requirement has two aspects. Institutions and their employees are obliged (pursuant to national law) to provide information to law enforcement authorities on their own initiative of "any facts" that "could be related" to a money laundering offense, and to furnish any information, documents, and records requested by these authorities. Presumably, the BSA approach of requests pursuant to a judicial order is contemplated rather than any casual request by any law enforcement authority. The first duty is the controversial one, because it emasculates the long-established tradition of bankers as confidants who follow the fundamental norm of protecting client information except when ordered to make disclosure by a court or grand jury. The underlying principle is that bank secrecy "must be lifted in cases of Criminal Law." The problem with this argument is that it turns a conclusion that is valid in some instances into a basis for all sorts of invasions of privacy. Furthermore, civil recovery against banking organizations is explicitly prohibited, even when there was no basis for reporting the transaction, in order to encourage cooperation.

The Directive protects persons and institutions that make disclosures from any legal redress, civil or criminal. Good faith disclosures of "any suspicion or belief" that a transaction is related to money laundering are absolutely privileged.[92] The dangers to individual liberty that are posed by the EC approach to unsolicited and unfounded disclosures are only too apparent.

Notes

1 84 Stat. 1114 (1970). The discussion throughout the chapter proceeds on the assumption that disclosures are accurate. Inaccurate disclosures raise quite different legal issues.
2 *Peterson v. Idaho First National Bank*, 83 Idaho 578, 367 P.2d 284 (1961).
3 28 USC ss. 7609-10.
4 *United States v. Powell*, 379 US 48 (1964). The IRS summons procedures are discussed in S. Huber, *Bank Officer's Handbook of Government Regulation*, 2nd edn (Warren, Gorham, and Lamont, 1989), para. 23.05.
5 Limited provision for recovery was made in the 1986 BSA amendments for costs associated with bank participation in investigations, but there is no reimbursement for compliance with the basic reporting requirements.
6 1970 US Code Cong. & Admin. News 4394 (legislative history of the BSA).
7 102 Stat. 4181 (1988), November 18, 1988, P.L. 100-690, 102 Stat 4181, 6001ff.
8 The Office of the Comptroller of the Currency (OCC) has primary responsibility for national banks, the Federal Reserve System (FRS) for state member banks and bank holding companies, and the Federal Deposit Insurance Corporation (FDIC) for insured state nonmember banks.
9 12 USC ss. 1829b(a)(1), 1953(a); 31 USC s. 1051. See Byrne and Johannes, "What You Should Know about the Money Laundering Law," *ABA Banking J.*, July 1985, p. 69.
10 31 USC s. 5322.
11 31 USC s. 5318.
12 See 51 Fed. Reg. 45108 (1986), 52 Fed. Reg. 2858 (1987), 52 Fed. Reg. 11436 (1987), 52 Fed. Reg. 23977 (1987), 54 Fed. Reg. 28416 (1989), 54 Fed. Reg. 33675 (1989), and 55 Fed. Reg. 20139 (1990).
13 31 CFR s. 103.38.
14 See Huber, *Bank Officer's Handbook*, paras 5.07, 5.08.
15 48 Banking Rep. 467 (1987).
16 *United States v. St. Michael's Credit Union*, 880 F.2d 579 (1st Cir. 1990).
17 31 CFR s. 103.22(a).
18 *United States v. Ospina*, 798 F.2d 1570 (11th Cir. 1986).
19 *United States v. Bucey*, 876 F.2d 1297 (7th Cir. 1989).
20 *United States v. American Investors, Inc.*, 879 F.2d 1087 (5th Cir. 1989).
21 31 CFR s. 103.11.
22 31 CFR s. 103.22(e).
23 31 USC s. 5326. For implementing regulations, see 54 Fed. Reg. 33675 (1989).

24 53 Banking Rep. 301 (1989).
25 31 CFR s. 103.25(a).
26 31 CFR s. 1052(j). For an introduction to the Freedom of Information Act, see Huber, *Bank Officer's Handbook*, p. 5.04. See also Huber, "Mandatory Disclosure of Information About Banks," *Annual Review of Banking Law*, 6 (1987), p. 53.
27 55 Fed. Reg. 20139 (1990), effective August 13, 1990. These regulations are discussed in greater detail than would otherwise be warranted because they are the latest BSA development.
28 31 USC s. 1101. The amount was raised from $5,000 to $10,000 in late 1984.
29 31 CFR s. 103.11.
30 54 Fed. Reg. 28416 (1989).
31 *United States v. Silva*, 415 F.2d 43 (2d Cir. 1983).
32 31 CFR s. 103.25(c).
33 31 USC s. 5317 (formerly codified at 31 USC s. 1102).
34 *United States v. $6,700.00 in U.S. Currency*, 615 F.2d 1 (2d Cir. 1980).
35 *One Lot Emerald Cut Stones and One Ring v. United States*, 409 U.S. 232 (1972) (forfeiture based on failure to follow customs procedures).
36 *United States v. $173,081.04 in U.S. Currency*, 835 F.2d 1141 (5th Cir. 1988).
37 *United States v. $1,497,081.78*, 777 F.2d 1451 (11th Cir. 1985).
38 12 USC s. 1829b, 1953. The Treasury regulations refer only to "banks," but this term is defined to include thrift institutions and credit unions. 31 CFR s. 103.11. This unusual approach is not followed in this chapter.
39 31 CFR s. 103.34(a).
40 31 CFR s. 103.34(b).
41 31 CFR s. 103.35.
42 31 CFR s. 103.36.
43 N. Penney and D. Baker, *The Law of Electronic Funds Transfer Systems* (Warren, Gorham, and Lamont, 1980), para. 15.03[3][b] n. 167.
44 HR 4044 (1990). See 54 Banking Rep. 328 (1990).
45 HR 3848, discussed at 54 Banking Rep. 678 (1990).
46 *United States v. Alamo Bank of Texas*, 880 F.2d 828 (5th Cir. 1989), cert. denied 493 U.S. 1071 (1990).
47 416 US 21 (1974).
48 *Hale v. Henkel*, 201 US 43 (1906). The privilege is inapplicable to unincorporated organizations, and it cannot be claimed by officials that might be incriminated by the records. *United States v. White*, 322 US 694 (1944) (union local); *Bellis v. United States*, 417 US 85 (1974) (dissolved law partnership).
49 See *United States v. City of Seattle*, 387 US 541 (1967).
50 425 US 435 (1976).
51 The weakness of the tax law analogy is discussed in the text accompanying notes 3–5 above.
52 The Right to Financial Privacy Act is discussed in Huber, *Bank Officer's Handbook*, p. 23.04.

53 Multistate bank operations raise difficult choice-of-law issues. For example, the bank may have its headquarters in state A, the customer lives in state B, and the transaction takes place in state C. Usury is the most important area in which banks have heretofore faced choice-of-law issues. See Huber, *Bank Officer's Handbook*, p. 20.04.
54 13 Cal. 3d 238, 529 P.2d 590, 118 Cal. Rptr. 166 (1974).
55 65 Off. Att'y Gen. 4 (1982).
56 *People* v. *Hale*, 139 Cal. App. 3d 431, 188 Cal. Rptr. 693 (1983) (insufficient funds check).
57 *Commonwealth* v. *De John*, 486 Pa. 32, 403 A.2d 1283 (Pa. 1979); *Charnes* v. *DiGiacomo*, 200 Colo. 94, 612 P.2d 1117 (Colo. 1980). An Illinois appellate court has adopted the same rationale. *Illinois* v. *Jackson*, 116 Ill. App. 3d 430, 452 NE2d 85 (Ill. App. 1983).
58 *Valley Bank* v. *Superior Court*, 15 Cal. 3d 652, 542 P.2d 944, 125 Cal. Rptr. 553 (1975).
59 *United States* v. *Kaatz*, 705 F.2d 1237 (10 Cir. 1983).
60 *Suburban Trust Co.* v. *Waller*, 44 Md. App. 335, 408 A.2d 758 (1979).
61 See Huber, *Bank Officer's Handbook*, p. 23.05.
62 *Schaut* v. *First Federal Savings & Loan Association*, 560 F. Supp. 245 (ND Ill. 1983).
63 Chapter 12 of the *United States Code Annotated*, titled *Banks and Banking*, fills five volumes containing over 3,800 pages (plus a 500-page index). The permanent regulations, which are found in chapter 12 of the *Code of Federal Regulations*, fill an additional 3,000 pages. Of course, many other federal and state statutes and regulations have a significant impact on banking organizations.
64 *United States* v. *First National Bank of Boston*, No. 85-52-MA (D. Mass., February 7, 1985).
65 Butterfield, "Bank of Boston Says Cash Role Was Unwitting," *New York Times*, February 22, 1985, p. 1, col. 2.
66 44 Wash. Fin. Rep. 1038, 1137 (1985).
67 46 Wash. Fin. Rep. 338 (1986).
68 See generally P. Lernoux, *In Banks We Trust* (New York, Doubleday, 1984), pp. 77–142.
69 Taylor, "Laundry Service: More Professionals Like Lawyers, Bankers Said to Hide Drug Loot," *Wall Street Journal*, July 25, 1983, p. 1, col. 1. As the title of this piece suggests, a number of bankers and lawyers have succumbed to temptation and participated in money laundering.
70 Smurfs are little blue creatures who are the stars of a Saturday morning television cartoon series called *The Smurfs*.
71 821 F.2d 844 (1st Cir. 1987). This decision cites the relevant case law.
72 31 USC s. 5322(b).
73 31 USC s. 5324.
74 48 Banking Rep. 679 (1987). The Treasury Department proposal was fiercely opposed by banking interests. 53 Fed. Reg. 6011 (1988).
75 See Huber, *Bank Officer's Handbook*, p. 17.03[2]–[3].

TRANSACTION REPORTING REQUIREMENTS 403

76 Any amount of cash and instruments can be deposited at an electronic terminal, but cash withdrawals are severely limited.
77 Issues relating to the regulation of banks with multistate operations will be of increasing importance, because the growth of interstate banking will be among the most important changes in the structure of American banking during the 1990s.
78 52 Fed. Reg. 11436 (1987).
79 31 CFR s. 103.71.
80 Hearing before the Senate Foreign Relations Subcommittee on Narcotics and Terrorism, quoted at 53 Banking Rep. 462 (1989).
81 American Bankers Association, *The Burden of Bank Regulation* (1989).
82 53 Banking Rep. 462 (1989).
83 COM(90) 106 Final. Office of Official Publication of the European Communities No. CB-CO-90-122-EN-C.
84 Article 9(1).
85 Ibid., article 2.
86 Ibid., article 3.
87 Ibid., article 4.
88 Ibid., article 7.
89 Ibid., article 3.
90 Ibid., article 5(1).
91 Ibid.
92 Ibid., article 5(2).

15

International Coordination of Insolvency Proceedings: A Transatlantic Perspective

JOEL P. TRACHTMAN

Chapter Outline

15.1 Introduction

15.2 The Hypothetical Facts

15.3 US Bankruptcy Code
    15.3.1 Sections 304 and 305
    15.3.2 Section 304(c): Universality and Territoriality

15.4 Application of Section 304(c) Factors by Courts
    15.4.1 *In re Culmer*
    15.4.2 *Toga*
    15.4.3 *Interpool*

15.5 Application of Sections 304 and 305 to Hypothetical Facts
    15.5.1 Section 304(c)(1), (2): Just Treatment of All Claimholders; Protection of US Claimholders

---

This paper was presented in connection with the author's lecture at the Queen Mary and Westfield College Centre for Commercial Law Studies Ninth Annual Conference on International Banking and Finance, London, June 1990, and speaks as of that date. Since that date, in addition to other case law developments, there have been at least two international bankruptcy cases of great notoriety and significance: the collapse of the Robert Maxwell empire and the BCCI débâcle. In the Maxwell case, Judge Hoffmann of the London High Court of Justice and Judge Brozman of the US Bankruptcy Court for the Southern District of New York approved an agreement to cooperate in certain matters. In the BCCI case, a private effort at coordination and pooling of assets appears to have been successful as of early November, 1992.

15.5.2   Section 304(c)(3): Prevention of Preferential or Fraudulent Transfers
15.5.3   Section 304(c)(4): Distribution in Accordance with US Priorities
15.5.4   Section 304(c)(5): Comity

15.6   A Comparative Perspective: How Would an English Court Treat Similar Issues?
15.6.1   Insolvency Act 1986, Section 426
15.6.2   *Felixstowe Dock and Railway Co. v. US Lines Inc.*

15.7   Attempts at International Coordination
15.7.1   The EC Draft Convention
15.7.2   Proposed Uniform Legislation
15.7.3   Council of Europe Convention

15.8   Conclusion

Appendix   Bankruptcy Reform Act of 1978, ss. 304, 305, 306, 508

15.1 Introduction

Bankruptcy has been a part of commerce and finance since early times, and international bankruptcy problems have followed the development of international commerce. Bankruptcy has gained greater currency recently, with the increasing sophistication and depersonalization of financial relationships, along with more aggressive and marginal institutional financing brought about by greater competition among financiers.

Another recent development is the increasing globalization of enterprise. Multinational or transnational enterprises are organized to maximize profits in a wide number of jurisdictions, using branches, subsidiaries, joint ventures, or contractual relationships to exploit global manufacturing or service opportunities and global markets. These enterprises have relationships, including financial relationships, commercial relationships, assets, branches, and subsidiaries, in a number of jurisdictions.

Government and legal structures have not kept pace with the globalization of business. They have particularly not kept pace in the area of resolving the financial problems of insolvent corporations. Each country has its own insolvency law, incorporating in various ways the principal insolvency law rationales of

- fairness among creditors,
- preservation of enterprise value,
- fairness and perhaps providing a fresh start to debtors, and
- minimization of economic dislocation.

Corporate insolvency law represents an area of intersection between private law and public law: between privately formulated contractual or other relationships of the insolvent corporation, and the public law establishing the rights of the various constituencies of the modern corporate enterprise (creditors of various types, debtors, shareholders, and employees). However, it has traditionally been viewed as an area of largely private interest, and a subject of private international law. Attempts to address the problems of international coordination by treaty have not met with wide success.

This chapter will examine the problems raised when national insolvency regimes attempt to address global business enterprises. It will do so in the context of an archetypal fact pattern. It will first examine the issues under the US Bankruptcy Code, and subsequently provide a brief comparative perspective from the standpoint of English law. It will then describe in brief general terms how proposed treaties or proposed uniformly adopted legislation could assist in providing coordination to deal more efficiently with insolvent global enterprises. It will not address important related issues, such as problems of international coordination in evidence gathering, which is necessary, for example, to determine if there are assets in a foreign jurisdiction worth pursuing, and the more general issue of enforcement of judgments in foreign jurisdictions.

15.2 The Hypothetical Facts

Multicorp Plc is an English multinational shipping corporation. It has a US branch consisting of administrative offices in New York, from which it arranges voyages, as well as berthing and bunkering provided by US suppliers. This branch maintains bank accounts in the US to support these operations. Multicorp Plc has borrowed £12 million from an English bank (Finebank) supported by a fixed and floating charge over all its assets in England, pursuant to a loan agreement specifying English governing law and an English forum. It also has many loans from many banks around the world, all secured by ship mortgages on Multicorp's ships. Multicorp Plc's only borrowing from a US bank is a loan of $10 million from Megabank, secured by a ship mortgage. The vessel subject to this mortgage is valued at $8 million on a distress sale basis. The Megabank loan agreement is governed by New York law, specifies a New York forum, and contains numerous events of default, including an event of default triggered by bankruptcy or insolvency of the borrower. After some significant business reverses, Multicorp Plc is insolvent.

Multicorp Plc applied for and, with the blessings of Finebank, obtained an administration order under English law, and an administrator has been appointed to seek to preserve Multicorp Plc as a going concern. Subsequently, Megabank has accelerated Multicorp Plc's obligations under its loan facility, and has taken action to enforce its ship mortgage and foreclose Multicorp Plc's rights in the vessel subject thereto. As its collateral will not satisfy its debt, it has sued Multicorp Plc in the US for repayment of its debt, hoping to satisfy the balance of its debt by enforcing against Multicorp's US bank accounts. It has made a motion for summary judgment on the merits, and has sought an order of prejudgment attachment with respect to the accounts. In addition, a US trade creditor of Multicorp Plc has filed a petition to place Multicorp Plc into liquidation under Chapter 7 of the US Bankruptcy Code.

The administrator for Multicorp Plc would find his purposes jeopardized by the US creditors' actions, and would seek advice of US counsel as to whether they may be blocked or delayed. He would also want to know how to obtain control over Multicorp Plc's US bank accounts, for disposition in the UK proceeding.

15.3 US Bankruptcy Code

There are many similarities between the UK and US bankruptcy law, especially since the legislation of the UK Insolvency Act 1986. However, there are also many differences, especially in procedure.

The US Bankruptcy Code, like section 426 of the Insolvency Act 1986, provides the potential for cooperation with foreign bankruptcy proceedings. Unlike section 426, which provides for cooperation with only a limited group of countries, the US Bankruptcy Code does not explicitly distinguish among types of countries, although in practice common law countries would be likely to be accorded greater cooperation.[1] Sections 304, 305, 306, and 508 of the US Bankruptcy Code are the principal provisions relating specifically to foreign bankruptcy or insolvency proceedings, and were added to the Bankruptcy Code in

1978.[2] In addition, a foreign representative can commence a full US bankruptcy proceeding under section 303 of the Bankruptcy Code. Prior to the enactment of these provisions, cooperation with foreign representatives was a matter of common law comity.[3] Comity remains a fundamental issue, or perhaps the sole issue, in determining cooperation with or deference to foreign bankruptcy proceedings. We will analyze below the meaning and function of comity under the Bankruptcy Code.

15.3.1 Sections 304 and 305

Sections 304 and 305 of the Bankruptcy Code are the principal provisions that concern us. Section 304 permits the commencement of a case in the US that is ancillary to a foreign proceeding. Only a "foreign representative," meaning a duly selected trustee, administrator, or other duly appointed representative of an estate in a "foreign proceeding," may commence such an ancillary case. The definition of "foreign representative" is contained in Bankruptcy Code, section 101(23). A "foreign proceeding" for these purposes is a judicial or administrative proceeding in a foreign country where the debtor has its domicile, residence, principal place of business, or principal assets at the time of commencement of the proceeding.[4] This definition would thus deny cooperation to a foreign administrator from a jurisdiction in which the debtor does not have its domicile, residence, principal place of business, or principal assets.

Before the implementation of section 304 in connection with a broad revision of US bankruptcy law, a foreign representative seeking to obtain assets located in the US could only commence a full US bankruptcy case,[5] or litigate in US non-bankruptcy courts. Section 304 provides the possibility of a limited case ancillary to the foreign proceeding. Under section 304(b), the court presented with the foreign representative's petition is permitted to enjoin actions against the debtor or its property, order the turnover of the debtor's property to the foreign representative, or order other appropriate relief. The court's decision must be guided by what will best assure an economical and expeditious administration of the local property, consistent with the six factors listed in section 304(c).

Under section 305, the foreign representative may seek dismissal or suspension of a separate US bankruptcy case in favor of the foreign proceeding, if the factors listed in section 304(c) warrant such dismissal or suspension. Thus, in a circumstance where concurrent bankruptcy proceedings in the US and abroad are pending, it is possible for the US proceeding to be dismissed or suspended in deference to the foreign proceeding.

15.3.2 Section 304(c): Universality and Territoriality

Section 304(c) sets forth the substantive factors that are intended to guide the court's decision under sections 304 and 305.[6] Section 304(c) first refers to assuring economical and expeditious administration of the local property, and then lists six factors with which the court's judgment must be consistent. This latter requirement for consistency is a potentially difficult task, as the six factors will not necessarily be mutually consistent. The six factors were designed to provide the court with great flexibility, but may be analyzed as a compromise between two conflict-of-laws principles: universality and territoriality.

The universality principle would allow the laws and procedure of a single jurisdiction, such as the jurisdiction of the principal place of business of the debtor, to govern a corporation's insolvency proceeding.[7] The universality principle represents agreement as to which jurisdiction's law will control, and universal acceptance of extraterritorial application of such law. The territoriality principle, in contrast, would hold that, regardless of the jurisdiction of the principal place of business, administration, or formation, local assets shall be administered under local laws and procedure. Especially in light of the flexibility of corporate structure, and depending on the connection used to determine the governing law and administration, the universality principle can be unsatisfactory from a substantive standpoint, in so far as it frustrates the regular and equal application of local laws to local assets. The universality principle thus fails fully to protect intrajurisdictional fairness and fails to allow the implementation of intrajurisdictional policy. (It is important to attempt to distinguish between substance and procedure: where only procedural aspects are yielded to foreign administration, little of the intrajurisdictional policy and fairness will be lost.) On the other hand, the territorial approach fails to allow the coordinated resolution of global insolvency problems, and may result in unfairness to foreign creditors; its weakness is in interjurisdictional fairness and implementation of interjurisdictional policy (whatever interjurisdictional policy may be). A third approach would be to harmonize bankruptcy law among jurisdictions and centralize its administration internationally, but this would obviously be the most difficult approach to achieve in practice.

The factors referenced in section 304(c) may be categorized individually by reference to the extent to which they reflect universality or territoriality. Factors (1) (just treatment of all claimholders) and (5) (comity) reflect universality. However, the universality of both of these factors is probably qualified because just treatment of all claimholders may argue for distributing the proceeds of US assets to US creditors, and because comity, at least as developed prior to the enactment of section 304, would not necessarily result in cooperation with or deference to the debtor's home jurisdiction. In fact, comity is a complex inquiry that itself seeks to balance the interest in international cooperation (i.e. universality) with local interests (territoriality).[8] The remaining four factors – protection of US claimholders, prevention of preferential or fraudulent dispositions of local property, consistency of distribution under foreign law with US priorities, and provision of an opportunity for a fresh start – all seek to determine the consistency of the foreign proceeding with the principal policies of US bankruptcy law.[9] Therefore, they reflect a territorial approach, requiring the implementation of US bankruptcy policy as a condition for cooperation with or deference to foreign proceedings. As they embody both these conflicting approaches, the factors will point in different directions in many situations. The moderation of the conflict between intrajurisdictional fairness and policy on the one hand and interjurisdictional fairness and policy on the other hand is thus left for the courts applying sections 304 and 305.[10]

This tension between territoriality and universality is familiar in all conflict-of-laws issues. However, it should be observed that nothing is said in the guidelines about the intensity of the interest which various countries may have in the debtor, the debtor's activities, or the creditors. That is, there is no private international law or choice-of-law thinking reflected in the section 304 guidelines.[11] We will return to this fundamental concern.

15.4 Application of Section 304(c) Factors by Courts

Despite the enactment of sections 304 and 305, the flexibility and discretion of comity still pervade the decisions by US courts to cooperate with or defer to foreign bankruptcy proceedings. We will look at two leading cases that applied the factors provided under section 304(c) in quite different ways, in order to understand the flexibility that these factors provide. We will then consider a recent case that illustrates some of the special considerations that may influence a court's judgment in this area. We will then consider how these factors could be applied to our hypothetical case.

15.4.1 In re Culmer

In re Culmer was the first major case to analyze section 304(c).[12] Mr Culmer was one of three Bahamian court-appointed liquidators of

Banco Ambrosiano Overseas Limited (BAOL), a banking company organized and licensed under Bahamian law and engaged in a banking business in Nassau.[13] The liquidators were appointed by a BAOL shareholders' meeting which also called upon the liquidators to apply to the Bahamas Supreme Court for voluntary liquidation under supervision of the Court. This order was applied for and obtained. The liquidators found it necessary to come to America because BAOL maintained various accounts at banks and financial institutions in New York.

The liquidators of BAOL wanted to protect the US accounts of BAOL from attack by creditors, and bring these assets into the Bahamian voluntary liquidation. They began by seeking and obtaining a temporary restraining order roughly parallel to the automatic stay that would be applicable to a full US bankruptcy case, barring the continuation or commencement of suits against BAOL, as well as the creation, perfection, or enforcement of liens, set-offs, or other claims against the property of BAOL.[14] The liquidators applied under section 304 to continue these prohibitions and also to require that all claimants to BAOL property release such property to the liquidators for administration in the Bahamian liquidation proceeding.

Other creditors of BAOL opposed the liquidators' petition under section 304(b). At issue was the proper application to the facts of the factors listed in section 304(c). The court found that the central question to be answered "is whether the relief petitioners seek will afford equality of distribution of the available assets."[15] In order to answer this question, the court reviewed Bahamian bankruptcy procedure. The court found that the Bahamas Supreme Court could "best assure an economical and expeditious administration of [the BAOL] estate."[16] The court also cited its finding that the Bahamas had the greatest interest in BAOL's liquidation, on the public-law-oriented basis that neither the US federal government nor the New York state government had any particular governmental interest in the matter. The creditors opposing the section 304 petition had small claims relative to those supporting the petition, and, if the petition were denied, would effectively benefit from a preference to which they were not entitled under either Bahamian law or US law.

Based on a detailed examination of the principles of Bahamian insolvency law, the court found that the Bahamian liquidation, under laws that are in substantial conformity with US insolvency law, satisfied the criteria of section 304(c), including the principle of equality of distribution. The court implicitly criticized the draftsmen of section 304(c) by stating that its factors have historically been considered in determinations of comity – this makes the inclusion of both comity and other factors redundant. The court proceeded to engage in a comity analysis, using the other section 304(c) factors as a subordinate basis for determining whether comity should be accorded the Bahamian proceeding.[17] The court thus placed great emphasis on comity.[18] Based on its understanding of the Bahamian proceeding analyzed pursuant to the factors listed in section 304(c), the court found that affording comity would not violate American law or public policy, the main focus of the comity analysis. On this basis, the court affirmed that it "is not obliged to protect the positions of fast-moving American and foreign attachment creditors over the policy favoring uniform administration in a foreign court."[19]

In support of its decision, the court noted that its decision was consistent with *Cornfeld* v. *Investors Overseas Services, Ltd*, a case that held that Canada (like the Bahamas) is "a sister common law jurisdiction with procedures akin to our own."[20] The *In re Culmer* court stated that for purposes of this analysis, Canada may be assimilated to the Bahamas, as the English Companies Act formed the basis for both the Canadian and Bahamian liquidation rules.[21]

Thus, *In re Culmer* stands for the propositions that

- comity is the decisive factor in determining whether to cooperate with or defer to a foreign proceeding, and
- the comity determination, at least for a court applying New York's comity doctrine,[22] is merely a determination of whether the foreign insolvency regime is sufficiently consistent with US law and policy, and whether the foreign court has jurisdiction.

This is a relatively generous internationalist approach, although it leaves open the questions of what US policy is sufficient to justify a rejection of the foreign insolvency regime, as well as what basis for foreign jurisdiction will be respected. Below, we consider a case that stands in sharp contrast to *In re Culmer*.

15.4.2 Toga

Matter of Toga Mfg Ltd involved a petition filed by a Canadian trustee for Toga Manufacturing Limited (Toga).[23] The Canadian trustee's section 304 petition sought the release of garnished funds by a state court holding the funds pending resolution of a dispute regarding priority, as well as an injunction against the commencement or continuation of actions against Toga or its assets. The dispute regarding priority was between Toga's largest secured creditor, Canadian Imperial Bank of Commerce (CIBC) and a US commercial judgment creditor, Hesse

Enterprises, Inc. (Hesse). Hesse had obtained two judgments against Toga: a consent judgment entered on April 1, 1982, and an arbitration award confirmed by a court judgment on May 21, 1982. Toga executed a consensual default agreement with CIBC on April 29, 1982, and CIBC appointed a receiver. Hesse served two sets of writs of garnishment: one on May 4, 1982, and the second on June 10, 1982. On October 18, 1982, an unsecured creditor of Toga instituted involuntary bankruptcy proceedings in Canada, and had its petition granted on November 16, 1982. The Supreme Court of Ontario appointed the trustee on November 16, 1982. On December 14, 1982, the trustee filed the section 304 petition.

Judge Graves began his analysis by comparing section 304 with two US Supreme Court cases from the early nineteenth century.[24] He explained that these nineteenth-century cases stood for a "pluralist" (territorial) bankruptcy conflict of laws theory, but that "adherence to this theory produces a result inimical to the policies" of US and Canadian bankruptcy law.[25] He then explained that section 304 embodies a qualified universal theory of conflict of laws, and proceeded to an analysis of the facts of this case under section 304(c).

Judge Graves began his section 304(c) analysis by taking judicial notice of the fact that Hesse would suffer no inconvenience or prejudice by being forced to litigate in Canada, thus determining that factor (2) argued for deference to the Canadian proceeding. He next considered factor (4) – distribution in accordance with US priorities. Judge Graves found, and the Canadian trustee conceded, that Hesse would be treated as an unsecured (ordinary) creditor in the Canadian proceeding, whereas Hesse would be a preferred lien creditor under US law, with the status of a secured creditor with respect to the property subject to the lien. Thus factor (4) argued against deference to the Canadian proceeding.

Judge Graves considered only one additional factor: comity. He referred to *Hilton* v. *Guyot*, a classic and often cited, although not faithfully followed, statement of the doctrine of comity.[26] *Hilton* v. *Guyot* has been criticized in so far as it may be read to call for reciprocity by the home jurisdiction as a requirement for enforcement of a judgment of such jurisdiction.[27] However, Judge Graves seemed to consider reciprocity a requirement for comity, as he described two Canadian cases: one denying effect to a US bankruptcy judgment ordering the turnover of property in Canada, and the second, a more recent case, allowing cooperation in Canada with a US trustee of a bankrupt estate. The opinion does not explain the purpose of this review.[28]

The court bases its holding against the Canadian receiver on its responsibility to "protect United States citizens' claims against foreign judgments inconsistent with this country's well-defined and accepted policies," and the "notion of international fair play and justice."[29] This holding is blatantly parochial, and therefore inconsistent with the apparent intent of section 304, yet it finds support in the explicit language of section 304(c)(4), as well as in the factors generally considered in comity determinations, which are implicit in section 304(c)(5).

The explicit language of section 304(c)(4) may be read to *require* that the applicable priorities of the foreign proceeding be consistent with US priorities. However, it appears that section 304(c) was intended to provide a flexible, multi-factor balancing test, rather than a checklist of tests to be satisfied in order to allow cooperation or deference. Judge Graves quoted the following portion of the legislative history of section 304: "[p]rinciples of international comity and respect for the judgments and laws of other nations suggest that the court be permitted to make the appropriate orders under all of the circumstances of each case, rather than being provided with inflexible rules."[30] This language seems to contradict an approach to section 304(c) that would decline to cooperate with or defer to a foreign proceeding on the basis of failure to satisfy a single factor of the six set forth therein.

More importantly, Judge Graves's holding demonstrates the great flaw in section 304(c): its indeterminacy by virtue of the fact that it is very difficult for any foreign proceeding to satisfy all of its prongs. First, if comity is a negative factor in the sense of Judge Graves's application – meaning that it requires a balance to be struck between forum policy and deference to foreign proceedings – it is almost by definition always possible to find a forum policy that is controverted by the foreign law. Otherwise, why (other than for reasons of inconvenience or prejudice) would the forum creditors seek to avoid the foreign proceeding? Clearly, comity works because forum policies are sacrificed to deference in circumstances deemed appropriate. However, section 304(c) provides little guidance to courts in determining when the circumstances are appropriate.

15.4.3 Interpool

This recent case illustrates some of the subtle problems that may arise in connection with international judicial cooperation in insolvency proceedings.[31] It involves the application of an Australian liquidator of KKL (Kangaroo Line) Pty Ltd (KKL) to dismiss a Chapter 7 liquidation case brought by US creditors of KKL, and to initiate a US case ancillary to the Australian proceeding. The Australian liquidation proceeding was brought by a Hong Kong shipping company and substantial creditor of KKL, Wah Kwong & Co.[32] Wah Kwong had control over certain aspects of KKL's operations, and the debt owed Wah Kwong was under certain circumstances only required to be repaid by mutual agreement. Under the Australian liquidation proceedings, KKL assigned its rights to any award in a particular arbitration proceeding to Wah Kwong.

The trial court noted that comity is the most important factor in the section 304 analysis, and noted also that a prerequisite to comity is that the foreign court follows "fundamental standards of procedural fairness."[33] The trial court stated that the decision whether to grant comity to the Australian liquidator depended on the level of protection of US creditors in the Australian proceeding. The trial court cited both *Toga* and *Culmer* to the effect that substantial consistency with US law is a prerequisite for deference, although it also stated that there is no requirement that Australian law be identical to US law. As a factual matter, the court found that the Australian proceeding lacked the important procedural protections found in US proceedings, as it allowed arrangements to be made between the liquidator and particular creditors without notice to other creditors. In particular, the court was concerned about the transfer to Wah Kwong of a priority interest in any arbitral award. The court also raised the unavailability of the remedy of equitable subordination in Australia, which was important here because of the possibility that Wah Kwong controlled KKL to the unfair detriment of other creditors.

The trial court concluded that both the laws and the public policy of the US would be violated if the case were permitted to proceed under Australian law, and accordingly denied the section 304 petition and granted the motion for Chapter 7 liquidation. This holding demonstrates the substantial issues raised by cooperation, despite the fact that the foreign jurisdiction involved was a "sister common law jurisdiction."

15.5 Application of Sections 304 and 305 to Hypothetical Facts

As described above, the administrator for Multicorp Plc wishes to block or delay both (1) Megabank's litigation against Multicorp Plc, including its attack on Multicorp Plc's vessel and US bank accounts, and (2) the Chapter 7 liquidation action brought by Multicorp Plc's US trade creditor. He also wishes to obtain control over Multicorp Plc's US bank accounts, for disposition in the UK proceeding. Megabank's litigation is subject to the automatic stay that came into effect upon the filing of the Chapter 7 liquidation petition. However, the administrator cannot rely on this stay remaining in place, as the petition could be dismissed, and, more relevantly, as the administrator will want to seek dismissal of the liquidation action under section 305, as well as cooperation under section 304. The cooperation will take the form of enjoining actions against Multicorp Plc or its assets, and ordering the release of these assets to the UK administrator. Let us assume that Megabank and the US trade creditor will oppose the petitions. The administrator will not be deterred by fears of being subject to US jurisdiction generally by virtue of his appearance, as section 306 explicitly allows limited appearances of foreign representatives in connection with sections 304 and 305.[34] The court may condition any order under section 304 or 305 on compliance by the foreign representative with such order. For example, in one case, the court conditioned release of local assets on the protection of local creditors.[35]

In light of the opposition, the court will hold a trial pursuant to section 304, which it will probably combine with the hearing required under section 305. The court will find that the UK procedure qualifies as a foreign proceeding within section 101(22) of the Bankruptcy Code, and that the administrator qualifies as a foreign representative under section 101(23) of the Bankruptcy Code. These decisions might not be so easy with respect to receivers appointed by private parties under floating charges.[36]

The court will next determine whether to grant the administrator's petition under section 304, and whether to dismiss the US Chapter 7 liquidation proceeding under section 305. This decision will be based on a review of the considerations specified in section 304(c). Here, we know that courts may take different approaches.

15.5.1 Section 304(c)(1), (2): Just Treatment of All Claimholders; Protection of US Claimholders Against Prejudice and Inconvenience

Despite *Interpool*, it should not be argued seriously that UK insolvency proceedings would not provide for just and unprejudicial treatment of all claimholders, in the abstract. However, in a particular case, such as *Interpool*, it might be argued that it would be unjust and prejudicial to require a US claimholder to participate in a UK insolvency proceeding. Consider our hypothetical case, where the US claimholder and the debtor have agreed on the application of New York law to their relationship, and the US claimholder relied on the expectation that this agreement would be enforceable, perhaps on the basis of a written legal opinion provided by counsel (which opinion as to enforceability would have provided an exception as to the possible effects of bankruptcy). The US claimholder, to the extent that UK insolvency proceedings would not provide all the value that would be available to him in a US proceeding, could argue that he was treated unjustly and prejudiced by deference to or cooperation with the UK proceeding. *Toga* stands for the proposition that the US claimholder should not be forced to accept less than he would have received in the US. One way in which this might occur is if in the UK proceeding, the vessel subject to Megabank's ship mortgage is to be retained by Multicorp Plc as part of a rehabilitation, thus depriving Megabank of this source of recovery. In addition, it might be argued that as in an English administration proceeding the administrator generally is selected by the directors, there is potential for prejudice to creditors.

15.5.2 Section 304(c)(3): Prevention of Preferential or Fraudulent Transfers

This factor would be relevant if property of the debtor had been transferred in a way that would be considered preferential or fraudulent and subject to disgorgement under US law, but that would not be subject to similar treatment under UK law. As US and UK law differ as to the types of payments that may be deemed preferential, fraudulent or at an undervalue, this factor could become important.

15.5.3 Section 304(c)(4): Distribution in Accordance with US Priorities

As noted above, if UK priorities of distribution would treat the US creditor differently from how he would be treated under US law, this would be a basis, as under *Toga*, for deciding to refuse to cooperate with or defer to the foreign proceeding. Of course, this position would be subject to all of the criticism that is levelled at *Toga*. UK insolvency law would respect a valid foreign ship mortgage, and accord it priority over all claims other than the costs of the liquidation. However, recall that Megabank is undersecured (and the trade creditor is unsecured), and would thus also be interested in the treatment of unsecured creditors. The UK system of priorities would provide that certain interests come ahead of unsecured creditors that might not come ahead of unsecured creditors in a US proceeding.

Thus, US unsecured creditors may feel that a UK insolvency proceeding would prejudice them. It is important to recognize that this is not a baldly parochial concern, as a US creditor would be likely to lend against collateral in the US on the basis of certain expectations regarding priority under US law. It would make commerce more cumbersome to require US creditors to examine the insolvency law of the borrower's home country in order to determine their respective priority. This issue would be accentuated where a *secured* creditor is subject to a priority in a foreign jurisdiction that differed, to his detriment, from the US system of priority.

15.5.4 Section 304(c)(5): Comity

We have seen that, under *Culmer* and *Toga*, comity can have varying meanings and can be read to call for different tests. The unanswered question is whether foreign proceedings may be denied cooperation on the basis of differences – whether procedural or substantive – that would provide less value to the US creditors than they would receive under US bankruptcy proceedings. If cooperation were always denied on the basis of such differences, then cooperation would be available only for proceedings under legal regimes that essentially mirror US law. If this ethnocentric attitude were adopted by each country, then cooperation would never be available to the US. This outcome is certainly not what Congress was seeking to achieve with sections 304 and 305 of the Bankruptcy Code. This leads to an interpretation of section 304(c) as a balancing test – with all of the shortcomings of a balancing test – that requires the US court, finding no particular factor necessarily dispositive, to seek as much as possible to balance the policies expressed in the Bankruptcy Code with the policy of international cooperation. This is the proper meaning of comity: compromising (but not giving up) domestic law and policy in the interest of international cooperation. It is a pragmatic way of dealing with a theoretically impossible situation.

Thus, a review of the section 304(c) factors would be relatively indeterminate without a concrete evaluation of the foreign bankruptcy procedure under these rules, and a determination of whether the court making the determination would follow the universalist approach of *Culmer*, or the more territorial approach of *Toga*, or perhaps something in between. A US bankruptcy court could decide to dismiss the Chapter 7 case brought by Multicorp's trade creditor, and assist the English administrator by enjoining Megabank's actions and turning over Multicorp Plc's US property, or might decide that it would be inappropriate to do so.

15.6 A Comparative Perspective: How Would an English Court Treat Similar Issues?

15.6.1 Insolvency Act 1986, Section 426

An English court dealing with facts similar to those set forth in the hypothetical case above, with the nationalities reversed, would consider English common law on cooperation with and deference to foreign bankruptcy proceedings, as well as section 426 of the Insolvency Act 1986 (which would not be applicable). These facts would involve a US shipping corporation with operations and assets in England, which had borrowed on a secured basis from an English bank, and which owed money to English trade creditors. The US trustee in bankruptcy comes to England seeking cooperation. Prior to the implementation of section 426, there was no English legislation providing for cooperation with foreign bankruptcy proceedings.[37] However, at English common law, the law of the place of incorporation would be recognized as the law governing a corporation's dissolution, and an administrator from the jurisdiction of incorporation would be recognized.[38]

The 1982 Cork Report on insolvency law, which formed a basis for the amendments to English insolvency law that included section 426, indicated that one of the aims of the law was to "ensure recognition and respect abroad for English insolvency proceedings."[39] The Cork Report emphasized the desire for reciprocal treatment as a reason for recognizing and respecting foreign insolvency proceedings.[40]

Section 426(4) *requires* an English court to assist a court in a "relevant country" and section 426(5) *provides discretion* for an English court to apply the insolvency law of that relevant country or territory in relation to matters specified in the request of the foreign court. In exercising its discretion to apply the foreign insolvency law, the English court must have regard to the rules of private international law. Even the requirement to provide assistance contains an implicit component of discretion as to the form of assistance and any conditions to assistance.[41] The major – and applicable – limitation here is the fact that "relevant country or territory" means only the Channel Islands, the Isle of Man, and any country designated by the Secretary of State. The Secretary of State has designated Australia, Canada, Hong Kong, Ireland, and New Zealand, in addition to a number of former colonies. Other European countries and the US are excluded. Until the scope of potential cooperation is expanded, it cannot be hoped that the aims expressed in the Cork Report – reciprocal recognition of English insolvency proceedings abroad – will be achieved by section 426.

The reference made by section 426(5) to the rules of private international law may serve the same function in English law as the reference to comity contained in section 304(c) of the US Bankruptcy Code. In addition, as noted above, sections 304 and 305 are viewed as non-exclusive, so they preserve the discretion of a US bankruptcy court to apply prior rules of comity, or private international law, to determine whether to cooperate with or defer to a foreign proceeding.

In England, as in the US, the reference to the rules of private international law detracts from the extent to which the statute innovates by departing from or codifying prior common law. It also renders unclear the goals of the legislators.

Indeed, the reference to the rules of private international law will require English courts to refer to common law in order to guide their discretion.[42] Of course, this body of private international law would be the source for rules of decision for courts dealing with cases not covered by section 426, which would be the vast majority, including our hypothetical case. This body of private international law includes rules relating to jurisdiction, rules relating to title to and security interests in property, choice-of-law rules, and public policies that may override general choice-of-law rules.[43] It is possible that an English creditor could commence insolvency proceedings against the US debtor, resulting in a situation of concurrent proceedings. The basis for English jurisdiction to wind up the US corporation would be that it carried on business in England.[44] The English court would have a general power to stay the English winding-up proceeding, including on the basis of *forum non conveniens*.[45] Thus, the English court could choose to defer to the US proceeding, on the basis that the US forum is the proper forum, or could choose not to defer, applying English law to the English proceeding.[46] However, Dicey and Morris states in Rule 178 that the "authority of a liquidator appointed under the law of the place of incorporation is recognised in England."[47]

15.6.2 Felixstowe Dock and Railway Co. *v.* US Lines Inc.

In a recent case arising from the insolvency of US Lines Inc., *Felixstowe Dock and Railway Co.* v. *US Lines Inc.*,[48] an English court declined to turn assets of a US debtor over to a US bankruptcy court. US Lines owed money to Felixstowe for dock charges. After US Lines filed for Chapter 11 reorganization, Felixstowe obtained a *Mareva* injunction to enjoin the removal of assets below a certain threshold. US Lines sought the lifting of the injunction on grounds of international comity, arguing that the US bankruptcy court should be permitted to deal with all of US Lines' assets. Felixstowe argued that English courts should deal with assets located in England, that the continuation of the *Mareva* injunction would not result in a preference to Felixstowe, and that its removal would cause Felixstowe substantial prejudice.

The court noted that the English courts had jurisdiction to wind up US Lines on the alternative grounds of its registration in England and its possession of assets in England.[49] It also noted that the Insolvency

Act does not provide jurisdiction to issue an administration order in respect of a foreign company. The court indicated that it would have accepted US Lines' position if the US bankruptcy proceeding were a liquidation, rather than a reorganization in which the funds subject to the *Mareva* injunction would be used for operations, rather than for distribution to creditors.[50] In connection with this distinction, the court expressed concern about two facts. First, while the excess of US Lines' consolidated liabilities over its assets was only approximately 2 percent, its English liabilities greatly exceeded its English assets. Second, part of US Lines' plan of reorganization was to close down its English and European operations. On this basis, the court determined that the UK plaintiffs would be slighted in the Chapter 11 reorganization process, and would therefore have "nothing to gain and much to lose from the transfer of their *Mareva* funds to the USA." The court decided to retain control of the *Mareva* funds, subject to distribution pursuant to an ancillary winding-up proceeding in England, if one were brought.

Thus, English law on deference to or cooperation with foreign insolvency proceedings – especially for those countries that have not been designated a "relevant country" – appears, like US law, to be relatively fluid and uncertain, based on rules of private international law or comity. Both legal regimes, at best, provide limited scope for reciprocal deference and cooperation, as well as mixed signals to the courts. In fact, Judge Hirst indicated in his *Felixstowe* opinion that he was not convinced that, if roles were reversed, a US court would release funds of an insolvent English company under similar circumstances.

15.7 Attempts at International Coordination

There have been many attempts to provide greater certainty and fairness in the resolution of multinational insolvencies. These attempts generally take the form of agreements, either by treaty or by proposed parallel action, to adhere to a policy of qualified universality: to accept that a particular jurisdiction's law will govern most aspects of the insolvency proceeding. These systems sacrifice the integrity of the domestic system in order to promote the integrity of an international system. Of course, sacrificing domestic objectives in order to promote international objectives is necessary in many areas and is becoming more pervasive in connection with the integration of the European Community, and even in connection with the dismantling of non-tariff barriers through GATT. There have been a number of unsuccessful or limited multilateral attempts to coordinate bankruptcy proceedings. For example, a number of European countries have concluded bilateral or even limited multilateral agreements. Five countries have ratified the Scandinavian Convention.[51] In addition, fifteen Latin American countries have ratified the Bustamente Code of Private International Law, which contains provisions on bankruptcy.[52] An initiative to implement a European Community regime for bankruptcy cooperation in accordance with article 220 of the Treaty of Rome lost momentum after a 1980 draft.

15.7.1 The EC Draft Convention

An agreement on coordination of bankruptcy proceedings was initially considered important to the creation of the internal market.[53] However, in light of wide variations in national laws, harmonization or approximation of laws under article 100 of the Treaty of Rome was deemed too ambitious.[54] Under the Single European Act, where harmonization is not achieved, home country regulation and host country (or forum) recognition of home country national standards is the general fall-back position. Similarly, in the area of insolvency, it was recognized that a measure of universality can serve in place of harmonization of national laws. Thus the rules of conflicts of law are harmonized, and made exclusive, but the substantive rules are not harmonized, as had been proposed in an earlier draft EC insolvency treaty. Even this limited approach proved too ambitious for the present, and the European Community's 1980 Draft Convention on Bankruptcy, Winding-Up, Arrangements, Compositions, and Similar Proceedings (the EC Draft Convention) has not proceeded toward adoption.[55]

The main problem in a system based on universality is determining which country's courts will have jurisdiction over a particular insolvency. That country's laws will also be made applicable to most matters related to the insolvency, especially procedural matters. Different countries may base jurisdiction on residence, domicile, location of principal place of business, location of assets, or other criteria. In order to eliminate conflicts of jurisdiction, it is necessary to specify a single, easy to identify, basis for jurisdiction.[56] The draftsmen of the EC Draft Convention adopted the debtor's center of administration within the European Community as the main single basis for qualified universal jurisdiction.[57] The center of administration will generally be presumed to be the registered office of a corporation. The court accorded jurisdiction under this regime would have exclusive jurisdiction with only limited exceptions, and its judgments would be recognized by other member states.

Generally, the law of the forum so selected would apply to both procedural and substantive aspects of the case. But to what extent may the law of the jurisdiction of the debtor's center of administration be accepted by other countries without prejudicing commercial certainty and policy interests in the domestic sphere? When dealing with a corporation with a foreign center of administration, must a local bank interested in set-off, or in lending against local collateral, comply with the laws of the jurisdiction of the center of administration? What about leases and conditional sale contracts? In response to these concerns, the EC Draft Convention represents an attempt to provide for a degree of harmonization of law where appropriate, for territoriality in some situations and for universality in other areas.

With respect to set-off, where each member state has a different approach, and where it was felt that these disparities would give rise to inequity, the solution proposed was to require each member state to permit set-off on a minimal basis.[58] This constitutes selective substantive harmonization.

For purposes of determining the priority of distribution of proceeds of assets, the law of the jurisdiction of location of the asset is generally applicable, with certain significant and complex exceptions.[59] This constitutes a major departure from the principle of universality in favor of the principle of territoriality. Thus, intrajurisdictional integrity is given primacy over interjurisdictional integrity, and the worldwide assets of the debtor are in effect subject to distribution on a blended priority basis, in proportion relating to the proportion of assets in the various jurisdictions. Similarly, with respect to leases of immovable property, the law of the jurisdiction where the property is located governs.[60]

With respect to recoveries of preferential or fraudulent payments, the law of the jurisdiction of the debtor's center of administration will generally govern.[61] However, if that bankruptcy law contains no such provisions, reference is made to the law governing the particular transaction under attack.[62] This constitutes selective territoriality.

15.7.2 Proposed Uniform Legislation

This approach is similar to a treaty that provides for universality and a single administration of a debtor's assets, in the sense that it calls for harmonization of private international law rules, not of substantive insolvency rules. The most recent effort in this area is the "Proposal for Consultative Draft of Model International Insolvency Co-Operation Act for Adoption by Domestic Legislation with or without Modification" (model act) prepared by the International Bar Association's

Subcommittee on International Cooperation in Bankruptcy Proceedings, and endorsed by the International Bar Association at its June 1989 meeting in Helsinki.[63] This approach has the advantage of providing greater flexibility for each adherent to accept a varying set of rules, consistent with domestic legislation, providing for mutual cooperation.

As a means of eliminating the perceived flexibility of the application of the factors set forth in section 304(c) of the US Bankruptcy Code, the proposed uniform legislation merely requires that the forum court assist a foreign court that has proper jurisdiction over the debtor and its estate. While this requirement is subject to the conditions that either (a) the jurisdiction of the foreign court have adopted the model international insolvency cooperation act, or (b) the foreign court be a proper and convenient forum and its administration be in the overall interests of the creditors, it is not subject to an explicit comity or private international law analysis or the consideration of other factors such as those contained in section 304(c). It is curious that the requirements in (b) do not apply in any case, and indeed the definition of "foreign proceeding" contained in section 6 of the model act requires that the foreign court have "proper jurisdiction," whatever that may mean to the forum court, in order for the cooperation requirements to apply. There is no provision for coordination where several fora may be considered to have proper jurisdiction, and seek assistance from one another. On the other hand, the model act requires that where a case ancillary to a foreign proceeding is commenced in the forum jurisdiction, the law of the foreign jurisdiction will be applicable, unless "after giving due consideration to principles of private international law and conflict of laws, the Court determines that it must apply the substantive insolvency law of [the forum]." The assisting jurisdiction is therefore free to determine, based on forum private international law without further guidance or uniformity, whether to apply its own law to its assistance. Thus the court has little flexibility in determining whether to assist, but largely uncurtailed flexibility in determining whether to apply its own law (with an expressed preference for the home jurisdiction's substantive law).

15.7.3 *Council of Europe Convention*

This recently signed treaty is intended to guarantee a minimum of legal cooperation in insolvency proceedings.[64] It is more limited in its aspirations toward a single administration than the EC Draft Convention.

The Council Convention follows the EC Draft Convention in providing that the jurisdiction where the debtor has the center of its "main interests" (the EC Draft Convention refers to a "center of administration," connoting less weight accorded to assets, and perhaps allowing greater manipulability) is competent to open a bankruptcy. Similarly to the EC Draft Convention, the place of the registered office is presumed to be the center of main interests. In addition, other jurisdictions where the debtor has an establishment may be competent to open a bankruptcy, if either (a) the debtor's main interests are not located in the territory of any party or (b) the debtor is not bankrupt or eligible for bankruptcy under the national law of the party where the debtor has its center of main interests.[65]

The liquidator appointed by the court or other competent authority that opens the bankruptcy may seek to protect the debtor's foreign assets, and may seek the assistance of local competent authorities. After a two-month waiting period to allow local bankruptcy proceedings to be brought, and an extended period for so long as the local proceedings have not been rejected, the liquidator may administer, manage, remove, or dispose of the debtor's foreign assets, subject to local law. During the waiting period, only preferred creditors, public law creditors, or creditors having a claim arising from the operation of an establishment or from employment in that party's territory (collectively, "preferred claimants") may commence or pursue individual legal actions against the debtor.[66] If bankruptcy proceedings are opened or blocked in the foreign territory, the liquidator cannot exercise his powers in that territory.[67] Under no circumstances may the liquidator override local security interests or public policy.[68]

The Council Convention provides for secondary bankruptcies or "satellite" bankruptcies, to be administered in parties where the debtor has an establishment or assets, after the opening of the main bankruptcy in the party where the debtor has its center of interests. Either the liquidator in the main bankruptcy or a person authorized under local law may commence the secondary bankruptcy.[69] In addition, any bankruptcy opened after the opening of a main bankruptcy where the debtor has its center of interests is a secondary bankruptcy. The governing law of the secondary bankruptcy is local bankruptcy law.[70] Local preferred claimants are to be paid from local assets, and remaining assets are transferred to the main bankruptcy for distribution in accordance with the main bankruptcy.[71] A bankruptcy that would otherwise be a secondary bankruptcy but is opened before the main bankruptcy may be asked to provide any local assets remaining at the end thereof to the main bankruptcy.

Thus the Council Convention provides a system for coordination of potentially numerous local proceedings, with these local proceedings transferring assets to the main bankruptcy generally only after certain local preferred interests have been paid. This treaty represents a compromise position that may find greater political acceptance than has the EC Draft Convention.

15.8 Conclusion

We have examined the US and UK unilateral approaches, a proposed uniform unilateral statutory approach, and two treaty approaches to the problem of coordination of bankruptcy proceedings. Why bother to coordinate? Fears of prejudice against foreign creditors appear to be overstated. The real issue is one of regularity and the integrity of government processes. It is necessary to provide coordination in order to diminish the potential advantage to creditors of speedy unilateral action to assert their rights against a debtor in jurisdictions where no bankruptcy proceeding may be pending. By diminishing the potential advantage of such action, we would be able to promote

- fairness among creditors,
- preservation of enterprise value,
- fairness and perhaps providing a fresh start to debtors, and
- minimization of economic dislocation.

These are the goals of domestic bankruptcy law; international coordination of domestic bankruptcy law is necessary to promote these goals, as well as international goals of mutual cooperation among countries. The central question raised by the problem of international coordination of bankruptcy law is: Whose law is to govern? This question must be answered in a relatively predictable way that will incorporate substantive elements. In other words, in determining governing law (or laws), factors such as the location of the various components of the debtor's operations (management, assets, and operations) and the relevant policy interests of the concerned states should be considered, in order to make the choice congruent with the policies sought to be implemented through insolvency law.

Notes

1 See text accompanying notes 20–1 below. See also *Remington Rand* v. *Business Systems, Inc.*, 830 F.2d 1260 (3rd Cir. 1987) (denying comity to Dutch bankruptcy order on due process grounds); *Drexel Lambert Group* v. *Galadari*, 777 F.2d 877 (2d Cir. 1985) (declining deference, subject to further inquiry as to fairness of a bankruptcy proceeding in Dubai, a jurisdiction with little experience or law in the area).

2 Bankruptcy Reform Act of 1978, 11 USC ss. 101–151326 (1988) (Bankruptcy Code). Copies of ss. 304, 305, 306, and 508 are appended to this chapter.
3 As s. 304 is phrased in permissive rather than mandatory terms, it has been asserted that comity continues to stand alongside the provisions of the Bankruptcy Code to allow US courts to recognize foreign bankruptcy judgments. *Cunard SS Co. v. Salen Reefer Services, AB*, 773 F.2d 452 (2nd Cir. 1985). See Harvey R. Miller and Lisa Rothenberg, "Transnational Bankruptcy and Reorganization Cases – A Potential Growth Area," in Southwestern Legal Foundation, *Private Investors Abroad: Problems and Solutions in International Business* (New York, Bender, 1988), pp. 3–39 ("Although Section 304 contains the doctrine of comity as one of the guidelines for determining appropriate relief, Congress left open the issue of whether a Section 304 proceeding should be the exclusive remedy of a foreign representative who wishes to stay or enjoin creditor actions in the United States.") See also L. F. E. Goldie, "The Challenge of Transnational Expectations and the Recognition of Foreign Bankruptcy Decrees – The United States Adjustment," *British Yearbook of International Law*, 58 (1987), pp. 303, 331–2. Professor Goldie points out that state, rather than federal, conflict-of-laws rules and concepts of comity may govern the comity determination by federal bankruptcy courts.
4 Bankruptcy Code, s. 101(22).
5 This option is available only if the debtor is an eligible debtor under s. 109 of the Bankruptcy Code, which requires that the person reside, have a domicile, have a place of business, or have property in the US in order to be a debtor. Bankruptcy Code, ss. 109(a), 303(b)(4).
6 See Appendix below for the text of s. 304(c).
7 Other connections could be substituted, such as jurisdiction of formation or jurisdiction of location of head office. However, the point is for each country to agree on a basis for allocating exclusive jurisdiction to a *single* country. Professor Trautman states that "it is almost universally agreed that jurisdiction for a business enterprise is its principal place of business," and suggests that the proposed US treaty with Canada failed because it substituted a preponderance of the assets test for a principal place of business test. Donald T. Trautman, "Foreign Creditors in American Bankruptcy Proceedings," *Harvard International Law Journal*, 29 (1988), pp. 49, 55.
8 "Comity means different things to different legislators, judges and commentators. Justice Story called 'comity of nations' the most appropriate phrase to express the true foundation and extent of the obligation of the laws of one nation within the territories of another. It is derived altogether from the voluntary consent of the latter; and is inadmissible, when it is contrary to its known policy, or prejudicial to its interests ... It is not the comity of the courts, but the comity of the nation, which is administered." J. Story, *Commentaries on the Conflict of Laws*, 2nd edn (Boston, Little, Brown, 1841), pp. 36–7.
9 It should be noted that this analysis of the section 304(c) factors is not necessarily obvious, and is not one that others necessarily share. In fact a

scholarly article written by a leading practitioner analyzes the factors quite differently. See Miller and Rothenberg, "Transnational Bankruptcy," pp. 3–29. Miller and Rothenberg view factors (3) and (4) as reflecting a universalist approach, in so far as they apply US policies in favor of all creditors, arguing that factors (2) and (5) suggest the territorial approach in so far as they protect local creditors. However, as noted above, factor (5) (comity) cuts both ways, and it is important to keep in mind that the difference between universality and territoriality relates to which laws are to be applied, not to which creditors are to be favored (although these will often be consistent).

10 Congress intended these factors to provide to courts "the maximum flexibility in handling ancillary cases." HR Rep. no. 595, 95th Congress, 1st session 324–25 (1977); Sen. Rep. no. 989, 95th Congress, 2d session 35 (1978).

11 Trautman, "Foreign Creditors," p. 51. Professor Trautman proceeds to note, as stated above, that the definition of "foreign proceeding" contained in 11 USC s. 109(19) is somewhat restricted in a way that may help to limit conflicts of jurisdiction, but he suggests that the term should be further restricted to reflect choice-of-law principles. This further limitation would require deference to the jurisdiction of the principal place of business.

12 25 Bankr. 621 (Bankr. SDNY 1982).

13 BAOL was a subsidiary of Banco Ambrosiano Holding of Luxembourg, which was a subsidiary of Banco Ambrosiano SPA.

14 The "automatic stay" is provided by s. 362 of the Bankruptcy Code. It is intended to preserve the assets of the debtor from attack during pendency of bankruptcy proceedings, and is thus crucial to the accomplishment of the purposes of a bankruptcy proceeding.

15 25 BR 621 at 628, citing *Israel British Bank (London), Ltd.* v. *Federal Deposit Insurance Corporation*, 536 F.2d 509, 513 (2d Cir.), certificate denied subs. nom. *Bank of the Commonwealth* v. *Israel British Bank (London) Ltd*, 429 US 978 (1976).

16 Ibid., referring to language of Bankruptcy Code, s. 304(c).

17 In this regard, it is interesting to note that the explicit reference in s. 304(c) (5) to "comity" was added as a last-minute afterthought. See Goldie, "Transnational Expectations," p. 303.

18 The court has been criticized for overemphasizing comity. See Stacy Allen Morales and Barbara Ann Deutcsh, "Bankruptcy Code Section 304 and US Recognition of Foreign Bankruptcies: The Tyranny of Comity," *Business Lawyer*, 39 (1984), pp. 1573, 1593 (arguing that *In re Culmer* may mark "a significant dismantling" of the law as intended by its authors).

19 25 BR 621, 629, citing *Banque de Financement, SA* v. *First National Bank of Boston*, 568 F.2d 911, 921 (2d Cir. 1977).

20 471 F. Supp. 1255 (SDNY 1979); ibid. 1259, quoting *Clarkson Co.* v. *Shaheen*, 544 F.2d 624, 630 (2d Cir. 1976).

21 25 BR 631, citing also *Canada Southern Railway* v. *Gebhard*, 109 US 527 (1883); *Kenner Products Co.* v. *Société Foncière et Financière*, 532 F. Supp.

478 (SDNY 1982). The court quoted from *Canada Southern Railway* v. *Gebhard*: "every person who deals with a foreign corporation impliedly subjects himself to such laws of the foreign government, affecting the powers and obligations of the corporation with which he voluntarily contracts, as the known and established policy of that government authorizes." 109 US 537–8.
22 For an interesting discussion of the Erie doctrine by which state law is applied in federal courts such as the federal bankruptcy courts, and of the possibility that the issue of recognition of foreign bankruptcy decrees might be governed by federal common law, see Goldie, "Transnational Expectations," p. 332, n. 152.
23 28 BR 165 (Bankr. ED Mich. 1983).
24 *Ogden* v. *Saunders*, 25 US (12 Wheat.) 213 (1827), and *Harrison* v. *Sterry*, 9 US (5 Cranch) 289 (1809).
25 28 BR 167.
26 159 US 113 (1895).
27 See *Direction der Disconto-Gesellschaft* v. *United States Steel Corporation*, 300 F. 741 (SDNY 1924), aff'd, 267 US 22 (1925). But see Kurt Hans Nadelmann, "The Bankruptcy Reform Act and the Conflict of Laws," *Harvard International Law Journal*, 29 (1988), pp. 27, 38–39 (suggesting that the reason for the addition of the reference to comity was to add a requirement for reciprocity).
28 *Macdonald* v. *Georgian Bay Lumber Co.*, 2 SCR 364 (Canadian Supreme Court 1878); *Williams* v. *Rice & Rice Knitting Mills Ltd.*, 3 DLR 225 (Canada 1926). Professor Goldie has expressed a view that Judge Graves cited these Canadian cases in order to be able to deny recognition of a Canadian judgment for failure of reciprocity. See Goldie, "Transnational Expectations," p. 331.
29 29 BR 170.
30 28 BR 169, quoting H. Rep. no. 95–595, 95th Congress, 1st session 324–5 (1977); S. Rep. no. 95–989, 95th Congress, 2d session 35 (1978).
31 *Interpool Ltd.* v. *Certain Freights of M/V Venture Star*, 102 Bankr. 373 (DNJ 1988), appeal dismissed 878 F.2d 111 (3rd Cir. 1989).
32 The author represented certain other debtors of Wah Kwong in related matters.
33 102 BR 373, 377, citing *Cunard SS Co.* v. *Salen Reefer Services AB*, 773 F.2d 452 (2d Cir. 1985).
34 Bankruptcy Code, s. 306.
35 *In re Lineas Aereas de Nicaragua, SA*, 10 BR 790 (SD Fla. 1981).
36 See Douglass G. Boshkoff, "United States Judicial Assistance in Cross-Border Insolvencies," *International and Comparative Law Quarterly*, 36 (1987), pp. 729, 742, citing 2 Collier Bankruptcy Practice Guide par. 19.04 [1] (1986); John Honsberger, "Conflict of Laws and the Bankruptcy Reform Act of 1978," *Case Western Reserve Law Review*, 30 (1980), pp. 631, 652.
37 See J. W. Woloniecki, "Co-operation between National Courts in International Insolvencies: Recent United Kingdom Legislation," *International and Comparative Law Quarterly*, 35 (1986), pp. 644, 647.

38 Ibid. The effect of the recognition and the availability of cooperation is another question, which is dealt with below.
39 *Insolvency Law and Practice – Report of the Review Committee*, para. 198 (1982), Cmnd. 8558, quoted by Woloniecki, "Co-operation between National Courts," pp. 648–9.
40 *Insolvency Law and Practice – Report of the Review Committee*, Cmnd. 8558 (HMSO, 1982), para. 1912.
41 Woloniecki, "Co-operation between National Courts," p. 653.
42 Philip St John Smart, "Carrying on Business as a Basis of Recognition of Foreign Bankruptcies in English Private International Law," *Oxford Journal of Legal Studies*, 9 (1989), pp. 557, 569.
43 See Woloniecki, "Co-operation between National Courts," p. 655 (providing a more detailed discussion of each of these issues).
44 Insolvency Act 1986, ss. 117, 221. See also A. V. Dicey and J. H. C. Morris, *Conflict of Laws* (London, Stevens, 1987), Rule 175, p. 1137, which provides for jurisdiction over foreign unregistered companies if there are assets situated in England and there are persons who would benefit from the making of a winding-up order. In *International Westminster Bank plc v. Okeanos Maritime Corporation*, 3 WLR 339 (Chancery 1987), the court took jurisdiction to liquidate a Liberian corporation despite the fact that the corporation had no assets in England, on the basis that there was a reasonable possibility of conferring benefit on the corporation's creditors, no more appropriate forum, and a sufficiently close connection with England.
45 Woloniecki, "Co-operation between National Courts," p. 657. See also Smart, "Forum Non Conveniens in Bankruptcy Proceedings," *Journal of Business Law* (March 1989).
46 See Dicey and Morris, *Conflict of Laws*, Rule 177, p. 1147.
47 Ibid., pp. 1150–1.
48 [1987] 2 LLR 76 (QB 1987).
49 Ibid., 86.
50 Ibid., 93.
51 November 7, 1933, 155 LNTS 136.
52 February 20, 1928, 86 LNTS 362. See articles 414–22.
53 Report on the Draft Convention on Bankruptcy, Winding-up, Arrangements, Compositions, and Similar Proceedings, *Bulletin of the European Communities*, Supplement 2/1982, 47 (1982) (hereafter Report on the Draft Convention).
54 Ibid., 50.
55 *Bulletin of the European Communities, Supplement* 2/1982 (1982).
56 Story, *Commentaries*.
57 EC Draft Convention, article 3. Where there is no center of administration in the Community, jurisdiction is accorded to the courts of any member country where the debtor has an establishment. Ibid., article 4.
58 EC Draft Convention, article 36.
59 Ibid., articles 43–52.
60 Ibid., article 39.

61 Ibid., article 15(1).
62 Ibid., article 37.
63 See *International Business Lawyer*, 17 (1989), p. 323.
64 Council of Europe, European Convention on Certain International Aspects of Bankruptcy (Istanbul, June 5, 1990) 30 ILM 165 (1991).
65 Ibid., article 4(2).
66 Ibid., article 11(2).
67 Ibid., article 14(1).
68 Ibid., article 14(2).
69 Ibid., article 18.
70 Ibid., article 19.
71 Ibid., articles 21, 22.

Appendix

Bankruptcy Reform Act of 1978, ss. 304, 305, 306, 508

§ 304. *Cases ancillary to foreign proceedings*

(a) A case ancillary to a foreign proceeding is commenced by the filing with the bankruptcy court of a petition under this section by a foreign representative.

(b) Subject to the provisions of subsection (c) of this section, if a party in interest does not timely controvert the petition, or after trial, the court may –
   (1) enjoin the commencement or continuation of –
      (A) any action against –
         (i) a debtor with respect to property involved in such foreign proceeding; or
         (ii) such property; or
      (B) the enforcement of any judgment against the debtor with respect to such property, or any act or the commencement or continuation of any judicial proceeding to create or enforce a lien against the property of such estate;
   (2) order turnover of the property of such estate, or the proceeds of such property, to such foreign representative; or
   (3) order other appropriate relief.

(c) In determining whether to grant relief under subsection (b) of this section, the court shall be guided by what will best assure an economical and expeditious administration of such estate, consistent with –
   (1) just treatment of all holders of claims against or interests in such estate;
   (2) protection of claim holders in the United States against prejudice and inconvenience in the processing of claims in such foreign proceeding;

(3) prevention of preferential or fraudulent dispositions of property of such estate;
(4) distribution of proceeds of such estate substantially in accordance with the order prescribed by this title;
(5) comity; and
(6) if appropriate, the provision of an opportunity for a fresh start for the individual that such foreign proceeding concerns.

§ 305. Abstention

(a) The court, after notice and a hearing, may dismiss a case under this title, or may suspend all proceedings in a case under this title, at any time if –
   (1) the interests of creditors and the debtor would be better served by such dismissal or suspension; or
   (2) (A) there is pending a foreign proceeding; and
       (B) the factors specified in section 304(c) of this title warrant such dismissal or suspension.

(b) A foreign representative may seek dismissal or suspension under subsection (a)(2) of this section.

(c) An order under subsection (a) of this section dismissing a case or suspending all proceedings in a case, or a decision not so to dismiss or suspend, is not reviewable by appeal or otherwise by the court of appeals under section 158(d), 1291, or 1292 of title 28 or by the Supreme Court of the United States under section 1254 of title 28.

§ 306. Limited appearance

An appearance in a bankruptcy court by a foreign representative in connection with a petition or request under section 303, 304, or 305 of this title does not submit such foreign representative to the jurisdiction of any court in the United States for any other purpose, but the bankruptcy court may condition any order under section 303, 304, or 305 of this title on compliance by such foreign representative with the orders of such bankruptcy court.

§ 508. Effect of distribution other than under this title

(a) If a creditor receives, in a foreign proceeding, payment of, or a transfer of property on account of, a claim that is allowed under this title, such creditor may not receive any payment under this title on account of such claim until each of the other holders of claims on account of which such holders are entitled to share equally with such creditor under this title has received payment under this title equal in value to the consideration received by such creditor in such foreign proceeding.

(b) If a creditor of a partnership debtor receives, from a general partner that is not a debtor in a case under chapter 7 of this title, payment of, or a transfer of property on account of, a claim that is allowed under this title and that is not secured by a lien on property of such partner, such creditor may not receive any payment under this title on account of such claim until each of the other holders of claims on account of which such holders are entitled to share equally with such creditor under this title has received payment under this title equal in value to the consideration received by such creditor from such general partner.

Index

account standards 77, 321, 337–9
aid agencies 263–4, 273
aircraft financing 364–76
Alamo Bank 387–8
'all moneys' clauses 100
American Depository Shares 177–8
amortizable bond premium 314
Asian Development Bank 97
asset securitization 35, 293, 342
asset swaps 352–3
auditors (role) 77
aval (guarantee) 246–8, 254–5

bad debt risk 321–2
Bank of England 65, 69, 72–3, 78, 318, 320–1, 324–7, 336–7, 341–2, 354
Bank Secrecy Act (US) 380–3, 385–97 *passim*
Banking Act (UK) 77, 320–1, 342
bankruptcy: Czech Republic and Slovakia 134–7; Hungary 146, 148–52; Poland 171–2; Russia 121–2; US 302–3, 311–12, 361, 363, 405–18
banks 316–17; location of accounts 118, 130–1, 145; records (confidential) 379–400; supervision 64–78
barter transactions 19, 22, 278–9
basis risk 294, 322–3
Basle Committee 71–8 *passim*, 320
BCCI 65, 67, 69, 73–5, 77–8, 81–4
bills of exchange 241–55
'blue sky' laws 178, 307
board of directors 328–32 *passim*
borrowing costs, reducing 352
Brady Plan 37–41, 90
buy-back 35–6, 40, 277–8, 284–6, 288–9

cap 47, 348–50
capital 102, 295–7, 316–17;
shortages 3–7; *see also* public fund-raising
cash settlement (swaps) 361–3
claimholders (bankruptcy) 416–17
co-finance projects 97
co-ownership (Poland) 166–7
co-production 278, 287
collar 47, 348–50
collateralized mortgage obligations 303–4, 309
comity (bankruptcy) 418
commercial paper 304–5
Commodity Credit Corporation 258
commodity swaps 46, 355
Companies Acts (UK) 100, 321, 326–39, 342, 367
company law: Czechoslovakia 126–8; Hungary 139–42; Poland 156–9; Russia 111–14
compensation 115, 142, 278
competitive equality 17, 67–8, 69, 70
Comptroller of Currency (US) 307, 310, 316
confidentiality (bank) 76, 379–400
consolidated annual accounts 329–37
consumer loans 299
convergence process 71–2, 76–7
Cork Report (1982) 419
Council of Europe Convention 424–6
counterpurchase 278, 280–4
countertrade 97, 275–90
coupon stripping 315
credit 305–6, 356–7, 360
credit card receivables 299–300
creditors 35–6, 121–2, 134–7, 149–53
Culmer case 410–12, 415, 418
currency 92; convertibility 117–18, 145, 163; swaps 45–6, 347–8; transaction

INDEX 435

reports 382–3, 387, 391–4, 397
customer transactions (records) 386–7
Czech Republic (and Euromarket) 126–39

debt: for bond swaps 35–6, 38, 41, 44; conversions (LDC) 32–55; debt–equity ratios 115, 144, 164; debt–equity swaps 34–6, 39, 41–2; restructuring 33–41; securities 312–13; servicing 91–8
Delors Report 6
deregulation 15, 368
'diamond structure' 329
disclosure 76, 179–82, 308–9, 389–91, 396–7
domestic currency transactions 382–4

Eastern Europe 4–6, 272–3
Economic and Monetary Union (EC) 76
Economic Recovery Tax Act (US) 17–18
electronic funds transfer 387
environmental issues 106–8, 120, 132, 146, 168
equal and rateable security 100–2
Eurocredits 34
Euromarket developments 109–10, 204; Czech Republic and Slovakia 126–39; Hungary 139–56; Poland 156–73; Russia 111–25
Euronote facilities 44–5
European Community 73, 370; Directives 74–5, 320, 329–30, 397–400; Draft Convention 422–6; export financing 267–8; insolvency 421–6
European Currency Units 21, 244–6
European Investment Bank 97
EXCEL program 271
Exchange Act 178–80, 182, 184, 186, 192–8, 201–2, 308
exchange control 94, 104
execution of documents 123–4, 138, 154

Eximbank 40, 257–62, 264, 272–3
Export Credits Guarantee Department (UK) 264–7, 268, 369
exports: assistance 257–67; financing arrangements 256–73; forfaiting 239–55
Exposure Draft 42 (1988 [UK]) 321–4, 337, 339
Exposure Draft 49 (1990 [UK]) 321, 337–41

factoring 241
FASB 77 295–6
Federal Deposit Insurance Corporation 69, 316, 395
Federal Home Loan Bank Board 307, 316
Federal Home Loan Mortgage Company 298, 311, 317
Federal Reserve System 65, 72, 76, 78, 310, 316
fee income (securitization) 296
Felixstowe Dock and Railway Co. case 420
financial failure 9–11
financial innovations 43–8
financial trends (global business) 13–29
Financial Services Act (UK) 354
FIRREA (US) 17, 69, 296–7, 307, 316
floors 47, 349, 350
Foreign Bank Supervision Act (US) 74
foreign broker–dealer 198–9, 211
Foreign Credit Insurance Association (US) 261, 272–3
foreign exchange: Czech Republic and Slovakia 130–1; Hungary 144–5; Poland 163–4; Russia 112–168
foreign investment: Czech Republic and Slovakia 129; Hungary 144; Poland 160–2; Russia 115–16, 117, 118
Foreign Military Sales program (US) 258, 260
foreign withholding requirements 315–16
forfaiting 239–55

forward market instruments 46–8
forward rate agreement 350–1
France (global equity offerings) 219
Freedom of Information Act (US) 383
funds/income funds 374–5

generally accepted accounting principle (GAAP) 180, 196, 212, 295
Geneva Conventions 243–4, 246, 249, 251, 254
Glass–Steagall Act 74
global business (financial trends) 13–29
global equity offerings (US) 174–222
global planning 26–9
global shrinkage 23–4
gold standard 15, 17, 19
government bonds 50–1
grantor trusts 299, 302, 313–14
guarantee (forfaiting) 242, 246–8, 254–5

hard currency countries 13–20, 22, 24–6, 29, 97
hedging arrangements 46, 91–8, 240
HLT loans 300–1, 303–4
Hungary (and Euromarket) 139–56

IMF 40, 95, 104
importing country (objectives) 276–7
Industry Acts (UK) 369
inflationary/deflationary cycles 15–18
insolvency proceedings 77; Europe 421–6; Poland 171–2; UK 418–21, 426; US 311–12, 404–21, 426
interest rate swaps 45–6, 345–7
Internal Revenue Service 380, 383, 386, 389, 391, 393, 396
International Bank for Reconstruction and Development 91, 101, 106
International Federation of Accountants 73, 77
International Finance Corporation 92, 271–2
International Lending Supervision Act (US) 69
International Swap Dealers Association 354
Interpool case 414–15, 416
investment: Euromarket 109–73; overseas 262–3, 272–3, 287; swap financing 352
Investment Company Act (US) 178, 192–3, 197–8, 211, 308–11
ISDA Agreement 359–60, 361–2, 363

Jack Committee 243, 244
Japan (global equity offerings) 219–20
Johnson Mathey 67, 69, 73
joint stock companies 112–14, 121–2, 127, 140, 156–7, 164
joint ventures 277, 373
junk bonds 41–2, 300–1, 303

Key and Scott Report 76

law and jurisdiction: Czech Republic and Slovakia 138–9; Hungary 155–6; Poland 172–3; Russia 124–5
Law of Property Act (UK) 245, 248, 367
LDC debt 32–55, 318, 319
League of Nations 27, 29
lease-backed securities 300
leasing 122–3, 137–8, 153–4, 169–70
legal issues: aircraft/ship financing 366–8; forfaiting 243–51; project finance 88, 102–6
legal regulation (bank supervision) 69–71
lender liability 107–8
leveraged buyout loans 301
liability management 352
LIBOR 323, 346–7, 350, 352
licenced production 287
limited liability companies 112, 127, 140, 156–7, 164, 172
limited partnerships 112, 140–1, 374
liquidation 122, 159–60, 171–2
liquidity 296, 322

loans 299–301, 303–4, 321, 324–7, 341

Maastricht Treaty 6
market discount obligations 314
merchant banking (LDC) 41–3
Mexican agreement 38–9, 49, 52–3, 61–3
mezzanine financing 373–4
Minsk Agreement 111
monetary instruments (cross-border) 384
money laundering 393, 397–400
mortgages 146–9, 165, 170–1, 298, 303–4, 307–11, 313–14, 316–17
Multi-Year Deposit Facility Agreement 53
Multilateral Investment Guarantee Agency 97–8
multinational corporations 20–3, 405–7

NASD 178, 215; NASDAQ 177, 179, 184, 194, 201; Rules 191–2, 197, 211, 220
National Credit Union Administration 382
negative pledge clauses 36, 40–1, 48, 49, 99, 100
non-performing loans 301

obligations (forfaiting) 242–3
OECD 257, 264, 267–70
off-balance-sheet treatment 324–7, 329
offset arrangements 278, 286–8
offshore transactions 118, 130, 145, 202
onlending rights 34
operating leases 375
original issue discount 314–15
overseas investment 262–3, 272–3, 287

'Papilsky' rules 191
parent company 328–41 *passim*
participation security 302–3
pass-through structures 299, 301–2
Poland (and Euromarket) 156–73
political risks (debt servicing) 91–8
Private Export Funding Corporation 260

private placements (US) 175, 193–9, 212–15
privatization 215–18, 266–7; Euromarket development 114–15, 128–9, 142, 159–60
profit repatriation (Poland) 161
project finance 87–108
promissory notes 45, 241–55
property laws 120, 131–2, 145–6, 164–8
public fund-raising 119–20, 127, 143, 157–9
public offerings 175, 178–93, 215–20

rate risk 356
Regulation S 199–204, 205
regulations (global equity) 176–204
reinvestment risk 323
relending rights 34
REMIC status 313–14
reservation of title 99–100
retention accounts 92–5
Right to Financial Privacy Act (US) 389, 391
risk: capital requirements based on 316–17; of financial failure 9–11; hedging 91–8; project finance 88, 107; segregation 98–9; swap 356–7
Russia (and Euromarket) 111–25

secured debt 303–4
securities 43–4, 74–5; *see also* asset securitization
Securities and Exchange Commission (US) 175–9, 182, 184–91, 195–9, 201, 206–16, 218, 221–2, 306–7, 309–11
Securities Investment Board (UK) 210, 215, 218
security concerns 98–102, 120–1, 132–4, 146–9, 170–1
SEED Act (US) 273
sellers' liens 99–100
shares (global offerings) 174–222
ship financing 364–76
'shrinking world' trend 23–4
Single European Act 422
Slovakia (and Euromarket) 126–39

Small Business Administration (US) 261–2
SMMEA 307–8
social issues 25–6
socioeconomic traditions 25–6
soft currency countries 14, 18–20, 25, 29
sovereign immunity 52, 104, 125, 139, 156, 173
Soviet Union 4, 5–6, 272–3
Special Buyer Credit Limit (US) 261
SPVs 321–3, 327–9, 331–7, 339–42
State Immunity Act (UK) 52
Statute of Frauds (UK) 358
stock market 9–10, 119–20, 143, 157, 220; London 208–10, 213, 216, 218; New York 177, 209–10, 219
stripped coupons/bonds 315
structured transactions 394–6
subcontractors 287
subsidiaries 328–41 *passim*
successor liability 387–8
swap financing 344–63
switch trading 283–4
syndication (forfaiting) 252–3

take and/or pay contracts 95–6
tax-exempt bonds 301
Tax Reform Act (US) 18
taxation (Euromarket) 115–16, 131, 153, 162–3
taxpayer identification numbers 386
technical risk (project finance) 88
technology transfer 287
thrifts 316–17
through-put contracts 95
Toga case 412–14, 415, 417–18

Trade and Development Program 263
trade receivables 299
transaction reporting requirements (US) 379–400
Treasury Department (US) 381–3, 386–7, 394–6
Treaty of Rome 267, 422
triangular counterpurchase 283, 284
trust accounts 92–5

UK: asset securitization 317–42; export assistance 264–7; global equity offerings 215–19; insolvency 418–21, 426
ultra vires rule 103, 127, 334
UNCITRAL report 276, 278, 290
'Uniform Law' 243, 254–5
United Nations 27, 29
US: asset securitization 294–317; export assistance 257–64; global equity offerings 174–222; insolvency 404–21, 426; transaction reporting 379–400
usufruct 164, 166
usury laws 104

voting rights 328–31, 334–5

'without recourse' endorsement 250–1
World Bank 90, 91, 97, 271

Index compiled by Jackie McDermott